LIBRARY OF NEW TESTAMENT STUDIES

660

Formerly the Journal for the Study of the New Testament Supplement series

Editor
Chris Keith

Editorial Board
Dale C. Allison, Lynn H. Cohick, R. Alan Culpepper, Craig A. Evans,
Jennifer Eyl, Robert Fowler, Simon J. Gathercole, Juan Hernández Jr.,
John S. Kloppenborg, Michael Labahn, Matthew V. Novenson, Love L. Sechrest,
Robert Wall, Catrin H. Williams, Brittany E. Wilson

The Ties That Bind

Negotiating Relationships in Early Jewish and Christian Texts, Contexts, and Reception History
Essays in Honor of Adele Reinhartz

Edited by
Esther Kobel, Jo-Ann A. Brant,
and Meredith J. C. Warren, in collaboration with
Andrew Bowden

t&tclark

LONDON • NEW YORK • OXFORD • NEW DELHI • SYDNEY

T&T CLARK
Bloomsbury Publishing Plc
50 Bedford Square, London, WC1B 3DP, UK
1385 Broadway, New York, NY 10018, USA
29 Earlsfort Terrace, Dublin 2, Ireland

BLOOMSBURY, T&T CLARK and the T&T Clark logo are trademarks of
Bloomsbury Publishing Plc

First published in Great Britain 2023
Paperback edition published 2025

Copyright © Esther Kobel, Jo-Ann A. Brant, Meredith J. C. Warren, and contributors, 2023

Esther Kobel, Jo-Ann A. Brant, and Meredith J. C. Warren have asserted their right under the
Copyright, Designs and Patents Act, 1988, to be identified as Editors of this work.

All rights reserved. No part of this publication may be reproduced or transmitted
in any form or by any means, electronic or mechanical, including photocopying,
recording, or any information storage or retrieval system, without prior
permission in writing from the publishers.

Bloomsbury Publishing Plc does not have any control over, or responsibility for,
any third-party websites referred to or in this book. All internet addresses given in this book were
correct at the time of going to press. The author and publisher regret any inconvenience caused if
addresses have changed or sites have ceased to exist,
but can accept no responsibility for any such changes.

A catalogue record for this book is available from the British Library.

Library of Congress Cataloging-in-Publication Data
Names: Reinhartz, Adele, 1953– honouree | Kobel, Esther, editor. | Brant, Jo-Ann A.,
1956– editor. | Warren, Meredith J. C., editor. | Bowden, Andrew, 1984– |
Title: The ties that bind : negotiating relationships in early Jewish and Christian texts : essays in
Honor of Adele Reinhartz / edited by Esther Kobel, Jo-Ann Brant and Meredith J.C. Warren ; in
collaboration with Andrew Bowden.
Description: London ; New York : T&T Clark, 2023. | Series: The library of New Testament studies,
2513-8790 ; 660 | Includes bibliographical references and index. |
Summary: "This volume examines the centrality of relationships in the understanding of identity
in early Christianity and Judaism"– Provided by publisher.
Identifiers: LCCN 2022056436 (print) | LCCN 2022056437 (ebook) |
ISBN 9780567702586 (hb) | ISBN 9780567702623 (pb) | ISBN 9780567702593 (epdf) |
ISBN 9780567702616 (epub)
Subjects: LCSH: Friendship–Religious aspects–Christianity. | Friendship–Religious
aspects–Judaism. | Interpersonal relations–Religious aspects–Christianity. |
Interpersonal relations–Religious aspects–Judaism. | Church history–ca. 30–100.
Classification: LCC BS2545.F75 T54 2023 (print) | LCC BS2545.F75 (ebook) |
DDC 220.6–dc23/eng/20230301
LC record available at https://lccn.loc.gov/2022056436
LC ebook record available at https://lccn.loc.gov/2022056437

ISBN: HB: 978-0-5677-0258-6
PB: 978-0-5677-0262-3
ePDF: 978-0-5677-0259-3
ePUB: 978-0-5677-0261-6

Series: Library of New Testament Studies, volume 660
ISSN 2513-8790

Typeset by Newgen KnowledgeWorks Pvt. Ltd., Chennai, India

To find out more about our authors and books visit www.bloomsbury.com
and sign up for our newsletters.

Contents

List of Figures — vii
List of Contributors — viii
Abbreviations — ix

Introduction — 1
    Esther Kobel and Jo-Ann A. Brant

Part 1 Gospel of John

1   Befriending the Beloved Disciple Requires Interventions — 13
    Amy-Jill Levine

2   Intimacy with Jesus: Construction of Closeness by Gender Diversity in John — 23
    Peter Wick

3   Was Pilate a "Friend of the Emperor" (John 19:12)? — 33
    Ruben Zimmermann

4   John among the Synoptics? Understanding the Institutional World of the Fourth Gospel in Light of Other Early Gospels — 44
    Anders Runesson

5   False Friends in the First Gospel — 53
    R. Alan Culpepper

Part 2 Letters of Paul

6   "Put Out of the Synagogue": A Pauline Unpacking of a Johannine Trope — 67
    Paula Fredriksen

7   Befriending Paul: The Letter to Philemon as a Test Case — 78
    Esther Kobel

8   Paul's "Beloved" Friends — 87
    Stephen Westerholm

Contents

9 "As to the Law—a Pharisee" (Phil 3:5c): Do We Have a Friend in Paul? 95
Kathy Ehrensperger

10 The Wet Nurse as a Model for Communal Relationships in 1 Thessalonians 106
Margaret Y. MacDonald

Part 3 Further Texts and Contexts in Jewish Antiquity

11 Wine, Dine, and Bind: Sacrificial Food and Community Formation in Asia Minor 119
Shayna Sheinfeld and Meredith J. C. Warren

12 Socializing with the Impure (or Not): Interactions and Impurity in Late Second Temple Judaism 130
Cecilia Wassén

13 How to Be Better Neighbors: Rewriting the Conquest in Greek Terms 140
Albert I. Baumgarten

14 Negotiating National and Sectarian Identities in the Dead Sea Scrolls: The Case of Words of the Luminaries and the Yaḥad's Covenant Ceremony 150
Esther G. Chazon

Part 4 Scriptures on the Silver Screen 2.0

15 Lovers or (Just) Friends? Jesus and Mary Magdalene in the Gospel of John and in Film 161
Caroline Vander Stichele

16 What a Friend We Have in Jesus: A Consideration of Jesus as Friend in Jesus Films 172
Richard Walsh

17 *Dividing the Red Soup*: An Antimodel in *Bruce Almighty* 181
Jan Willem van Henten

18 The Quick and the Dead in Film Treatments of the Raising of Lazarus 189
Jo-Ann A. Brant

Bibliography 201
Bibliography of the Works of Adele Reinhartz (1983–2022) 223
Index 237

Figures

3.1	Coins from Pilate, 29 CE	41
15.1	Jesus blesses Mary, *Mary Magdalene*	165
15.2	Mary greets the resurrected Jesus, *Mary Magdalene*	166
15.3	Mary's place at the Last Supper, *Mary Magdalene*	169
18.1	*From the Manger to Cross*	191
18.2	*King of Kings*	192
18.3	*The Greatest Story Ever Told*	195
18.4	*The Last Temptation of Christ*	197
18.5	Jesus in *Mary Magdalene*	198

Contributors

Albert I. Baumgarten, *Bar Ilan University, Israel*

Jo-Ann A. Brant, *Goshen College, USA*

Esther G. Chazon, *The Hebrew University of Jerusalem, Israel*

R. Alan Culpepper, *Mercer University, USA*

Kathy Ehrensperger, *University of Potsdam, Germany*

Paula Fredriksen, *Boston University, USA, and The Hebrew University of Jerusalem, Israel*

Esther Kobel, *Johannes Gutenberg-University Mainz, Germany*

Amy-Jill Levine, *Vanderbilt University Divinity School, USA*

Margaret Y. MacDonald, *Saint Mary's University, Canada*

Anders Runesson, *University of Oslo, Norway*

Shayna Sheinfeld, *Augsburg University, USA*

Jan Willem van Henten, *University of Amsterdam, The Netherlands*

Caroline Vander Stichele, *Tilburg University, The Netherlands*

Richard Walsh, *Methodist University, USA*

Meredith J. C. Warren, *University of Sheffield, UK*

Cecilia Wassén, *Uppsala University, Sweden*

Stephen Westerholm, *McMaster University, USA*

Peter Wick, *Ruhr University Bochum, Germany*

Ruben Zimmermann, *Johannes Gutenberg-Universität Mainz, Germany*

Abbreviations

General

apocr.	apocryphon
art. cit.	article cited
c.	century
c.	circa
cf.	*confer*, compare
dir.	director
e.g.	*exempli gratia*, for example
esp.	especially
et al.	*et alii*, and others
fig.	figure
frag.	fragment
Hebr	Hebrew
ibid.	*ibidem*, in the same place
n.	note
POV	point of view
repr.	reprint
s.v.	*sub verbo*, under the word
trans.	translation

Bible Texts and Versions

CEB	Common English Bible
JANT	The Jewish Annotated New Testament
LXX	Septuagint
MT	Masoretic Text
NABR	New American Bible, Revised Edition
NCB	St. Joseph New Catholic Bible
NEB	New English Bible
NKJV	New King James Version
NRSV	New Revised Standard Version
RSV	Revised Standard Version

Ancient Corpora

Old Testament

1–2 Chr	1–2 Chronicles
1–2 Kgs	1–2 Kings
1–2 Sam	1–2 Samuel
Dan	Daniel
Deut	Deuteronomy
Esth	Esther
Exod	Exodus
Gen	Genesis
Isa	Isaiah
Josh	Joshua
Judg	Judges
Lam	Lamentations
Lev	Leviticus
Neh	Nehemiah
Num	Numbers
Ps/Pss	Psalms
Song	Song of Songs

Deuterocanonical Works

1–4 Macc	1–4 Maccabees
Bar	Baruch
Jdt	Judith
Pr Azar	Prayer of Azariah
Sir	Sirach/Ecclesiasticus
Tob	Tobit

New Testament

1–2 Cor	1–2 Corinthians
1–2 Thess	1–2 Thessalonians
1–2 Pet	1–2 Peter
2 Tim	2 Timothy
Eph	Ephesians
Gal	Galatians
Heb	Hebrews
Jas	James
Matt	Matthew
Phil	Philippians
Phlm	Philemon
Rev	Revelation

| Rom | Romans |
| Tit | Titus |

Dead Sea Scrolls and Related Works

11QT	Temple Scroll
1QM	War Scroll
1QpHab	Pesher Habakkuk
1QS	Rule of the Community
4Q504	Words of the Luminaries
4Q252	Commentary on Genesis A, formerly Patriarchal Blessings or Pesher Genesis
4QD^a	Damascus Document
4QMMT	Miqṣat Ma'aśê ha-Torah
4QToḥorot A	Toḥorot A

Rabbinic Literature

Ber.	Berakhot
Gen. Rab.	Genesis Rabbah
Kel.	Kelim
Mak.	Makkot
Nid.	Niddah
Šabb.	Šabbat
Sanh.	Sanhedrin
Šeb.	Šebi'it
Šeqal.	Šeqalim
Yoma	Yoma

Old Testament Pseudepigrapha

Jub.	Jubilees
Let. Aris.	Letter of Aristeas
Pss. Sol.	Psalms of Solomon
Sib. Or.	Sibylline Oracles
T. Benj.	Testament of Benjamin

Ancient Authors

Aelius Theon

| Prog. | *Progymnasmata* |

Aphthonius

Prog. *Progymnasmata*

Apuleius

Metam. *Metamorphoses/The Golden Ass*

Aristotle

Eth. eud. *Eudemian Ethics*
Eth. nic. *Nichomachean Ethics*

Aulus Gellius

Noct. Att. *Attic Nights*

Cicero

Leg. *De legibus*
Phil. *Orationes philippicae*

Dio Chrysostom

Ven. *The Hunter (Eubeoan Discourse)*

Epictetus

Diatr. *Diatribai (Dissertationes)*

Eusebius

Hist. eccl. *Ecclesiastical History*

Irenaeus

Haer. *Against Heresies*

Josephus

Ag. Ap. *Against Apion*
Ant. *Jewish Antiquities*
J.W. *Jewish War*
Life *The Life*

Justin Martyr

Dial. *Dialogue with Trypho*

Lucian

Tox. *Toxaris*

Martial

Epig. *Epigramme*

Nicolaus the Sophist

Prog. *Progymnasmata*

Philo

Abraham *On the Life of Abraham*
Contempl. *Life On the Contemplative Life*
Embassy *On the Embassy to Gaius*
Flaccus *Against Flaccus*
Good Person *That Every Good Person Is Free*
Moses *On the Life of Moses*
QE *Questions and Answers on Exodus*
Spec. Laws *On the Special Laws*

Philip of Side

Hist. eccl. *Historia ecclesiastica*

Plato

Resp. *Republic*

Plutarch

Cons. ux. *Consolatio ad uxorem*
Mor. *Moralia*

Quintilian

Inst. *Institutio oratoria*

Seneca

Aug.	*Divus Augustus*
Cal.	*Gaius Caligula*
Ep.	*Epistulae Morales*
Tib.	*Tiberius*
Tit.	*Divus Titus*

Suetonius

Aug.	*Divus Augustus*
Cal.	*Gaius Caligula*
Tib.	*Tiberius*
Tit.	*Divus Titus*

Tacitus

Ann.	*Annales*
Dial.	*Dialogus de oratoribus*
Germ.	*Germania*

Tertullian

Nat.	*To the Heathen*

Modern Works, Series, and Collections

AB	Anchor Bible
ABRL	Anchor Bible Reference Library
AE	*Année épigraphique*
AGJU	Arbeiten zur Geschichte des antiken Judentums und des Urchristentums
AIRF	Acta Instituti Romani Finlandiae
AJEC	Ancient Judaism and Early Christianity Series
AJSR	*Association for Jewish Studies Review*
ANF	Ante-Nicene Fathers
BAGD	Baur, Walter, William F. Arndt, F. Wilbur Gingrich, and Frederick W. Danker. *Greek-English Lexicon of the New Testament and Other Early Christian Literature*, 2nd ed. Chicago: University of Chicago Press, 1979 (Bauer-Arndt-Gingrich-Danker)
BAR	*Biblical Archaeology Review*
BBR	*Bulletin for Biblical Research*
BDAG	Danker, Frederick W., Walter Bauer, William F. Arndt, and F. Wilbur Gingrich. *Greek-English Lexicon of the New Testament and Other Early*

	Christian Literature, 3rd ed. Chicago: University of Chicago Press, 2000 (Danker-Bauer-Arndt-Gingrich)
BDB	Brown, Francis, S. R. Driver, and Charles A Briggs. *The Brown-Driver-Briggs Hebrew and English Lexicon: With an Appendix Containing the Biblical Aramaic*. Peabody MA: Hendrickson, 1996.
BETL	üBibliotheca Ephemeridum Theologicarum Lovaniensium
BibInt	Biblical Interpretation Series
BJ	*Bonner Jahrbücher*
BK	*Bibel und Kirche*
BNP	*Brill's New Pauly: Encyclopaedia of the Ancient World*. Edited by Hubert Cancik. 22 vols. Leiden: Brill, 2002–2011.
BR	*Biblical Research*
BzA	Beitrage zur Assyriologie
BZNW	Zeitschrift für die neutestamentliche Wissenschaft
CB	*Cultura Biblica*
CBQ	*Catholic Biblical Quarterly*
CH	*Church History*
CIG	*Corpus Inscriptionum Graecarum*
CIL	*Corpus Inscriptionum Latinarum*
CIP	Corpus Inscriptionum Iudaeae/Palestine
ConBNT	Coniectanea Neotestamentica Series
Conc(I)	*Concilium. Brescia*
DJD	Discoveries in the Judaean Desert
DSD	*Dead Sea Discoveries*
DSSR	*The Dead Sea Scrolls Reader*. Edited by Donald W. Parry and Emanuel Tov. 6 vols. Leiden: Brill, 2004–5
EBR	*Encyclopedia of the Bible and Its Reception*
ECL	Early Christianity and Its Literature
EJL	Early Judaism and Its Literature
ENS	Episcopal News Service
EvT	*Evangelische Theologie*
ExpTim	*Expository Times*
FilTh	*Film und Theologie*
GLAJJ	*Greek and Latin Authors on Jews and Judaism*
GR	*Greece and Rome*
HCOT	Historical Commentary on the Old Testament
HCS	Hellenistic Culture and Society
HeyJ	*Heythrop Journal*
HTR	*Harvard Theological Review*
HUCM	Monographs of the Hebrew Union College
ICC	International Critical Commentary
IDelos	Roussel, Pierre, and Marcel Launey. *Inscriptions de Délos: Décrets postérieurs à 166 av. J.-C. (nos. 1497-1524). Dédicaces postérieures à 166 av. J.-C. (nos. 1525-2219)*. Académie des Inscriptions et Belles-lettres. Paris: Librairie Ancienne Honoré Champion, 1937.

IG	*Inscriptiones Graeca. Editio Minor.* Berlin: de Gruyter, 1924–
IGRR	*Inscriptiones Graecae ad Res Romanas Pertinentes*
IJO	*Inscriptiones Judaicae Orientis*
Int	*Interpretation*
JAAR	*Jaarbericht van het Vooraziatisch-Egyptisch Gezelschap (Genootschap) Ex oriente lux*
JAJ	*Journal of Ancient Judaism*
JANT	*Jewish Annotated New Testament*
JBL	*Journal of Bibilcal Literature*
JES	*Journal of Ecumenical Studies*
JHS	*Journal of Hellenic Studies*
JJMJS	*Journal of the Jesus Movement in Its Jewish Setting*
JJS	*Journal of Jewish Studies*
JQR	*Jewish Quarterly Review*
JRA	*Journal of Roman Archaeology*
JRS	*Journal of Roman Studies*
JRTI	*Journal of Religious & Theological Information*
JSJ	*Journal for the Study of Judaism in the Persian, Hellenistic, and Roman Periods*
JSJSup	Journal for the Study of Judaism in the Persian, Hellenistic, and Roman Periods Supplement Series
JSNT	*Journal for the Study of the New Testament*
JSNTSup	Journal for the Study of the New Testament Supplement Series
JSOT	*Journal for the Study of the Old Testament*
JSOTSup	Journal for the Study of the Old Testament Supplement Series
JSP	*Journal for the Study of Pseudepigrapha*
KAW	Kulturgeschichte Der Antiken Welt
KuI	*Kirche und Israel*
LCL	Loeb Classical Library
LitTh	*Literature and Theology*
LNTS	The Library of New Testament Studies
LSTS	The Library of Second Temple Studies
MGWJ	*Monatschrift für Geschichte und Wissehnschaft des Judentums*
Neot	*Neotestamentica*
NIDB	*New Interpreter's Dictionary of the Bible.* Edited by Katharine Doob Sakenfeld. 5 vols. Nashville: Abingdon, 2006–9
NovT	*Novum Testamentum*
NTL	New Testament Library
NTM	New Testament Message
NTOA	Novum Testamentum et Orbis Antiquus
NTS	*New Testament Studies*
OECT	Oxford Early Christian Texts
OGIS	*Orientis Graeci Inscriptiones Selectae.* Edited by Whilhelm Dittenberger. 2 vols. Leipzig: Hirzel, 1903–5
OTGu	Old Testament Guides

RBL	*Review of Biblical Literature*
RBS	Resources for Biblical Studies
REJ	*Revue des études juives*
RevQ	*Revue de Qumran*
RNS	Religion News Service
RPC	*Roman Provincial Coinage*
SBEC	Studies in the Bible and early Christianity
SBLDS	Society of Biblical Literature Dissertation Series
SBLMS	Society of Biblical Literature Monograph Series
SCI	*Scripta Classica Israelica*
SEÅ	*Svensk exegetisk årsbok*
SemeiaSt	Semeia Studies
SIDA	*Scripta Instituti Donneriani Aboensis*
SP	Sacra Pagina
SPhiloA	*Studia Philonica Annual*
SR	*Studies in Religion/Sciences Religieuses*
STDJ	Studies on the Texts of the Desert of Judah
SUNT	Studien zur Umwelt des Neuen Testaments
TAM	Tituli Asiae Minoris
TDNT	*Theological Dictionary of the New Testament*
ThZ	*Theologische Zeitschrift. Basel*
TLZ	*Theologische Literaturzeitung*
TSAJ	Texte und Studien zum antiken Judentum
UTB	Uni-Taschenbücher
VC	*Vigiliae Christianae*
WGRW	Writings from the Greco-Roman World
WUNT	Wissenschaftliche Untersuchungen zum Neuen Testament
ZNW	*Zeitschrift für die Neutestamentliche Wissenschaft und die Kunde der älteren Kirche*

Introduction

Esther Kobel and Jo-Ann A. Brant

In the greater field of research on early Judaism and Christianity, relationships—and the topic of friendship as a particular manifestation of relationship—have received some attention, but not as much as deserved. Yet for Adele Reinhartz, the jubilarian to be honored with the present book, friendship along with other kinds of relationships have occupied a central position in her research activities for decades. Adele Reinhartz has explicitly tackled this topic by documenting her attempts at *Befriending the Beloved Disciple* in the Gospel of John in her book of that name. In this seminal work and later in *Cast Out of the Covenant*, along with many other publications, the impressive list of which appears on pages 223–35 this immediately becomes obvious. In her oeuvre, it is also possible to track how she has liberated herself from constraints that might have boxed her in as a Jewish, female biblical scholar, allowing her to challenge themes of anti-Judaism in New Testament literature, to raise up the neglected or overlooked characters in biblical narratives with her significant insights and abilities. Adele Reinhartz has significantly helped shape the current discourse and research on the forces, motivations, and actions that led to the separation of Judaism from Christianity in antiquity. Time and again, she enters into dialogue between the two in modernity. With her almost unique position as a Jewish researcher working predominantly on early Christian texts, she has examined especially the Gospel of John, images of women in biblical texts, the so-called Parting of the Ways, and the history of the Bible's impact in movies and in TV series.

In addition to her highly significant scholarly contributions and other academic virtues, Adele has demonstrated her superior capacity and strength to lead through the many administrative roles that she has taken on in service to other scholars, including the two recent examples of serving as the editor of the *Journal of Biblical Literature* from 2012 to 2018 and as the president of the Society of Biblical Literature in 2020.

The academic world into which Adele first entered in the late 1970s and early 1980s was fraught with androcentrism and chauvinism. Her tenacity and competence as a scholar and solidarity with other female scholars have pushed the bar much closer to meaningful equality. Many younger scholars have benefited from her friendship and mentorship. Many of these are women, three of whom are editors of this volume. Those who have worked with Adele value her vigilance in maintaining collegial workspaces that are free of hatred and that seek to include a diversity of voices.

It is because of Adele's extraordinary ability to foster and maintain so many meaningful relationships with her colleagues and students that the editors have chosen the topic of friendship and relationships for this *Festschrift* in her honor. Each of the contributors found their inspiration from scholarly directions set by Adele. While the *Festschrift* is organized around texts and mediums, this introduction to its contents is organized around the themes central to Adele Reinhartz's career.

Befriending the Beloved Disciple and *Cast Out of the Covenant*

Two of Reinhartz's books take center stage in many of the chapters. As a Jewish scholar working primarily with New Testament texts, principally the Gospel of John, Adele developed a multidimensional hermeneutic in *Befriending the Beloved Disciple*, which facilitates engagement with texts that contain troubling and even offensive material. Her approach seeks a means of entering into dialogue with a text about which one feels some ambivalence. This hermeneutic demands a level of honesty and justice from both the reader and the text. As a result, Reinhartz's questioning of the depiction of the Jews and Judaism in the Gospel of John cannot be dismissed. Her approach avoids the traps of both a hermeneutic of goodwill that runs the risk of glossing over problematic elements and a hermeneutic of suspicion that can distort the principal focus or potential meaning of a text.

In a more recent work, *Cast Out of the Covenant,* Adele uses rhetorical analysis to build upon her previous work to lay down a compelling case that anti-Judaism is part of the constitutive fabric of this Gospel. She demonstrates that the Fourth Gospel's rhetoric of disaffiliation and fear motivate Jesus's followers to leave the synagogue rather than being expelled. In her discussion of the depiction of Jews and Judaism in this and other works, she has challenged the sort of apologetics that have downplayed the role that the Gospel of John has played in the Parting of the Ways between Judaism and Christianity. It certainly holds true, as one of the authors of this volume states, "While the debate about the nature of the Fourth Gospel will surely continue, scholarship has reached a point, not least thanks to Reinhartz's work, where the interpretive and methodological options—and their implications—are clearer than they have ever been" (Runesson, 44). Some such implications are in focus in the very first article in the volume. Amy-Jill Levine, "Befriending the Beloved Disciple Requires Interventions" (Chapter 1, 13–22), plays with the title and adopts the intention of the first of the above-mentioned works in order to support Reinhartz's conclusion in the second work mentioned here. She addresses the ongoing need for intervention for Christians who persist in denying the anti-Judaism of the Gospel of John. She demonstrates the continued reliance of some scholars upon the *Birkat Haminim* theory and the attempts of many to excuse John's anti-Jewish polemic as a symptom of pain of being kicked out of synagogue. Levine provides examples that illustrate that it is possible to love John as a fellow believer-in-Christ while frankly criticizing "the hateful message" of his Gospel (14). She then provides additional arguments that explain why John's words become a catalyst for hatred by distinguishing between eschatological supersession that envisions a salvation that includes Jews and the "hard supersessionism" in John's replacement theology. She challenges the attempt to parse John's Ἰουδαῖοι (*Ioudaioi*)[1] into subcategories to limit the scope of the anti-Judaism to a group that all modern readers will feel comfortable villainizing. Levine thereby removes the temptation to say that John does not mean all Jews, but simply those Jews, such as those "who identify with the Jerusalem Temple and its system under Roman imperial control," or those who "want to bring down Jesus," by pointing out that John "knows the words 'chief priests' and 'Pharisees' but nonetheless bleeds these terms into 'Jews'" (16–17). She points out that attempts to avoid the word "Jew" imply that the term is necessarily derisive and demonstrates how such apologetics create other problems.

Two authors respond to Reinhartz's conclusions about the Gospel of John by adopting her hermeneutical strategy of maintaining a scholarly and "friendly" relationship with a text in order to question whether they can befriend Paul. In "'As to the Law—a Pharisee' (Phil 3:5c): Do We Have a Friend in Paul?" (Chapter 9, 95–105), Kathy Ehrensperger asks, "Do they [the implications of Paul's Pharisaic identity] render Paul a friend to be trusted when it comes to the overcoming of anti-Judaism in Christian tradition—or does he stay at the margins, contributing to the ongoing problems?" (95). She carefully looks at Paul's language of νόμος and ἔργα νόμου in Romans and Galatians and then ζῆλος in Galatians and Philippians through the lens of recent scholarship on the Pharisees. As a result, she concludes that Paul's discourse on the law is directed to non-Jews and is not a polemic against the Torah. Ehrensperger contextualizes Paul's teaching within his allegiance to the pragmatic approach of the Pharisees to living according to the Torah by seeking accommodations to "everyday life needs and conditions" (99). She demonstrates that Paul's zeal is neither a form of ethnocentrism in his Jewish self-understanding that he rejects for his life in Christ nor a malevolent zeal for "the traditions of his ancestors" that motivates his early persecution of Christians. She contends that Paul's point is that "his commitment to the traditions of his ancestors ... does not render him the most obvious candidate for a mission to the gentiles" (100). Rather, what separates Paul from other zealous Jews is "that he teaches non-Jews how they can relate to the one God of Israel at the dawning of the messianic time, without beginning a process of becoming Jews, that is, members of the people of Israel" (102). Nevertheless, in order to become such members through Christ's agency, the Torah remains the means of orienting them to a life in conformity with Christ. Moreover, building on the work of Albert Baumgarten (one of Adele's doctoral advisors), who describes the Pharisees as working toward reconciliation between the larger Jewish public, Ehrensperger sees Paul's work as following the trajectory of Pharisaic objectives. These observations lead her to conclude that "in this Paul we could well have a friend, possibly conversation partner, in our attempts to respect each other in difference" (105).

---

[1] In this volume, the first appearance of every Greek word in the main text of each essay is always provided in Greek (as opposed to transliteration). When authors also provide transliterations of the Greek, these have not been removed. Where no transliterations of Greek have been provided, transliterations have not been added. When authors discuss a Greek term in the footnotes only by means of transliteration, the original Greek has not been added. Additionally, for essays referring only to Hebrew transliterations, the original Hebrew has not been added.

Esther Kobel, in "Befriending Paul: The Letter to Philemon as a Test Case" (Chapter 7, 78–86), applies Reinhartz's hermeneutic to Paul's letter to Philemon—specifically to his treatment of slavery therein—in order to test whether a letter as well as a book can be treated as a friend. In doing so, she reminds us that Adele's hermeneutic calls for frank speech that is characteristic of true friendship. While applying each of Adele's stances from *Befriending the Beloved Disciple*, she asks two questions: "What kind of friend is Paul to each sort of reader with regard to these aspects of relationships?" and "What are the ethical implications of each reading position?" (79). After drawing our attention to the many relationships with various roles associated with persona in the letter and to the fact that the letter is addressed to more people than one man, Kobel begins by adopting the stance of a compliant reader, noting the positive and negative consequences of allowing Paul to serve as the reader's mentor. His encouragement of "love, faith, and fellowship in Christian congregations" (82) also contains encouragement on the part of Onesimus to respect the institution of slavery by returning to his master. Adopting a resistant reading in which Paul becomes an opponent, she examines how the egalitarian language of siblings in Christ remains theoretical and that in reality, Onesimus remains an object subjected to the desires of one master or another. As a sympathetic reader, Kobel treats Paul as a colleague. She looks at the rhetorical effect of Paul's relationship language and notes the power of language to shape a reality that more closely reflects Paul's theoretical egalitarianism. In her final stance, she treats Paul as "the other" by placing the text at arm's distance. Kobel notes that Paul relies upon the power relationships between himself and Philemon to ask that Onesimus be manumitted. Nowhere in the letter does Paul suggest that other slaves in the household similarly be set free; slaves needed to manage a household large enough to accommodate a meeting of the church. The letter is sent and arrives in a world in which the institution of slavery is entrenched, an institution upon which the community of Christ depends. In the end, Kobel demonstrates the fruitfulness of the ongoing application of Adele's hermeneutics.

Paula Fredriksen, "'Put Out of the Synagogue': A Pauline Unpacking of a Johannine Trope" (Chapter 6, 67–77), picks up Adele's conclusions about the role that the Gospel of John plays in the Parting of the Ways between the church and the synagogue. Fredriksen examines Paul's relationship with the synagogue to add evidence to the assertion that John's "cast out of the synagogue" is a fictional construct that serves his plot by casting the *Ioudaioi* in the role of hoisting Jesus on the cross and his polarizing rhetoric that reduces truth to the view of the author in order to remove Judaism as a viable choice. She substantiates the findings of Ehrensperger that, while Paul does not demand that his non-Jewish audience become circumcised, he does demand adopting social behaviors that their contemporaries would consider "Jewish" and living according to Jewish ethics. Fredriksen carefully looks at how Paul relates to synagogues in light of current research, according to which synagogues were institutions that accommodated "a broad bandwidth of religious affiliation" and whose members in the diaspora demonstrated "social permeability" (71). She notes that Paul consents to the discipline of the synagogue rather than simply rejecting its authority and walking away and that the synagogues recognize rather than repudiate Paul by disciplining him. In doing so, she draws a strong contrast between Paul's experience and the depiction of synagogues in the Gospel of John. By marshaling strong historical evidence that Jewish institutions, including those in Judea, continued to receive "Christ-confessors" well into the fourth century CE, she convincingly argues and supports Reinhartz's thesis that both the threat and fear of being "put out of the synagogue" in the Fourth Gospel must be treated as fictions rather than facts.

Anders Runesson in "John among the Synoptics? Understanding the Institutional World of the Fourth Gospel in Light of Other Early Gospels" (Chapter 4, 44–52) takes a second look at the depiction of Jewish institutions in the Gospel of John. His goal is not to deny that John encourages parting ways with the synagogue so much as to see the degree to which John is still shaped by this institution and whether he differs from the Synoptic Gospels in his treatment of civic and institutional spaces. In his survey of synagogue scenes, he observes that the Johannine Jesus, like that of the other three canonical Gospels, aims "to influence public Jewish society rather than wanting to withdraw from it" (49) and finds this to be oddly dissonant with the religio-political ostracism that John mentions. Moreover, even though John is concerned with extending the relevance of Jesus "to Samaritans and beyond," he does not reimagine "the institutional structures in which he [John] places Jesus" (52). Runesson's work suggests that while John uses a rhetoric of expropriation to transfer the positive elements of Jewish tradition to the domain of Christ followers and then a rhetoric of disaffiliation to build a barrier between the two communities—as Reinhartz contends in *Cast Out of the Covenant*—John and the story he narrates are still Jewish enough to make Christ-followers dependent upon Jewish institutions.

In the last chapter in the volume, Jo-Ann A. Brant, "The Quick and the Dead in Film Treatments of the Raising of Lazarus" (Chapter 18, 189–99), as a way of honoring Reinhartz's contribution to the study of film, looks at how film treatments negotiate the tension in the Gospel of John between Lazarus, who seems very Jewish and says nothing about his faith in Jesus, and John's disparagement of Jews. She finds that the reception history documented in many films affirms Reinhartz's conclusions by pointing out a pattern running through films dating from the late nineteenth century, which represent Lazarus's resurrection as a baptism into the Christian community and a departure from Judaism. In many cases, the Jews and Jewish institutions come to signify the realm of death. The films under scrutiny dramatize the Johannine Jesus's claim that those who trust in Jesus are the living and never die even if they are dead (1:12; 5:24; 8:52; 10:10-11) while those who do not trust in him have no life in them (6:53). Brant notes a significant shift beginning in the 1960s in which filmmakers exploit the disruption of Lazarus's resurrection to the relationship between the living and the dead to explore tensions in the relationship between Christian dogmas and the realities of Jesus's death. She does not find that this shift necessarily avoids the trap of misrepresenting late Second Temple Judaism, but as Reinhartz demonstrates in works like *Jesus of Hollywood*, the story of Lazarus's resurrection becomes more meaningful and intriguing when it is liberated from a telling that justifies Christianity's hard supersessionism.

Negotiating Potentially Fraught Relationships

Adele Reinhartz has been committed to negotiating potentially fraught relationships, both scholarly and ancient. Besides the relationship between Judaism and Christianity in late antiquity, a number of contributors have broadened the horizon to include other members of the Greco-Roman world or narrowed the focus to what might be considered intra-muros relationship.

In Albert I. Baumgarten's piece, "How to Be Better Neighbors: Rewriting the Conquest in Greek Terms" (Chapter 13, 140–9), readers will find an example of the scholarship that has shaped Adele's career. Adele completed her graduate studies in the religious studies department at McMaster University, studying with E. P. Sanders and Baumgarten during a time when the department was heavily invested in the project on "Jewish and Christian Self-Definition," funded by the Canadian Social Sciences and Humanities Research Council. That project sought to understand Second Temple and early Rabbinic Judaism on their own terms rather than through the lens of Christianity. Adele shares Baumgarten's grounding in a deep understanding of the literatures, cultures, and philosophies of the broader Mediterranean world that Jews had to negotiate in order to maintain their own self-definitions. In his contribution, Baumgarten looks at how Jewish authors in the Greco-Roman world sought "to remove the sting" (142) of the conquest narratives to facilitate easier relationships with their gentile neighbors by using arguments derived from the Greco-Roman world. He makes clear the sensitivity of ancient Jewish scholars to anti-Judaism and their desire to be considered good neighbors.

Esther Chazon in "Negotiating National and Sectarian Identities in the Dead Sea Scrolls: The Case of Words of the Luminaries and the Yaḥad's Covenant Ceremony" (Chapter 14, 150–8) looks at how the Yaḥad (the so-called Qumran) community was able to appropriate outsiders' texts and reconcile them with their own sectarian identity. She looks at the role of the Community Rule's covenant ceremony in constructing Yaḥad sectarian identity in part by adapting biblical models and scriptural quotations to both promote in-group cohesiveness and maintain separation from outsiders. She thereby observes how the Words of the Luminaries "is conspicuously devoid of distinctive, sectarian markers" (153) but that it does share key biblical texts with the Community Rule. Thus, recitation of these texts helped them claim a historic Israelite identity, which in turn confirmed their sectarian identity as the elect. Chazon finds that the reliance upon these texts also allowed the community to remain open to the eschatological inclusion of or alignment with other Israelites in the face of foreign enemies. Her study provides an important insight into the capacity of a sectarian community to renegotiate relationships.

Cecilia Wassén's "Socializing with the Impure (or Not): Interactions and Impurity in Late Second Temple Judaism" (Chapter 12, 130–9) explores another factor that requires negotiation within Jewish communities. We can see Reinhartz's influence in how Wassén avoids adopting a contrived and thus one-dimensional perception of Second Temple Judaism with regard to purity. She does so by finding evidence of diverse practices, principally with reference to stepped pools and accommodations that make it impossible to construct a simple schema differentiating sacred space from ordinary space and Galilee from Judea. She does find that increased emphasis on washing in various forms goes a long way toward mitigating the spread of impurity. Although menstruants would not have been permitted to enter the temple precincts, Wassén finds no warrant for contending that these women would have been isolated within their own communities. She draws a picture of Jewish communities managing purity with an eye to practicality and facilitation of social interaction. Throughout the article, she illustrates how her observations should inform the reading Mark 5:24-43, the story about the woman with a hemorrhage.

Equally devoted to social matters of everyday life, Margaret MacDonald's contribution to the volume picks up a constant theme in Adele's work, namely the ambiguous place of women within early Christian societies. In "The Wet Nurse as a Model for Communal Relationships in 1 Thessalonians" (Chapter 10, 106–15), she looks at Paul's curious references to himself as a wet nurse and an infant in 1 Thess 2:5-8, both roles that seem self-demeaning when he more typically refers to himself as a father, a role that denotes his authority as well as loving intimacy. MacDonald argues that the nurse metaphor is a strategy for building bridges between social gulfs as Paul attempts "to establish a rapport with the community as a person who works" (106). The metaphor conjures up a metaphorical plane in which all members of the community are children. MacDonald explores the power of metaphor to shape reality, an interest that Reinhartz has displayed throughout her published works. In the first half of the chapter, MacDonald describes the respected place of the wet nurses within ancient Mediterranean societies as providers of both nourishment and early education as well as her vulnerability as a female slave with a lack of autonomy over her body and forced removal of her own biological children. She then places the metaphor within Paul's broader metaphorical design that stresses the longing for his children from whom he is separated by distance and oppression. She also looks at the metaphor's effect upon the members of the Thessalonian community, which was probably largely "composed of 'slave, free handworkers, and perhaps some freedmen'" (114). Thus, "the appeal to manual labour and to the work of a wet nurse (most often a slave) is part of a rhetorical strategy where Paul reverses the values of elite society, which found such efforts taxing and even increasingly demeaning" (115).

Meredith J. C. Warren and Shayna Sheinfeld, "Wine, Dine, and Bind: Sacrificial Food and Community Formation in Asia Minor" (Chapter 11, 119–29), frame their chapter by acknowledging the collegiality of their own meal fellowship with Adele. They then discuss the differences between how Paul and the author of Revelation navigate the issue of consuming sacrificed food in the context of using meals to maintain friendships and to establish community relationships. They find that Paul uses the concept of perception to guide the choice of whether or when to eat meat or drink wine that have been subject to the "wrong" rituals, whereas John of Patmos simply prohibits their ingestion. The differences in the two New Testament authors' limitation of table fellowship would then have generated very different moods while dining. They imagine that John's gathering would have been much more fraught with tension than that of Paul, with the result that John's community would have been much more socially isolated.

True Friendships

At the heart of this volume stands an interest in friendships, those with Adele forged through similar passions and commitments and those that were foundational to the societies of the Greco-Roman world. A number of contributors have consequently taken friendship as their starting point.

In "Lovers or (Just) Friends? Jesus and Mary Magdalene in the Gospel of John and in Film" (Chapter 15, 161–71), Caroline Vander Stichele analyzes the relationship's depiction in the film *Mary Magdalene* (2018). In doing so, she builds upon Adele Reinhartz's readings of the relationship between Jesus and Mary Magdalene in John 20 as either a disciple or romantic lover[2] as well as upon her discussion of Mary Magdalene in *Jesus of Hollywood* (2007). As a result, Vander Stichele finds a third possible reading in which Mary assumes the role of the beloved disciple whose exclusive and unique relationship with Jesus signifies a close friendship.

In "Paul's 'Beloved' Friends" (Chapter 8, 87–94), Stephen Westerholm begins with the startling observation that the words φίλος and φιλία never appear in the Pauline corpus and that they are used sparsely in other New Testament texts. Nevertheless, Westerholm finds grounds within Paul's writings to claim that he had a "genius for friendship" (89). He demonstrates that, beyond Paul's call and practice of maintaining good relationships with all, there is evidence that he had a number of close friendships. He lifts out terms that differentiate the degree of friendship that Paul experiences with the communities to which he writes as well as the language that sets some individuals apart enough to warrant considering them to be close friends. In the end, Westerholm leaves us with a picture of a man who has a capacity for true friendship while maintaining a wide range of friendly relationships.

R. Alan Culpepper begins his contribution with an observation similar to that of Westerholm of the limited use of φίλος in Matthew, a Gospel filled with warm relationships. In "False Friends in the First Gospel" (Chapter 5, 53–63), he turns his attention to Matthew's unique use of the word ἑταῖρος ("comrade" or "companion") to denote a degree of friendship in two parables and with reference to Judas. In each case, he finds that "a subordinate has erred, wronged, or challenged a superior, who responds with the ostensibly polite address followed by a condemnation" (55). By setting this usage in the context of the rhetorical use of syncrisis, Culpepper contends that Matthew's Jesus is implicitly comparing Judas to the discontent laborers and unprepared wedding guests. When examination of the use of ἑταῖρος in other ancient sources reveals no parallel to Matthew's usage, Culpepper looks at how false friendships are described in ancient treatises and concludes that the Matthean application of the term ἑταῖρος to Judas underscores his betrayal of all that true friendship entails.

In "Was Pilate a 'Friend of the Emperor' (John 19:12)?" (Chapter 3, 33–43), Ruben Zimmermann adds evidence to the case that the accusation that Pilate will be no friend of the emperor if he releases Jesus and situates the use of the title within the

---

[2] Adele Reinhartz, "To Love the Lord: An Intertextual Reading of John 20," in *The Labour of Reading: Desire, Alienation, and Biblical Interpretation*, ed. Fiona C. Black, Roland Boer, and Erin Runions (Atlanta, GA: SBL Press, 1999), 53–69.

Johannine polemic against Jesus's opponents. He begins by looking at the contexts in which the terminology of "friend of the emperor" was used and concludes that it was indeed a "conferred title that gives a specific status to the relationship between a political officeholder and the emperor or king." He then goes on to demonstrate that it is highly implausible that Pilate received this honor by examining the extant evidence for the titles that were conferred upon him. Moreover, he refutes the argument that Pilate had a close relationship with Sejanus that would have allowed him to claim the title. Zimmermann ends by proposing that the evangelist places the familiar concept of "Friend of the Emperor" on the lips of Jesus's Jewish opponents to indict them in the future for placing their allegiance to the emperor over their faithfulness to their God.

Peter Wick in "Intimacy with Jesus: Construction of Closeness by Gender Diversity in John" (Chapter 2, 23–32) narrows his focus to true friendship and how it is expressed among men and between men and women. After setting the Gospel's concept of friendship within the discussion of the *topos* in ancient sources, Wick finds that male friendships in the Fourth Gospel conform to the ideal of friendship centered on shared virtues but that they lean toward some features that are discussed in other sources, yet are not considered necessary to friendship. These are the lack of reciprocity and the epitomization of dying for a friend. When he broadens the horizon to the Central Eurasian cultural complex of "the hero and his friends" that has been articulated by Christopher Beckwith, Wick can place the Johannine ideal at the center of this conceptual framework. Turning to Jesus's friendships with women, he shows that φιλία has been replaced by ἔρως. In the end, he finds that the gender distinctions serve narrative purposes but, at the level of the Johannine community, these distinctions between men and women manifest both forms of intimacy in their relationships.

For his article "What a Friend We Have in Jesus: A Consideration of Jesus as Friend in Jesus Films" (Chapter 16, 172–80), Richard Walsh provides a secondary title "Looking for Friends (in all the Wrong Places)." Building upon Reinhartz's observations about the inadequacies of the representation of Jesus and his story in Jesus biopics and Jesus's own failure to be friendly, Walsh looks at ways in which Jesus has been characterized as a friend in *The Greatest Story Ever Told* (1965) and *Jesus of Nazareth* (1975). In the former, Walsh traces out the narrative lines in which first Lazarus and then Judas try to be a friend of the impossibly demanding Jesus. In his treatment of the latter, *Jesus of Nazareth*, Walsh draws attention to a more disturbing characterization of Jesus as a friend. The problem is not so much how he expresses friendship but rather that his nemesis in the story, Barabbas, correctly identifies who Jesus befriends: the Roman Empire.

In "*Dividing the Red Soup*: An Antimodel in *Bruce Almighty*" (Chapter 17, 181–8), Jan Willem van Henten looks at how even a light-hearted comedy turns on a biblically based understanding of what constitutes healthy human relationships. In his examination of a critical scene in the film in which the protagonist Bruce reenacts the parting of the Red Sea by miraculously creating a dry path in the middle of a bowl of tomato soup, van Henten highlights the scene's dependence on the book of Exodus and Cecille B. DeMille's two versions of *The Ten Commandments*. He then points out first how the film dramatizes the negative consequences to Bruce's relationship that result from his playing God and then how the problem is resolved by Bruce accepting his role as God's helper by valuing justice, mercy, and love and offering others concrete help.

The Ties That Bind—*ad me'ah ve'esrim*

The breadth of scholarship represented in this volume testifies to the scope of the influence that Adele Reinhartz has had upon the work of others. When we, the editors of the volume, generated an initial list of possible contributors, we quickly realized that we would have to prioritize those whom we would ask first and then proceed down the list if refusals created more space. The speed and enthusiasm with which contributors positively responded meant that many who would have liked to have been included could not be. We can assuage any feelings of regret about the omission of other names with the knowledge that these scholars will continue to attest to their respect for Adele by building upon her contributions. We might even be bold enough to say that there exists a community of scholars unified by their connection with Adele, all of whom are extremely grateful for "the ties that bind" us together with her.

The fact that the contributions could be gathered in this volume was supported by a range of people in addition to the authors, whom we thank for their commitment. Dr. Andrew Bowden and Mag. Theol. Janina Serfas (both Mainz) carefully proofread the contributions, while Susanne Patock (also Mainz) assisted with formatting, for which they all deserve great thanks. We thank Dominic Mattos for his straightforward inclusion of the volume in the LNTS series, and Lucy Davies for her careful supervision of the publication.

The greatest and final thanks go to Adele, whose friendship gave us the reason in the first place to undertake this project on the occasion of her seventieth birthday. With the very best wishes for the future, *ad me'ah ve'esrim* on behalf of all involved.

Part 1

Gospel of John

1

Befriending the Beloved Disciple Requires Interventions

Amy-Jill Levine

In her introduction to the Gospel of John in *The Jewish Annotated New Testament* (*JANT*), Adele Reinhartz clearly and forcefully names the anti-Judaism in this text:

> "The Jews" are the archenemies of Jesus and his followers; they are oblivious to the truth and relentless in pursuit of Jesus to the point of masterminding his demise. Their behavior towards Jesus and their failure to believe demonstrate that they have relinquished their covenantal relationship with the God of Israel and show them to be instead the children of the devil.[1]

She doubles down on this view in her *Cast Out of the Covenant*, whose title reveals the Gospel's replacement theology.[2] In her *Marginalia Review*, she concludes, "Having long had a conflicted relationship with the 'Beloved Disciple,'—since my doctoral research in the late 1970s—it is time to break up."[3] Pastoral care can sometimes restore abusive relationships; given John's consistent abusive language toward Jews, this is a relationship, however, that cannot be sustained.

Similar to how the "Paul within Judaism" school refuses to begin with the premise that Paul found something wrong with Judaism, so Reinhartz refuses to begin with the premise that the Jews, however defined, drove the followers of Jesus to trauma, expulsion, or otherwise did something so heinous (other than to refuse to accept the proclamation of Jesus as Lord) to prompt the Gospel's negative rhetoric.

If John's Gospel is fundamentally tainted with anti-Judaism, then Christians who still befriend the Beloved Disciple will need to reassess this friendship and perhaps set up interventions.

---

[1] Adele Reinhartz, "The Gospel according to John," in *The Jewish Annotated New Testament*, ed. Amy-Jill Levine and Marc Zvi Brettler, 2nd ed. (New York: Oxford University Press, 2017), 168–218, here 168.
[2] Adele Reinhartz, *Cast Out of the Covenant: Jews and Anti-Judaism in the Gospel of John* (Lanham, MD: Lexington Books, 2018).
[3] Adele Reinhartz, "Reflections on My Journey with John: A Retrospective from Adele Reinhartz," *Ancient Jew Review*, April 11, 2018, https://www.ancientjewreview.com/read/2018/2/24/reflections-on-my-journey-with-john-a-retrospective-from-adele-reinhartz (checked May 13, 2022).

Friendly Interventions

We can befriend people who do heinous things. At Riverbend Maximum Security Prison in Nashville, where I have taught for twenty years, I have befriended men convicted of murder, rape, aggravated armed robbery, and child sexual abuse. This friendship, however, takes place in the context of safeguards. Befriending a man convicted of child abuse, and who still admits to such urges, is not the same thing as inviting him to live next door to my children.

One can also befriend people who have heinous thoughts. I have managed to remain friends with individuals whose political views I abhor. We agree not to discuss politics, and the silence preserves the friendship. So too might the case be with John's Gospel: there are many likable, even profound aspects to the text, but not all of it needs to be proclaimed in public.

It would be good for friends of John (FOJs) to engage with Lev 19:17, "You shall not hate in your heart anyone of your kin; you shall reprove your neighbor, or you will incur guilt yourself." This verse precedes the more famous Lev 19:18, "You shall not take vengeance or bear a grudge against any of your people, but you shall love your neighbor as yourself." By extrapolation, the Christian reader might love John, a fellow believer-in-Christ, and at the same time, with love, rebuke the hateful message the text conveys.

This work is being done. For example, in 2022, the Diocese of Washington offered Resolution C014 to the Eightieth General Convention of the Episcopal Church to "recommend revisions to the Church's appointed lectionary readings for Holy Week [John 18–19 is read on Holy Friday] to remedy passages that use language that has been interpreted as anti-Semitic."[4] Whether this resolution will lead to solutions remains unknown; since 2006, the Episcopal Church has been developing homiletic guides regarding biblical passages as well as hymns that can be and have been interpreted as promoting Jew-hatred. Resolutions on this topic continued almost annually for the next decade. As I stated in testimony regarding C014, "Since you keep repeating the guidelines, and the guidelines don't work, then the problem is not with the guidelines; it's with the readings. Change the lectionary."[5]

Similar concerns are being heard in pockets of the Roman Catholic Church. On April 14, Maundy or Holy Thursday, 2022, Jim McDermott wrote in the Jesuit magazine *America*, "The Gospel of John has been used to justify anti-Semitism—so we should

---

[4] Cited in David Paulsen, "Churches Consider Alternate Good Friday Liturgies, Bible Translations over Concerns of Anti-Jewish Interpretations," *Episcopal News Service* (ENS), April 12, 2022, https://www.episcopalnewsservice.org/2022/04/12/churches-eye-alternate-liturgies-bible-translations-amid-anti-jewish-concerns-on-good-friday/ (checked May 13, 2022).

[5] Quoted in Paulsen, "Churches Consider." See also Emily McFarlan Miller, "Episcopal Church Mulls Changes to Holy Week Readings Seen as Antisemitic," *Religion News Service* (RNS), April 14, 2022, https://religionnews.com/2022/04/14/episcopal-church-mulls-changes-to-holy-week-readings-seen-as-antisemitic/ (checked May 13, 2022).

stop reading it on Good Friday."[6] Among his sources, he quotes Adele Reinhartz on the emotional impact made by the repeated use of "the Jews" (Greek: οἱ Ἰουδαῖοι, *hoi Ioudaioi*) in the Johannine passion narrative.

Shifting one reading for another (e.g., John to Luke for Holy Friday) or eliminating certain verses from a reading of John's Gospel is not the same thing as dismantling doctrine. No group should sacrifice their own soteriologies on the altars of interfaith sensitivity. Changing the lectionary to avoid Jew-hatred— blaming Jews for the death of Jesus; calling Jews money-loving, hypocritical, and other nasty names[7]—is doable.

Changing liturgical readings is not the same thing as changing doctrine. On soteriological matters, determining what constitutes Jew-hatred becomes murkier. For example, also in 2022, the Diocese of New York offered Resolution C030, which seeks to reassess "lectionaries authorized for use in The Episcopal Church that contain language that has been interpreted as antisemitic, anti-Jewish, or supersessionist"; the goal is for the Standing Committee in Liturgy and Music to offer alternative readings for worship. Not all supersessionist views catalyze hatred. Supersessionism is part of most if not all religious traditions and, depending on its form, is not inherently evil. The rabbinic movement superseded the Sadducees by writing out of the world to come those who deny that the Torah teaches resurrection of the dead (m. Sanh. 10:1). Trinitarian Christians, after Nicaea, superseded other Christian movements with different christologies, pneumatologies, and theologies.

Christian eschatological supersessionism that proclaims Jesus to be the "way and the truth and the life" (John 14:6) and that asserts "all Israel" (Rom 11:26), meaning all Jews, "will be saved" *through him* need not catalyze hatred. Since both Judaism and Christianity are unfinished—the former waiting for the messiah; the latter for the Messiah to return—I have no problem with waiting for the details of the messianic age to be sorted out. The problem is the hard supersessionism known as replacement theology in which the promises to Israel pass over to the Church.[8] This is the type of supersessionism promulgated by the (now but not always; it appears in Codex Sinaiticus) noncanonical Epistle of Barnabas. According to this text, the covenant with Israel (i.e., the Jews) was broken, permanently, with the Golden Calf. The question is whether John's Gospel strays into replacement theology—which I think it does via its cosmic dualism and its consequent erasure of the *Ioudaioi* to their own history in relation to Abraham and David—and, if John does that, what can FOJs do about it.

---

[6] Jim McDermott, "The Gospel of John Has Been Used to Justify Anti-Semitism—So We Should Stop Reading It on Good Friday," *America*, April 14, 2022, https://www.americamagazine.org/faith/2022/04/14/good-friday-gospel-john-jews-242822 (checked May 13, 2022).

[7] Because both Jews and Christians typically see the Pharisees as the forerunners of the rabbinic movement, lectionary readings concerning the Pharisees are also in play. See Joseph Sievers and Amy-Jill Levine, eds., *The Pharisees* (Grand Rapids, MI: Eerdmans, 2021).

[8] Amy-Jill Levine, "Supersessionism: Admit and Address Rather Than Debate or Deny," *Religions* 13:155 (2022), https://doi.org/10.3390/rel13020155 (checked May 13, 2022).

Interventions That Threaten to Excuse Rather Than Correct

Still popular is the conviction that historical understanding of the Gospel will correct anti-Jewish readings.[9] McDermott advises, "Whenever you are dealing with a passage from Scripture that does not seem to make sense, a good strategy is to dig a little deeper. Is our translation truly accurate to the time and culture in which the text was written? What did the passage mean within its proper historical context?"[10] That we cannot be sure where, when, by whom, or to whom the Gospel is written should be a first indication that historical-critical intervention may not work.

The most popular iteration of the historical reconstruction today is that John's *Ioudaioi* represent an "ideological category" (in reference to "those who identify with the Jerusalem Temple and its system under Roman imperial control").[11] This contextualization reaches back (unintentionally) to the antisemitic writings of Renan, Grundmann, and their ilk by positing a Galilean versus Judean divide, with the Galileans charismatic, egalitarian, laissez-faire on purity and the temple, gentile oriented, and otherwise looking more or less like liberal Protestants.[12] The Judeans are cosmopolitan (a dog whistle), money-loving, obsessed with ritual purity, and devoted to a temple system that exploits the poor. Howard-Brook concludes that because Jesus "claims he is the living Temple of God" [better phrased: John's Gospel promulgates this view; it is not clear that Jesus made the claim himself], "you don't have to come to Jerusalem three times a year and spend all your money there. You can go anywhere and experience God." In this configuration, John's *Ioudaioi* are not just the "religious elite" but include the residents of Jerusalem who support the local government and thus "wanted Jesus brought down."[13]

This approach misreads Judaism, which never restricted the divine to the temple. The divine can be experienced anywhere, such as at the Jordan River with John's

---

[9] See extended discussion with examples in Amy-Jill Levine, "Christian Privilege, Christian Fragility, and the Gospel of John," in *The Gospel of John and Jewish-Christian Relations*, ed. Adele Reinhartz (Lanham, MD: Lexington/Fortress, 2018), 87–110; and Amy-Jill Levine, "Jesus and the Liberal Academy: From First Century Jew to Twenty-First Century Anti-Fascist," in *Exegeting Exegesis*, vol. 2 of *What Does Theology Do, Actually?* ed. Phillip A. Davis Jr., Daniel Lanzinger, and Matthew R. Robinson (Leipzig: Evangelische Verlagsanstalt, 2023).

[10] McDermott, "Gospel of John."

[11] Wes Howard-Brook, cited in McDermott, "Gospel of John." The quotes in the following paragraph are from this source. See also on the "Judeans" as "elite" Wes Howard-Brook, "Why We Need to Translate *Ioudaioi* as 'Judeans,'" in *Jesus Wasn't Killed by the Jews: Reflections for Christians in Lent*, ed. Jon M. Sweeny (Maryknoll, NY: Orbis Books, 2020), 76–83, for example, "in the narrative context of the Gospel of John, the *Ioudaioi* are those who are ideological defenders and economic beneficiaries of the Roman Judean collaboration" (Howard-Brook, "Translate *Ioudaioi*," 81), while Jesus "is seeking, like the prophets before him, to call the elite and their supporters to radical reform" (Howard-Brook, "Translate *Ioudaioi*," 82). In this article, he does not mention what the reforms are. In John's Gospel, social-justice issues take a far back seat to christological claims.

[12] History of scholarship in Roland Deines, "Jesus the Galilean: Questioning the Function of Galilee in Recent Jesus Research," in *Acts of God in History: Studies Towards Recovering a Theological Historiography*, ed. Christoph Ochs and Peter Watts, WUNT 317 (Tübingen: Mohr Siebeck, 2013), 53–93.

[13] McDermott, "Gospel of John."

immersions. It misrepresents the temple via allusions to bankruptcy, especially given that the temple worked on a sliding scale. It misrepresents Jesus's Jewish followers, including Paul, who worshiped in the temple and found that "worship" (Rom 9:4: λατρεία) valuable. Finally, it indicts all Jewish residents of Judea as arrayed against Jesus, even as it depicts Jesus not as an apocalyptic eschatological prophet who expected the inbreaking of the kingdom of God but as an anti-Roman social justice warrior.

An alternative FOJ view is to read the Gospel as a window (if perhaps mullioned stained glass) into a Johannine community. That a text is not a community is one of many problems with this approach. For this contingent, John's polemic is a response to that community's rejection if not persecution by "the Jews." McDermott cites Reinhartz to make this claim:

> As to why John was so persistent and strident in his attacks on *hoi Ioudaioi*, Dr. Reinhartz identifies three possible interpretations, which are not mutually exclusive: John is trying to punish the Pharisees for expelling his community from the synagogue; John is trying to assert the distinctiveness and superiority of his community over that of the Pharisees; or it is a product of John's overall dualistic rhetorical framework.[14]

Yet Reinhartz rejects two of these interpretations: J. L. Martyn's popular two-stage reading of the Gospel and the idea that synagogues are expelling Christ confessors because of christological concerns.

Other FOJs, recognizing that words take on different connotations depending on the context, insist that the dozens of negative appearances of *Ioudaioi* in the Fourth Gospel refer to "Jewish leaders" or "Jewish authorities." McDermott states, "Scholars generally agree that despite how it sounds, John did not mean 'all Jews.' Dr. Reinhartz notes how John uses the term interchangeably with the Pharisees, at one point even in the same passage."[15] Reinhartz's point, as I understand her, is that John uses the various terms interchangeably and *therefore means all Jews*, since the interchangeable use creates one undifferentiated group of *Ioudaioi* defined by their opposition to Jesus and so their rejection of being children of God or heirs of Abraham. John's dedifferentiation follows Matthew, who begins the process by creating groups of Pharisees and Sadducees (Matt 3:7; 16:1, 6, 11, 12; Matthew's is the only Gospel where this pair occurs)[16] and replacing Mark's neutral "scribe" (Mark 12:29-34) with a malevolent "Pharisee" (Matt 22:34-40). John continues the pattern by omitting Sadducees and scribes and merging Pharisees into *Ioudaioi*.

The parsing of John's *Ioudaioi* into subcategories leads to the claim that the Gospel is *only* against the "Jewish leaders" or "Jewish authorities"; it therefore is not defaming all Jews. The argument fails. John knows the words "chief priests" and "Pharisees" but nonetheless bleeds these terms into "Jews." The addition of terms such as "leaders" or

---

[14] McDermott, "Gospel of John."
[15] McDermott, "Gospel of John."
[16] Henry Pattarumadathil, "Pharisees and Sadducees Together in Matthew," in *Pharisees*, ed. Joseph Sievers and Amy-Jill Levine (Grand Rapids, MI: Eerdmans, 2021), 136–47.

"authorities" to John's text may exacerbate the problem. People with pew Bibles see and therefore hear "Jews" in the text, regardless of what the lector says. The discrepancy between what is said and what is written calls attention to the (reference to the) Jews as a problem. The shift in terminology opens the accusation of wokeness even as it avoids the problem rather than engages it.[17]

Perhaps some FOJs want to place "Jew" in the same category as now-forbidden words applied to other groups. People who should know better continue to use the term "Jew" as a verb, meaning to bargain down a price.[18] In fall 2021, a former faculty colleague emailed me to describe how, during a lecture on Second Temple Judaism, a student disrupted the class and "registered strong dissent on the use of the words 'Jew' and 'Jewish'"; the student then self-identified as a "proud member of the tribe of Hebrews." The colleague asked, "Is the use of the word 'Jewish' or 'Jew' such an odious and unacceptable lexical choice to be avoided at all costs?" I wondered why the question needed to be asked.

In February 2022, the Duden German dictionary initially glossed over the term *Jude* with the correct note that the term is sometimes used as a derogatory slur. The dictionary retracted that gloss after criticism. Joseph Schuster, the head of the Central Council of Jews in Germany, stated, "Even if 'Jew' is used pejoratively in schoolyards or only hesitantly by some people, and the Duden editors are certainly well-meaning in pointing out this context, everything should be done to avoid solidifying the term as discriminatory."[19] This approach to the term "Jew" may be behind the increasingly frequent substitution of "Jewish person" even in conversation.

Perhaps this concern to avoid the word "Jew" is why the Common English Bible (CEB) shifts "Jew" to "Jewish" at John 4:9: the Samaritan woman at the well meets not "a Jew" but "a Jewish man."[20] The CEB for John 3:13 mentions "the Jewish Passover,"[21] and both 5:1 and 6:4 similarly note "a Jewish festival"; Nicodemus is not a "leader of the Jews" but a "Jewish leader" (3:1); for John 1:19, the CEB speaks not of the Jews in Jerusalem, but the Jewish leaders.[22] The same overtranslation of Jewish leaders appears in 2:18, 20; 5:10, 15, 18; 7:11; 8:22; 9:18, and so on. A variant, "Jewish opposition," surfaces in 6:41; 7:35; 8:48, 52, 57; and 7:1 has "Jewish authorities" as does 7:13. "Jews"

---

[17] On the "Jew" versus "Judean" argument see n. 11 above as well as Amy-Jill Levine, *The Misunderstood Jew: The Church and the Scandal of the Jewish Jesus* (San Francisco, CA: HarperOne, 2004), 159–60; Adele Reinhartz, "The Vanishing Jews of Antiquity," in *Jew and Judean: A Marginalia Forum on Politics and Historiography in the Translation of Ancient Texts*, ed. Timothy Michael Law and Charles Halton, *Marginalia/Los Angeles Review of Books*, June 24, 2014, 10–23.

[18] Jane Kaufman, "OSU Investigating Professor's 'Jewing down' comment," *Cleveland Jewish News*, December 22, 2021, https://www.clevelandjewishnews.com/news/local_news/osu-investigating-professor-s-jewing-down-comment/article_f247f81b-1017-509c-8473-3ce2c30810d2.html (checked May 13, 2022).

[19] Shira Hanau, "German Dictionary Changes Definition of 'Jew' after Complaint from Local Jewish Community," *Jewish Telegraph Agency*, February 17, 2022, https://www.jta.org/2022/02/17/global/german-dictionary-changes-definition-of-jew-after-complaint-from-local-jewish-community (checked May 13, 2022).

[20] CEB ad loc., ed. Joel Green, *The CEB Study Bible* (Nashville, TN: Abingdon, 2013); notes on John by J. Ramsey Michaels.

[21] CEB NT, 173.

[22] CEB NT, 171.

finally appears at 4:22, "salvation is from the Jews." For 6:52, where some Jews could be seen as positive, the CEB offers, "Then the Jews debated among themselves, asking, 'How can this man give us his flesh to eat?'" In like manner, 8:31 notes "the Jews who believed in him." Thus, the only "Jews" are either representatives of the biblical tradition in distinction to the Samaritans or the ones who believe in Jesus. There is no comment on 8:44 save the note on "murderer from the beginning" and a reference to 1 John 3:12. This translation does not resolve the problem; the litany of Jewish leaders, authorities, opposition, and so on solidifies that pretty much anyone "Jewish" is to be avoided.

How much FOJ arguments and retranslations stem from convictions that reject the idea that there is something rotten in the heart of the Gospel remains an open question. How much of Reinhartz's own Jewish identity (or mine) will be seen as coloring conclusions of John's anti-Jewish rhetoric also remain open questions. And yet, in today's rush to read the Bible from one's own social location or subject position (postcolonial, trans, disabled, etc.), the one identity marker that typically goes missing from most discussions of John and the Jews—that is, discussions not by Jews—is that of Christian identity. When a (nominally, e.g., by affiliation with a seminary, having an MDiv) Christian academic makes a comment that lands in the FOJ category, without also stating whether disagreement with a text is possible, whether one can separate tradition from redaction, or whether the Gospel is seen as "sacred," such a statement ignores the social-location element of greatest relevance to the subject area.

Historical-critical work is not going to resolve the problem of whether John is anti-Jewish. Even the definition of what constitutes something as "anti-Jewish" remains unsettled. Less controversial is the claim that John has led to anti-Jewish interpretations or, bluntly, Jew-hatred. Since extracting the Gospel from Scripture is not an option, and since proclaiming an anti-Jewish message should not be a possibility, effective responses will require insights from ethics and theology; only through such postbiblical filters of what Christianity represents can people in good faith continue to befriend this text and to proclaim it.

Listening to the "Experts"

Adele Reinhartz's work has moved from the academy to the general public. It has also influenced Johannine scholarship. Ideally, her breakup with the Beloved Disciple will influence scholarly approaches more. In comparison with most study guides, annotated Bibles, and commentaries, only Adele Reinhartz, as far as I can tell, sees John as casting the Jews out of the covenant.

The majority of textbooks and annotated Bibles I surveyed take the route of exculpation by historical context: positing that the evangelist wrote from within the Jewish community, they conclude that the Gospel cannot be anti-Jewish. They also latch onto *aposynagōgos* (ἀποσυνάγωγος) language in John 9, 12, and 16 to conclude that the Johannine language is reactionary and thus explicable. A few warn against concluding that the Jews in John's Gospel, if not throughout the New Testament and into history, are "children of the devil" (John 8:44), but most go no farther than telling readers to be careful not to perpetuate negative stereotypes. *How* readers are supposed to do this is left in the hands of the students.

Given the excellent work that the Roman Catholic Church has done in both Vatican documents and statements by National Bishops Conferences, I would have expected biblical resources to be particularly attentive to anti-Jewish elements. Even the best of the studies—including studies that engage with Reinhartz's work—leave room for improvement. For example, in the first of her two-volume contribution on the Gospel of John in the Wisdom Commentary series, Mary Coloe, a member of the Sisters of the Presentation of the Virgin Mary (PVBM), begins with the claim that John's "Gospel, more than any other New Testament book, requires that all characters—women, men, Jews, Gentiles—all participate equally in the divinization of creation when the 'Word became flesh' (1:14)."[23] The problem: God may have so loved the world, but the world did not respond positively. Nor could it, since not all are called to be children of God. The prologue begins the differentiation: "But to those receiving him, he gave to them authority to become children of God, to those who had faith in his name" (1:12). In 6:65, Jesus states, "no one is able to come to me unless it is given to him by the Father." Finally, Jesus tells his disciples, "You did not choose me, but I chose you" (John 15:16).

Referencing the *aposynagōgos* statements in John 9, 12, 16, she begins, "Even if this refers only to a local synagogue ... ."[24] In this reading, *that* Jews were expelling Christ-followers is not in doubt; the issue is the extent of the problem. She finds John's threats—"for the Jews had already agreed that anyone who confessed him to be the Christ *would be put out* of the synagogue" (9:22b); "for fear that they *would be put out* of the synagogue" (12:42b); "They *will put you out* of the synagogues" (16:2)—to be *fait accompli* since "such a decision may have come about following the rabbinic discussions at Jamnia/Yavneh during the 80s." She thus assumes the outdated view of Yavneh as an ancient post-temple conclave that influenced Diaspora synagogues. Finally, she reproduces the version of the *Birkat Haminim* that mentions the Nazareans.[25]

As Reinhartz discusses in several places, the council at Yavneh may be a rabbinic invention, and, even had some gathering occurred, "it is now acknowledged by most scholars that *Birkat Haminim* was not yet incorporated into Jewish liturgy in the late first century."[26] In *JANT*, she writes that the expulsion theory, modeled on the *Birkat*,

---

[23] Mary Coloe, *John 1–10*, Wisdom Commentary 44A (Collegeville, MN: Liturgical Press, 2021), xiv.
[24] Coloe, *John 1–10*, li. For comparison, Jo-Ann A. Brant finds the connection of the Gospel to the *Birkat* and to Jamnia unlikely: "Scholars began to recognize that the decisions attributed to Yavneh occurred over many years, and that orthodox Judaism is a product of retrospection promoted in part by the rise of Orthodox Christianity," in *John*, Paideia: Commentaries on the NT (Grand Rapids, MI: Baker Academic, 2011), 11. Conversely, Francis J. Moloney locates the context of the Gospel in the "final breakdown between the Johannine community and the local synagogue" with the Christ-believers "forcibly excluded from the synagogue." See his *The Gospel of John*, SP 4 (Collegeville, MN: Liturgical Press, 2005), 2, 11. Moloney, *Gospel of John*, 297, goes as far as to locate the *aposynagōgos* comments in terms of the "experience of the Johannine Christians before the *Bet Din* (religious court) in Jamnia."
[25] Coloe, *John 1–10*, lii.
[26] Reinhartz, *Cast Out of the Covenant*, 117. See Ruth Langer, *Cursing the Christians? A History of the Birkat Haminim* (New York: Oxford University Press, 2011); Ruth Langer, "Birkat Ha-Minim. A Jewish Curse of Christians?" in *The Jewish Annotated New Testament*, ed. Amy-Jill Levine and Marc Zvi Brettler, 2nd ed. (New York: Oxford University Press, 2017), 653–4, and Reinhartz, *Cast Out of the Covenant*, for bibliography on the relationship of the benediction to the Fourth Gospel.

"is flawed on both literary and historical grounds."[27] Among the few commentators to suggest an alternative reconstruction is Warren Carter, who finds it more plausible that the Johannine community "may have decided that they did not want to associate with a synagogue community that resisted their claims. They voluntarily withdrew but, in pain and anger, understood their withdrawal as a forced separation."[28]

After describing and then reinforcing these presumed historical circumstances, Coloe concludes, "but the waters here are muddy!"[29] Yet her explications seemed clear to me. Indeed, she's planted the seed of Jewish expulsion, which she then cultivates. For example, Coloe states that high Christology (e.g., John 1:1) "led to conflict with other Jews, and eventually those believers openly confessing their faith in Jesus were expelled from the synagogue (9:22; 12:42; 16:2) in this locale."[30] The muddy hypothesis becomes fact.

The Roman Catholic New American Bible Revised Edition (NABR, as in "won't you be my NABR?") for John's Gospel begins with replacement theology: "The first sign is the transformation of water into wine at Cana (Jn 2:1-11); this represents the replacement of the Jewish ceremonial washings and symbolizes the entire creative and transforming work of Jesus."[31] The point is incorrect both historically and theologically. Historically, people at the wedding already would have washed; so the issue cannot be replacement of ritual purity.[32] Theologically, the Church follows Paul in maintaining that the "gifts and callings of God are irrevocable" (Rom 11:29).

The notes then offer a tendentious comparison of the Gospel's treatment of Jews with its discussion of women:

> The polemic between synagogue and church produced bitter and harsh invective, especially regarding the hostility toward Jesus of the authorities—Pharisees and Sadducees—who are combined and referred to frequently as "the Jews" (see note on Jn 1:19). These opponents are even described in Jn 8:44 as springing from their father the devil, whose conduct they imitate in opposing God by rejecting Jesus, whom God has sent. On the other hand, the author of this gospel seems to take pains to show that women are not inferior to men in the Christian community: the woman at the well in Samaria (Jn 4) is presented as a prototype of a missionary (Jn 4:4–42), and the first witness of the resurrection is a woman (Jn 20:11–18).

John's Gospel never mentions Sadducees. The juxtaposition of John 8:44 with the Samaritan woman is tantamount to saying, "Well, yes, we do say Jews are children of the devil, but we're really progressive [with an implicit contrast with the Jewish community's take on women's issues] on women's issues."

---

[27] Reinhartz, "The Gospel according to John," 169.
[28] Warren Carter, *John: Storyteller, Interpreter, Evangelist* (Grand Rapids, MI: Baker Academic, 2006), 170.
[29] Coloe, *John 1–10*, lii.
[30] Coloe, *John 1–10*, lix.
[31] https://bible.usccb.org/bible/john/0 (checked May 13, 2022).
[32] Reinhartz, "The Gospel according to John," comments on John 2:7: "*Fill the jars*, since they needed to be refilled, the washing likely had already taken place." *JANT*, 178.

While the note on John 1:11 glosses "his own [people]" with "Israelites" (not Jews), the note on 1:19 confirms the attempt to restrict Johannine *Ioudaioi* to leaders:

> The Jews: throughout most of the gospel, the "Jews" does not refer to the Jewish people as such but to the hostile authorities, both Pharisees and Sadducees, particularly in Jerusalem, who refuse to believe in Jesus. The usage reflects the atmosphere, at the end of the first century, of polemics between church and synagogue, or possibly it refers to Jews as representative of a hostile world (Jn 1:10–11).[33]

While helpful in distinguishing tradition from redaction, the note creates additional problems. First, there is no reason to distinguish, either in the Gospel or in any stage of history, the average Jew who "refuses to believe in Jesus" (as if belief is a choice!) and the leaders who share such lack of belief. Second, the note does not explain the refusal. Do Jews refuse because Jesus failed to bring about the messianic age as they understood it? Do they refuse because they were predestined to do so, since in the Fourth Gospel Jesus calls his own (John 10:3; not everyone makes the cut)? Third, what synagogue polemics?

By chapter 3, the notes drop the distinction between Jews and Jewish leaders so that the opponents are Jews all the way down: "The shift from singular through Jn 3:10 to plural in Jn 3:11 may reflect the early church's controversy with the Jews." By implication, there are no "Jews" in "the early church." For 4:9, we learn, "Samaritan women were regarded by Jews as ritually impure, and therefore Jews were forbidden to drink from any vessel they had handled." Missing are the extensive rabbinic debates on Samaritan halakah, the fact that Antipas's mother was a Samaritan, and Samaritan views of Jews. Ritual impurity, unmentioned in the text and irrelevant to it, goes undefined. For John 8, we learn that "Dt 22:23–24 prescribes stoning for a betrothed virgin" found in an adulterous situation; the notes ignore the fact that the woman's accusers are not about to stone her, that the issue is a matter of legal interpretation, that such stoning is never carried out in the Bible, and that the rabbis make capital punishment almost impossible.

And now?

Some churches have been wrestling with John's depiction of the Jews for decades. Little progress has been made. FOJs continue to explain, and explain away, the problem rather than wrestle with the texts and change their lectionaries. Perhaps were more FOJs to read Adele's works, especially the more recent studies, they would be better able to do the necessary wrestling. They can befriend John, but just as some friendship is maintained by not discussing politics, they may leave John's anti-Jewish rhetoric outside the sanctuary and relocate it to the classroom. Just as some friendship is maintained despite the crimes people commit, so friendship with John can be maintained, but John should not be allowed to commit more harm. The story of Adele Reinhartz's breakup with the Beloved Disciple should serve as a warning to any who want to befriend the Beloved Disciple.

---

[33] https://bible.usccb.org/bible/john/1 (checked May 13, 2022).

2

Intimacy with Jesus: Construction of Closeness by Gender Diversity in John

Peter Wick

The Gospel of John promises Jesus's followers an intimate closeness to Jesus. This intimacy is promised to both men and women. But women and men are promised two very different ways of closeness and also qualities of closeness. A diversity is constructed here through the differentiation of the sexes. However, both forms of intimate closeness are promised beyond the Gospel to the whole congregation, that is, to both men and women.

The Disciples as Friends

First, the intimacy between Jesus and the men will be examined here. In the farewell discourses, Jesus calls his disciples friends in the Fourth Gospel (John 13–17). The term "friend" (φίλος) as a relationship description between Jesus and his disciples hardly plays a role in the Synoptic Gospels. It is therefore remarkable that the term "friend" (φίλος) becomes the climax for the disciple–Jesus relationship in John's Gospel. John the Baptist refers to himself as the friend of the bridegroom in his relationship with Jesus (John 3:29). Jesus speaks of Lazarus as a friend of his and his disciples (John 11:11).[1] The speech of the vine and of abiding in Jesus with the subsequent words of friendship with Jesus forms the center of the farewell speeches.

Hellenistic Concepts of Friendship in the Gospel

How is this friendship to be understood in John 15:9-17? Hellenistic ideals of friendship play an important role in the background to this text. But how does the text draw on them and what meaning does it evoke?

---

[1] For important essays on the question of the Hellenistic background of these friendship statements, see Klaus Scholtissek, "'Eine größere Liebe als diese hat niemand, als wenn einer sein Leben hingibt für seine Freunde' (Joh 15,13)," in *Kontexte des Johannesevangeliums: Das vierte Evangelium in religions- und traditionsgeschichtlicher Perspektive*, ed. Jörg Frey and Udo Schnelle, WUNT 175 (Tübingen: Mohr Siebeck, 2004), 413–39, and Martin M. Culy, *Echoes of Friendship in the Gospel of John*, NTM 30 (Sheffield: Sheffield Phoenix, 2010).

The central *topoi* of ancient friendship discourses are status-related equality and reciprocity among friends.[2] Reciprocity is linked to utilitarian thinking. Friends benefit each other. Such reciprocal utilitarian thinking hardly plays a role in John 15. The disciples do not directly benefit Jesus. In the immediately preceding speech about the vine, this is indirectly the case: the vine depends on the branches to bear fruit. However, the style of the image emphasizes the opposite direction: without the connection to the vine, the branches are useless. Equality is not the theme of the image of the vine.[3] But the ideal of equality is encountered all the more clearly in John 15:9-17: Jesus grants his disciples, who until now had the status of servants, the honor of friendship and places them on the same level in terms of relationship with himself, who is one with God the Father. Equality is therefore not a prerequisite for this friendship but is only realized through it. Mutual benefit is not the goal. This is in tension with the Hellenistic ideal of friendship.

Aristotle grounds equality particularly in a doctrine of virtue. Friends are oriented toward the same virtues.[4] Jesus raises the disciples to friends through the common orientation toward love, which is founded in the Father's love for him and in his love for them, and which is at the same time a model for their dealings with each other.

Friendships are gladly made at the evening banquet, the δεῖπνον (*deipnon*), which is followed by the συμπόσιον (*symposion*). The farewell speeches immediately follow the evening meal (*deipnon*) at which Jesus washed the feet of his disciples. They can be understood as speeches that took place at the *symposion*, which followed the *deipnon*.

Another ideal is present: possessions are common to friends.[5] This also applies to knowledge. Friends have no secrets from each other and speak to each other in frankness.[6] The only friends of God in the Hebrew Bible, Abraham and Moses, are each initiated by God into his plans of judgment toward Sodom and Gomorrah (Gen 18:16-33) and the people in the wilderness (Exod 32:7-14), respectively, and they discuss these matters with him. Jesus shares with the disciples all that he has heard from the Father. Since he is one with the Father and the disciples are united with him in friendship, they become God's friends at the same time, at least in an ulterior way. Insofar as the world rejects God and his Son, it also hates Jesus's disciples (John 15:18-19).[7]

The disciples share in the rights of access to God. What Jesus could ask of the Father, they are also entitled to in his name. Everything Jesus knows about his Father he shares with his friends. However, it is important to note that the disciples have nothing to offer in return. They benefit unilaterally from Jesus's gifts. There is no actual reciprocity of friendship. The gradient of dependence is once again consolidated with reference to the figurative word of the vine in John 15:16: "You did not choose me but I chose you.

---

[2] Scholtissek, "Liebe," 430.
[3] Chrys Caragounis, "'Abide in Me.' The New Mode of Relationship between Jesus and His Followers as a Basis for Christian Ethics (John 15)," in *Rethinking the Ethics of John: 'Implicit Ethics' in the Johannine Writings*, vol. 3 of *Contexts and Norms of New Testament Ethics*, ed. Jan Gabriel van der Watt and Ruben Zimmermann, WUNT 291 (Tübingen: Mohr Siebeck, 2012), 250–63, here 261.
[4] Aristotle, *Eth. nic.* 1166b.
[5] Aristotle, *Eth. nic.* 1159b, 1186b; Plato, *Resp.* 462C; Plutarch, *Mor.* 490E.
[6] On frankness in friendship, see Scholtissek, "Liebe," 428–30.
[7] Thus, Scholtissek, "Liebe," 428.

And I appointed you to go and bear fruit, fruit that will last, so that the Father will give you whatever you ask him in my name."[8] The Johannine Jesus clearly records here that a hierarchical divide remains. The disciples' actions are ultimately grounded in his electing action and love alone.

In Hellenistic texts on friendship, dying for a friend is treated as a borderline situation of friendship. The possibility is discussed, but there is no obligation to give one's life for a friend.[9] But in John 15:13, it is spoken of as the highest measure of friendship-love. Jesus is ready to die for his friends.[10] The same is not demanded of his disciples directly, but indirectly it is. For he gives them his love as an example.

A More Radical and Asymmetrical Form of Friendship

A more hierarchical concept of friendship aims at a more radical form of friendship, which—it is postulated by Greeks and Romans—is to be found east of the imperial border. In Tacitus, a contemporary of the evangelist, and in Lucian of Samosata (120–180 CE), writing a good half century later, this concept of friendship becomes tangible: men crowd around a hero and court his friendship until they are chosen by him as a friend. In a kind of blood community, they commit themselves entirely to the goals of their heroic friend. They are prepared to sacrifice their lives for him. To outlive them in battle is considered a disgrace, because it would be a sign of a lack of commitment to their friend. Conversely, they participate fully in the privileges and wealth of their friend and dine at his table.

Christopher Beckwith, a specialist in the study of so-called Central Eurasia in antiquity and the Middle Ages, in his monograph *Empires of the Silk Road* (2009),[11] places the preface under the title "The Hero and His Friends," because he considers this type of friendship to be part of a Central Eurasian cultural complex. He also draws on Lucian and Tacitus, among others.

In his dialogue *Toxaris*, Lucian describes the competition between a Greek and a Scythian named Toxaris over the question of which culture offers the better conception of friendship. In *Toxaris* it sounds like this:

> For I would have you know this also—Scythians think that there is nothing greater than friendship, and there is not anything upon which a Scythian will pride himself more than on aiding a friend and sharing his dangers. (*Toxaris* 7)[12]
>
> First of all, I wish to tell you how we make our friends. ... [W]hen we see a brave man, capable of great achievements, we all make after him, and we think fit to

---

[8] All English Bible quotations refer to the NRSV.
[9] Scholtissek, "Liebe," 421–2, 433.
[10] Thomas Söding, "Einsatz des Lebens. Ein Motiv johanneischer Soteriologie," in *The Death of Jesus in the Fourth Gospel*, ed. Gilbert van Belle (Leuven: Leuven University Press, 2007), 363–84, here 365, 382.
[11] Christopher I. Beckwith, *Empires of the Silk Road. A History of Central Eurasia from the Bronze Age to the Present* (Princeton, NJ: Princeton University Press, 2009).
[12] *Lucian*, trans. A. M. Harmon, 8 vols., LCL (Cambridge, MA: Harvard University Press, 1962), 115.

behave in forming friendships as you do in seeking brides, paying them protracted court and doing everything in their company to the end that we may not fall short of attaining their friendship or be thought to deserve rejection. And when a man has been singled out and is at last a friend, there ensue formal compacts and the most solemn of oaths that we will not only live with one another but die, if need be, for each other; and we do just that. For, once we have cut our fingers, let the blood drip into a cup, dipped our sword-points into it, and then, both at once, have set it to our lips and drunk, there is nothing thereafter that can dissolve the bond between us. (*Toxaris* 37)

Tacitus writes about the Germanic tribes (*germani*):

When the battlefield is reached it is a reproach for a chief to be surpassed in prowess; a reproach for his retinue not to equal the prowess of its chief: but to have left the field and survived one's chief, this means lifelong infamy and shame: to defend and protect him, to devote one's own feats even to his glorification, this is the gist of their allegiance: … for it is from their leader's bounty that they demand that glorious warhorse, and that murderous and masterful spear: banquetings and a certain rude but lavish outfit are equivalent to salary. (Tacitus, *Germania* 14)

Here it is not equals who make friends with each other, but a hero who chooses friends from among those who compete for them. In fact, not only does John 15 show impressive similarities to this, but it also shows that other peculiarities of John's Gospel can be interpreted more deeply through this pattern of friendship. Only after the similarities have been pointed out will it be asked whether and how it is justifiable to relate Scythian and Germanic sources to the Gospel of John.

Unlike the Synoptics, according to John, Jesus, apart from Philip, does not call the disciples to follow him, but they press toward him of their own accord and want to stay with him (1:38). Jesus does not call the circle of twelve either. He provokes and frightens his disciples with the speech that they must chew his flesh and drink his blood (6:51-56). Even though the drinking of blood is meant symbolically, unlike Toxaris, many turn away from Jesus because of this speech. Only the hard core of twelve disciples remains. So the disciples come to Jesus in this chapter and are tested by him. Only a few remain. These are apparently the twelve who are first mentioned in 6:67.[13] In John 15, they will learn that they do not become friends of his because of this but because he has chosen them to be so.

Moreover, the willingness of the disciples to die for the "hero" and friend does not seem to be the borderline case of friendship in John's Gospel but rather a matter of course. After Jesus escaped from Judea because he was in danger of death there, he wants to return to his friend Lazarus, even though this means risking his life for his friend (11:1–12:11).[14] Thomas knows about the danger of death in this region

---

[13] See Esther Kobel, *Dining with John. Communal Meals and Identity Formation in the Fourth Gospel and Its Historical and Cultural Context*, BibInt 109 (Leiden: Brill, 2011), 88–9.

[14] Cf. Scholtissek, "Liebe," 427.

and urges his fellow disciples: "Let us also go to die with him!" (11:16). Peter wants to lay down his life for Jesus and leave it for him (13:37-38). Only in this Gospel does Peter, who is mentioned by name, defend his friend with the sword (18:10). In 21:19, the Risen Lord announces that Peter will indeed suffer death in the future for his sake.

In 15:9-17, Jesus offers the disciples a very specific friendship that has many similarities to *Toxaris*[15] and also to *Germania*. The condition of this friendship is that his disciples have remained with Jesus and in his love and now love each other with this love. Judas does not become a friend because he has not stayed and has already left Jesus (John 13). This friendship is clearly hierarchical. Jesus alone has chosen his friends. The participation is one-sided. The disciples, through their new status as friends, participate in Jesus's goods and privileges: in his joy, in his knowledge, in his power of prayer, in his ability to work lasting fruit, and above all and first in his salvific commitment of his life, which is the highest form of this love for friends. They themselves fail with such love when Jesus is crucified, although they thought they were ready for it. They obviously understand the willingness to die for the friend as a matter of course.

However, the concept of this more radical friendship of the East is apparently deliberately broken and turned around in the style of Johannine theology. The friends do not succeed in laying down their lives for the "hero" but the hero lays down his life for the friends. The death of the "hero" does not drag the others with him into death but opens up life in abundance for them. The giving of life by the friends is not intended by the Johannine Jesus. Later, beyond the text, it becomes a possibility for Peter (cf. 21:19). Jesus grants intimacy to his disciples through this radical concept of *philia* as male friendship.

Bride and Groom, Husband and Wife as Counterparts (John 2 and 4)

Women are not included in this male friendship concept. In the Gospel of John, *eros* (ἔρως) is a form of love that is enigmatically present in the women's stories.[16] In contrast to *agape* (ἀγάπη) and *philia* (φιλία), it does not appear at all as a concept. Nevertheless, *eros* resonates in Jesus's encounters with women in this Gospel and gains greater weight with each encounter. Jesus performs his first sign at the wedding in Cana (John 2) at the ritual union of a man and a woman. There, with wine, he serves the festive joy of bridegroom and bride, only to be called bridegroom, who already has the bride with his community of disciples, mentioned a little later by John the Baptist (3:29). But not only man and woman meet at the wedding in Cana, but also Jesus and

---

[15] Richard I. Pervo, "With Lucian: Who Needs Friends? Friendship in the *Toxaris*," in *Greco-Roman Perspectives on Friendship*, ed. John T. Fitzgerald, RBS 34 (Atlanta, GA: Scholars Press, 1997), 163–80.

[16] For an examination of ἔρως in the Gospel of John, see Jo-Ann Brant, "Husband Hunting. Characterization and Narrative Art in the Gospel of John," *BibInt* 4 (1996): 205–23.

his mother, whom he addresses as a woman (2:3-5). Jesus does not want to respond to the intervention of this woman, his mother, but then does.

In chapter 4, Jesus meets a Samaritan woman at Jacob's well (4:6). A deep conversation develops between the two. The Samaritan woman is not only the one who answers, but she also steers the conversation several times. She becomes Jesus's "counterpart" a dialogue partner and finally the proclaimer of the Messiah. All readers who were familiar with the Holy Scriptures of the Old Testament associated this scene with those in the Old Testament. In the Bible, several men find their wives at wells, namely, Jacob Rachel (Gen 29:6-11) and Moses Zipporah (Exod 2:15-22) and the marriage of Rebekah and Isaac is initiated at a well (Gen 24:13-27). At the same time, the well becomes a central erotic symbol for the woman in the Song of Songs (Song 4:12, 15). Thus, Jesus's encounter with the woman at the well has very strong erotic connotations.

The Reinterpreted Service of Love (John 12)

The enigmatic *eros* is even more evident at the banquet in Lazarus's house in Bethany. "There they gave a dinner for him. Martha served, and Lazarus was one of those at the table with him" (12:2). In Bethany there was a supper (δεῖπνον). Lazarus as a man was present. Martha performed table service (διακονέω). This story appears to reinforce normative gender roles. But for that very reason, it now takes an offensive turn. "Mary took a pound of costly perfume made of pure nard, anointed Jesus' feet, and wiped them with her hair. The house was filled with the fragrance of the perfume" (v. 3).

When a woman loosens her hair, as is assumed here, and anoints a man's feet, this can initiate the erotic play. Thus, in the *Golden Ass*, Lucius says to the maid at the beginning of lovemaking (Apuleius, *Metam.* 2.16.7-9): "But humour me even more: unloose your tresses and let them flow, and embrace me lovingly with your hair rippling like waves." Later, the same Lucius relates (*Metam.* 10.21.4), "Furthermore I had saturated myself with a generous quantity of the finest wine and aroused my desire for sex with the heady fragrance of the ointment." In *Deipnosophistae* 12.553 [Yonge], Athenaeus quotes Eubulos as saying, "Lying full softly in a bed-chamber; around him were most delicate cloaks, well suited for tender maidens, soft, voluptuous; such as those are, who well perfumed and fragrant with oils of amaracus, do rub my feet."

A woman unraveling her hair, anointing a man's feet, and also drenching her hair with this scented oil must have aroused strong erotic associations in contemporary readers and listeners. The first interpretation is obvious: a love game begins between a woman and a man. The context of the Last Supper supports this interpretation, for it was precisely the *symposion* after the meal that offered space for such advances in antiquity. The Song of Songs also links wine, anointing oil, the scent of the bride, and the scent of the bridegroom in an erotic way (Song 1:2-4).

Mary dries Jesus's feet, dripping with anointing oil, with her hair (cf. John 12:3). The fragrance that fills the house now emanates from both Jesus and Mary. The most obvious interpretation of this event is an erotic one. This is an interpretation that explains the present event—the narrated present tense.

This interpretation, however, is not pronounced, but another: "But Judas Iscariot, one of his disciples (the one who was about to betray him), said, 'Why was this perfume not sold for three hundred denarii and the money given to the poor?'" (John 12:4-5). Mary afforded a great luxury for Jesus. She wasted anointing oil worth at least a year's wages of a day laborer. Thus, Jesus not only begins his public ministry with a "luxury miracle" (miracle of wine at Cana in John 2:1-12), but also near the end of his public ministry the luxury of this anointing oil reappears.

Judas's proposal for what would have been a more ethical alternate use for the oil is shown to be insincere. The author uses an aside, "He said this not because he cared about the poor, but because he was a thief; he kept the common purse and used to steal what was put into it" (v. 6), to counter the interpretation that the erotic use of the oil was a waste.

But now Jesus gives a completely different interpretation: "Jesus said, 'Leave her alone. She bought it so that she might keep it for the day of my burial'" (12:7). The loosening of a woman's hair because of a man can also be interpreted as a gesture of mourning when that man is dead. The anointing of his body with precious oils can be understood as a benefit and last duty toward a corpse. Thus, the mourning of a mother for her daughter is described in Phlegon of Tralles's *Book of Marvels* (1.8 [Hansen]): "When Charito saw this evidence she uttered a cry, tore her clothes, cast her headdress from her head and fell to the ground." So the anointing of Jesus's feet points to the future (future tense). But since he is not dead, this interpretation is not the closest.

Thus, this text describes an event, the anointing of the feet. This is interpreted in three ways. The first erotic interpretation is not stated but is suggested by contemporary patterns of understanding. This interpretation is not rejected. The second interpretation, the interpretation as waste, is rejected. "You always have the poor with you, but you do not always have me" (12:8). A third interpretation is offered by Jesus himself, which only gains weight in the future: the anointing of the feet as an anticipation of actions on the day of burial.

The Embrace Not Yet Allowed (John 20)

The dimension of *eros* is also very present in Mary's encounter with the Risen Lord (20:11-18). Only in John is the tomb in a garden (κῆπος) and only here is the body of the executed anointed with myrrh and aloes and oils of fragrant spices. The "garden" and all these spices in combination with each other otherwise only occur in the Song of Songs, the erotic love poem of the Hebrew Bible.

The following takes place in this garden: "Early on the first day of the week, while it was still dark, Mary Magdalene came to the tomb and saw that the stone had been removed from the tomb. ... But Mary stood weeping outside the tomb" (20:1, 11). Mary does not begin to lament, as would have been expected as a mourning rite, but she weeps. Grief, pain of separation, sorrow because of the loss of the beloved Jesus, the supposed theft of the body, and the disciples' inability to help are too much. Driven by her longing, she begins to search.

Mary peers into the supposedly empty tomb. She sees two angels. But she is not frightened. She only gives a curt answer to the angels' question. Without waiting for another word from the angels, she turns away from them. Because of her sorrow, she is not interested in angels (20:11-14). "Jesus said to her, 'Woman, why are you weeping? Whom are you looking for?' Supposing him to be the gardener, she said to him, 'Sir, if you have carried him away, tell me where you have laid him, and I will take him away.' Jesus said to her, 'Mary!' She turned and said to him in Hebrew, 'Rabbouni!' (which means Teacher)" (20:15-16). Succinctly the evangelist tells of a Mary who, since she wept, was constantly on the move, turning and turning. Three times she has already turned, away from the angels, away from the "gardener," and again toward the "gardener," who is in truth the Risen One.

The two angels and Jesus first address Mary with the impersonal "woman." The second time, Jesus calls Mary, who is already turning away, by her name. Jesus is the good shepherd; he calls Mary by her name. She is his, because she knows him (10:3).

Mary does not recognize her Lord by seeing him. Seeing is not enough for her to believe. She believes because she hears his voice. Mary stands here for the church, which is dependent on the eyewitnesses but does not come to faith by seeing, but must and may believe because of the Word. "Jesus said to her, 'Do not hold on to me, because I have not yet ascended to the Father. But go to my brothers and say to them, "I am ascending to my Father and your Father, to my God and your God"'" (20:17).

Do not hold on to me! The verb ἅπτω does not denote a gentle or tactile touch but denotes an energetic touching or taking.[17] In Greek, the imperative in the present tense alludes to the fact that Mary was already about to act. But what was she about to do? The imprecise Latin translation *noli me tangere* probably corresponds to a certain understanding. According to this translation and many exegetes to this day, Mary wanted to touch Jesus to make sure that it was really him and that it was not an optical illusion or a phantom standing before her. But such an interpretation not only fails to do justice to her hearing and recognizing Jesus but also to the Greek word; it has frequently led to major problems with the next but one passage of the Gospel. There we find the story of the so-called unbelieving Thomas. He does not want to believe until he has put his hands into the stigmata of Jesus. The Risen One offers him this without further ado. Thomas may touch, but why not Mary?

The scene in which Jesus commands Mary "Do not hold on to me!" is, according to its literary genre, an erotic scene. Sjef van Tilborg compared Mary's encounter with Jesus to the Hellenistic romance novel and recognized that in formal terms it resembles a recognition scene between a pair of lovers in this literature. There, lovers find each other after painful separation and many difficulties; they do not recognize each other at first; they hear each other's voice, recognize each other, call each other's name, and embrace each other in exuberant emotionality. Finally, they finish their greeting.[18] In fact, our story follows this pattern. But in the place of the embrace, Jesus says

---

[17] Cf. Theodor Zahn, *Das Evangelium des Johannes*, vol. 4 of *Kommentar zum Neuen Testament*, 6th ed. (Leipzig: Deichert, 1921), 675.

[18] Sjef van Tilborg, *Imaginative Love in John* (Leiden: Brill, 1993), 203–6.

μή μου ἅπτου. He does not forbid Mary the doubter's probing touch, but he forbids her embrace. "Do not hold on to me" thus carries the meaning, "Do not fall around my neck." The lover commands the beloved not to join herself to him yet. *Eros* must not yet be satisfied and suspended. This interpretation solves the problem with the "unbelieving" Thomas. With him it is a matter of a probing touching, which is not good but permitted, but with Mary it is a matter of a passionate embracing, which is good but still forbidden.

Such an erotic interpretation is supported by the many allusions to the Song of Songs.[19] As in John 20, in this erotic poem a woman named Shulammite seeks her beloved king by night and asks the sentinels (Song 3:1-3). The seeking Mary talks accordingly with the angels and asks the supposed gardener, "Sir, if you have carried him away, tell me where you have laid him." The Song of Songs goes on to say, "Scarcely had I passed them, when I found him whom my soul loves. I held him, and would not let him go until I brought him into my mother's house, and into the chamber of her that conceived me" (Song 3:4).

When Mary has already left the angels behind, she finds Jesus. Shulammite holds her beloved and does not let him go. The Song of Songs coincides with the recognition scenes of ancient romance novels. However, the Song of Songs and the Gospel of John diverge at this point. Immediately before Mary is able to hold Jesus like Shulammite and does not want to let go, John sounds the μή μου ἅπτου: "Do not embrace me! Do not hold me!"

Before the inner eyes of the listeners, the seeking Mary turns and turns and turns. "Return, return, O Shulammite! Return, return, that we may look upon you" (Song 6:13). Our scene takes place in a garden, in front of the tomb, to which myrrh, aloes, and fine spices had been brought three days before. In the Song of Songs, the bridegroom sings to his bride, "A garden locked is my sister, my bride, a garden locked, a fountain sealed" (Song 4:12). In this garden grows everything that we find in the Gospel of John in terms of fragrance: nard, myrrh, aloe, and fragrant spices, "a garden fountain, a well of living water ..." (Song 4:15). The erotically charged terms "well," "spring," and "living water" already occurred in John 4. Jesus speaks to the Samaritan woman at a well, a spring, about living water in the passage already mentioned.

In John's Gospel, women always simultaneously embody the whole congregation and anticipate it as individuals. According to this Gospel, the congregation is the bride, Jesus the bridegroom. Therefore, according to the theology of the evangelist, the Song of Songs as a bridal song must be fulfilled especially between the women and Jesus, but then also in a figurative sense between Jesus and his congregation. Jesus makes his first sign in the Fourth Gospel at the miracle of wine at a wedding in Cana (John 2; cf. Song 2:4). The Samaritan woman as the first proclaimer of the Messiah stands for the proclaiming church, the mother Mary in John 2 for the intercessory church. In and through Mary and Martha, faith in the resurrection is first unfolded as a representative of the church of Jesus Christ (John 11). Mary, in a very erotic scene for ancient readers,

---

[19] Ann Roberts Winsor, *A King Is Bound in the Tresses. Allusions to the Song of Songs in the Fourth Gospel* (New York: Peter Lang, 1999), 35-48.

anoints Jesus's feet with fragrant spice oil and dries them with her loosened hair. Jesus and Mary exude the same fragrance. She represents the community that is one in love with its Lord.[20]

So "do not hold on to me" literally means not only "do not hold on to me," but "seize me not," or "take not possession of me as a lover." This erotic tension becomes the mark of the church, which longs for the union with her Lord in heaven, but cannot grasp him physically, emotionally, or with rational thought, as long as it is still on earth as a visible body. The Johannine community desires its Lord in heaven but accepts his commandment: *Noli me tangere* and lives on earth in the tension of the *eros*. This tension longs for heaven and will be lived on earth through *agape*.

Conclusion

Thus, the evangelist draws from old traditions that correspond to a very conservative gender role image. Male bonding and friendship and the erotic closeness and longing of man and woman for each other both give shape and profile to *agape* within the congregation. But just as the individual women represent the whole church, the disciples together in their community also represent the whole church. Everything speaks for the fact that in each case the church of men and women in their community is meant. Thus, both traditions about the church are made fruitful for both genders. Narratively, the gender boundaries will be reinforced precisely in order to strengthen two quite different radical forms of intimacy. In their ecclesiological dimension, however, they are both relevant for women and men. Gender diversity is here in the service of a plurality of promises that are not to be fulfilled in a gender-bound way.

---

[20] Winsor, *A King Is Bound in the Tresses*, 17–34.

3

Was Pilate a "Friend of the Emperor" (John 19:12)?

Ruben Zimmermann

In the Johannine account of the trial, the phrase "Friend of the Emperor" (φίλος τοῦ Καίσαρος) is used for Pontius Pilate. The phrase appears at the end of a series of speeches involving the Jewish authorities as accusers, Jesus as the accused, and Pontius Pilate as the Roman governor acting as judge. Pilate ultimately considers releasing Jesus. Thereupon, the Jewish authorities accuse him of risking no longer being a "Friend of the Emperor": "From then on Pilate tried to release him, but the Jews cried out, 'If you release this man, you are no friend of the emperor. Everyone who claims to be a king sets himself against the emperor'" (John 19:12 NRSV). The passage has provoked repeated questions for researchers: is the formulation φίλος τοῦ Καίσαρος a well-known phrase indicating a specific relationship or even an honorary title that Pilate had been given? Is it the fear of losing this title that dissuades Pilate from his plans to release Jesus? Could this be a historically reliable recollection of facts?[1] I will demonstrate that contemporary sources, including coins from the material culture, make it highly plausible that there was formal use of the title "Friend of the Emperor" in the Roman empire. With respect to Pilate, however, there is no clear evidence that the equestrian held this title. Given the contrastive structure of the narrative of the Fourth Gospel, it is more likely that the evangelist took up the well-known concept in order to express scathing opposition to the "friend(s) of Jesus" (e.g., John 15:13-15).

The Title "Friend of the Emperor" (φίλος τοῦ Καίσαρος)

The first question to answer is whether φίλος τοῦ Καίσαρος was an official, or at least a designated, honorary name, as first argued by Adolf Deißmann and now widely

---

[1] Historical reliability of John is now more frequently postulated; see, for instance, Tom Thatcher, "Aspects of Historicity in the Fourth Gospel: Phase Two of the John, Jesus, and History Project," in *Aspects of Historicity in the Fourth Gospel*, vol. 2 of *John, Jesus, and History*, ed. Paul N. Anderson, Felix Just, and Tom Thatcher (Atlanta, GA: SBL Press, 2009), 1–6.

accepted.[2] Critical of this argument, Jens Herzer sees this as merely a privileged status and not an official title.[3]

A look at the sources reveals a wide range of variation in the terminology used in ancient texts and archeological evidence.[4] Greek terms include the rather rare genitive combinations (comparable to John's use), such as φίλος τοῦ Καίσαρος (analogous to Lat. *amicus Caesaris*), φίλος τοῦ Σεβαστοῦ (*amicus Augusti*), or φίλος τοῦ βασιλέως. Adjectives occur more frequently, such as φιλοκαίσαρ, φιλοσεβαστός, or even φιλορωμαῖος.

The genres of these texts also vary. Inscriptions on buildings or on coins can be found next to notes by historians (e.g., emperor's *vitae*) or philosophical discourses. One can assume a more titular use of a phrase in the case of an inscription on a building than, for example, in the case of elaborated discourses by historians or philosophers. Nevertheless, the specific use in each case demands its own appraisal in order to arrive at an overall picture. Given the manifold examples of epithets, the presentation of findings can be done only in an illustrative way. I will first utilize a descriptive approach and focus on occurrences that have not been discussed in detail in previous research.[5] In the subsequent section, these findings will be read against the wider historical horizon of political friendship.

The term φίλος τοῦ Καίσαρος (as in John) is used several times by Epictetus (*Diatr*. 4.1.45-49)[6] when discussing whether it is desirable, in terms of a free, happy and contented life, to become a "Friend of the Emperor." Epictetus gives different consequences of this friendship, such as fear, compulsion, and invitations to meals, that are supposed to show that being a "Friend of the Emperor" misses the mark of the desired increase of freedom and happiness. Epictetus uses the phrase Καίσαρος φίλος or ὁ φίλος (τοῦ) Καίσαρος only with reference to a single friend. Furthermore, Epictetus uses phrases such as "becoming a friend" (*Diatr*. 4.1.46: ὅταν οὖν γένηται Καίσαρος φίλος) or "being a friend" (*Diatr*. 4.1.45: τοῦ φίλος εἶναι Καίσαρος). The

---

[2] See Gustav Adolf Deissmann, *Licht vom Osten: Das Neue Testament und die neuentdeckten Texte der hellenistisch-römischen Welt*, 4th ed. (Tübingen: J. C. B. Mohr [Paul Siebeck], 1923), 423, n. 3. See also the translation Gustav Adolf Deissmann, *Light from the Ancient East: The New Testament Illustrated by Recently Discovered Texts from the Graeco-Roman World*, 2nd ed. (London: Hodder & Stoughton, 1927; repr., Grand Rapids, MI: Baker, 1978), 383.

[3] See Jens Herzer, *Pontius Pilatus: Henker und Heiliger*, Biblische Gestalten 32 (Leipzig: Evangelische Verlagsanstalt, 2020), 41: "Ein offizieller Titel war *amicus Caesaris* wohl ohnehin nicht, eher ein 'privilegierter Status,' Ausdruck amtlicher Vertrautheit und vor allem der Loyalität gegenüber dem Kaiser."

[4] See Chryssoula Veligianni, "*Philos* und *philos*-Komposita in den griechischen Inschriften der Kaiserzeit," in *Aspects of Friendship in the Graeco-Roman World*, ed. Michael Peachin (Portsmouth: JRA, 2001), 67–9.

[5] See Ernst Bammel, "Φίλος τοῦ Καίσαρος," *TLZ* 77 (1952): 205–10; Helen Bond, *Pontius Pilate in History and Interpretation* (Cambridge: Cambridge University Press, 1998), 189–90; Brian E. Messner, "'No Friend of Caesar': Jesus, Pilate, Sejanus, and Tiberius," *Stone-Campbell Journal* 11 (2008): 47–57; Rainer Metzner, "Exkurs 6: Freund des Kaisers," in *Die Prominenten im Neuen Testament: Ein prosopographischer Kommentar*, NTOA/SUNT 66 (Göttingen: Vandenhoeck & Ruprecht, 2008), 327–8.

[6] See *Epiktet. Teles, Musonius: Ausgewählte Schriften Griechisch-Deutsch*, ed. and trans. Rainer Nickel, Sammlung Tusculum (Darmstadt: Wissenschaftliche Buchgesellschaft, 1994), 244–7. Epictetus also knows the term οἱ φίλοι τῶν βασιλέων used in the following section.

whole passage includes a temporal dimension that distinguishes between the present state (as the emperor's friend) and the past (*Diatr.* 4.1.47: νῦν ἢ πρὶν γενέσθαι φίλος τοῦ Καίσαρος).

From *Diatr.* 4.1.95-97 (φίλος ἔσομαι Καίσαρος "I want to become a friend of the emperor"), one sees that people explicitly strove to attain this title and the rights and privileges associated with it. One may therefore conclude that the term φίλος τοῦ Καίσαρος has a titular status for the philosopher. Furthermore, there was apparently a clearly definable point from which one was allowed to claim the status for oneself, indicating a bestowal or recognition of the title. Epictetus, however, leaves open the question of who was able to attain this title in the first place. Yet another instance interests us. According to *Diatr.* 3.4.2, the terms "friend" (φίλος) and "governor" (ἐπίτροπος), also used for Pilate, are mentioned in the same breath. The governor of Epirus is here called friend and representative of the emperor (τοῦ Καίσαρος φίλον καὶ ἐπίτροπον).[7]

As another example, I turn to two inscriptions from Thyatira in Asia Minor that speak of the "friend of Sebastus" (φίλος τοῦ Σεβαστοῦ in acc.), meaning "friend of Augustus," which is used to refer to a certain Marcus Gnaeus Licinius Rufinus.[8] Licinius Rufinus, born in Thyatira (185 CE), and who like Pilate came from the *equites*, held several equestrian court offices from about 211 to 223 CE before becoming consul in the late 220s or early 230s CE. Although the difference in time and place does not allow definitive conclusions about the first century, the appearance of the designation φίλος τοῦ Σεβαστοῦ among other honorific titles in the inscriptions attests to the use of the term φίλος as a titular rank in connection with an imperial name.

Analogous to φιλοσεβαστός (the adjective common in Asia Minor),[9] we also encounter φιλοκαίσαρ,[10] another term linguistically proximate to φίλος τοῦ Καίσαρος, used especially for client kings.[11] Accordingly, a considerable number occur within inscriptions by the kings of the Bosphorus.[12] A specific way to advertise the friendship with Rome and the emperor was to use this title on coins. The terminology φιλοκαίσαρ appears on a number of provincial coins.[13] Of special interest are three coins from

---

[7] See Udo Schnelle, Michael Labahn, and Manfred Lang, eds., *Texte zum Johannesevangelium*, vol. I.2 of *Neuer Wettstein: Texte zum Neuen Testament aus Griechentum und Hellenismus* (Berlin: de Gruyter, 2001), 806.

[8] See Augustus Böckhius, *Corpus Inscriptionum Graecorum*, vol. 2 (Berlin: Akademie der Wissenschaften zu Berlin, 1843; repr., Hildesheim: Olms, 1977): CIG 2.3499 lines 3-4 (= IGRR 4, 1216 = TAM 5, 2, 986) and *CIG*, 2.3500 line 5 (= IGRR 4, 1215 = TAM 5, 2, 984). The first one reads: Μ. Γναῖον Λικίνιον Ῥουφῖνον, τὸν λαμπρότατον ὑπατικόν, φίλον τοῦ Σεβαστοῦ, κτίστην κ(αὶ) εὐεργέτην τῆς πατρίδος, οἱ βυρσεῖς. See Werner Eck, "Der Kaiser und seine Ratgeber. Überlegungen zum inneren Zusammenhang von amici, comites und consiliarii am römischen Kaiserhof," in *Herrschaftsstrukturen und Herrschaftspraxis. Konzepte, Prinzipien und Strategien der Administration im römischen Kaiserreich*, ed. Anne Kolb (Berlin: Akademie, 2006), 67-78, here 71-2.

[9] See Bammel, "Φίλος," 210.

[10] See on this term the overview by G. H. R. Horsely, ed., *New Documents Illustrating Early Christianity*, vol. 3 (North Ryde: Macquary University Press, 1983), 87-9.

[11] See David C. Braund, *Rome and the Friendly King: The Character of Client Kingship* (New York: St. Martin's, 1984), 105-8.

[12] The index of the *Corpus Inscriptionum Regni Bosporani*, ed. by Vasilij V. Struve (Moskva: Izdat. Nauka, 1965), lists seventy-five occurrences of φιλόκαισαρ.

[13] See Michael P. Theophilos, "John 15.14 and the ΦΙΛ-Lexeme in Light of Numismatic Evidence: Friendship or Obedience," *NTS* 64 (2018): 33-43. Theophilos lists twelve coins with the

Judaea that celebrate the friendship between the Jewish client kings Agrippa I and Agrippa II, who were reinstated in Judaea and are also mentioned in the New Testament.[14] The inscription of *RPC* 1.4983 reads: "Great King Agrippa, friend of Caesar (ΦΙΛΟΚΑΙΣΑΡ)." In *Against Flaccus*, Philo of Alexandria also confirms that Agrippa I was called φίλος Καίσαρος.[15] Apart from its attribution to client kings, it appears that the term was used equally for senators, equestrians, and even private individuals.[16]

While the terms φιλοκαίσαρ and φιλορώμαιος are often used synonymously, Vasile Lica has argued for distinct usages and statuses associated with them.[17] Using the example of Rholes (Ρώλης), who was given the title φίλος καὶ σύμμαχος by Octavianus (see Dio Cassius, *Historia Romana* 51, 24, 6-7), Lica contends that he became "Friend of the Emperor" but not *"amicus et socius populi Romani."* The latter was a higher title conferred only by the Senate since republican times.[18] Her observation that the specific adjectives did carry differentiated meanings and were not simply used synonymously is confirmed by my final example.

The Books of Maccabees contain the designation φίλος τοῦ βασιλέως, usually in the plural form οἱ φίλοι τοῦ βασιλέως (e.g., 1 Macc 2:18; 3:38). In 1 Maccabees, the phrase is explicitly bestowed as a title. King Alexander Epiphanes courts the favor of Jews close to Demetrius, king of Ptolemais. Alexander first preempts Demetrius and offers to make Jonathan high priest and "Friend of the King":

> "King Alexander to his brother Jonathan, greetings. We have heard about you, that you are a mighty warrior and worthy to be our friend (ἐπιτήδειος εἶ τοῦ εἶναι ἡμῶν φίλος). And so we have appointed you today to be the high priest of your nation; you are to be called the *king's Friend (φίλον βασιλέως)* and you are to take our side and keep friendship with us (συντηρεῖν φιλίας πρὸς ἡμᾶς)." He also sent him a purple robe and a golden crown [emphasis added]. (1 Macc 10:18-20)

Although the "Friend of the King" is not the same as the "Friend of the Emperor," apparently the term "friend" in relation to a political ruler (here the king) is used as a conferred title and, in this case, signifies a political-military alliance.

In summary, the investigation into these examples of the use of the term φίλος in connection with an emperor or a king indicates a conferred title that gives a specific

---

inscription φιλοκαίσαρ from the first century CE, particularly three coins from Judaea (*RPC* 1.4979; 1.4983; 1.4985 = OGIS I 419, 420, 424), five coins from Philadelphia/Lyd. (*RPC* 1.3027-1.3031), and four coins from Tripolis/Lyd. (*RPC* 1.3054-1.3057). Numbers follow the edition by A. Burnett et al., eds., *From the Death of Caesar to the Death of Vitellius (44 BC-AD 69)*, vol. 1 of *Roman Provincial Coinage* (London: British Museum, 1992).

[14] Agrippa I in Acts 12:1-4 and Agrippa II in Acts 25:13-26, 32.
[15] See Philo, *Flaccus* 40: ὅτι γε βασιλέα καὶ φίλον Καίσαρος.
[16] See Richard P. Saller, *Personal Patronage under the Early Empire* (Cambridge: Cambridge University Press, 1982), 59.
[17] Vasile Lica, "φιλορώμαιος oder φιλοκαίσαρ?" *BJ* 192 (1992-3): 225-30.
[18] Lica, φιλορώμαιος, 230: "Rholes (war) rex amicus et socius, aber nicht des römischen Volkes, sondern des Octavian persönlich. Wenn wir ihn einer Kategorie von Bundesgenossen zuordnen, die zu Anfang des Prinzipats gültig war, dann war Rholes ein amicus Caesaris, ein φιλοκαίσαρ."

status to the relationship between a political officeholder and the emperor or king. Whoever received this title demonstrated this status through coins and inscriptions, thus indicating the power associated with it. Even in Epictetus's philosophical treatise, a titular use of the term can be assumed to be plausible.

The Political Dimension of Friendship in Ancient Discourse

In the next step, I place the phrase in the horizon of the ancient discourse on friendship. The topic of friendship was widely discussed in different contexts in antiquity.[19] In addition to classical writings by Plato and Aristotle,[20] increased interest can also be found in various philosophical currents during the Roman Principate. One thinks of Cicero's *Laelius de amicitia*, Seneca's *Epistulae Morales*, or Oration 22 of Themistios's Περὶ φιλίας.[21]

In addition to individual friendships between private persons, the concept of friendship has played a role in political contexts since ancient Athenian democracy.[22] Despite certain differences, the two dimensions need not be played against each other. Whereas in personal friendships equality and openness (παρρησία)[23] come more to the fore, political friendship is based more on exchange and considerations of utility.[24] The latter is visible, for example, in patron–client relationships, which were also described using the category of "friendship."[25] An aristocratic patron (*patronus*) assured support to nonaristocratic clients (*clientes*), for example, in court, while the clients, in turn, supported the *patron* in elections.[26] The clients were called "friends" of the patron,

---

[19] See David Konstan, *Friendship in the Classical World* (Cambridge: Cambridge University Press, 1997); John T. Fitzgerald, ed., *Graeco-Roman Perspectives on Friendship*, RBS 34 (Atlanta, GA: SBL Press, 1997); Katarina Mustakallio and Christian Krötzl, eds., *De Amicitia: Friendship and Social Networks in Antiquity and the Middle Ages*, AIRF36 (Rome: Institutum Romanum Finlandiae, 2009).

[20] See Plato's dialogue, *Lysis*, or Aristotle's discourses on friendship within his ethical writings, for example, *Eth. nic.* 8 and *Eth. eud.* 7.

[21] See Michael Schramm, *Freundschaft im Neuplatonismus: Politisches Denken und Sozialphilosophie von Plotin bis Kaiser Julian*, BzA 319 (Berlin: de Gruyter, 2013), 244–99.

[22] See Mirjam Zimmermann and Ruben Zimmermann, "Freundschaftsethik im Johannesevangelium: Zur öffentlichen und politischen Reichweite eines ethischen Konzepts," in *Biblical Ethics and Application: Purview, Validity, and Relevance of Biblical Texts in Ethical Discourse*, ed. Ruben Zimmermann and Stephan Joubert, WUNT 38 (Tübingen: Mohr Siebeck, 2017), 165–71.

[23] See, for instance, Philodemus, Περὶ παρρησίας, and Seneca, *Ep.* 3, 2–3, on which, see Clarence E. Glad, "Frank Speech, Flattery, and Friendship in Philodemus," in *Friendship, Flattery, and Frankness of Speech: Studies on Friendship in the New Testament World*, ed. John T. Fitzgerald, NovTSup 82 (Leiden: Brill, 1996), 21–59; in general, Peter-Ben Smit and Eva van Urk, eds., *Parrhesia: Ancient and Modern Perspectives on Freedom of Speech* (Leiden: Brill, 2018).

[24] Cf. especially in relation to Arist. *Eth. eud.* 7.9-10; Malcolm Schofield, "Political Friendship and the Ideology of Reciprocity," in *Kosmos: Essays in Order, Conflict and Community in Classical Athens*, ed. Peter Cartledge, Paul Millett, and Sitta von Reden (Cambridge: Cambridge University Press, 1998), 37–51, here 51: "political friendship is an exchange relationship."

[25] See Richard P. Saller, "Patronage and Friendship in Early Imperial Rome: Drawing the Distinction," in *Patronage in Ancient Society*, ed. A. Wallace-Hadrill (London: Routledge, 1989), 49–62; Aloys Winterling, "Freundschaft und Klientel im kaiserzeitlichen Rom," *Historia* 57 (2008): 298–316.

[26] Winterling, "Freundschaft und Klientel," 300.

but likewise patrons could also be called "friends" of the clients.[27] Even though the patronage–friendship was modified over the course of time, it persisted in Imperial Rome as an essential pillar in the functioning of the political system.[28]

A more specific kind of political friendship was the friendship with a king. A few formulations occur in the Septuagint. The "friend of David" appears a number of times (2 Sam 15:37; 16:16-17; also 1 Kgs 4:5), and in 1 Chr 27:33 (LXX) the φίλος τοῦ βασιλέως is mentioned alongside the "king's counselor" (σύμβουλος). However, the functional use of the term "friend" comes from the Greek ruling houses. For example, Diodorus Siculus reports that the Macedonian kings Alexander and Cassander were surrounded by friends in the function of their advisors.[29] Thus, not surprising, in the Ptolemaic or Seleucid kingdoms, advisors such as heads of executive offices (jurisdiction, diplomacy, military) in the vicinity of the king were called "friends."[30]

During the reign of the king Ptolemy V (197–194 BCE), different classes of "friends," such as "honored friends" or "friends of the first rank," are documented within a court rank title list. This list, according to Wolfgang Orth, was also valid for the Seleucid Empire.[31] The Books of Maccabees give ample evidence of this ranking,[32] such as the specific expression "friend of the first rank" (τῶν πρώτων φίλων) in 1 Macc 10:65 and 2 Macc 8:9. According to 4 Macc 12:5 (// 2 Macc 7:24), Antiochus IV Epiphanes even attempts to bribe the youngest of seven brothers to testify against his elder siblings by giving him the title of "friend."[33]

In the Roman principate, high officials are named "*amicus Caesaris/Augusti.*"[34] Suetonius reports about Titus: "He surrounded himself with such excellent friends, that the succeeding princes adopted them as most serviceable to themselves and the state" (*Tit.* 7:2 [Thomson]). The honorary title "Friend of the Emperor" was also regarded as a step up the career ladder during the Principate and was mentioned in the same breath as senator and consul (Epictetus, *Diatr.* 4.8.1).[35]

Clearly the title was coveted. However, favor and privilege could also change quickly and lead to ill will and persecution, or even murder. Thus, Tacitus or Suetonius

---

[27] See Robert K. Sherk, ed., *The Roman Empire: Augustus to Hadrian* (New York: Cambridge University Press, 1988), 235.
[28] See the overview in Winterling, "Freundschaft und Klientel," 302–5.
[29] Cf. Alexander of Macedon (Diodorus Siculus, *Bibliotheca historica* 17.31.6; 17.39.2; 17.100.1); with Cassander (Diodorus Siculus, *Bibliotheca historica* 18.55.1).
[30] See Wolfgang Orth, "Seleukidische Hoftitel und politische Strukturen im Spiegel der Septuaginta-Überlieferung," in *Septuaginta Deutsch: Erläuterungen und Kommentare zum griechischen Alten Testament, Band 1*, ed. Martin Karrer and Wolfgang Kraus (Stuttgart: Deutsche Bibelgesellschaft, 2011), 65–77, here 66: "Freunde des Königs ... erweisen sich als besonders wichtige Stützen der Machtausübung."
[31] See Orth, "Seleukidische Hoftitel," 66–7.
[32] See 1 Macc 10:20, 15:28, 32; 2 Macc 7:24; Let. Aris. 40–41, 44, 190, 208, 225, 228, 318; Josephus, *Ant.* 12.366, 13.146, 225; *Life* 131.
[33] See 1 Macc 6:28; 12:43; 13:36; 3 Macc 5:3, and so on. See Orth, "Seleukidische Hoftitel," 67.
[34] See Ernst Badian, "Amicitia," *BNP* 1 (1996): 590–1; furthermore, Fergus Millar, *The Emperor in the Roman World (31 BC–AD 337)* (Ithaca, NY: Cornell University Press, 1977), 110–20.
[35] Cf. Epictetus, *Diatr.* 4.1.45–50; Martial, *Epig.* 5.19.15–16; Ailios Herodianos 4.3.5; Tacitus, *Ann.* 6.8. Winterling, "Freundschaft und Klientel," 309–12, sees here a new form of *amicitia* in imperial favor accompanying the loss of power of the aristocracy and emerging as a competing principle alongside the patron–client *amicitia*.

report cases when a friendship's termination led to the merciless persecution by former friends.³⁶

Finally, the friendship of client kings or rulers with the emperor is of special importance. As the inscriptions and coinage above demonstrate, the emperor created a relationship of dependence through the bestowal of the title of friendship. This secured the privileges of the client kings but at the same time demanded close loyalty. As seen above, according to coins and inscriptions, the Jewish kings Agrippa I and II, and Herod the Great before them, were such "friends of the Emperor."³⁷

Pilate as Roman *Praefectus Iudaeae*

We have seen so far that the term "Friend of the Emperor" was used as a title. While common among client kings in provinces (such as the Bosphorus and also Palestine), it could also be used for Romans in different functions. The question now arises whether it is plausible that Pontius Pilate held this title.

After Archelaus had to relinquish the regency over the province of Judea in 6 CE, the area was officially counted as part of the province of Syria but ruled by Roman prefects. Pilate ruled as the fifth *praefectus Iudaeae* from 26–37 CE.³⁸ Whether he actually bore the title of praefectus is not clear in the sources. The neutral term ἡγεμών ("ruler") is used in the Gospels of Matthew and Luke.³⁹

According to Tacitus, Pilate is called "Procurator," a title that became more common beginning in the 40s CE after Claudius's reorganization of the provinces.⁴⁰ Josephus and Philo also use ἐπίτροπος for Pilate.⁴¹ On the so-called Pilate Inscription of Caesarea Maritima, however, Pilate is called "Praefectus," which corresponds to the Greek equivalent ἔπαρχος. Most historians therefore argue for this title as the usual one for Pilate's rule.⁴²

The stone with the so-called Pilate Inscription was damaged in the fourth century during reconstruction work when it was hewn in the process of making a step in the theater of Caesarea. A part of the inscription is missing and what remains is fragmentary:⁴³

---

³⁶ See Tacitus, *Ann.* 6.29.2; Suetonius, *Aug.* 66.2; Suetonius, *Cal.* 26.3; Suetonius, *Tib.* 55, see the texts in Schnelle, *Wettstein*, 810–11.
³⁷ Cf. *IG*² 3441; *AE* 1995 Nr. 1578, located in Veligianni, "*Philos*," 67.
³⁸ The names of the predecessors are Coponius (6–9 CE), Ambibulus (9–12 CE), Annius Rufus (12–14 CE), and Valerius Gratus (15–26 CE).
³⁹ See Matt 17:2, 11, 14, and so on, and Luke 20:20; see also Josephus, *Ant.* 18: Πιλᾶτος δὲ ὁ τῆς Ἰουδαίας ἡγεμών.
⁴⁰ Herzer, *Pilate*, 29, assumes from this that Tacitus is using the later common term for Pilate anachronistically.
⁴¹ See Philo, *Embassy* 37.299: Πιλᾶτος ἦν τῶν ὑπάρχων ἐπίτροπος ἀποδεδειγμένος τῆς Ἰουδαίας; Josephus, *J.W.* 2.169: Πεμφθεὶς δὲ εἰς Ἰουδαίαν ἐπίτροπος ὑπὸ Τιβερίου Πιλᾶτος … .
⁴² See Alexander Demandt, *Pontius Pilatus* (München: Beck, 2012), 45–7; Herzer, *Pilatus*, 29, therefore, also ascribes the highest historical probability to this title, even though Josephus applies the title only to the predecessors of Pilate.
⁴³ See Walther Ameling, Hannah M. Cotton, and Werner Eck, *Caesarea and the Middle Coast 1121–2160*, vol. 2 of *Corpus Inscriptionum Iudaeae/Palestine (CIP): A Multi-lingual Corpus of the Inscriptions from Alexander to Muhammad* (Berlin: de Gruyter, 2011), 228 (fig. 1277).

...]S TIBERIEUM
N]TIVUS PILATUS
[PRAEF]ECTUS IVDAE[A]E
[REF]EC[IT].

The various attempts at reconstruction generally agree about the second and third line,[44] while the proposals for first and fourth lines remain hypothetical due to their fragmentary character.[45] For our context, the well-preserved adjective TIBERIEUM is decisive due to the ending (-eum), which suggests that Pilate had erected or renovated a building in honor of the Emperor Tiberius. Thus, the inscription expresses the close relationship between the prefect and the emperor. This relationship is documented by other sources, especially coins minted by Pontius Pilate in the years 29–32 CE. The inscription IOYLIA KAISAROC (to the emperor's mother, Livia Drusilla) and TIBERIOY KAISAROC pays explicit homage to the emperor (see Figure 3.1).[46]

While one cannot assume high historical reliability for the letter of Agrippa to Gaius Caligula in Philo's account (*Embassy* 299–305), the homage to Tiberius also appears in the votive shields.[47]

Since Heinrich Graetz, one commonly encounters the argument that Pilate was in the favor of Lucius Aelius Sejanus,[48] prefect of the Praetorian Guard under Tiberius. Sejanus thus occupied an extremely important position of power in Rome that probably became even greater after Tiberius moved his residence to Capri. According to Roman historians, Tiberius called him his companion and even "my friend."[49] He was given the *ornamenta praetoria* of the Roman army and most probably also the title "Friend of the Emperor."[50] According to Tacitus, *Ann.* 6:8, the confidants of Sejanus were also appointed as "Friends of the Emperor": *Quisque Seiano intimus, ita ad Caesaris amicitiam validus*. Ernst Bammel concludes from this that the equestrian

---

[44] See Ameling et al., *CIP*, 228–9.

[45] The above-mentioned edition favors the reconstruction of Géza Alföldy, who takes from the indication in Josephus's *J.W.* 1.408-416 (reconstruction of the harbor by Herod the Great and dedication of a lighthouse to Drusus, stepson of Emperor Augustus and brother of the later Emperor Tiberius) that Pilate had the lighthouse restored and then dedicated directly to Tiberius. The supplemented inscription would then read "*Nautis Tiberieum Pontius Pilatus Praefectus Iudaeae refecit*" (For the sailors ... Pontius Pilate, prefect of Judaea, had the Tiberieum restored). Cf. Ameling et al., *CIP*, 228–9; see Géza Alföldy, "Pontius Pilatus und das Tiberieum von Caesarea Maritima," *SCI* 18 (1999): 85–108; this is also followed by Herzer, *Pilatus*, 31. An alternative reconstruction adds "Incolis" to line 1, which would then be translated as "*for the inhabitants ...*"; see Karl Jaroš, *In Sachen Pontius Pilatus*, KAW 93 (Mainz: von Zabern, 2002), 39–40.

[46] On Pilate's coins, see Helen K. Bond, "The Coins of Pontius Pilate. Part of an Attempt to Provoke the People or to Integrate Them into the Empire?" *JSJ* 27 (1996): 241–62.

[47] According to Demandt, *Pilatus*, 51, the inscription on the shield possibly reads "TIBERIO CAESARI PONTIUS PILATUS." See a more critical appraisal on Philo's report in Herzer, *Pilatus*, 109–25.

[48] See Heinrich Graetz, *History of the Jews* (Philadelphia, PA: Jewish Publication Society of America, 1893), 2:138–9; Bammel, "Φίλος," 207: "eine Kreatur Sejans"; Paul Maier, "Sejanus, Pilate, and the Date of the Crucifixion," *CH* 37 (1968): 3–13; Metzner, "Freund," 327; Messner, "No Friend," 48–9 (reports the "Sejanus Theory" in detail).

[49] See Cassius Dio 58.4: κοινωνὸς τῶν φροντίδων and Σηιανός τε ὁ ἐμός. Tacitus, *Ann.* 4.74: *socius laborum*.

[50] Tac., *Ann.* 4.2; Suetonius, *Tib.* 48; according to Bammel, "Φίλος," 207, Sejanus "war selbstverständlich φίλος."

Figure 3.1 Coins from Pilate, 29 CE (© R. Zimmermann, own collection).

Pilate was also included among the *amici*.[51] This cannot be excluded, but there is no proof for the close connection between Sejanus and Pilate in ancient sources. Only a late remark by Eusebius of Caesarea connects the two, but this is obviously tied to a broader expression of anti-Judaic polemic.[52]

---

[51] See Bammel, "Φίλος," 208.
[52] See Eusebius, *Hist. eccl.* 2.5.7.

Against the overestimation of Sejanus's importance for Pilate[53] stands the fact that in the year 31 CE, at the height of his power (he had just been appointed consul), Sejanus fell out of favor with the emperor and was killed along with his family and friends. Alongside Tacitus (*Ann.* 4.1-3; 6.18-19), Suetonius (*Tib.* 54–55, 61), Dio Cassius (*Historia Romana* 58.14.1), and Philo (*Embassy* 159–160) report the fall of Sejanus, bringing his confidants down with him.[54] Josephus, *Ant.* 18:250, gives the impression that Sejanus also became *persona non grata* in the province. In order to discredit him, Josephus writes that Herod Antipas was suspected of having been a follower of Sejanus in 39 CE. Pilate, however, was obviously not affected by the fall of Sejanus and continued to be the Praefectus of Judaea until 37 CE, when the Syrian prefect Vitellius deposed him through a scheme to instate his own favorite, Marcellus.

In summary, the extant sources show a close relationship between Pilate and Emperor Tiberius. Both the "Pilate Inscription" from Caesarea Maritima and coinage demonstrate loyalty to the emperor, making it plausible that Pilate also possessed the honorary title of "Friend of the Emperor." Nevertheless, the coinage provides particularly strong evidence against this assessment. Other coins from the same period and region explicitly evince the title φιλοκαίσαρ. Therefore, one must ask: Why would Pilate have missed this opportunity to brag about his title and at the same time express loyalty to the emperor by the people?

In view of the fragmentary nature of the sources, a final judgment is hardly possible here. If one evaluates the positive source evidence, one must come to the conclusion that, apart from John 19:12, no source supports the view that the title "friend of Caesar/of the emperor" was given to Pilate.[55]

Summary and Prospects

The phrase "Friend of the Emperor" was used as a formal title in the Roman Empire. However, only John 19:12 contains evidence that the equestrian Pilate held this title. In the Fourth Gospel, the title is put on the lips of the accusing Jews with rhetorical intent. According to them, Pilate is no friend of the emperor if he releases a pretender to the kingship like Jesus. The Fourth Gospel does not say that he is "no longer" a friend of the emperor or that he loses a previously given title. Historically, if Pilate sought this title, conflict with Jewish authorities could have possibly complicated the nomination. More likely, however, is that in the narrative role reversal within the trial,[56] the Jews

---

[53] For a critical view on this relationship, see Herzer, *Pilatus*, 40–1, Demandt, *Pilatus*, 60. Messner also disagrees with the hypothesis of a close connection between Sejanus and Pilate but nevertheless sees the aftermath of Sejanus's fall as a precondition for the threat set up by the Jewish elite in John 19:12. He concludes: "The abnormal Roman political atmosphere after Sejanus provides an adequate context for Pilate's actions, because prior to AD 31 the Jews would have had very little legal ground for action against Pilate." Messner, "No Friend," 57.

[54] See for details Messner, "No Friend," 55–6.

[55] Demandt, *Pilatus*, 61, summarizes: "(Freund des Kaisers) war Pilatus zumal im formalen Sinne, nie."

[56] See Ruben Zimmermann, "'Deuten' heißt erzählen und übertragen. Narrativität und Metaphorik als sprachliche Grundformen historischer Sinnbildung zum Tod Jesu," in *Deutungen des Todes Jesu im Neuen Testament*, ed. Jörg Frey and Jens Schröter, WUNT 181 (Tübingen: Mohr Siebeck, 2005), 345–51; see on Pilate as character D. Francois Tolmie, "Pontius Pilate: Failing in More Ways Than

are presented as the ones who care for the emperor's honor and, as explicitly said, are themselves honoring the emperor as their only king (John 19:15)—clear evidence of blasphemy. This relates to the narrative unfolding of the concept of friendship in the Fourth Gospel.[57] The contrastive structure of the narrative plausibly signifies that the evangelist takes up the well-known concept of "Friend of the Emperor" in order to pointedly express opposition to the "friend(s) of Jesus" (e.g., John 15:13-15).[58]

Terminologically, the formulation also fits into the Fourth Gospel's narratological motif of friendship with its use of the term φίλος as a recurring element. But must historical memory and narrative presentation be played against each other? Historical information and narrative presentation combine in specific ways. In historical terms, the Johannine text preserves the memory that Pilate had a close association with the emperor, which also finds expression elsewhere in specific titles. This historical reminiscence is then linked to and intensified by the evangelist's concept of friendship, something understood as social and political in John (as well as in ancient discourse). In this combination of history and narration, then, Pilate can be called "Friend of the Emperor."

One," in *Character Studies in the Fourth Gospel. Narrative Approaches to Seventy Figures in John*, ed. Steven A. Hunt, D. Francois Tolmie, and Ruben Zimmermann, WUNT 314 (Tübingen: Mohr Siebeck, 2013; repr., Eerdmans, 2016), 578–97.

[57] See Zimmermann and Zimmermann, "Freundschaftsethik," 171–9; The friendship metaphor is also used by Adele Reinhartz, *Befriending the Beloved Disciple: A Jewish Reading of the Gospel of John* (New York: Continuum, 2005), 160–2.

[58] See also Warren Carter, "Community of Friends (15:12-15)," in his *John and Empire: Initial Explorations* (New York: T&T Clark, 2008), 278–81.

4

John among the Synoptics? Understanding the Institutional World of the Fourth Gospel in Light of Other Early Gospels*

Anders Runesson

Introduction

The Gospel of John is a problem in ways the Synoptics are not. As Adele Reinhartz's extensive work on the Fourth Gospel has shown, this text can be read in ways detrimental to Jews and Judaism, and, indeed, so it has been read by the church for more than a millennium and a half, with disastrous consequences for the Jewish people.[1] Others, such as Wally Cirafesi, have argued that other historical readings are possible, which situate John within first-century Judaism.[2] While the debate about the nature of the Fourth Gospel will surely continue, scholarship has reached a point, not least thanks to Reinhartz's work, where the interpretive and methodological options—and their implications—are clearer than they have ever been. In this short essay, I will not enter the much larger debate about John and Judaism but instead focus on a limited aspect of the text, which may in turn add perspectives to the debate through a comparative approach. The task I have set before me will be to explore civic and other possible institutional spaces depicted in this Gospel in light of the other three

---

* It is an honor for me to dedicate this essay to Adele Reinhartz, a long-time friend and colleague. Her contribution to New Testament studies has been, throughout, an inspiration and continues to keep me on my toes. We were both influenced, I believe, by our work at McMaster University, although she left as I arrived. I knew already then that no one could fill her shoes. Also, in Oslo, I have done my best to critically engage the intersection of New Testament and Jewish studies, an interest that we very much share and an area where I have learned a great deal from her work. I am grateful for her friendship and the example she has set, and I look forward to many more years of discussions and the exchange of ideas.

[1] To list in a footnote Adele Reinhartz's many publications on John's Gospel and how it portrays "the Jews" (*hoi Ioudaioi*) would be impossible in a short article like this. I refer here instead to her most recent magisterial study *Cast Out of the Covenant: Jews and Anti-Judaism in the Gospel of John* (Lanham, MD: Lexington Books/Fortress Academic, 2018). See also her edited volume, *The Gospel of John and Jewish–Christian Relations* (Lanham, MD: Lexington Books/Fortress Academic, 2018); cf. Reimund Bieringer, Didier Pollefeyt, and Frederique Vandecasteele-Vanneuville, *Anti-Judaism and the Fourth Gospel* (Louisville, KY: Westminster John Knox, 2001).

[2] Wally V. Cirafesi, *John within Judaism: Religion, Ethnicity, and the Shaping of Jesus-Oriented Jewishness in the Fourth Gospel*, AJEC 112 (Leiden: Brill, 2021).

Gospels included in the New Testament, in order to see whether such a comparison has the potential to shed light on the (Jewish) nature of the narrative world in which the author(s) have placed their characters. Does John part ways with the other three, or do we find similar narrative-social patterns across these texts? What, more precisely, is the relationship between them? And what would either conclusion imply about John and the Jewish world that he describes (positively and negatively)? I will argue that, from an institutional perspective, John's world is not so different from that of the others; in fact, Luke-Acts rather than John seems to offer contrasting material, as John aligns more with Mark and Matthew than with the Third Gospel in its descriptions of Jewish institutions.[3]

Why Institutions Matter

A brief word on why a focus on Jewish institutions might be helpful in the analysis of the Gospels (and other New Testament texts) is in order. Ideology and theology do not appear *ex nihilo* and are never the result of the mind of a single author only. Socially, humans weave themselves together in varied and complex patterns creating, maintaining, or dissolving relationships, so that their thoughts, writings, and actions cannot be disentangled from the type of collective agreements we call institutions; one needs, therefore, a body to locate a soul. As Paula Fredriksen recently noted, "People build institutions; but institutions shape people."[4]

It follows, arguably, that effective analyses of patterns of thought and historical developments should involve, at some level, consideration of the contemporary socio-institutional realities within which the texts and/or events recounted were embedded.[5] In the context of the present essay, I am interested not primarily in theology or ideology, but rather in what kind of knowledge John and the Synoptics had of Jewish institutional realities and how they used this knowledge to construe their stories. This, in turn, may reveal something about how they wanted to portray their Messiah's relationship to Jewish society, and perhaps also shed light on the *Sitz im Leben* of these ancient writers.

---

[3] This is, thus, not a traditional contribution to the Synoptic problem, a field of study that has received some bad press recently; see, for example, Ekaputra Tupamahu, "The Stubborn Invisibility of Whiteness in Biblical Scholarship," *Political Theology Network*, https://politicaltheology.com/the-stubborn-invisibility-of-whiteness-in-biblical-scholarship/ (checked August 19, 2022); cf. the discussion of that article in Greg Carey, "Looking for White in the Synoptic Problem," *Political Theology Network*, https://politicaltheology.com/looking-for-white-in-the-synoptic-problem/ (checked August 19, 2022). Rather, my interest in this topic comes from many years of studying ancient synagogues as well as the Jesus movement and other forms of Judaism in relation to ancient Jewish institutions.
[4] Paula Fredriksen, "Where Do We Go from Here? Conflict and Co-existence in Institutional Contexts," in *Negotiating Identities: Conflict, Conversion, and Consolidation in Early Judaism and Christianity (200 BCE–600 CE)*, ed. Karin Hedner Zetterholm, Anders Runesson, Cecilia Wassén, and Magnus Zetterholm, CB (Lanham, MD: Lexington/Fortress Academic, 2022), 381.
[5] I have developed this further in Anders Runesson, "Placing Paul: Institutional Structures and Theological Strategy in the World of the Early Christ-Believers," *SEÅ* 80 (2015): 43–67; see also Anders Runesson, *Judaism for Gentiles: Reading Paul beyond the Parting of the Ways Paradigm*, in collaboration with Rebecca Runesson, WUNT 494 (Tübingen: Mohr Siebeck, 2022).

In the following, we shall look first at scenes in the Gospels that are related to synagogues and then discuss how these scenes change especially in Luke-Acts as perspectives turn global. Of course, in order to enable such analyses, it is crucial to take as point of departure a working hypothesis of what "synagogues" actually were in antiquity. I have written extensively on this topic elsewhere and shall not repeat those discussions here.[6] The key to uncover the narrative dynamics of the Gospels in this regard is the recognition that behind the many and varied terms for synagogues in antiquity[7] lie two types of institutions, reflecting how Greco-Roman societies more generally were structured: the official civic institutions through which society was run, and the often quite small,[8] unofficial associations catering to various types of networks (occupational, ethnic/geographic, cultic, neighborhood, household).[9] While some associations were exclusively dedicated to the worship of a specific deity, all of these institutions included some kind of cultic activities. In terms of titles, names of officials, the honoring of patrons, and several other functions, associations mimicked to various degrees the civic institutions.[10] A final point to keep in mind is that, while civic institutions were dominated by men, associations could be exclusively male or exclusively female, or have a mixed membership of both men and women; they could also include members from different social strata, so that slaves and free citizens could be members of the same association(s).[11]

On a basic level, then, when mentioned in the New Testament texts, "synagogues" need to be understood as references to either public civic institutions or various types of Jewish associations whose patron deity was the God of Israel, who accommodated the needs of various networks. While Jewish civic institutions existed where Jews oversaw

---

[6] See, especially, Anders Runesson, *The Origins of the Synagogue: A Socio-Historical Study*, ConBNT 37 (Stockholm: Almqvist & Wiksell International, 2001). For relevant sources, see Anders Runesson, Donald D. Binder, and Birger Olsson, *The Ancient Synagogue from Its Origins to 200 CE: A Source Book*, AGJU 72 (Leiden: Brill, 2008).

[7] Among the many Greek terms used for these institutions, the most common were *synagōgē*, *proseuchē*, and *ekklēsia*. On *ekklēsia* as a synagogue term, see, especially, Ralph J. Korner's comprehensive study, *The Origin and Meaning of* Ekklēsia *in the Early Jesus Movement*, AJEC 98 (Leiden: Brill, 2017).

[8] While a few associations could count their membership in the hundreds, many or most would have had between ten and twenty-five members.

[9] On this categorization, which includes some overlap between networks, see most recently John S. Kloppenborg, *Christ's Associations: Connecting and Belonging in the Ancient City* (New Haven, CT: Yale University Press, 2019), 23–40; Richard Last and Philip A. Harland, *Group Survival in the Ancient Mediterranean: Rethinking Material Conditions in the Landscape of Jews and Christians* (London: T&T Clark, 2020), 9–13.

[10] See Kloppenborg, *Christ's Associations*. Examples of honorary inscriptions in civic and associative contexts, respectively, include *IGRR* 4.786 (civic), and *IDelos* 1699 (association, ethnic/geographical [Italians living on the Island of Delos]). For discussion of these inscriptions, I am grateful to Rebecca Runesson (University of Toronto), who also sends her very best wishes to the honoree of this book.

[11] On the number of female members in associations, see the discussion by Last and Harland, *Group Survival*, 23–6. On women as leaders in synagogue settings, see also Bernadette Brooten, *Women Leaders in the Synagogue: Inscriptional Evidence and Background Issues* (Providence, RI: Brown Judaic Studies, 1982). On the unique social opportunities enabled by the associative setting more generally, see also Koenraad Verboven, "The Associative Order: Status and Ethos among Roman Businessmen in Late Republic and Early Empire," *Athenaeum* 95 (2007): 1–33.

city and town administration (in Judea and Galilee), evidence of Jewish associations comes from both the land and the diaspora.

Synagogue Scenes: John among the Synoptics

The story of this specific Messiah is set within the land considered Jewish by all four Gospels.[12] While Rome ultimately controlled the area, they ruled through the local Jewish administrative system, embodied in the civic institutions of the Jerusalem temple and the public "synagogues." The temple administration represented Jerusalem but extended to some degree its influence also to Judea and Galilee through local civic institutions ("synagogues").[13] While application of Jewish law was dependent on local tradition throughout the land, the Jerusalem authorities were responsible before Rome to keep the peace not only in Judea but also in Galilee. If the Gospels narratively place Jesus in the civic institutions of the land, then they also present his message as politically charged and relevant beyond what we today would call the "religious" sphere of society. It would also be a claim that this Messiah and his followers were deeply immersed in Jewish society and its religio-political aspirations. If, on the other hand, they remove Jesus from these public institutions and contextualize the movement in unofficial associative settings similar to those that may be reconstructed from the sectarian texts among the Dead Sea Scrolls and the archaeological remains at Qumran,[14] then our authors, while still presenting an image of what they believed to be *the* way to embody Jewish life, would present a Jesus more concerned with his own group than engaging directly and politically with Jewish society.[15] Interpretively, then, the way we understand these institutions have rather important implications for how we read the Gospels and their messages.

Taking a bird's-eye view of the Gospels' "synagogue" landscapes, we may note the following details about terminology and officials involved. *Synagōgē* (συναγωγή) dominates almost exclusively (Mark 8x, Matthew 9x, Luke 15x, John 2x), although Matthew's narrative also includes two occurrences of *ekklēsia* (ἐκκλησία, Matt 16:18; 18:17). Officials connected to these institutions are identified in various ways: Mark

---

[12] Matthew is the most explicit about this, as this Gospel designates this part of the Roman Empire "the land of Israel" (*gē Israēl*; Matt 2:20, 21).

[13] An intriguing example of the connection between Jerusalem and Galilee in this regard is the iconography of the so-called Magdala Stone, found in the assembly room of the Magdala synagogue, which features a three-dimensional representation of the temple. For discussion, see Jordan J. Ryan, *The Role of the Synagogue in the Aims of Jesus* (Minneapolis, MN: Fortress, 2017).

[14] On the covenanters and their associative setting, see Yonder Moynihan Gillihan, *Civic Ideology, Organization, and Law in the Rule Scrolls: A Comparative Study of the Covenanters' Sect and Contemporary Voluntary Associations in Political Context*, STDJ 97 (Leiden: Brill, 2012).

[15] There are several such examples of Jewish groups forming networks around their own vision of Jewish life, including the Essenes (Philo, *Good Person.* 80–83, noting that their *synagōgai* were considered "sacred spots"; cf. Josephus, *J.W.* 2.128–132), and the Therapeutae (Philo, *Contempl. Life* 30–33). Of course, forming groups catering to specific needs and interests does not imply isolation from society; on the contrary, most often the opposite was true. There is a (social) difference, however, between targeting and engaging public civic institutions on the one hand and forming unofficial associations to spread one's ideas on the other.

and Luke use *archisynagōgos* (ἀρχισυνάγωγος, Mark 4x in the same pericope, Luke twice). *Archōn* (ἄρχων) is used by Matthew twice and Luke once (but see Luke 12:58; 14:1). *Hyperētēs* (ὑπηρέτης, Hebr. *hazzan*; usually translated "attendant") is used once (Luke 4:20; cf. m. Sotah 7:7, where a similar ritual function is described), but see Matt 5:25, where the term is used with reference to court proceedings, a civic activity that took place in public "synagogues" (e.g., m. Mak. 3:12). The title *grammateus* ("scribe") is used frequently in the Gospels, often without giving an institutional context. The office is, however, connected with civic institutions, as is shown in Mark 1:21-22 and 12:39 (*synagōgē*). It is reasonable to assume a link between this office and civic institutions when the term is used more generally, especially because "teaching" is noted as one part of a scribe's duties in relation to whole populations at specific places, and such teaching took place in "synagogues." (In Matt 13:52, a *grammateus* trained in the secrets of the kingdom is held forth as an ideal disciple able to use and adapt both new and old in his work, with the implication that such an official would be influential and partial to the Jesus movement in the town where he was employed.[16]) Regarding *presbyteros*, this title is most often connected to the Jerusalem temple in the Gospels (John uses the term only once, and in a pericope not originally located in this Gospel: 8:9[17]), although Luke on one occasion places them in a setting involving a "synagogue" (in Capernaum; Luke 7:3-5).

As in other parts of the Mediterranean world, Jewish associations often mimicked the terminology used in civic institutions. How, then, is it possible to distinguish references to civic institutions from associations in the Gospels? The answer is simple and leaves space for discussion and debate in individual cases: through (narrative) context. Briefly, when we find in the Gospels institutions designated by synagogue terms and the setting reveals one or more of the following features, the narrative intention is likely to place the actors in public Jewish civic institutions (examples given are not exhaustive):

1. an institution mentioned in the singular and/or related to a specific (named) town (Mark 1:21; 3:1; Matt 13:54; Luke 4:16; John 6:59);
2. an institution representing the population of a town as a whole (see references above under the first item), and note also the connection between population/"our people" and a "synagogue" building in Luke 7:5);
3. an institutional context that implies public visibility (cf. Mark 12:39; Matt 6:2, 5; 23:6; Luke 11:43; 20:46; John 18:20);
4. an institution in which punishments are placed that usually are carried out in civic institutions (e.g., Mark 13:9; Matt 10:17; 23:34; Luke 12:11—note the pairing of various civic institutions here and in Luke 21:12; cf. also the pairing of "synagogues" with "councils" in Matt 10:17).

---

[16] I am using the male pronoun here because civic institutions in the Mediterranean world, including in Judea and Galilee, were dominated by male officials. This situation changes as we turn to associations, as we noted earlier and shall return to later in the text.
[17] The setting is, however, narratively placed in the Jerusalem temple, which matches how the other Gospels most often use this term.

Conversely, institutions designated by synagogue terms and narratively placed in settings in which none of the above is the case, and the institution caters to a smaller group of like-minded people or networks, and/or the smaller group decides its own rules/halakah, then the narrative intention is likely to describe an unofficial associative setting.

While some cases are difficult to adjudicate,[18] the overwhelming impression is that when synagogue terms are used, more specifically *synagōgē*, all four Gospels refer to Jewish civic institutions. These are institutions where the people of an entire town come together, where justice is administered, where Torah is taught to the entire population of a specific location, where leaders (*archōn*; *archisynagōgos*), scribes, and attendants are employed and elders (sometimes) make an appearance. As Donald Binder and Lee Levine have shown, these civic functions were also represented in the Jerusalem temple,[19] whose political functions are key for our understanding of ancient Jewish society in Judea as well as in Galilee. While the Gospels mention several such local-specific civic institutions, these types of institutions are very likely also understood in the paradigmatic references to "their synagogues" in Galilee (Mark 1:39; Matt 4:23; 9:35; Luke 4:15), Judea (Luke 4:44[20]), or the entire land (John 18:20[21]).[22]

From this survey, we may conclude that all four Gospels portray Jesus and the movement around him as part of, directly involved in, and aiming to influence public Jewish society rather than wanting to withdraw from it. Of course, this does not mean that these proclaimers of the kingdom of heaven were always favorably received, even if several passages, such as Matt 13:52, suggest that they sometimes were. The type of reception (positive or negative) is irrelevant to our question about the aim and self-perceived social location of the movement as described in the Gospels; resistance to a new movement "invading" civic space does not in and of itself make a Jewish movement less Jewish. This includes not only punishments inflicted on members of the movement in public "synagogues" mentioned by the Synoptics but also the three references to exclusion and ostracism from such civic institutions mentioned by John (9:22; 12:42; 16:2).[23]

---

[18] Such as Matt 12:9, where it is not clear whether the author(s) with "their synagogue" refer to a Pharisaic association (cf. Matt 12:2, 14), or the public institution of a specific town outside of which he placed the halakic discussion between Jesus and some Pharisees about what constitutes "work" on a Sabbath.

[19] Donald D. Binder, *Into the Temple Courts: The Place of the Synagogues in the Second Temple Period* (Atlanta, GA: SBL Press, 1999); Lee I. Levine, *The Ancient Synagogue: The First Thousand Years* (New Haven, CT: Yale University Press, 2005).

[20] While "Judea" is used here, it is possible that the author uses this term to designate the entire land, including Galilee (cf. John 18:20).

[21] On this verse, see the discussion in Birger Olsson, "'All My Teaching Was Done in Synagogues' (John 18,20)," in *Theology and Christology in the Fourth Gospel: Essays by the Members of the SNTS Johannine Writings Seminar*, ed. Gilbert van Belle, Jan G. Van der Watt, and P. J. Maritz, BETL 184 (Leuven: Leuven University Press, 2005), 203–24.

[22] The expression "their synagogues" thus has nothing to do with the author distancing himself from these institutions (as in "theirs, not ours"); it is simply a way to refer to the public gathering places of various Galilean and Judean towns.

[23] On these passages, which are contextualized in Jerusalem, see Jonathan Bernier, *Aposynagōgos and the Historical Jesus in John: Rethinking the Historicity of the Johannine Expulsion Passages*, BibInt 122 (Leiden: Brill, 2013); Cirafesi, *John Within Judaism*.

John, then, despite his few mentions of "synagogues,"[24] can be placed institutionally alongside the Synoptics; they all display knowledge of how Jewish towns and cities were administered in the land of Israel, and they place their main character and his followers in these settings, not in opposition to them. While we do not have space here to discuss this in more detail, it is interesting to note that while Mark and Luke mention Jesus's teaching, healing, and exorcism in civic space, and Matthew mentions only teaching and healings, John reports teaching, exclusively, as related to these institutions.

Beyond these described civic spaces, there are two clear examples of associative settings related to synagogue terms in the Gospels. Both are found in Matthew (16:18; 18:17) and the term used is *ekklēsia*. The context in Matthew reveals an emerging association of Jewish[25] followers of Jesus, which establishes its own bylaws and exclusion mechanisms, effective only for the members of this group.[26] The establishment of such a Christ-oriented group, however, in no way excludes, in this narrative, the participation of its members in public Jewish society and its civic institutions. While John's story mentions ostracism of followers of Jesus from civic institutions (which in the real world would be socially devastating if implemented), we do not find in the Fourth Gospel any hint of associative settings designated by synagogue terms and catering to followers of this Messiah only. Considering that such Christ-groups certainly existed when John was written, and that this Gospel is the only one mentioning (religio-political) ostracism, it is somewhat odd that we do not find clearer traces of such settings in this Gospel. Perhaps even more interesting is that if we turn to Luke-Acts, we find a narrative development in which the Third Gospel's focus on the civic institutions in Judea and the Galilee is replaced by descriptions of associative settings as the story takes the disciples outside the land.

From Judea to the Ends of the Earth: Luke's Difference

In contrast to the other three Gospels, Luke extends in Acts the story of Jesus to include the travels of his followers across the Mediterranean world, spreading the message that the Messiah of the Jewish people, after his resurrection, has implications for all nations, since the world, as they knew it, was soon coming to an end.[27] While I cannot

---

[24] John mentions "synagogues" only twice. While the first reference is to the civic institution of Capernaum (John 6:59), the second mention is a paradigmatic statement about "all" of Jesus's teaching being done publicly where "all" Jews come together: in the "synagogues" and in the Jerusalem temple (John 18:20).

[25] In this story, all followers of Jesus are Jewish; mission to non-Jews is explicitly forbidden (Matt 10:5-6), a prohibition that remains in effect until Matt 28:18-20. Non-Jews who approach Jesus do just that: approach him asking for a share of the blessings coming with the kingdom (primarily bodily health); they never belong among his disciples or follow him as he travels the land.

[26] Cf. in this regard the Didache, which is an example of such a rule, closely related to the Matthean Gospel.

[27] Matthew only hints at such an initiative in his last two verses, and claims, contrary to Luke, that this worldwide mission is to take its point of departure from Galilee, not Jerusalem. John, while including claims of the relevance of Jesus's message beyond the Jewish people (e.g., John 12:20-24), contains no explicit stories describing ventures beyond Judea.

go into any detail here, keeping an eye on the institutional settings as we read Acts, remembering the criteria for identifying civic and associative settings, respectively, reveals that the author of this two-part story seems to have a very clear idea about how the institutional settings shift for Jews as the story moves beyond the land.

In his story of Jesus, which takes place in Galilee and Judea, when Luke places his characters in institutions designated by synagogue terms he exclusively relates them to public space and events and decision-making processes appropriate for such settings. As the story of the movement he left behind is introduced, however, Luke places Jesus's followers and others both in civic space and in associative settings. Jewish civic space is only described in Luke-Acts as events take place in Judea and not in the diaspora. In the diaspora, Luke is careful to portray civic space as gentile space, as we see in the story of Gallio's court proceedings in Acts 18:12-17. Luke is aware, however, of Jewish associations in the land, mentioning the "synagogue of the Freedmen" in Jerusalem (Acts 6:9[28]), and, of course, the association of Christ-oriented Jews, including some Christ-following Pharisees, in Acts 15.

In the story-world's diaspora, a concordance will swiftly take the reader to a number of Jewish associations in which Luke places followers of Jesus as subgroups (note the plural in, e.g., Acts 9:2, 20; 13:5, 15). This author also describes some (but not all: cf. e.g., Acts 13:42-43) of these associations as rather swiftly rejecting and sometimes excluding Christ-followers, resulting in the creation of specific (Jewish) associations dedicated to the cult of the God of Israel through a Messianic lens (Acts 18:6-8). Most of these associations are described as mixed both in terms of ethnic identity and gender (e.g., Acts 18:4, 26). It is not unlikely, however, as Rebecca Runesson has argued, that Luke is portraying a Jewish women-only association in Acts 16:13-15.[29] The historical plausibility of the existence of gendered (male or female) Christ associations, in addition to those that were mixed, is quite strong, as some occupations, and thus also the guilds that organized them, were exclusively male and female, respectively.[30] This is not the place to develop this further, but it is of some interest to note that while the civic institutions of Judea and the Galilee include both men and women in the Synoptics, Luke seems aware that associations could be gendered.

---

[28] Depending on how the Greek is understood, this reference may be to one or more Jewish associations, catering to immigrants from various places in the diaspora. We have either one "synagogue of the Freedmen" within which we find members from different geographical locations (Cyrenians etc.), or we may understand *synagōgē* to apply to each of the geographical locations mentioned, so that we have in total five synagogues/associations. Joseph A. Fitzmyer, *The Acts of the Apostles: A New Translation with Introduction and Commentary*, AB 31 (New York: Doubleday, 1998), 358, understands the passage to refer to one synagogue of freedmen, whose members came from different diaspora locations (taking *kai* in the first instance as adverbial).

[29] Rebecca Runesson, "Dangerous Associations: Re-assessing Acts 16:13-15 in Light of the Bacchanalia Conspiracy" (paper presented at the Annual Meeting of the SBL, Book of Acts Section, Houston, TX, November 20, 2021). It is possible, but impossible to prove, that it may have been Luke's intention to portray here a Jewish occupational association, given the description of Lydia's profession as a dealer in purple cloth. R. Runesson argues, however, that Luke has reworked a tradition that originally depicted an all-female Dionysiac group.

[30] Cf., for example, Richard S. Ascough, *Paul's Macedonian Associations: The Social Context of Philippians and 1 Thessalonians*, WUNT 2/161 (Tübingen: Mohr Siebeck, 2003).

In sum, Luke's different descriptions of "synagogue" institutions do not arise because of a flawed understanding of Jewish institutional realities. All four Gospels describe Jewish civic structures rather realistically. Instead, Luke stands out because the author depicts in detailed ways in his second work the associative settings of both the land and, especially, the diaspora. What we see in Acts 16:13-15 is, institutionally, not what we find in Luke 4:16-30.

Conclusion

Notwithstanding all the differences between John and the Synoptics, institutionally John is still to be found as one among the four. While John's program is unmistakably concerned with extending the relevance of this Jewish Messiah to Samaritans and beyond, his theological agenda is not articulated through reimagining or rewriting the basic institutional structures in which he places Jesus. John, as the other three Gospels, describes Jewish public institutions as he aims to bring his characters to life in the land. While Matthew does include two passages signaling the emergence of a Jewish association of Christ-followers designated *ekklēsia*, Luke's narrative takes this to the next level in his second book. Throughout, however, Luke is careful to distinguish between civic and associative space as he tells his story of Jesus and his movement, and then how the latter expands from the Galilee to Jerusalem and to the ends of the world. This consistency across all four writings may tell us something both about the historical Jesus and the narrative habits of the variously interrelated groups that kept his memory alive. As research continues to deepen and expand in these areas, John's Gospel is as important a text as any of the Synoptics. Adele Reinhartz's defining contribution to Johannine studies will continue to play a crucial role as the field moves forward on these issues.

5

False Friends in the First Gospel

R. Alan Culpepper

Judas betrays Jesus with a kiss in all three Synoptic Gospels, but only in Matthew does Jesus respond, calling him ἑταῖρε, "friend."[1] Jesus uses this term three times in Matthew (20:13; 22:12; 26:50), but the term does not appear anywhere else in the New Testament.[2] Why does he not use φίλος in these contexts? Do the terms distinguish different relationships, or is one more appropriate than the other in certain situations? For example, in English, "country" and "nation" are synonymous in some contexts, but one would not say "one country under God" or "For God and nation"!

BDAG describes a ἑταῖρος as "a person who has someth[ing] in common with others and enjoys association, but not necessarily at the level of a φίλος or φίλη, *comrade, companion*," hence, "*fellow-member*" of one's group, or "a general form of address for someone whose name one does not know."[3]

In the following paragraphs, we will examine (1) the occurrences of ἑταῖρος in Matthew; (2) the function of the address, ἑταῖρε, in Matthew's characterization of Judas; (3) contexts in which ἑταῖρος occurs outside the New Testament; and (4) the characteristics of false friends in discourses on friendship in antiquity.

Occurrences of ἑταῖρος in Matthew

Jesus is the only one who uses ἑταῖρε in the First Gospel, twice in parables and once addressing Judas. As we will see, there are commonalities in the three contexts, and the first two prepare the reader to understand the implications of the third occurrence.

The parable of the merciful vineyard owner (Matt 20:1-16), which appears only in Matthew, illustrates Jesus's pronouncement, "many who are first will be last, and

---

[1] Devoting an essay on false friends to Adele Reinhartz is the height of incongruity. Adele is the model of a true friend. For thirty years, we have agreed and disagreed, but always agreeably, shared insights, critiqued one another's work, pursued common convictions, and enjoyed meals together at conferences in exotic places. שָׁלוֹם וּבְרָכָה!
[2] BDAG, s.v. "ἑταῖρος," BDAG, 398, lists "of playmates Mt 11:16 v.l.," but the term there is ἑτέροις. Only G 700 *pm* lat sa contain the variant reading ἑταίροις. BDAG also suggests that "instead of being an itacized variant of ἑτέροις, the reading ἑταῖροι Lk 23:32 P[75] may well imply *political partisans* (cp. Lysias 43, 28)."
[3] BDAG, s.v. "ἑταῖρος," 398.

the last will be first" (19:30), which is repeated in reverse order at the end of the parable (20:16). An elite landowner hires laborers throughout the day to work in his vineyard. At the end of the day, he pays them all the same wage, a denarius. Those who worked all day are incensed when they receive the same wage as those who came last and worked only one hour. The parable culminates in the confrontation between the landowner and one of those who expected to receive more because he worked longer (20:10). The setting is tense. Those who came first "grumbled" or "murmured," a wonderfully onomatopoeic word—ἐγόγγυζον (cf. Exod 15:22–17:7). The laborers' complaint is that the vineyard owner made the less deserving workers equal to them by giving them the same wage, disregarding the greater merit of those who worked all day, even during the heat of the day. They have a legitimate complaint. Otherwise, the parable would have no punch. The reader/hearer waits for the landowner's response, the climax of the parable: "Friend (ἑταῖρε), I am doing you no wrong" (20:13). In this context, the polite address stands in contrast to the absence of any address in the worker's complaint. Alternatively, it may indicate that the vineyard owner did not know the laborer's name (BDAG, 398). The "first" laborers had agreed to work for a denarius. They would have been happy with their pay if they had not seen the others receive the same amount. The vineyard owner responds with a Semitic idiom, "Is your eye evil because I am good?" A good eye was a sign of purity or generosity (T. Benj. 4.2), while an "evil eye" was a metaphor for a grudging or selfish spirit. The wages ordered by the vineyard owner are based not on the laborers' merits but on the owner's generosity.

The parable of the guest without a wedding garment (Matt 22:11-14), which is an epilogue to the parable of the wedding guests (22:1-10), is uniquely Matthean, reflecting Matthean editing, if not wholesale composition.[4] A version of this parable, which teaches the same lesson as the parable of the wise and foolish maidens in Matt 25:1-13, can be found in b. Šabb. 153a, where: "The king rejoiced at the wise but was angry with the fools. 'Those who adorned themselves for the banquet,' ordered he, 'let them sit, eat and drink. But those who did not adorn themselves for the banquet, let them stand and watch.'"[5] In Matthew, when the king sees the guest without wedding clothes, he says, "Friend (ἑταῖρε)," and asks how he got into the banquet, implying that he had no right to be there. As Anders Runesson explains, the people at the banquet "have to be clothed in righteousness, which, in Matthew, is defined in terms of Torah observance."[6]

In Matthew, Judas has conspired with the authorities, who seek to arrest Jesus and kill him (Matt 26:4), asked for money (Matt 26:14-15), and arranged the signal that would identify Jesus. The feigned affection adds to Judas's treachery, and in time became a cipher for it (Luke 22:48), but the verb "to kiss" (καταφιλεῖν) does not connote anything out of the ordinary. On the contrary, the sign was calculated to appear normal

---

[4] W. D. Davies and Dale C. Allison, Jr., *The Gospel according to Saint Matthew*, vol. 3, ICC (London: Bloomsbury, 1997), 194, suspect "free Matthean composition." So also Ulrich Luz, *Matthew 21–28*, trans. James E. Crouch, Hermeneia (Minneapolis, MN: Fortress, 2005), 48–9.

[5] Trans. Rabbi H. Freedman (https://halakhah.com/shabbath/index.html).

[6] Anders Runesson, *Divine Wrath and Salvation in Matthew: The Narrative World of the First Gospel* (Minneapolis, MN: Fortress, 2016), 384.

and not to arouse suspicion.[7] Judas greets Jesus with χαῖρε ("greetings"), and Jesus responds with ἑταῖρε ("friend"). Commentators suggest an allusion to Sir 37:2, "Is it not a sorrow like that for death itself when a dear friend (ἑταῖρος καὶ φίλος) turns into an enemy?"[8] The ambiguity of Jesus's response (ἐφ' ὃ πάρει), literally, "Friend, for which you are here," need not concern us here.[9] It may be an ironic, rhetorical question: "Friend, *that's* what you are here for? [emphasis added]." Jesus knows what Judas has done and expresses both sorrow and judgment.

The three Matthean contexts in which ἑταῖρε occurs suggest a distinct frame of reference. In each context, a subordinate has erred, wronged, or challenged a superior, who responds with the ostensibly polite address followed by a condemnation.[10] The laborer protested the vineyard owner's generosity, the guest without a wedding garment violated social convention, showing disrespect for the king, and Judas betrayed Jesus with a kiss.

Characterization by Implied Syncrisis

Classical orators praised virtuous persons by comparing them with others of noted virtue and condemned evil persons by comparing them with others known for their wickedness. Aphthonius the Sophist (fourth century CE) defines syncrisis (σύγκρισις) as "a comparison, made by setting things side-by-side, bringing the greater together with what is compared to it" (*Prog.* 31; Kennedy 113–14). Nicolaus the Sophist (fifth century CE) adds, "Or it can also be defined thus: syncrisis is parallel scrutiny of goods or evils or persons or things, by which we try to show that the subjects under discussion are both equal to each other or that one is greater than the other" (*Prog.* 60; Kennedy 162). By comparing one crime or misdeed to another, the orator amplifies the deed to gain a harsher punishment: "For a traitor deserves anger, but much more when he is a general" (Theon, *Prog.* 109; Kennedy 45).

The progymnastic tradition established a defined set of topics (*topoi*) by which persons could be compared, and syncrisis influenced ancient *bioi*, most notably, but certainly not exclusively, in Plutarch's parallel lives. Michael Martin compiled a full list of *topoi* and concluded that "on the whole, the Third Gospel displays a close conformity in several regards to progymnastic topical instruction, and in this respect it is no different from other *bioi* of its time."[11] Nevertheless, syncrisis may be used in more limited ways: "Though the syncrisis is occasionally accomplished through explicit comparison of the subjects (as in Philo's *De vita Mosis* [Life of Moses]), it is

---

[7] See further Gustav Stählin, "φιλέω," *TDNT* 9:113–71, here 121, 139–41; Luz, *Matthew 21–28*, 412–17.
[8] Davies and Allison, *The Gospel According to Saint Matthew*, 3:509.
[9] See R. Alan Culpepper, *Matthew*, NTL (Louisville, KY: Westminster John Knox, 2021), 527.
[10] Karl H. Rengstorf, "ἑταῖρος," *TDNT* 2:699–701, here 701.
[11] Michael W. Martin, "Progymnastic Topic Lists: A Compositional Template for Luke and Other *Bioi*?" *NTS* 54 (2008): 18–41, here 41. See further Mikeal Parsons and Michael Wade Martin, *Ancient Rhetoric and the New Testament: The Influence of Elementary Greek Composition* (Waco, TX: Baylor University Press, 2018), 231–74.

primarily carried out implicitly through parallel narration (as in Plutarch's *Alcibiades* and *Marcias Coriolanus*)."[12] In the case of the Matthean texts where the address ἑταῖρε occurs, we are dealing with syncrisis in a limited scope: not the main character of a *bios* but a minor character, not the full list of *topoi* but only the character's deeds and their outcome, and not an explicit but an implicit comparison.

Matthew is primarily Jewish rather than Greco-Roman, but by the first century Greco-Roman concepts were generally familiar in Palestine, so it is not out of the question that Matthew employed this rhetorical device. Martin Hengel conclusively established "the infiltration of Greek education" in Palestine in the Hellenistic period: "Hellenism also gained ground as an intellectual power in Jewish Palestine early and tenaciously."[13]

We have established that ἑταῖρος occurs widely in Greco-Roman literature but in the New Testament only in Matthew, where it occurs three times. In each context, a superior addresses a subordinate with the vocative ἑταῖρε after the subordinate has done something worthy of reproach. In each case, the subordinate has disobeyed, failed, or crossed his superior. The day laborer challenged the owner for paying the latecomers the same as those who worked all day. The wedding guest appeared at the feast without a wedding garment. In each of these parables, the superior acknowledges the subordinate as a ἑταῖρος, then condemns him for his offense. When the address, ἑταῖρε, recurs after Judas kisses Jesus, the reader recalls the earlier occurrences and can reflect on the similarities in the three contexts. Characters in parables (embedded narratives) earlier in the Gospel serve as points of comparison.[14] Jesus's address to Judas, therefore, establishes an implied syncrisis. The first two contexts serve as a frame for the third; Judas, like the dismissed laborer and the guest without a garment, is condemned by his master.

Matthew's technique is classical syncrisis, albeit indirect characterization of Judas by implicit comparison. When the Matthean Jesus addresses Judas, "ἑταῖρε," the reader/hearer understands that Matthew has implicitly associated Judas with the grumbling laborer and unprepared wedding guest. To the grumbling laborer the master says, "Take what belongs to you and go" (20:14). The guest without a wedding garment suffers a harsher penalty: "Then the king said to the attendants, 'Bind him hand and foot, and throw him into the outer darkness, where there will be weeping and gnashing of teeth'" (22:13). Yet, Judas's offense is even greater; he shares responsibility for Jesus's death with the leaders in Jerusalem.

Is this usage of ἑταῖρε as an address to one who has wronged a superior attested elsewhere, or is it unique to Matthew? Put another way, would an ancient reader/hearer have recognized this use of the term immediately, or like a modern reader, seen

---

[12] Martin, "Progymnastic Topic Lists," 40.

[13] Martin Hengel, *Judaism and Hellenism: Studies in Their Encounter in Palestine during the Early Hellenistic Period*, trans. John Bowden, 2 vols. (Philadelphia, PA: Fortress, 1974), 1:103, 104.

[14] Mary Ann Tolbert, *Sowing the Gospel: Mark's World in Literary-Historical Perspective* (Minneapolis, MN: Fortress, 1989), 232, 237, interprets the parables of the Sower (Mark 4:3-9, 14-20) and the Vineyard and the Tenants (Mark 12:1-12) as "parabolic plot synopses" that provide frames for interpreting events and characters in the larger Gospel narrative.

it only in the pattern of its occurrences in Matthew? These questions require us to survey contexts in which ἑταῖρος occurs outside the New Testament.

The Meaning of ἑταῖρος in Ancient Writings

Karl Rengstorf's observation that ἑταῖρος was used "from the time of Homer" for "'one who is associated with another,' the specific sense being determined by the context" is accurate both in its specificity and its generality.[15] In Homer, the term denotes comrades, fellow soldiers (*Iliad* 1.179), but also Achilles's close relationship with Patroclus (*Iliad* 1.345). Although companions may be dear, "*hetairoi* refers to Odysseus's shipmates, while *philoi* indicates his dear ones back in Ithaca."[16] Odysseus's comrades are characterized by formulaic tags: "noble comrades" (ἐσθλοὶ ἑταῖροι; *Odyssey* 2.391; 5.110; 5.133; 7.251; 23.331; cf. *Iliad* 4.113; 16.327) and "godlike comrades" (ἀντιθέοις ἑτάροισι; *Odyssey* 15.54; 19.216). By the fourth century BCE, the term designated the king's close associates in Macedonia. Adrian Goldsworthy describes their status:

> All Argead kings had their Companions (*hetairoi*), who feasted with them, fought by their side, or were given important commands, and whose advice they sought. These men included members of established aristocratic families and the newly favored. ... Tradition allowed the Companions to address the king freely and to disagree with him.[17]

The vocative ἑταῖρε appears in the Homeric Hymn to Hermes, where Apollo calls Hermes "you friend of dark night" and says, "You shall be known as the prince of thieves for evermore" (290 [West, LCL]).

The appeal to an unnamed pupil in Theognis, "Learning this lesson, dear friend [φίλ᾿ ἑταῖρε], ..." (1.753 [Gerber, LCL]), foreshadows the extensive use of the vocative in Plato's dialogues. Compare the following examples:

> Socrates: "And realizing this I tell you, my good friend (ὦ φίλε ἑταῖρε), I'm keen to become your pupil." (*Euthyphro* 5c [Emlyn-Jones Preddy, LCL])

> Socrates: "For she [philosophy], my dear friend (ὦ φίλε ἑταῖρε), speaks what you hear me saying now." (*Gorgias* 482a [Lamb, LCL])

> "Well then," said Socrates, "if this is true, my friend (ὦ ἑταῖρε) ... ." (*Phaedo* 67b [Emlyn-Jones Preddy, LCL])

Many such examples could be cited in Plato as well as Xenophon, which illustrate the use of the vocative addressing a student or adherent in the context of a

---

[15] Rengstorf, "ἑταῖρος," 699.
[16] See David Konstan, *Friendship in the Classical World* (Cambridge: Cambridge University Press, 1997), 31–3.
[17] Adrian Goldsworthy, *Philip and Alexander: Kings and Conquerors* (New York: Basic Books, 2020), 88.

philosophical discussion. One also finds the terms for a friend elided: φιλέταιρός (Plato, *Lysis* 212A). Consistently, however, the term appears only in Socrates's words, never addressed to Socrates, which confirms the ambiguity of the term as an address to an associate who is not an equal but a subordinate, conferring status with no hint of condemnation. The same usage occurs in many later school texts, including Hippocrates (fifth to fourth century BCE; *Epistles* 12.37; 13.3; 16.2; 17.119), Musonius Rufus (first century CE; *Discourse* 9.106), and Longinus (first century CE; *On the Sublime* 1.2.6; 9.6.7; 9.10.2; 26.2.4). Epictetus counseled his students to judge the character of a friend:

> But if you hear these men assert that in all sincerity they believe the good to be where moral purpose lies, and where there is the right use of external impressions, then you need no longer trouble yourself as to whether they are son and father, or brothers, or have been schoolmates a long time and are comrades (ἑταῖροι); but though this is the only knowledge you have concerning them, you may confidently declare them "friends" (φίλοι), just as you may declare them "faithful" and "upright." (*Discourses* 2.22.29 [Oldfather, LCL])

This selection of texts suggests the need to examine the role of a ἑταῖρος as an equal or subordinate in relation to the speaker, and the relationships between a ἑταῖρος, a true friend, and a flatterer. Before doing so, we will trace the rather different course of occurrences of ἑταῖρος in the LXX and Jewish writings, where the term generally translates רֵעָה or רֵעַ, "friend," "companion," or "fellow,"[18] which are often rendered by πλησίον ("neighbor") in the LXX.

In the historical writings, the occurrences of ἑταῖρος are similar to those in the pre-Socratic Greek texts, often denoting a comrade in arms (Judg 4:17). Samson's ἑταῖρος was also his best man (Judg 14:20). Amnon's ἑταῖρος, Jonadab, "a very crafty man," suggested to Amnon a plan for raping Tamar (2 Sam 13:3). While the classic example of friends in the history of Israel is David and Jonathan (1 Sam 18:1-4), Hushai the Archite was David's ἑταῖρος, companion and advisor (2 Sam 15:32, 37; 16:17). Similarly, although the LXX ambiguously refers to both Abiathar the priest and Joab the son of Saruia, the commander in chief, as Solomon's ἑταῖρος (1 Kgs 2:22 LXX), the term again seems to denote the king's chief counselor. Two chapters later, that role is assigned to Zabud, son of Nathan (1 Kgs 4:5 LXX). It is tempting to draw a connection between the references to David's companion and Jesus's use of the term in his address to Judas in Matthew, especially since Matthew emphasizes Jesus's Davidic kingship (1:1, 17; 2:2; 21:5, 9; 22:41-46) and Matthew is the only Gospel in which Jesus promises his disciples that they will sit on twelve thrones and rule over Israel (19:28). The use of ἑταῖρε in the two earlier, parallel references in Matthew, however, militates against finding a special sense in the address to Judas.

The term moves to more personal relationships in the wisdom literature, where Proverbs counsels, "Make no friends [LXX: ἑταῖρος] with those given to anger, and do

---

[18] Francis Brown, Samuel Rolles Driver, and Charles Augustus Briggs, "רֵעָה", BDB (Boston, MA: Houghton Mifflin, 1907; repr. with corrections, Oxford: Clarendon, 1966), 945; "רֵעַ," BDB, 946.

not associate with hotheads" (22:24). Job laments that he has become the ἑταῖρος of ostriches (Job 30:29); and in the Song of Songs, the maiden complains, "Why should I be like one who is veiled [a harlot] beside the flocks of your companions?" (1:7, where the LXX translates חֲבֵרֶיךָ as ἑταίρων σου).

In the later writings of the LXX, the leading men of Nebuchadnezzar's court are called his ἑταῖροι, "companions" (Dan 5:1-2), while Sirach uses the term for "friends":

> Some companions (ἑταῖρος) help a friend (φίλῳ) for their stomachs' sake. (37:5)
>
> A friend (φίλος) or companion (ἑταῖρος) is always welcome, but a sensible wife is better than either. (40:23)
>
> [Do not be ashamed] of dividing the inheritance of friends (ἑταίρων). (42:3)

The same range of meaning is found in 3 Maccabees, where Ptolemy's ἑταῖροι and drinking companions are mentioned together (2:26) and Daniel and his two companions are τρεῖς ἑταίρους (6:6). Notably, the vocative ἑταῖρε does not occur in the LXX.

In Philo, the status of a ἑταῖρος is closer to a true friend than a flatterer: "In private friendships (φιλίαις) flatterers (οἱ κόλακες) prove enemies (ἐχθροί) instead of comrades (ἑταίρων)" (*Allegorical Interpretation* 2.10). Similarly,

> In reality pleasure is a foe to sense, albeit thought by some to be a close friend. But just as no one would call the flatterer (κόλακα) a comrade (ἑταῖρον), since flattery is friendship (φιλίας) diseased. (*Allegorical Interpretation* 3.182 [Colston, LCL])

Josephus knows the same range of meaning: his soldiers, comrades (*Ant.* 12.302), and a governor's subordinates (*Ant.* 11.101). Josephus's response to the Jews under his command when they threatened him with their swords because he considered surrendering to the Romans exhibits parallels to Jesus's response to Judas at his arrest. When Josephus sees that the Jews preferred to die at their own hands rather than surrender, he responds, "Why, comrades (ἑταῖροι), ... this thirst for our own blood?" (*J.W.* 3.362 [Thackeray]). Josephus himself explains, "Fearing an assault, and holding that it would be a betrayal of God's commands, should he [Josephus] die before delivering his message, [he] proceeded, in this emergency, to reason philosophically with them" (*J.W.* 3.361 [Thackeray, LCL]). In spite of the similar elements in the situation, however, Josephus, does not use the address with any hint that they were not, or were no longer, truly his ἑταῖροι.

Failing to find true parallels to the Matthean use of ἑταῖρε—namely, as an address to a subordinate who has violated his relationship to the speaker—we turn from the use of the term in antiquity to some of the ancient treatises on friendship.[19]

---

[19] For occurrences in patristic sources, see Didache 14.2; Irenaeus, *Haer.* 5.33.3-4; Eusebius, *Hist. eccl.* 3.39.1; and Philip of Side, *Hist. eccl.* (LCL 25: 112-13).

False Friends in Antiquity

Any reader, ancient or modern, will recognize immediately the treachery of Judas's act of betrayal, making an appeal to philosophical discourses unnecessary. On the other hand, a grasp of how the ancients thought about friendship sensitizes modern readers to the norms by which ancient hearers or readers would have judged Judas.[20] Varieties of friendships, expectations of a true friend, signs of flatterers or false friends, and exhortations regarding prudence in such relationships all occupied an important place in ancient Greek and Roman discourse. Diogenes Laertius, citing Timaeus, claims Pythagoras "was the first to say, 'Friends (φίλων) have all things in common' and 'Friendship (φιλίαν) is equality'" (8.10 [Hicks, LCL]),[21] and the Pythagoreans were known for their "friendship."[22] In this section, we will briefly survey three of the most important exemplars of this literature for insights into the qualities associated with false friends: Aristotle (384–322 BCE), Cicero (106–43 BCE), and Plutarch (c. 45–120 CE). In some contexts, false friends are characterized directly; elsewhere inferences must be made from what is said about true friends.

Books 8 and 9 of Aristotle's *Nicomachean Ethics* are foundational for ancient reflections on friendship, adumbrating questions raised earlier in Plato's *Lysis*. Aristotle reasons that happiness requires virtue, virtue contributes to happiness, and friendships advance both happiness and the pursuit of virtue. "Friendship" (φιλία) included a wider range of relationships in antiquity than it does today. Hence, Aristotle suggests that there are three reasons why one might cultivate a friendship: pleasure, utility, and virtue. Friendship can produce pleasure and benefit, but in its highest form one person is attracted to another because of his or her virtue. Friendships based on pleasure or utility are not true friendships because one seeks the pleasure or benefit rather than good for the other person: "A friendship based on utility dissolves as soon as its profit ceases; for the friends did not love each other, but what they got out of each other" (1157a14–16 [Rackham, LCL]). Friendship also requires mutual goodwill (εὔνοια): "To be friends therefore, men must (1) feel goodwill for each other, that is, wish each other's good, and (2) be aware of each other's goodwill, and (3) the cause of their goodwill must be one of the lovable qualities mentioned above" (1156a3–5 [Rackham, LCL]).

Matthew omits Mark's explanation that Jesus called twelve disciples "to be with him, and to be sent out to proclaim the message, and to have authority to cast out demons" (Mark 3:14-15), but Matthew reports that Jesus instructed the disciples, and they spent time with him while he preached and healed in Galilee. Presumably, the disciples recognized Jesus's virtue and assumed there would be benefit in following him.

---

[20] The following discussion is limited to those elements pertinent to our interpretation of ἑταῖρος in Matthew, especially in reference to Judas. For a more comprehensive analysis of friendship in antiquity, see especially Konstan, *Friendship in the Classical World*.

[21] Cf. Plato, *Lysis* 207C, "Friends are said to have everything in common" (Lamb, LCL 166: 20–1).

[22] R. Alan Culpepper, *The Johannine School: An Evaluation of the Johannine School Hypothesis Based on an Investigation of the Nature of Ancient Schools*, SBLDS 26 (Missoula, MT: Scholars Press 1975), 49–50.

Goodwill is not a feeling but a fixed disposition, a matter of character (*Eth. nic.* 1157b29). Good friends are therefore incapable "ever to do each other wrong" (1157a23). Such friendships also require that "towards comrades (ἑταίρους) and brothers ... we should use frankness of speech" (1165a29-30 [Rackham, LCL]). The great-souled person "must be open both in love and in hate ... and speak and act openly" (1124b26-28 [Rackham, LCL]). On the other hand, one who pretends or deceives is "a worse malefactor than those who counterfeit the coinage, inasmuch as his offence touches something more precious than money" (1165b12-14 [Rackham, LCL]). Parenthetically, Theophrastus, who succeeded Aristotle as head of the Lyceum, characterized the pretender by saying, "He praises to their faces those whom he has attacked in secret" (*Characters* 2.1 [Rusten, LCL]).

Theophrastus's treatise *On Friendship* has been lost, but Aulus Gellius (*Noct. Att.* 1.3.10-13) says that Cicero borrowed from Theophrastus when he wrote his treatise *On Friendship*. In this discourse, which celebrates Cicero's friendship with Atticus, Laelius reflects on his friendship with Scipio. Cicero maintains, "The whole essence of friendship [is] the most complete agreement in policy, in pursuits, and in opinions" (*On Friendship* 4.15 [Falconer, LCL]), and therefore, "friendship cannot exist except among good men" (5.18 [Falconer, LCL]). By "good men," Cicero explains, he means, "those who so act and so live as to give proof of loyalty and uprightness, of fairness and generosity ... and have great strength of character" (5.19 [Falconer, LCL]). Accordingly, "friendship is nothing else than an accord in all things, human and divine, conjoined with mutual goodwill and affection" (6.20 [Falconer, LCL]). As Laelius concludes his opening statement on the nature of friendship, praising the great good there is in friendship, he recalls the audience's response to a scene in a recent performance:

> Whenever, therefore, there comes to light some signal service in undergoing or sharing the dangers of a friend, who does not proclaim it with the loudest praise? What shouts recently rang through the entire theatre during the performance of the new play, written by my guest and friend, Marcus Pacuvius, at the scene where, the king being ignorant which of the two was Orestes, Pylades, who wished to be put to death instead of his friend, declared, "I am Orestes," while Orestes continued steadfastly to assert, as was the fact, "I am Orestes!" The people in the audience rose to their feet and cheered this incident in fiction; what, think we, would they have done had it occurred in real life? (7.24 [Falconer, LCL])

In his response, Scaevola adds that "in friendship there is nothing false, nothing pretended" (8.27 [Falconer, LCL]), and "friendship is desirable, not because we are influenced by hope of gain, but because its entire profit is in the love itself" (9.31 [Falconer, LCL]). Laelius agrees: "The greatest bane of friendship is the lust for money" (10.34 [Falconer, LCL]). Later, he explains, "For it is not so much the material gain procured through a friend, as it is his love, and his love alone, that gives us delight" (14.51 [Falconer, LCL]). Yet, "some men often give proof in a petty money transaction how unstable they are" (17.63 [Falconer, LCL]). On the contrary, the evidence of "the unswerving constancy, which we look for in friendship, is loyalty" (18.65 [Falconer, LCL]). Therefore, "let there be no feigning or hypocrisy; for it is more befitting a candid man to hate openly than to mask his real thoughts with a lying face" (18.65 [Falconer LCL]).

In friendship, Cicero counsels, "care must be used, first, that advice be free from harshness, and second, that reproof be free from insult" (24.89 [Falconer, LCL]). Again, following Aristotle, Cicero affirms the importance of virtue: "Hypocrisy is not only wicked under all circumstances, because it pollutes truth and takes away the power to discern it, but it is also especially inimical to friendship, since it utterly destroys sincerity, without which the word friendship can have no meaning" (25.92 [Falconer, LCL]).

In one of his letters to Atticus, during a difficult period, Cicero confessed how much he needed his friend: "I must tell you that what I most badly need at the present time is a confidant—someone with whom I could share all that gives me my anxiety, a wise, affectionate friend to whom I could talk without pretense or evasion or concealment" (*Letters to Atticus* 1.18 [Shackleton Bailey, LCL]).

Plutarch, in *How to Tell a Flatterer from a Friend* (*Mor.* 48E–74), describes the various artifices and tricks of a flatterer (κόλαξ). Strictly, Judas is not a flatterer, but his kiss is certainly deceitful. In various particulars, therefore, Plutarch's warnings about a flatterer's deceptions suggest how ancients might have interpreted Judas's treachery. The setting of Judas's act is critical, "For it is cruel to discover friends that are no friends at a crucial time which calls for friends, since there is then no exchanging one that is untrustworthy and spurious for the true and trustworthy" (*Mor.* 49D [Cole Babbitt, LCL]). His manner is also characteristic of a flatterer, who, "imitating the pleasant and attractive characteristics of the friend, always presents himself in a cheerful and blithe mood, with never a whit of crossing or opposition" (50B [Cole Babbitt, LCL]). Plutarch quotes Plato, "For as Plato says, 'it is the height of dishonesty to seem to be honest when one is not' [*Republic* 361A], and so the flattery which we must regard as difficult to deal with is that which is hidden, not that which is openly avowed" (50F [Cole Babbitt, LCL]). False friendship, certainly betrayal, reveals one's character and lack of virtue. Echoing Aristotle, Plutarch affirms that "since the disposition and character are the seed from which actions spring, such persons are thus perverting the very first principle and fountain-head of living" (56B [Cole Babbitt, LCL]). By various deceptions, a flatterer "arrays himself to masquerade in the badges and insignia proper to a friend" (59B [Cole Babbitt, LCL]). Greetings offer a flatterer the opportunity to pretend friendship:

> Take the case of one person meeting another: a friend sometimes, without the exchange of a word, but merely by a glance and a smile, gives and receives through the medium of the eyes an intimation of the goodwill and intimacy that is in the heart, and passes on. But the flatterer runs, pursues, extends his greeting at a distance, and if he be seen and spoken to first, he pleads his defence with witnesses and oaths over and over again. It is the same with actions: friends omit many of the trifling formalities, not being at all exacting or officious in this respect, not putting themselves forward for every kind of ministration. (62CD [Cole Babbitt, LCL])

Judas kisses Jesus, a common but in this case an especially telling act, "for a gracious act on the part of a friend is like a living thing: it has its most potent qualities deep within it, and there is nothing on the surface to suggest show or display" (63D [Cole Babbitt, LCL]). In contrast, "the flatterer's activity shows no sign of honesty, truth, straightforwardness, or generosity" (63F [Cole Babbitt, LCL]). Turning others against a friend is "a crime against friendship, which in his [the flatterer's] hands becomes a counterfeit coin as it were" (65B [Cole Babbitt, LCL] 197:344–5). Therefore, Plutarch declares, "Without more ado we must say to such a man: 'Stranger, you seem to me now a different man than aforetime' [Homer, *Odyssey* 16.181]" (53B [Cole Babbitt, LCL]).

Conclusion

Matthew's distinctive use of ἑταῖρε led us first to review the three contexts in which this term occurs in Matthew and to the conclusion that Matthew's use of the term to signal a superior's rebuke of a subordinate's failing characterizes Judas by means of syncrisis. A survey of the usage of this term in Greco-Roman and Jewish sources revealed no true parallels to the three Matthean contexts. Finally, a necessarily cursory survey of classic treatises on friendship suggests ways Judas exemplifies the conduct of a false friend. His betrayal reveals a lack of character and a disregard for virtue. He is disloyal, seeks monetary benefit, and conspires in secret. He is not there for his friend in his time of crisis, and he does not act openly or speak frankly. At the crucial moment, he assumes the mask of a flatterer; deceptively displaying a token of friendship, he greets his friend with a kiss.

Part 2

Letters of Paul

6

"Put Out of the Synagogue": A Pauline Unpacking of a Johannine Trope

Paula Fredriksen

In her important book, *Cast Out of the Covenant*, Adele Reinhartz looks closely at the language of the Fourth Gospel. She argues against the received paradigm, which holds that the explanation for the Gospel's polarizing rhetoric, especially as regards the *Ioudaioi*, has social-historical roots. In this view, the evangelist's work witnesses to an experience of expulsion: he and his community have been "put out of the synagogue."

This understanding of the Gospel's social history is most associated with J. Louis Martyn, who pioneered and promoted the "expulsion" argument.[1] It rests on a wide webbing of inferences drawn from chronologically dispersed sources, both rabbinic and patristic. Pride of place goes to the *Birkat Haminim*. The rabbinic terms *min/minim*, often translated as "heretic/heretics," means "type" or "sort," and it also appears sometimes as "sect." A text redacted (probably) in the mid-third century, Tosefta Ber. 3:25, mentions a *Birkat Haminim*. Within a liturgical sequence of blessings to be said in daily prayer, this particular text pronounces a malediction on Not-us, that is, on "them," the *minim*: May "they" be uprooted—that is, by God.

Some New Testament scholars have argued that the Tosefta's *minim* obliquely describe the social situation of the group of Jewish Christ-followers represented in and by John's Gospel (written, in Greek, some one hundred and fifty years earlier). These *minim* stand in for those Jewish Christians of the "Johannine community" whom the synagogue had expelled. John's Gospel, in turn, backdates the malediction: despite its earliest appearance in a third-century Hebrew text, the "curse" itself, like John's Gospel, must have originated in the second half of the first century (with a historical Council of Yavneh, post 70 CE, mobilized in support). Justin Martyr's repeated accusations in his mid-second-century *Dialogue with Trypho*, that "you Jews" curse "us" in the synagogue, in turn reinforce this interpretation (*Dial.* 16:4; 93:4; 95:4; 96:2; 108:3; 123:6; 133:6; 137:2).[2]

---

[1] J. Louis Martyn, *History and Theology in the Fourth Gospel*, 3rd ed. (Louisville, KY: Westminster John Knox Press, 2003).

[2] For a defense of Martyn, see Martinus C. de Boer, "The Johannine Community under Attack in Recent Scholarship," in *The Ways That Often Parted: Essays in Honor of Joel Marcus*, ed. Lori Baron, Jill Hicks-Keeton, and Matthew Thiessen (Atlanta, GA: SBL Press, 2018), 211–41, citing opponents: Reuven Kimelman, "*Birkat ha-Minim* and the Lack of Evidence for an Anti-Christian Jewish Prayer in Late Antiquity," in *Aspects of Judaism in the Graeco-Roman Period*, vol. 2 of *Jewish*

Other scholars have challenged the early dating of this notorious "benediction," while noting that its mechanism points to *self*-exclusion. In the imagined enactment of this prayer, a Jewish male would chant the *brachah*, somehow realize that the *minim* of the malediction actually referred to himself or to his group, and then walk away—in effect, voluntarily quitting the praying community.[3] This softens the idea of a forcible expulsion but still preserves the etiological social-historical framing for it: the synagogue, in this view, actively sought to shed itself of Jesus-following Jews.

Not so, says Reinhartz. Rather, she urges, the evangelist, through his own polarizing *"rhetoric of disaffiliation"*[4] sought to *create* difference, to insist that his community distinguish itself from those groups represented by his story's Ἰουδαῖοι (*Ioudaioi*). Within this context and for the upbuilding of group identity, John strategically deploys his premier image of exclusion: those who follow Christ are actively "put out of the synagogue" (John 9:22; 12:42; 16:2).

So many other issues encumber our efforts to assess Johannine rhetoric, both historiographical (the so-called parting of the ways, itself well problematized elsewhere by Reinhartz)[5] and historical (how and when does Christ-following become self-consciously something other than, even hostile to, Judaism?). The relation of intra-Jewish invective to anti-Jewish invective and, thence, to antisemitism;[6] correlating questions about the author and audience's ethnicity (Jewish? Non-Jewish?[7]); and the social dynamics that frame and, in a sense, explain the charged vituperation of John's Gospel. We have many more questions than we have answers, and we know much less than we would like to know. Our utter lack of information about this text itself—Who is this author? When did he write, and where?—only compounds our difficulties. This Gospel, not unlike its narrative protagonist, presents us with a mysterious stranger.

Comparanda: Paul and His ἐκκλησίαι (*Ekklēsiai*)

In this essay, I propose to gain some traction up the slippery slopes of Johannine rhetoric by leaving this text temporarily to one side to turn to an earlier figure

---

    and Christian Self-Definition, ed. E. P. Sanders (Philadelphia, PA: Fortress, 1981), 226–44, Ruth Langer, *Cursing the Christians? A History of the Birkat ha-Minim* (New York: Oxford University Press, 2011).

[3] Adele Reinhartz, *Cast Out of the Covenant: Jews and Anti-Judaism in the Gospel of John* (Lanham, MD: Lexington Books/Fortress Academic, 2018), 111–30, gives Reinhartz's account of Martyn's "expulsion" theory. On page 118, she cites Steven Katz's observation, that "as long as a person did not consider himself a *min* the benediction would be irrelevant and his participation in synagogue life would continue"; Steven Katz, "Issues in the Separation of Judaism and Christianity after 70 CE: A Reconsideration," *JBL* 103 (1984): 43–76, here 74.

[4] Reinhartz, *Cast Out of the Covenant*, xxii; also 131–57 (her own "propulsion" theory).

[5] Adele Reinhartz, "A Fork in the Road or a Multi-Lane Highway? New Perspectives on 'The Parting of the Ways' between Judaism and Christianity," in *The Changing Face of Judaism, Christianity and Other Greco-Roman Religions in Antiquity*, ed. Ian Henderson et al. (Gütersloh: Gütersloher Verlagshaus, 2006), 280–95.

[6] John Marshall, "Apocalypticism and Anti-Semitism: Inner-Group Resources and Inter-group Conflicts," in *Apocalypticism, Anti-Semitism and the Historical Jesus*, ed. John S. Kloppenborg and John Marshall (London: T&T Clark International, 2005), 68–82.

[7] Reinhartz, *Cast Out of the Covenant*, esp. 159–63.

about whom, by comparison, we know quite a lot: the apostle Paul. Paul's ethnoreligious identity is not in doubt. He is a Jew and proclaims this identity proudly in scriptural terms. Paul is an Israelite (Phil 3:5; 2 Cor 11:22; Rom 9:3; 11:1); he is a Benjaminite (Phil 3:5; Rom 11:1); he is a Hebrew born to Hebrew parents who brought him into the covenant on his eighth day of life (Phil 3:5). A flawlessly observant Pharisee (Phil 3:6; cf. Gal 1:14), Paul traces his biological descent from Abraham and Israel's patriarchs (2 Cor 11:22; Rom 9:4-5; 11:1). The tribes who wandered in the wilderness were his "fathers" (1 Cor 10:1). Being a Jew in all its biological, ethical, and religious dimensions is hardwired into Paul's very φύσις (*physis*), his "nature" (Gal 2:15). The ethnoreligious identity of the Fourth evangelist may be elusive. Paul's is not.

The same holds true for Paul's audiences, the communities within which he pursues his calling to be a messenger of the εὐαγγέλιον (*euangelion*). In his seven undisputed letters, the ethnicity—thus, the religious allegiances—of his addressees seems clear: they are ex-pagan gentiles, non-Jews who used to worship non-Jewish gods. The group in Thessalonica had turned to God from idols (1 Thess 1:9; 4:5). The assemblies in Corinth and in Galatia, Paul claims, were formerly mired in "pagan" sins, especially idolatry and its perennial accompaniment, πορνεία (*porneia*, 1 Cor 6:9-11; Gal 5:19-21; cf. 1 Thess 4:5; Rom 1:18-32). And in Romans, writing to a community he does not yet personally know, Paul at several points specifically names his addressees as ἔθνη (*ethnē*, Rom 1:6, 13; 11:13; cf. 16:26).

In short, Paul's audience, unlike John's, is (reasonably) identifiable. They are for the most part non-Jews whom Paul, through the gospel, has called upon to Judaize— that is, to act Jewishly—in the brief interregnum between "now" and "soon" (Christ's approaching advent as Davidic warrior-messiah). To what degree does Paul require gentile followers to "act like Jews"?[8] Circumcision for male Christ-followers? Definitely not, Paul heatedly insists. But he demands other socially conspicuous behaviors that he and his contemporaries of whatever ethnicity would consider "Jewish." Prime among these is Paul's requirement that his gentiles "in Christ" renounce their native gods and cease sacrificing before cult images. Furthermore, he insists, they are to live according to idealized Jewish ethics: chaste marriages; internal community regulation; exemplary and peaceful group deportment; support of the poor, both locally and back in Jerusalem. In these ways, despite their sinful gentile *physis* (Gal 2:15; cf. Rom 11:24, where following Christ and thus gaining salvation are nonetheless παρὰ φύσιν, *para physin*, *against* gentile nature), enabled and empowered by πνεῦμα (*pneuma*), Paul's gentile assemblies can "fulfill the law" (e.g., Gal 5:14; Rom 13:8-10)—or as much of the

---

[8] See Shaye J. D. Cohen, *The Beginnings of Jewishness: Boundaries, Varieties, Uncertainties*, HCS 31 (Berkeley: University of California Press, 1999); and Steve Mason, "Jews, Judaeans, Judaizing, Judaism: Problems of Categorization in Ancient History," *JSJ* 38 (2007): 457–512, for the semantic and social range of this ethnic verbing. For this view of Paul himself as someone who encourages non-Jews to assume (some) Jewish behaviors, see Paula Fredriksen, "Judaizing the Nations: The Ritual Demands of Paul's Gospel," *NTS* 56 (2010): 232–52; also, Paula Fredriksen, *Paul: The Pagans' Apostle* (New Haven, CT: Yale University Press, 2018), esp. 94–130.

law as he deems necessary for their inclusion in the ἐκκλησία τοῦ Χριστοῦ (*ekklēsia tou Christou*).⁹

Paul addresses (mainly) ex-pagan gentiles: this much seems clear. And he orients them in his gospel message by frequent reference to God's λόγια (*logia*, e.g., Rom 3:2) and γραφή (*graphē*, e.g., 1 Cor 15:3), Jewish Scriptures written in Greek. Abraham; the Messiah (*christos*); God the Father; God's kingdom; David; Adam; the law; Zion; the wilderness generation; indeed, the very idea of the resurrection of the dead, whether of Jesus or of everyone else: these are all distinctly, even idiosyncratically, Jewish ideas. How can Paul assume so much acquaintance with these ideas on the part of those listeners who, until he reached them, were comfortably, actively immersed in their own Mediterranean religious cultures? Here we touch upon that community organization to which Paul (implicitly) and John (explicitly) allude: the synagogue.

Israel Abroad

Greek-speaking diaspora Jews may have dotted farmlands, countryside and χώρα (*chōra*); but those (like Paul) who had good educations, especially in rhetoric, lived within antiquity's premier religious institution: the Greco-Roman city.¹⁰ In the baths and in the schools; in the courts and in the curiae; in theaters, amphitheaters, and hippodromes whether as spectators or as participants, diaspora Jews rubbed shoulders with urban neighbors both human and divine.¹¹ The rhythms of Greco-Roman urban life set their broader social calendars. But these populations, to the degree that they chose to do so, could also live by "Jewish" time, measuring the week in seven-day increments, celebrating ancient pilgrimage holidays while remaining at home. Jewish timekeeping in the pagan city was enabled by a form of communal organization: Jews had synagogues.

The term συναγωγή (*synagōgē*) might designate the assembly of the local Jewish community itself; προσευχή (*proseuchē*, "prayer house") certainly implies an actual

---

⁹ For a description of Jewish law in Paul's letters, see Yael Fisch, "The Origins of Oral Torah: A New Pauline Perspective," *JSJ* 50 (2020): 1–25, noting the recent consensus, independently achieved, by Martin Goodman, Steve Mason, Martin Jaffee, and Steven Fraade, art. cit. 3–4 and notes.

¹⁰ For literary attestation of widespread presence of Jews throughout the Mediterranean, see, for example, Strabo *apud* Josephus, *Ant.* 14.114-115; Philo, *Flaccus* 46; 1 Macc 15:22-23; Acts 2:5-11. Archaeological evidence confirms this; see Lee I. Levine, *The Ancient Synagogue: The First Thousand Years* (New Haven, CT: Yale University Press, 2000). On the ancient city as a religious institution, see David Potter, "Roman Religion: Ideas and Actions," in *Life, Death and Entertainment in the Roman Empire*, ed. David S. Potter and David J. Mattingly (Ann Arbor: University of Michigan Press, 1999), 113–67; Robin Lane Fox, *Pagans and Christians* (New York: Alfred I. Knopf, 1987), 27–101 (especially to divert divine anger); John Scheid, *The Gods, the State, and the Individual: Reflections on Civic Religion in Rome*, trans. Clifford Ando (Philadelphia: University of Pennsylvania Press, 2016). On these gods as local powers, fellow residents, citizens, and *decuriones* of their cities, cf. Cicero, *Leg.* 2.26; Tertullian, *Nat.* 2.8.7; Clifford Ando, *The Matter of the Gods* (Los Angeles: University of California Press, 2008), 123, 162–4; also Christian Marek, *In the Land of a Thousand Gods*, trans. Stephen Randall (Princeton, NJ: Princeton University Press, 2016), 509–18.

¹¹ Fredriksen, *Paul*, 32–49, for ancient Mediterranean Jews within pagan society; see also Zeev Weiss, *Public Spectacles in Roman and Late Antique Palestine* (Cambridge, MA: Harvard University Press, 2014), who surveys the Jews in the Western diaspora.

"Put Out of the Synagogue" 71

building.[12] Remnants of these urban institutions have been found in areas stretching from Sicily to Syria, from the Black Sea to North Africa. Where there were Jews, it seems, there were synagogues.[13]

Archaeological evidence for these Jewish community organizations, especially inscriptions, reveals a striking level of social permeability. Pagans both divine and human also dropped by. One famous (and controverted) synagogue manumission inscription, installed whether by a pagan ("god-fearer"[14]) or a Jew, calls as witnesses Zeus, Gaia, and Helios (*IJO* 1, BS20). Another inscription mentions a huge benefaction to the community—constructing the οἶκος (*oikos*) at Acmonia—conferred by a near contemporary of Paul's, one Julia Severa, a priestess in the imperial cult (*IJO* 2.168).[15] My point here is the broad bandwidth of religious affiliation (and of superhuman powers) accommodated by synagogue communities. Literary evidence from irritated outsiders, whether offended pagans or, later, from exasperated church fathers, only confirms this impression. For centuries to either side of the mid- to late-first century, Jewish community institutions went on receiving and including non-Jews, whether pagan or, eventually, Christian.[16]

Paul himself, alas, nowhere directly names synagogues as a matrix for his mission. His assumption that his recently pagan gentile listeners could follow arguments drawn from Jewish traditions and Scriptures, however, certainly supports the inference. In the mid-first century, the synagogue would have been the only means for pagans to have the familiarity with Jewish figures and ideas that Paul presupposes: they could hear them read aloud and discussed, in the vernacular, once a week. How the synagogue communities felt about and reacted to Paul's using them to garner Judaized pagans

---

[12] Other terms for these Jewish associations include *politeuma, collegia, synodos, koinon, thiasos*, and *communitas*.

[13] Diaspora Judaism is explored in Anders Runesson, David D. Binder, and Birger Olson, *The Ancient Synagogue from Its Origins to 200 C.E.* (Leiden: Brill, 2010), 118–254; John M. G. Barclay, *Jews in the Western Mediterranean Diaspora: From Alexander to Trajan (323 BCE–117 CE)* (Berkeley: University of California Press, 1996); and Erich Gruen, *Diaspora: Jews Amidst Greeks and Romans* (Cambridge, MA: Harvard University Press, 2002).

[14] Further on this term, see n. 17.

[15] For the text and translation, cf. Runesson et al., *Ancient Synagogue*, Nos. 121 and 103; for discussion of many of these sources, cf. Margaret Williams, *The Jews among the Greeks and Romans: A Diasporan Sourcebook* (Baltimore, MD: Johns Hopkins University Press, 1998); also Pieter W. van der Horst, *Saxa iudaica loquuntur* (Leiden: Brill, 2014), esp. 46–66 ("Early Jewish Epigraphy: What Can We Learn?").

[16] On Mediterranean mixing in synagogues from the early Roman period to Late Antiquity, see Paula Fredriksen, "What 'Parting of the Ways?'" in *The Ways That Never Parted*, ed. Adam H. Becker and Annette Yoshiko Reed (Tübingen: Mohr Siebeck, 2003), 35–63; more recently, Paula Fredriksen and Oded Irshai, "'Include Me Out': Tertullian, the Rabbis, and the Graeco-Roman City," in *Identité à travers l'éthique: Nouvelles perspectives sur la formation des identités collectives dans le monde gréco-romain*, ed. Katell Berthelot, Ron Naiweld, and Daniel Stökl ben Ezra (Turnhout: Brepols, 2015), 117–32. Primary sources from pagan outside observers are collected, translated, and discussed in Menachem Stern, *Greek and Latin Authors on Jews and Judaism*, 3 vols. (Jerusalem: Israel Academy of Sciences and Humanities, 1974–84); from various church fathers, Marcel Simon, *Verus Israël: A Study of the Relations between Christians and Jews in the Roman Empire, AD 135–425* (Oxford: Oxford University Press, 1986); for later canonical and imperial laws attempting to unmix Christians and Jews, see the primary sources collected by Amnon Linder, *The Jews in the Legal Sources of the Early Middle Ages* (Detroit, MI: Wayne State University Press, 1997); and Amnon Linder, *The Jews in Roman Imperial Legislation* (Detroit, MI: Wayne State University Press, 1987).

is another matter, one which we will consider shortly. For now, I simply underscore the interethnic, thus interreligious diversity to be found within these diaspora "ethnic reading houses."[17]

Furthermore, Jewish communities whether abroad or at home also accommodated a broad range of *intra*ethnic diversity. Abroad, different Jews variously "foreignized" or "hellenized," picking up local gods and holidays wherever they lived their lives, interpreting their ancestral customs within the broader framing of Greco-Roman culture.[18] Even within Alexandria, in what must have been a tiny Greek-speaking and reading Jewish elite (those wealthy enough to be well educated in pagan philosophy and literary theory as well as in Septuagintal texts), we find wide disagreement over such key issues as covenantal circumcision and Sabbath observance (Philo, *Abraham* 16.89-93). Jewish fathers sent their sons to the ephebate, dedicated to Heracles and Hermes.[19] Jewish athletes ran (like their competitors) in the nude.[20] Disagreement was lived with; diversity prevailed. What central authority existed to have things be otherwise?

Distinctions with (sharp) differences also shaped Jewish life in Herod's kingdom. Josephus famously named three different "schools": Sadducees, Pharisees, and Essenes (*J.W.* 2.119-122). Describing the run-up to the rebellion of 66–73 CE, he added "the school of Judah the Galilean," meaning "insurrectionists," to this roll (*Ant.* 18:12-23). There was little love lost between these groups, who marched to their own drummers. (The Essenes's solar calendar put them literally in a different time zone from the rest of the country; and they famously loathed Jerusalem's high priests.) Taken all together, these named groups represented only a small fraction of the total Jewish population of Herod the Great's kingdom.[21] The vast majority were the *am ha-aretz*. By definition neither priests nor scholars, they played who knows what variations on the themes that constituted late Second Temple Jewishness. What is important to note about all of this internal difference (whatever the grudges, resentments, or disagreements it may have entailed) is that, for the most part, it was simply lived with. Again, even in Judea and the Galilee, variety was not the exception but the rule.

---

[17] Frances Young's phrasing, *Biblical Exegesis and the Formation of Christian Culture* (Cambridge: Cambridge University Press, 1997), 13. On god-fearers as sympathetic (but active) pagans, see Paula Fredriksen, "'If It *Looks* Like a Duck, and It *Quacks* Like a Duck …': On *Not* Giving Up the Godfearers," in *A Most Reliable Witness: Essays in Honor of Ross Shepard Kraemer*, ed. Susan Ashbrook Harvey et al. (Providence, RI: Brown Judaic Series, 2016), 25–34.

[18] Cf. discussion with primary sources in Paula Fredriksen, "Philo, Herod, Paul, and the Many Gods of Ancient Jewish 'Monotheism,'" *HTR* 115 (2022): 23–45. "Foreignization" and "Hellenization" also penetrated Judean Jewishness, most markedly in Jerusalem, in the run-up to the Maccabean revolt, 2 Macc 4:13.

[19] The names of ephebes Jesus son of Antiphilos and Eleazar son of Eleazer appear on a stele dedicated to Heracles (brawn) and to Hermes (brain), Gerd Lüderitz, *Corpus jüdischer Zeugnisse aus der Cyrenaika* (Wiesbaden: L. Reichert, 1983), 6–7.

[20] For references in literature and papyri, see Fredriksen, *Paul*, 198, n. 24.

[21] Estimates for the total Jewish population of Herod's kingdom have ranged from 0.5 million to 2.5 million. While not reliable, Josephus's numbers give a *sense* of the impact that these groups could have had: Pharisees, about six thousand (and concentrated in Jerusalem and Judea, *Ant.* 17.42); Essenes, about four thousand (*Ant.* 18.21); priests (among whom, Sadducees) and Levites, 20,000 (*Ag. Ap.* 2.108), thus altogether representing only 6% of the lowest total population guesstimate of half a million.

"Put Out of the Synagogue" 73

How does thinking with "the synagogue" help us understand Paul and, I will argue, thereby help us understand John as well?

Dispute, Discipline, and Discourse

Paul's intended audience in all his letters seems to be ex-pagan gentiles. He hints, though, that in the course of his travels he also reached out to fellow Jews. "To the Jews I became as a Jew, in order to win Jews ... I have become all things to all people, so that I might secure some of them" (1 Cor 9:20, 22). The community in Antioch, before his forced retreat, seems to have been significantly mixed (Gal 2). Paul's gospel brings the news of impending salvation "to the Jew first, and also to the Greek" (Rom 1:16). A half-century later, Acts routinely presents Paul as proclaiming his message within diaspora synagogues (with dismal results), thus, to Jews as well as to pagans ("god-fearers" in Luke's text). But Acts needs to be used with caution: the prima facie plausibility of Luke's presentation cannot outweigh all the places where his story clashes with the information that we have from Paul himself.[22] Still, we have reasonably secure evidence that Paul addressed synagogue communities at least five times where he was subjected to disciplinary punishment:

> Five times at the hands of the Jews I have received the forty lashes less one. Three times I have been beaten with rods; once I was stoned. Three times I have been shipwrecked, a night and a day adrift at sea. On frequent journeys, in danger from rivers, from robbers, from my own people and from the pagans; danger in the city, in the wilderness and at sea; danger from false brothers,[23] in toil and in hardship. (2 Cor 11:24-27)

Paul's woes, listed here, involved multiple agents: synagogue authorities (the thirty-nine lashes), Roman magistrates (beating with rods), angry urban crowds (demographically obscure, but most likely pagans), and, of course, other Jews, whether outside of the Christ movement or—perhaps worse—those within, whose message to interested gentiles differed from Paul's own ("false brethren"). We will consider these various antagonists later. For now, we concentrate on those whom Paul shares with the narrative characters in John's Gospel: the synagogue authorities.

We start with Paul. Why is he disciplined in this way, and what does it mean that he is? Various religious or theological causes have been adduced to explain muscular Jewish disapproval of the early Christ movement's mission and message, with Paul both on the giving (Gal 1:15; 1 Cor 15:8; Phil 3:6) and on the receiving ends of this disapproval (2 Cor 11:24). The source of such theological conflict is seen as the content or consequence of the gospel message. But the questions remain: what, and why? In the past, New Testament scholars have named (1) the scandal of a (specifically) *crucified* messiah—that is, a messiah known to have died a death cursed by God (nodding to

---

[22] For a quick orientation, see Fredriksen, *Paul*, 61–2.
[23] Cf. 2 Cor 11:13-15 and 22-23.

Deut 21:23 via Gal 3:10-14); (2) the scandal of legal laxity on the part of the *ekklēsia*, which permitted too great mixing of Jews and gentiles (cf. the Antioch Incident, Gal 2:11-13); and (3) the scandal of legal laxity on the part of Christ-apostles themselves, whose level of personal law observance (whether because Jesus himself had preached against law observance or because of the social exigencies of the gentile mission) had precipitously fallen off.

Scholarly speculations have their seasons. The crucified messiah, once much invoked, has encountered problems of historical attestation. No ancient Jewish text—not even those of Josephus, who recounts many such executions—holds crucifixion *eo ipso* to indicate death under a divine curse.[24] And the Jerusalem community presents counterevidence. That group lived in the city largely unmolested for four decades, and it too proclaimed a crucified messiah.

The first version of the legal laxity argument, too, runs into the problem of counterevidence. Diaspora synagogues themselves, as we have seen, accommodated and even welcomed the presence of pagan gentiles (not to mention evocations of witnessing gentile gods). Why then should its authorities object to Christ-following Jews mixing with *ex*-pagan gentiles? The second version of the legal laxity argument rests on circular reasoning: it presupposes that following Christ entails not being law observant. If we jettison that assumption, the "explanation" itself evaporates. And our evidence of vigorously various enactments of ancient Jewishness tells fatally against it: not even in the Jewish homeland, still less in the diaspora, not even within elite Jewish circles in first-century Alexandrian *salons*, were Jews on the same page. No translocal and enforceable standard interpretation of Jewish ancestral traditions has ever prevailed.[25]

À la mode currently, a fourth theological explanation is Christological monotheism. This argument runs as follows. The first generation of the Christ movement—including the Jerusalem community, from its post-crucifixion beginnings—thought that Jesus *was* God. Not a second god or a lower god, but somehow Christ, for his post-crucifixion followers, was radically included "within the identity of God," as Richard Bauckham has frequently phrased it. (John's Gospel has been read as claiming the same.) Paul fought against this transgressive view—after all, good Jews were strict monotheists—and later, after his Christophany, he championed it. For this reason, namely, Paul's too-high proto-Nicene Christology, synagogue authorities on five different occasions inflicted the thirty-nine lashes.[26]

Besides its utter improbability,[27] this argument has other problems. For one thing, ancient Jews were *ancient* "monotheists." They lived in the same divinity-cluttered

---

[24] E. P. Sanders unpacked (and dismantled) this "crucifixion-as-curse" argument in *Paul, the Law, and the Jewish People* (Philadelphia, PA: Fortress, 1983), 25.

[25] For review of these explanations and their problems in greater detail, see Paula Fredriksen, "Who Was Paul?" in *The New Cambridge Companion to St. Paul*, ed. Bruce Longenecker (Cambridge: Cambridge University Press, 2020), 6–30.

[26] For recent statements of this view and my arguments against it, see the essays assembled in Matthew V. Novenson, ed., *Monotheism and Christology in Greco-Roman Antiquity*, NovTSup 180 (Leiden: Brill, 2021).

[27] Not least, it makes the Christological controversies of the late second through early fourth century all but inexplicable. Adela Collins notes, "This recognition of ambiguity [in early Christologies] … is supported by the Christological controversies of the fourth century. If the texts of the New

cosmos as did the next first-century person (cf. Paul's complaints at 2 Cor 4:4 about the "god of this age"). The god of Israel, for Jews, might be the highest god, but that simply puts him first among a larger numinous grouping, "gods." There were highest gods, high gods, and lower gods (some of whom, like Heracles or Julius Caesar, started life off as humans). Paul, further, seems to have no trouble distinguishing between God the father and his son, the messiah. And their relationship, as the family language implies, is hierarchical. Saying that Christ was in a μορφὴ θεοῦ (*morphē theou*) before he descended to a μορφὴ δούλου (*morphē doulou*, Phil 2:6-7) just means that Christ, "the man from heaven" (1 Cor 15:47), had had a pneumatic body (as did most divine beings).[28] Could we look back at Rom 9:5 without Nicea (still some three centuries off over Paul's historical horizon line) getting in the way, its meaning would be unremarkable because its implied caesura would be obvious.[29]

What happens if we put aside some distinctively Christian (thus, later) theological reason for Paul's behavior before his call to apostleship, and for his synagogue woes thereafter? We might see more clearly how Paul drew the ire of more than just Jewish authorities. His "persecutors" include Roman magistrates, incensed pagans, and angry, resistant pagan gods.[30] What drew all these antagonists together was the ancient city and its traditional religious ecosystem. Cities could prosper only if heaven was happy. Cult kept humans on their gods' good side. Conversely, refusal to show gods the honors due them—precisely what the early Christ-movement in the Diaspora was demanding of sympathetic pagans—put the whole city at risk.

Before 250 CE, and the administrative improvisations under Decius, there was no mechanism in place to monitor popular cultic compliance.[31] But every ancient person knew the potential consequences of offending the gods—fire, famine, flood, earthquake, disease, and disaster. Paul and those within the Christ movement were unafraid: their messiah, after all, was about to return definitively to subdue or destroy these lower, lesser divine entities (1 Cor 15:24-26; Rom 8:38-39; Phil 2:10-11—a lot of superhuman knees; cf. the martial imagery of 1 Thess 4:16). But agitated urban populations—and authorities, whether Jewish or Roman attempting to keep the peace—enjoyed no such apocalyptic insouciance. Punishment placated both the gods' humans and perhaps even the gods themselves.

This essay argues that these social dynamics, and not first-order theological ones, explain the actions of all these mid-first-century agents. Whereas Paul would have had

---

Testament had been unambiguous, there would have been fewer disagreements about what the texts meant"; Adela Collins, "'How on Earth Did Jesus Become a God?' A Reply," in *Israel's God and Rebecca's Children*, ed. David B. Capes et al. (Waco, TX: Baylor University Press, 2007), 55–66, here 64.

[28] Fredriksen, *Paul*, 133–41.

[29] καὶ ἐξ ὧν [that is, Israelites] ὁ χριστὸς τὸ κατὰ σάρκα ὁ ὢν ἐπὶ πάντων θεὸς εὐλογητὸς εἰς τοὺς αἰῶνας· ἀμήν. A comma between κατὰ σάρκα and ὁ ὢν makes "Christ" in apposition to "God." Understanding a full stop between the two allows Paul's blessing in Rom 9:5 to echo the same in Rom 1:25 and to have him be a first-century Jew rather than a fourth-century Christian theologian.

[30] On Paul's numinous resistance—to be defeated by the returning Christ—see Fredriksen, *Paul*, 73–93; 313, s.v. "gods."

[31] See, especially, James B. Rives, "The Decree of Decius and the Religion of the Empire," *JRS* 89 (1999): 135–54. Decius had to adopt and adapt tax *libelli* to do the job, many papyri of which have survived in Egypt.

no control over abuse from pagan powers (magistrates, mobs, or gods), he would have *consented* to receive the synagogue's disciplinary lashing. Otherwise, he could always have just walked away.[32]

It is this point—the contrast between Paul's actual historical experience and John's Christ-followers' narrative experience—that I want to emphasize. As noted succinctly by E. P. Sanders, "*Punishment implies inclusion.*"[33] Paul from his own point of view belonged within the diaspora community, and the authorities of 2 Cor 11:24 agreed with him. This, despite local politics. Because Paul alienated many pagan residents of their diaspora city—thus compromising the safety of the local community—they would have had good reason to repudiate the apostle and his mission and to exclude him from the synagogue. Instead, they *included* him. And by his assent to receive corporeal discipline, Paul included himself.

But in John's narrative, such Jewish community leaders exclude Jewish Christ-followers. Why? No alienated pagans put John's synagogue communities at risk: his characters are constituted within an entirely Jewish narrative setting. The evangelist, rather, states plainly the reasons for this expulsion: the Christology of his gospel. Anyone who "acknowledges" or "confesses" or "knows" the Christological identity of John's protagonist is "put out of the synagogue." These antagonists, in other words, serve to highlight, or backlight, John's very developed Christological message.

Paul's Christology is no less "high" than John's: for both, Christ represents the divine being closest to God. Whatever mid-century disagreements that Paul had with James (and, thus, with Peter, Barnabas, and the rest of the *ekklēsia* in Antioch, Gal 2:11-13), differences of Christology do not seem to have figured among them. Despite practical disputes over how—not whether—to incorporate ex-pagan gentiles, on Jesus's status as *christos* all these late Second Temple Jews seem joined. All proclaimed a divine, crucified, raised, and returning messiah. But neither Paul nor those Christ-following Jews resident in Jerusalem for forty years were "put out" of any Jewish institution: not the synagogue, not the temple, not the holy city itself. And even as Christology grew higher and higher with the passage of time—say, through 387 CE, in Chrysostom's post-Nicene Antioch—and even as theology *adversus Iudaeos* grew louder and louder, synagogues continued to receive "Christ-confessors" (much to the bishop's annoyance). If a late Roman Jewish urban association received pagan gentiles and Christian gentiles, why would it not also receive Christian Jews?

These comparative historical data about Paul cumulatively support the case that Reinhartz, through her rhetorical analysis, has made about John. John's *Ioudaioi* are a narrative device, not a historical community. Their fictive action—the expulsion of Christ-confessors—services the evangelist's emplotment. John's Christ must be "lifted up" (John 8:28, note who is doing the lifting; 12:32). The hostile *Ioudaioi* get the job done (18:35-19:16, naming [John's] Christology as their motivation for insisting on crucifixion).

---

[32] On this aspect of submission, cf. Anthony E. Harvey, "Forty Strokes Save One: Social Aspects of Judaizing and Apostasy," in *Alternative Approaches to New Testament Study* (London: SPCK, 1985), 79–86.

[33] Sanders, *Paul, the Law, and the Jewish People*, 192 (italics in the original).

The actual ethnicity of the author and of his audience really does not matter to the story's structure and its semiotics, wherein "Jews" serve to symbolize the uncomprehending lower world of darkness and death. They also encode the obverse of what the knowing listener knows: that she, like Christ and thanks to Christ, will have life eternal. Polarizing rhetoric reduces the clutter of choice: truth inheres only with the view of the author. For this reason, the Fourth Gospel's story is rhetorically compelling. And for this same reason, its *Ioudaioi* are *propelling*: they enact the author's demand that the listener discern the vital distinctions between light and darkness. Between God and Satan. Between Above and Below. Between Christ and "the Jews."

7

Befriending Paul: The Letter to Philemon as a Test Case

Esther Kobel

Prologue

In her seminal work *Befriending the Beloved Disciple: A Jewish Reading of the Gospel of John*,[1] the honoree of this volume skillfully makes use of the book-as-friend metaphor.[2] Drawing on the American literary critic Wayne Booth's work, Adele Reinhartz interacts with the "Beloved Disciple," the implied author, who stands as the personification of the Fourth Gospel. She vividly engages in four different "readings" of the Fourth Gospel: compliant, resistant, sympathetic, and engaged. Each approach views the "Beloved Disciple" differently: as mentor, opponent, colleague, and as "other."

If a Gospel can potentially become a friend of sorts, we can certainly also claim the same for a letter. Letters were a common means of communication in antiquity: archaeological digs in the Mediterranean world have revealed thousands of them.[3] They served to maintain contact between geographically distant people. Marcus Tullius Cicero (106–43 BCE) defines letters as a conversation with absent friends (*amicorum conloquia absentium*, *Phil*. 2.7). By means of a letter the writer can temporarily overcome the gap between sender and addressee. In addition to geographical distance, to some degree, letters can also bridge a gap in time.

In the following, I will adopt Adele Reinhartz's concept and enter into a conversation with Paul. Together with his coworkers, Paul wrote letters to the communities that he

---

[1] Adele Reinhartz, *Befriending the Beloved Disciple: A Jewish Reading of the Gospel of John* (New York: Continuum, 2001). The approach of this outstanding and award-winning book deserves attention on its own. For me personally, it was an eye-opener into the Fourth Gospel. It set me on fire and eventually led to its translation into German and to a doctorate on the Gospel of John under Adele's cosupervision during my time in Ottawa and beyond. Adele has been a wise, open-minded, warm, and straightforward mentor ever since we first met in 2000 when I was a young graduate student in Switzerland. Over the years, she has become a dear friend with whom I love to discuss a great variety of topics and share a good laugh. I have learned an immense amount from Adele and am infinitely grateful for her friendship.
[2] Reinhartz, *Befriending the Beloved Disciple*, 18.
[3] For example, Hans-Josef Klauck, *Die antike Briefliteratur und das Neue Testament: Ein Lehr- und Arbeitsbuch* (Paderborn: Ferdinand Schöningh, 1998).

had founded or that he wished to visit in the near future. Like these communities, I am also separated by space and time as well as culture. I will engage with one of these communities and discuss the ways Paul either enables me—as a twenty-first-century, female, German-speaking, Christian reader from the Reformed tradition—to become his friend or prevents me from becoming one. My interest and focus are how Paul's message affects people and their relationships among themselves and with Paul.

I will begin with a brief overview of relationships in Phlm,[4] thereby exploring an "ecclesiological tale" of sorts. Then, following Adele Reinhartz's hermeneutical concept, I will ask two related questions: (1) What kind of friend is Paul to each sort of reader with regard to these aspects of relationships? (2) What are the ethical implications of each reading position?[5]

Relationships in Phlm

Phlm is shaped by various aspects of relationships.[6] Leaving aside the connection between the living humans referred to in Phlm and Christ, who is mentioned no less than eight times within its twenty-five verses, many other aspects can be considered.

To begin with, "Paul's letter to Philemon" is not a letter from one man to another but rather a letter from a number of people to a group.[7] Alongside Paul, the *praescript* mentions Timothy, who is again—as in other instances (cf. 1 Cor 1:1; 2 Cor 1:1; Gal 1:1)—called "the brother," an expression often used in Pauline letters in reference to fellow Christ-believers. This coauthorship already indicates that we are not dealing with a private letter between Paul and Philemon containing Paul's personal opinion but that other individuals must also be accounted for. This notion is supported by the fact that Paul names an array of people who send greetings and are thereby included in the relationships that become visible: his coprisoner in Christ Epaphras and his coworkers Mark, Aristarch, Demas, and Luke. The sender thus remains a group even when in the body of the letter the first-person singular is used. The addressees mentioned by name are Philemon, Apphia, and Archippus in addition to the community in Philemon's

---

[4] I will use "Phlm" when referring to the letter and "Philemon" when referring to the person.

[5] For each perspective, some scholars who have already distinguished themselves before me in the respective way of reading will join us and have their say. I will restrict the company to the most recent ones within the vast literature on Phlm and add only a few very influential ones from previous decades.

[6] To name only some recent publications, cf. David R. Wallace, "Friendship in Philemon," *BBR* 30 (2020): 561–82; Harry O. Maier, "Paul's Letter to Philemon: A Case Study in Individualisation, Dividuation, and Partibility in Imperial Spatial Contexts," in *Religious Individualisation: Historical Dimensions and Comparative Perspectives*, ed. Martin Fuchs et al. (Berlin: de Gruyter, 2020), 519–39; Ulrike Roth, "Paul, Philemon, and Onesimus: A Christian Design for Mastery," *ZNW* 105 (2014): 102–30; Craig S. de Vos, "Once a Slave, Always a Slave? Slavery, Manumission and Relational Patterns in Paul's Letter to Philemon," *JSNT* 23 (2001): 89–105. For an overview of recent research on Phlm in general, cf. D. Francois Tolmie, "Tendencies in the Research on the Letter to Philemon since 1980," in *Philemon in Perspective: Interpreting a Pauline Letter*, ed. D. Francois Tolmie and Alfred Friedl, BZNW 169 (Berlin: de Gruyter, 2010), 1–27.

[7] This has been pointed out by other scholars earlier, c.f., for example, the section "The public nature of the letter" in Sara C. Winter, "Paul's Letter to Philemon," *NTS* 33 (1987): 1–15, here 1–2.

house. The fact that the letter is addressed not only to Philemon but also to a number of other people also confirms that the letter belongs in the context of a community. This aspect must be considered in more detail.

The use of the term "beloved" (ἀγαπητός Phlm 1) for Philemon conforms to Greco-Roman epistolary conventions.[8] Besides being beloved, Philemon is explicitly named a coworker (συνεργός Phlm 1). Apphia, in parallel to Philemon, is called a sister (ἀδελφή Phlm 2), while Archippus is addressed as a fellow soldier (συστρατιώτης Phlm 2). It becomes clear that Phlm addresses a socially diverse group of people. While the real authors know the real recipients and share a common history, these are only remotely accessible for the modern reader, and the gaps in the text are categorically wider than for the real addressees. Furthermore, these people also have their individual relationships with Paul and his cosenders. What has been described in the *praescript* is only a glimpse into a much more dynamic relational situation. Harry O. Maier has recently offered an impressive list of both roles invoked by the letter and *dramatis personae*, demonstrating that "we are dealing with practices and dynamic relations that have the power to affect one another rather than with static identities."[9] Philemon is no doubt the *paterfamilias* of the house and the owner of the slave Onesimus. Maier identifies no less than thirteen practices and relationships for Philemon alone:[10] (1) dear friend (v. 1), (2) coworker (v. 1), (3) house church host (v. 2), (4) love for the saints and faith (v. 5), (5) evangelist (v. 6), (6) patron (vv. 2, 7, 19, 20, 21), (7) brother of Paul (vv. 7, 20), (8) brother of Onesimus (v. 16), (9) servant/slave (vv. 8, 21), (10) slave owner (vv. 11, 16), (11) partner (v. 17), (12) Paul's client (v. 19), and (13) "prayer" (v. 22). Maier cogently holds that "one witnesses a straightforward script that combines notions of friendship together with those of patronage, but also a social account of one giving a piece or part of oneself to another that results in a change in the other."[11] This pointedly sums up a multifaceted relationship with just one—but still the primary—addressee.

Paul also mentions Apphia. This is the only time that Paul addresses a woman by name in any *praescript*. Although no specific relationship to any of the males is hinted at, early traditions claim that she is Philemon's wife.[12] While the possibility cannot be ruled out completely, her being mentioned explicitly might imply that she had a higher position within the community. The term "sister" is otherwise used only for Phoebe (Rom 16:1). Apphia allows a glimpse into the early Christ-believing communities' lives and women's active roles therein; she certainly overturns the proposal that Phlm addresses two men and consists of all-male interaction.[13]

---

[8] Oda Wischmeyer has pointed out that Paul here in his use of ἀγαπητός draws on a Jewish tradition in which this adjective carries the notion of election in "Das Adjektiv ΑΓΑΠΗΤΟΣ in den paulinischen Briefen: Eine traditionsgeschichtliche Miszelle," *NTS* 32 (1986): 476–80.

[9] Maier, "Paul's Letter to Philemon," 528–9.

[10] Maier, "Paul's Letter to Philemon," 529.

[11] Maier, "Paul's Letter to Philemon," 530.

[12] Theodore of Mopsuestia regards Apphia as Philemon's wife and Archippus as their son. See John T. Fitzgerald, "Theodore of Mopsuestia on Paul's Letter to Philemon," in *Philemon in Perspective: Interpreting a Pauline Letter*, ed. D. Francois Tolmie and Alfred Friedl, BZNW 169 (Berlin: de Gruyter, 2010), 333–63, here 357–8.

[13] Sabine Bieberstein, "Disrupting the Normal Reality of Slavery: A Feminist Reading of the Letter to Philemon," *JSNT* 23 (2001): 105–16, here 106.

This brief discussion clarifies that Phlm is not simply a private letter from one individual to another but also a letter to a wider audience. Phlm is addressed to a community that gathers in Philemon's house, and Paul and his cosender can expect that Apphia, Archippus, and the other people present in his house could advocate on their behalf or at least exercise a certain influence on Philemon. Furthermore, each of the *dramatis personae* has their own individual perspectives on the issues raised in this letter.

The primary issue is the question of how to deal with Onesimus, Philemon's slave who—like his master—has become a Christ-believer under Paul's guidance. Usually, Phlm is understood to be a letter written by Paul to the slave owner Philemon on behalf of Onesimus, a runaway slave, with the request that he may return without penalty to his owner and household. Paul asks Philemon to receive Onesimus no longer as a slave but as a beloved brother (οὐκέτι ὡς δοῦλον ἀλλ' ὑπὲρ δοῦλον, ἀδελφὸν ἀγαπητόν Phlm 16). This specific request and Paul's inconclusive dealing with slavery within Phlm shall be addressed in my following four attempts to befriend Paul.

Four Attempts to Befriend Paul

Paul as Mentor: A Compliant Reading of Phlm

As a compliant reader, when I accept the ecclesiological tale as proclaimed by Paul and his entourage, they in turn become mentors and guides. What then are the ethical consequences of a compliant reading?[14]

According to the typical understanding of Phlm, Paul asks Philemon to accept the fugitive Onesimus back into the household and to consider him as a brother in Christ and more than a slave.[15] Onesimus assumingly complies with this scheme and returns to his master with the letter of reference, hoping for spiritual kinship. Many have understood the letter's intent as a request that Philemon manumit Onesimus. Others have held that Onesimus returns to the household, only changing his status in a spiritual sense while remaining a slave in social status.

Recently, D. Francois Tolmie adopted Reinhartz's approach with a specific focus on ethics in Phlm, outlining some aspects of a compliant reading in which "the exegete allows the hierarchy of norms detected in the letter to guide the appropriation."[16] These primary norms that he singles out are "spiritual kinship," "divine will," "the good," and "what is proper."[17] Tolmie demonstrates that a compliant reading serves modern readers well as an appropriation of the letter's ethics for their own context in a meaningful way,

---

[14] Cf. Reinhartz, *Befriending the Beloved Disciple*, 54.
[15] Cf. G. Francois Wessels, "The Letter to Philemon in the Context of Slavery in Early Christianity," in *Philemon in Perspective: Interpreting a Pauline Letter*, ed. D. Francois Tolmie and Alfred Friedl, BZNW 169 (Berlin: de Gruyter, 2010), 143–68, here 162–5.
[16] D. Francois Tolmie, "The Ethics of the Letter to Philemon," *Neot* 54 (2020): 47–66, here 60–2, quotation 60.
[17] Tolmie, "Ethics of the Letter to Philemon," 60.

naming, for example, the letter's encouragement for Christ-believers to consider the relationship between love, faith, and fellowship in Christian congregations.

Compliant readings come, however, with some issues, especially regarding the appropriation of Paul's concept of spiritual kinship. Read from a compliant stance, Phlm can refer to Onesimus as an ex-fugitive slave who realizes and accepts his responsibility, willingly returning to his master as a slave after having become a Christ-believer. What has been suggested and put forward as an argument is the notion that a runaway slave's behavior is against God's will and is therefore un-Christian.[18] And even worse according to this argument, Paul confirms that slavery is an institution in accordance with the will of God, because he sends a fugitive slave back to his master.[19] In this way, compliant readings of Phlm with simple arguments have been regularly used to support slavery in modern times.[20] Needless to say that from a postabolitionist Western view, such disastrous consequences from the *Wirkungsgeschichte* of the letter can only be condemned.

Paul as Opponent: A Resistant Reading of Phlm

As a resistant reader, I will address some problematic issues in the relationships depicted in Phlm.[21] Onesimus is a slave and, as such, not even legally a human being according to Roman law.[22]

The fact that slaves as well as women were considered to be siblings in the Christ-group points to the programmatic change in community relationships and hints toward egalitarian structures that did not consider class, status, or gender (cf. Gal 3:28 and 1 Cor 12:12-13). Phlm shows that such equality is not a given and that establishing a "discipleship of equals," in the sense Elisabeth Schüssler Fiorenza intends,[23] needs work.

Onesimus, a slave, could become a member in the Christ-believing community, which could be considered a liberating step, especially in light of the Christ-believers' terminology of "brothers and sisters." At the same time, however—and this is where the resistance appears—a glaring discrepancy becomes obvious between this virtual equality and the likelihood that Onesimus legally remained a slave.

In her feminist analysis of Phlm, Sabine Bieberstein argues that Onesimus's ambiguous status makes visible cracks in the logic of slavery, but Paul and his coauthors

---

[18] For example, J. Albert Harrill, "The Use of the New Testament in the American Slave Controversy: A Case History in the Hermeneutical Tension between Biblical Criticism and Christian Moral Debate," *Religion and American Culture* 10 (2000): 149–86.

[19] For examples using this argument, see Tolmie, "Ethics of the Letter to Philemon," 62.

[20] See examples in John M. G. Barclay, "'Am I Not a Man and a Brother?': The Bible and the British Anti-Slavery Campaign," *ExpTim* 119 (2007): 3–14, here 13.

[21] Cf. Reinhartz, *Befriending the Beloved Disciple*, 81.

[22] For an overview of literature on the concept and a reevaluation of it, see Kostas Vlassopoulos, "Greek Slavery: From Domination to Property and Back Again," *JHS* 131 (2011): 115–30. Still very important on the topic in general, see William L. Westermann, *The Slave Systems of Greek and Roman Antiquity*, Memoirs of The American Philosophical Society 40 (Philadelphia, PA: American Philosophical Society, 1955).

[23] Elisabeth Schüssler Fiorenza, *Discipleship of Equals: A Critical Feminist Ekklēsia-Logy of Liberation* (London: SCM Press, 1993); Elisabeth Schüssler Fiorenza, "Discipleship of Equals," *Jahrbuch der Europäischen Gesellschaft für (die) Theologische Forschung von Frauen* 16 (2008): 67–90.

never fully moved beyond the system of slavery since he never rejects slavery as such.[24] A feminist approach thus enables us to see that Onesimus remains a victim and certainly a person whose wishes are not addressed and whose voice is not heard. He is not a subject in the sense of an independent human being but essentially a voiceless object.

By demonstrating that Paul and Onesimus stand in the relationship of a (real) master and his slave, Ulrike Roth suggests that Paul has a substantially greater involvement with the institution of slavery. Central to her thesis is a dual interpretation of the κοινωνία that characterizes the letter, both in terms of Paul's theological thinking and in terms of a very specific arrangement between Paul and Philemon, such as often existed in private relationships. This arrangement had practical consequences for the ownership of the slave. Roth's convincing argument boils down to the insights that Phlm exposes Paul as a slave owner and that "the letter is a silent witness of the co-ownership of the slave Onesimus" by Philemon and Paul. Roth reveals that Paul's active involvement in slavery through personal slave ownership goes "far beyond the present realization of the level of Paul's participation and implication in the slave system."[25] Paul asks to be allowed to continue exploiting Onesimus's services as a slave and thereby fully acknowledges worldly slavery.

Therefore, while the concept of siblings in Christ is very noble in theory, for a resistant modern reader its theoretical character is not enough. Very likely a concept of this sort had revolutionary character in the first century CE because its core idea diametrically contradicted reality. If, however, "siblings in Christ" remains an entirely theoretical concept and Christ-believers perpetuate the oppressive structures in real life, such a concept at best only loses some of its force and—far worse but very likely—contributes to the disastrous developments already mentioned in the previous reading.

Paul as Colleague: A Sympathetic Reading of Phlm

As a sympathetic reader, I focus on the matters that might unite the authors and myself while ignoring those that might separate us. My *modus operandi* is comparative. In order to sympathize with Paul and his coworkers, I identify those elements within this letter that resonate positively in some way with my own tradition and experience.[26]

One major point with which I particularly sympathize in this Pauline letter is its rhetoric. While Phlm is similar to other Pauline letters in terms of its elements, this letter stands out because of its tone as well as abundance of terms and expressions of endearment—even across gender and class. The force of relational language is compelling. The entire letter communicates strong bonds between authors and addressees, as well as Onesimus who, as the probable letter carrier, creates a physical link between them. A few examples may illustrate this: Paul remembers Philemon in his prayers, is intimately connected with him through their shared love for Jesus and toward the "saints," and receives joy and comfort because of this love (Phlm 4–7). Paul

---

[24] Bieberstein, "Disrupting the Normal Reality of Slavery," 115.
[25] Roth, "Paul, Philemon, and Onesimus," 120–1.
[26] Cf. Reinhartz, *Befriending the Beloved Disciple*, 99.

characterizes Onesimus as σπλάγχνα, literally his inner organs—which in modern Western culture is usually equated with the heart. This term carries the notion that Paul has a deep affection for him (Phlm 12). And Paul asks Philemon to consider Onesimus as a brother and to receive him as he would receive Paul (Phlm 17).

The authors treat the Christ-believing community to be one family with Paul in the role of the father, indicated by the use of γεννάω to describe Onesimus's becoming a Christ-believer. Bonds shared by parents and children would have been one of the strongest.[27] The aim of strengthening bonds is obvious and compelling. In particular, the way Paul uses family metaphors beyond class, even for a slave, is very appealing in the current day.

The compelling aspect of relational vocabulary and metaphors not only gives the letter a pleasant tone. There is good reason to assume their potential to go further, since language not only depicts but also shapes reality, or at least a certain version of reality or a certain perspective on it. Language reacts to reality and to changes therein. This is evident in the continuous creation of new terms. Thus, words have an effect and therefore language is always also action.

We do not know what happened in Philemon's house when Onesimus arrived with a letter fraught with relational language. But convinced of the power of language, I do cherish the idea that the use of strong relational metaphors emphasizing family bonds and community connections to be potentially valuable for creation of ties that bind people and for strengthening existing bonds bridging gender or class.

Paul as Other: An Engaged Reading of Phlm

As "other," I attempt a friendship by naming and addressing the major issues that stand between the letter writers and myself. I seek to engage directly with fundamental issues as well as to address my own stand on them.[28]

The major issue between myself and Paul and his associates in terms of relationships is the issue of slavery. In what follows, I take seriously the fact that we are "others." This "otherness" is intensified through the temporal, geographical, and cultural gap between us. We are all children of our time, and accordingly it is not surprising that my modern view differs from what I deduce as the authors' possible intention or the recipients' reaction. The intention, in fact, is one crucial aspect that deserves further comment. Exactly how can the recipients understand the request that Onesimus be received "no longer as a slave but as a beloved brother—especially to me but how much more to you both in the flesh and in the Lord"[29] (οὐκέτι ὡς δοῦλον ἀλλ᾽ ὑπὲρ δοῦλον, ἀδελφὸν ἀγαπητόν, μάλιστα ἐμοί, πόσῳ δὲ μᾶλλον σοὶ καὶ ἐν σαρκὶ καὶ ἐν κυρίῳ. Phlm 16)? Does this mean that Philemon and his house should receive Onesimus back and accept him into the community of Christ-believers while removing any doubt that he remains a slave with all that this state entailed? Or are they asking that Onesimus be accepted as a fellow Christ-believer and additionally be set free?

---

[27] For example, 1 Thess 2:7, 11.
[28] Cf. Reinhartz, *Befriending the Beloved Disciple*, 131.
[29] All translations of Bible texts into English: NRSV.

Once more, scholars' opinions differ: a minority believes that neither here nor in other Pauline letters can a challenge to the system of slavery be identified.[30] Some even blame Paul for this.[31] Another group understands the letter to announce a change in relationship between former master and former slave, with variations in the degree of clarity in terms of what it actually asks for.[32] Most notably, John M. G. Barclay argues that the letter is ambiguous and deliberately open ended.[33] The third and majority group interprets the phrase as clearly asking for Onesimus to be set free.[34] From a modern Western point of view, this might seem like the only feasible interpretation. Acknowledging, however, that the circumstances were very different requires a more nuanced approach that considers the request in its historical and cultural setting.

G. Francois Wessels convincingly argues that "abolishment of slavery did not even fall within the realm of possibility in Paul's day."[35] He further holds that "manumission of a specific slave was not hard to imagine."[36] According to Wessels, phrases in Phlm, such as in Phlm 16 or the idea that Philemon welcome Onesimus as he would Paul (Phlm 17) or "knowing that you will do more than I say" (Phlm 21) strongly imply that the senders are implicitly asking for Onesimus's manumission.

Why, however, would the senders not ask explicitly? Barclay answers that "there must be some tension here between the Pauline ideas of brotherhood and the practical realities of slavery" that caused ambiguity.[37] Wessels rejects this view and argues that the senders are paying tribute to the power relations at play, recognizing that a refusal of a wish by a leader of a house church would cause "disastrous consequences for Paul's position of authority."[38] In addition, Paul's understanding of a Christ believing group not only as a spiritual community but also "in the flesh" must mean that Onesimus be received as a brother in Christ, without setting him free—that is, manumitting him—is not conceivable.

I am tempted to accept this interpretation. I fear, however, that it ignores the difficulties that would arise through the manumission of a runaway slave, namely, anomalies and troubles in the relationship between Philemon as a believer in Christ and Onesimus as a believer in Christ, including the reaction of other slaves in the household. How would Philemon look if he set a delinquent fellow-slave free and not all others who devotedly served him? Who would pay for Onesimus's manumission and, by extension, that of other Christ-believing slaves in the house? How would such an action affect Philemon's status in society? Without slaves he could not run the house of the size suitable for a community to convene.[39] Thus, in the bigger picture with slavery

---

[30] For examples, see Wessels, "Letter to Philemon in the Context of Slavery," 162–3.
[31] For example, Siegfried Schulz, *Gott ist kein Sklavenhalter: Die Geschichte einer verspäteten Revolution* (Zürich: Flamberg; Hamburg: Furche, 1972), 167–93.
[32] For examples, see Wessels, "Letter to Philemon in the Context of Slavery," 163.
[33] John M. G. Barclay, "Paul, Philemon and the Dilemma of Christian Slave-Ownership," NTS 37 (1991): 161–86.
[34] For examples, see Wessels, "Letter to Philemon in the Context of Slavery," 163–4.
[35] Wessels, "Letter to Philemon in the Context of Slavery," 164.
[36] Wessels, "Letter to Philemon in the Context of Slavery," 164.
[37] Barclay, "Paul, Philemon and the Dilemma of Christian Slave-Ownership," 182.
[38] Wessels, "Letter to Philemon in the Context of Slavery," 165.
[39] For a lucid discussion of these and further issues see Barclay, "Paul, Philemon and the Dilemma of Christian Slave-Ownership," 175–7.

woven into the very fabric of Greco-Roman society, there are more complications to be expected than appear at first glance.

Epilogue

The application of Adele Reinhartz's hermeneutical approach to Paul and his cosenders in Phlm has shown that it is perfectly suited to enter into a dialogue with them.

The letter and its diverse readings reveal that Phlm has both empowering aspects and problematic notions. By encouraging Onesimus to return to his master and asking that he be upgraded to a "brother" among the Christ-believers in Philemon's house, Paul's vision of equality becomes tangible, and this remains appealing. Unsurprisingly, however, regarding the real-life aspects for a twenty-first century woman living in a postabolitionist society, there are points where I have my reservations about the unquestioned acceptance of worldly slavery. I most certainly vehemently disagree with and denounce the *wirkungsgeschichtliche* consequences of certain readings of Phlm that have supported slavery. Nevertheless, the rhetoric of the letter, especially by means of its relational language and the historical context in which it was written, are appealing, inviting me again and again to meet and engage with Paul and his associates.

What I hope to have demonstrated by this example exploration—which remains somewhat rudimentary due to the nature of a short article—of some aspects of relationships within the short letter to Philemon and his house is that Adele's multiperspective approach to the Gospel of John can become a fruitful endeavor for other aspects in Phlm and, therefore, implicitly for various other concerns in other Pauline writings and beyond.

8

Paul's "Beloved" Friends

Stephen Westerholm

The apostle Paul had his enemies, but this is no time to be talking about them. He also had friends, and plenty of them. They have attracted much less attention than his enemies, as good news does less than bad; but what better time to talk about Paul's friends than in a tribute to a friend with a great gift for friendship?

The Bigger Picture

We may talk about Paul's friends, but he himself never does—not, at least, in so many words.[1] In none of the New Testament letters attributed to Paul does the word "friend" (φίλος) or "friendship" (φιλία) even occur. On the other hand, the Acts of the Apostles does speak of Paul's friends—on two unlikely occasions. According to Acts 19:31, there were, in Ephesus, Asiarchs "friendly toward Paul [αὐτῷ φίλοι]" who urged him not to enter the theater when the city was in uproar. Strictly speaking, φίλοι, here used with the dative case, must be an adjective ("well disposed toward" [+ dative]) rather than the cognate noun "friends." Nothing in the narrative suggests that these officials had come to share Paul's faith.[2] According to Acts 20:31, Paul was in Ephesus for three years. During that time, he not only, as expected, spread the gospel, but apparently

---

[1] Not, that is, in the Greek text. For our purposes, the NRSV is not helpful here. Although it usually renders ἀδελφοί "brothers and sisters," it often resorts to paraphrase: "believers" (e.g., 2 Thess 3:15); "members of God's family" (Gal 1:2); "members of the church" (1 Tim 6:2); "whole community" (Eph 6:23); and, frequently, "friends" (Rom 7:4; 1 Cor 14:26, 39; Gal 4:12, 28, etc.). In the process, the point in speaking of ἀδελφοί is lost to view, as is anything that might be learned from the *absence* of reference to "friends." For understandings of friendship in ancient Greece and Rome, see David Konstan, *Friendship in the Classical World* (Cambridge: Cambridge University Press, 1997); John T. Fitzgerald, "Paul and Friendship," in *Paul in the Greco-Roman World: A Handbook*, vol. 1, ed. J. Paul Sampley (London: Bloomsbury T&T Clark, 2016), 331–62, here 331–51.

[2] On the contrary, Asiarchs would have been "expected to participate publicly in all events of civic religion, both those honoring the emperor and those devoted to Artemis" (Craig S. Keener, *Acts: An Exegetical Commentary, Volume 3: 15:1–23:35* [Grand Rapids, MI: Baker Academic, 2014], 2909). On the nature of the office of Asiarch, see R. A. Kearsley, "Some Asiarchs of Ephesos," in G. H. R. Horsley, *New Documents Illustrating Early Christianity: A Review of the Greek Inscriptions and Papyri Published in 1979* (The Ancient History Documentary Research Centre, Macquarie University, 1987), 46–55; Keener, *Acts*, 3:2908–9: "it was the highest office a citizen could achieve in Ephesus."

also—this we might not have expected—established good relations with certain local authorities. According to Acts 27:3, Paul, as a prisoner on his way to Rome, was allowed to visit "friends" in Sidon and to receive care from them: this suggests that he was on good terms with Julius, the centurion responsible for conveying him to Rome (27:1; see also vv. 42-43). As for Paul's "friends" in Sidon, we may assume that they *were* believers, although Acts has said nothing about a mission to Sidon—this is, in fact, the first reference in Acts to the city—or about any acquaintance of Paul in the city.

Apart from these references, Acts mentions only that the centurion Cornelius had "friends" whom he invited to hear Peter (10:24). References to friends in other parts of the New Testament are equally sparse. Some of those *not* friendly toward Jesus dismiss him as "a friend of tax collectors and sinners" (Matt 11:19 par. Luke 7:34). Elsewhere in the Synoptic Gospels, a centurion has friends (Luke 7:6); Herod and Pilate, in examining Jesus, *become* friends (Luke 23:12); and friends appear in various parables (Luke 11:5-8; 14:10; 15:6, 9, 29). Once Jesus addresses his disciples as "friends" (Luke 12:4); once he urges his host to invite the poor rather than friends to a meal (14:12-14); once he commends the use of one's resources to make friends of the poor (16:9); and once he warns his followers that family and friends will betray them (21:16). There are several passing references to friends in the Fourth Gospel: John the Baptist speaks of the "friend of the bridegroom" (3:29), Lazarus is identified as a friend of Jesus and his disciples (11:11), and Pilate is warned that he will be no friend of Caesar if he releases Jesus (19:12). Of more significance, Jesus speaks of his disciples as "friends" rather than mere servants, inasmuch as he takes them into his confidence (15:14-15); and he notes that no greater love can be shown than in giving one's life for one's friends—as he will do (15:13). The Epistle of James notes that Abraham was called "God's friend" (2:23). In the only reference to "friendship" (φιλία) in the New Testament, James notes that "friendship of the world" amounts to enmity toward God: "whoever, then, wishes to be a friend (φίλος) of the world becomes an enemy of God" (4:4). Third John requests that greetings be exchanged between friends (3 John 15).

And that, my friends, is a list of every occurrence of φίλος, "friend," and φιλία, "friendship," in the New Testament. John 13:13-15 is perhaps the closest we come to a celebration of friendship. Several texts show that friends can be good to have (e.g., Luke 16:9; Acts 19:31; 27:3), but nowhere is attention drawn to the benefits of friendship; and nowhere is the cultivation of friendship, as such, encouraged. On the contrary: those who follow Jesus's teaching will be distinguished from others precisely by their concern to treat well those *beyond* their circle of friends (Matt 5:43-48; Luke 14:12-14; 16:9). Since those they regard as friends may well betray them, it is clear that loyalty to Jesus must take priority over human friendship (Luke 21:16; cf. 14:26-27). Indeed, for those single-mindedly "seek[ing] the kingdom of God and its righteousness" (Matt 6:33), what time will be left over for the quotidian demands and pleasures of earthly friendships?

And Paul? Because we know so much more about Paul than about any other early follower of Jesus, it is easy to forget how little we know about him. That he never mentions friends or friendship in his few extant writings may be purely an accident of history; in other contexts, he might well have used the terms. Certainly (as we shall see), he speaks in his letters of a number of people whose friendship with the apostle is evident: we may even say that he had a "genius for friendship."[3] On the other hand, the same considerations that tempered talk of friendship in the Gospels were operative for Paul as well. He echoes the words of Jesus in calling on believers to show goodness beyond the sphere of the like-minded to include even their enemies (Rom 12:14, 21; cf. Gal 6:10). He surely thought that loyalty to the cause of Jesus and the gospel should take precedence over any competing demands based on human relationships (cf. 2 Cor 6:14-18). And no one can have been more consumed in the pursuit of God's kingdom than Paul was with his mission. It would seem to follow that the cultivation of friendship *for friendship's sake* could hold no attraction for him.

Yet good relations with others, both inside and outside the community of faith, were a high priority for the apostle. As much as was possible (of course, loyalty to the faith must come first), his readers were to "be at peace" with *everyone* (Rom 12:18). They were to behave in ways that even outsiders would respect (Rom 12:17; 2 Cor 8:21). They were to give offense to none (1 Cor 10:32), but rather to do good to all (Gal 6:10), to celebrate with others in their times of joy and to weep with others in their times of sorrow (Rom 12:15; since relations with outsiders are the subject of v. 14, there is no reason, in v. 15, to limit to fellow-believers those to whom sympathy is to be shown). Paul had no problem with a member of the Corinthian church accepting a dinner invitation from an "unbeliever" (1 Cor 10:27). Perhaps, then, we ought to be neither dubious nor surprised at references in Acts to Paul's good relations with Asiarchs and a Roman centurion!

When Paul urges his readers to do good to all, he immediately adds, "but especially to those of the household of faith" (Gal 6:10). Within the community of faith, believers are to show family love for each other, to consider others better than themselves, to seek others' good rather than their own, to be of the same mind with each other, and so on (Rom 12:9-10, 16; 1 Cor 10:24; Phil 2:2-4, etc.). These are all *general* exhortations: the same spirit is to be shown to all. To greet with a "holy kiss" was a mark, not of friendship, exchanged with a few, but of fellowship, exchanged within the entire community of believers (Rom 16:16; 1 Cor 16:20; 2 Cor 13:12; 1 Thess 5:26). There appears to be no place in Paul's thinking for *select* friendships.[4]

And yet, there can be no doubt: Paul had friends.[5]

---

[3] F. F. Bruce, *The Pauline Circle* (Grand Rapids, MI: Eerdmans, 1985), 8.
[4] Fitzgerald, "Paul and Friendship," 351–61, rightly draws attention to Paul's usage of language typical of friendship relationships in speaking of how those within the community of faith should relate to each other: "All Christians are implicitly friends, even those who have not yet met one another" (361). But to speak of a "friendship" that embraces a whole community (including those one has never met) is to extend the term beyond its general usage, in the ancient world as well as our own. (Fitzgerald also highlights Paul's usage of friendship language to describe relations between God and human beings who, through Christ, have been "reconciled" to God [354–8]—a topic not considered here.)
[5] That is, it is clear from Paul's letters that there were those whom *we* would call his "friends," even if—for reasons about which I speculated above—*he* does not.

Communities of Friends

When addressing, in the vocative case, his readers as a whole, Paul generally labels them ἀδελφοί, "brothers and sisters"; the usage, found in non-Pauline epistles as well (e.g., Heb 3:1, 12; 10:19; Jas 1:2, 16; 2 Pet 1:10; 1 John 3:13), was hardly confined to early Christian circles,[6] although it had a particular point among the latter: those "adopted" (Rom 8:15; Gal 4:5) or "born" (1 John 3:9; 5:1) into the family of God as God's children are naturally brothers and sisters of one another (cf. Rom 8:29). (Paul can also refer to fellow-Jews as "his brothers and sisters," but these are his kin *according to the flesh* [Rom 9:3].) The vocative address comes naturally to Paul when he wants to exhort his readers (Rom 12:1; 15:30; 16:17; 1 Cor 1:10; 7:24, etc.); or to speak of something he wants them, or thinks they ought, to know (Rom 1:13; 7:1; 11:25; 1 Cor 10:1; 15:1, etc.); or to mention something specific about them or his relationship with them (1 Cor 1:11, 26; 2:1; 3:1; 1 Thess 2:1, 9, 14, 17, etc.). At times, Paul adds a possessive pronoun (μου, "my") to ἀδελφοί (e.g., Rom 7:4; 9:3; 1 Cor 11:33); where not stated, it is nonetheless implied. Occasionally, Paul refers to his converts, "brothers and sisters" all, as his "children"—particularly when he wants to emphasize his concern, or his love, or his concerned love for his spiritual offspring (1 Cor 4:14-15; 2 Cor 6:13; Gal 4:19).

But "brothers and sisters," even spiritual "brothers and sisters," are not necessarily friends. Occasionally, Paul replaces ἀδελφοί with ἀγαπητοί, "beloved" (Rom 12:19; 2 Cor 7:1; 12:19), or ἀγαπητοί μου, "my beloved" (1 Cor 10:14; Phil 2:12); or he may combine "beloved" *with* "brothers and sisters" (1 Cor 15:28; Phil 4:1).[7] To paraphrase "beloved" with "friend(s)" seems reasonable enough (NRSV 1 Cor 10:14; Phlm 1); those whom Paul labels his "beloved" were, we may infer, his friends (cf. 1 Thess 2:8). It is perhaps surprising, then, that Paul once addresses the Roman believers, most of whom he had not met, as "beloved" (Rom 12:19). Disregarding authorial intent, we may see here an echo of Rom 1:7 ("beloved of God")—but I doubt that Paul was thinking along those lines. Perhaps he had in mind those among the Roman believers whom he *did* know and with whom he *did* have a warm relationship; more likely, without reflection, he used of the Roman believers a term common in epistolary addresses, and one that he had become accustomed to using with his converts.

But there are other, and better, indications of warm relationships between Paul and his readers than the terms used in vocative addresses. In writing to the Galatians, Paul recalls the extraordinary devotion with which they had initially received him—only to lament the very different stance toward him that they had lately adopted (Gal 4:13-16).

When Paul speaks of the Thessalonian believers as his "hope," "joy," "crown of boasting," and "glory" (1 Thess 2:19-20), and of the Philippians as his "joy and crown" (Phil 4:1), he is thinking primarily of the account he must one day give of his

---

[6] See Dale C. Allison Jr., *A Critical and Exegetical Commentary on the Epistle of James* (New York: Bloomsbury T&T Clark, 2013), 145, n. 66, for references to usages in Jewish literature, and 145, n. 67, for the suggestion that it was taken over in Christian hortatory literature from "the homiletical style of the synagogue."

[7] Again, Paul is by no means unique in addressing as "beloved" those communities of believers to whom he writes; see, for example, Jas 1:16, 19; 1 Pet 2:11; 4:12; 2 Pet 3:1; 1 John 2:7; 3:2; Jude 3, 17.

commissioned activities: how good to have these believers to show as the "fruit" of his labors (note, explicitly, 1 Thess 2:19; also Phil 1:22; 2:16; and, conversely, his fears that his labors might prove to be in vain [Gal 2:2; 4:11; Phil 2:16; 1 Thess 3:5])! But surely we may say that those he calls his pride and joy were not only his spiritual "children" but also his friends. And, indeed, we find marked expressions of affection in Paul's letters to these communities (1 Thess 2:8, 17; Phil 1:8; 4:1; but note also 1 Cor 16:24; 2 Cor 6:11-12; 7:3; 12:15).

Paul could have *communities* of friends in Thessalonica, Philippi, and Corinth inasmuch as he had personal relationships with all (or nearly all) of the believers in those cities. In the case of the Philippians, these relationships must have been particularly warm: they repeatedly sent him gifts (Phil 4:15-18; see also 1:5, 7; 2 Cor 11:9); enthusiastically supported his charitable endeavors (2 Cor 8:1-5); and delegated Epaphroditus, one of their members, to assist Paul in prison (Phil 2:25-30).[8]

Individual Friends

No doubt Paul was generally on friendly terms with the coworkers he mentions in his letters.[9] In what follows, however, I confine attention to those about whom there are more explicit indications of friendship (even if Paul himself refrains from using the term). For the same reason, I exclude references to individuals as Paul's "brother," "sister," or "kin." "Brother" and "sister" generally mean no more than "fellow-believer," although "brother" may, at times, mean something like "colleague in mission" (e.g., 1 Cor 16:11, 19-20; Gal 1:2; Phil 4:21-22);[10] friendship need not, in any case, be implied. As for Paul's "kin" (συγγενεῖς), the term certainly means "fellow-Jews" in Rom 9:3; elsewhere, it probably has the same meaning, although there is nothing impossible in the suggestion that it means "relative(s)" in Rom 16:7, 11, and 21. Still, we need not pause over those of whom Paul says no more than that they are his "kin." Since most of Paul's references to individuals whom we may regard as his friends are found in Romans 16, a chapter with its own distinctive issues, I begin with references from other letters before devoting a separate section to Romans.

There are no relevant references to individuals in 1 Thessalonians or Galatians. In 1 Cor 4:17, Paul refers to Timothy as his "beloved and faithful child in the

---

[8] See Fitzgerald, "Paul and Friendship," 352-4; Ken L. Berry, "The Function of Friendship Language in Philippians 4:10-20," in *Friendship, Flattery, and Frankness of Speech: Studies on Friendship in the New Testament World*, ed. John T. Fitzgerald (Leiden: Brill, 1996), 107-24. Peter Lampe ("Paul, Patrons, and Clients," in *Paul in the Greco-Roman World: A Handbook*, vol. 2, ed. J. Paul Sampley [London: Bloomsbury T&T Clark, 2016], 204-38, here 223) notes that, although the Philippians' support of Paul might suggest that they were his patrons, he, as their spiritual "father," can also be seen as *their* patron. He concludes that it is better to describe their relationship as one of *amicitia*, "friendship."

[9] On these, see E. Earle Ellis, "Paul and His Co-workers," *NTS* 17 (1971): 437-52; also David Smith, "Paul's 'Friends': Rethinking Paul in Light of His Social Network," *Stone-Campbell Journal* 22 (2019): 77-87. Note, however, that the Acts of the Apostles does speak of a breakup of Paul's partnership with Barnabas (Acts 15:36-40; cf. Gal 2:13).

[10] Ellis, "Co-workers," 445-51.

Lord"—immediately after addressing the Corinthians themselves as "beloved children" (4:14). The apostle's solicitude for this particular "beloved child" is evident at 16:10-11, where Paul urges the Corinthians neither to intimidate nor disdain him.[11] That *we* would label Paul's relationship with Stephanas, Fortunatus, and Achaicus as one of friendship seems clear enough from 1 Cor 16:17-18: the apostle speaks of the joy and refreshment he received from their visit and tells the Corinthians to give them due recognition. Paul found refreshment and joy as well when Titus returned to him from Corinth (2 Cor 7:6, 13). In large part, this was due to the good news Titus brought to an anxious apostle; but concern for the well-being of a friend, who had not appeared at an appointed rendezvous (2:13), must also have been a factor. Already in Paul's reliance on Titus as his intermediary with the troublesome Corinthians, we see evidence of a trusting friendship.

With Philemon, a "beloved brother" (Phlm 1) and convert of Paul's (v. 19), his relationship must have been very good indeed, since the apostle feels free to make (indirectly, to be sure) a considerable request of this friend: not only the forgiveness of his slave Onesimus, who has run away and quite possibly stolen goods from his master, but (it seems) also the release of Onesimus to serve Paul in prison (vv. 8-14). Confident that no offense will be taken, the apostle then proceeds to express his expectation that Philemon will provide him with hospitality once—in answer to Philemon's prayers— he has been released from prison (v. 22). Nor, in this context, should we overlook the warmth with which Paul refers to Onesimus, who, like Philemon, is both a (spiritual) "child" of his (v. 10) and his "beloved brother" (v. 16): Paul calls him τὰ ἐμὰ σπλάγχνα, "my very heart" (so freely rendered, BAGD 938). Philemon and Onesimus were both Paul's spiritual "children"; from what he says about them, we may also consider them his friends.

Something has already been said of Paul's warm relations with the Philippian believers, and of Epaphroditus, the Philippian who brought to Paul the church's gift and who served Paul during the latter's imprisonment. After referring to Epaphroditus as his "brother, fellow-worker, and fellow-soldier" (Phil 2:25), Paul speaks of a life-threatening sickness from which Epaphroditus had recovered, and of how the latter had "jeopardized his life" to complete his mission. A plausible interpretation is that Epaphroditus "took ill en route to Rome, but pressed on anyway to fulfill his commitment to the church and Paul, and thus exposed himself to the very real possibility of death."[12] Mutual affection is in any case apparent in Epaphroditus's commitment to Paul, and in the apostle's anxiety over the sickness and near loss of his friend (2:27-28).

Something like paternal affection and pride (and, we may say, friendship) are evident in what Paul writes about Timothy to the Philippians: no one can match Timothy in his concern for the Philippians' well-being (2:20); like father and son, the two have worked together (2:22). Although Euodia and Syntyche were not on good terms with each other, Paul recalls the way both had expended themselves alongside

---

[11] Christopher Roy Hutson ("Was Timothy Timid? On the Rhetoric of Fearlessness [1 Corinthians 16:10–11] and Cowardice [2 Timothy 1:7]," *BR* 42 [1997]: 58–73) opposes the common reading of these verses as implying Timothy's timidity.

[12] Gordon D. Fee, *Paul's Letter to the Philippians* (Grand Rapids, MI: Eerdmans, 1995), 283.

him "in the gospel" (4:2). For some reason, Paul does not name the "true yoke-fellow (γνήσιε σύζυγε)" whom he asks to assist these women (4:3).[13]

Turning to the disputed epistles, we find no relevant reference to an individual in 2 Thessalonians, and only a single reference to Tychicus ("a beloved brother and faithful servant in the Lord") in Ephesians (6:21). Tychicus is spoken of in similar terms in Col 4:7, a letter in which Epaphras, Onesimus, and Luke are also referred to as "beloved" (1:7; 4:9, 14)—Luke, famously, as "the beloved physician." That Aristarchus, Mark, and "Jesus who is called Justus" have been a "comfort" (παρηγορία) to Paul suggests that we should include these (explicitly Jewish) coworkers of Paul in the list of his friends (Col 4:10-11).

From the Pastoral Epistles, mention need only be made of Onesiphorus, who on numerous occasions had "refreshed" Paul, and who, at a time when others found it prudent to disassociate themselves from the imprisoned apostle, "was not ashamed" to seek him out in Rome (2 Tim 1:15-18).[14]

Romans 16

In none of the acknowledged epistles apart from Romans does Paul request that greetings be conveyed to named individuals, although the Philippians are asked to greet "every saint in Christ Jesus" (Phil 4:21) and, as noted above, the Corinthians and Thessalonians are to "greet one another with a holy kiss" (1 Cor 16:20; 2 Cor 13:12; 1 Thess 5:26). In the disputed epistles, greetings are to be conveyed to "the brothers and sisters in Laodicea, and to Nympha and the church in her house" (Col 4:15); to "those who love us in the faith" (Tit 3:15); and to "Prisca and Aquila, and the household of Onesiphorus" (2 Tim 4:19). Nowhere do we find anything that would prepare us for the lengthy list, in Rom 16:3-15, of named individuals to whom greetings are to be conveyed.

Since Paul's mission had not yet taken him to Rome (Rom 1:10-15; 15:22-23), some have thought it likely that this section of Romans is part of a letter initially sent to Ephesus, where Paul knew many people whom he might have wanted to greet.[15] The consensus today, however, is that Romans 16 was sent to believers in Rome.[16] Nothing like this list occurs in any of Paul's letters to churches he knew well; on the other hand,

---

[13] Of course, Paul's failure to name this coworker has invited speculation. For different proposals, see Fee, *Philippians*, 393-5. Fee himself notes that Luke at least "fits all the available historical data" (395).

[14] That Paul greets and prays for "the household of Onesiphorus" (2 Tim 1:16; 4:19) and wishes for Onesiphorus only mercy on judgment day (1:18) has suggested to many that the latter was now dead, leaving only his household to be greeted. See, for example, J. N. D. Kelly, *A Commentary on the Pastoral Epistles* (Grand Rapids, MI: Baker, 1981), 169-70. But other explanations are possible (I. Howard Marshall, in collaboration with Philip H. Towner, *A Critical and Exegetical Commentary on the Pastoral Epistles* [Edinburgh: T&T Clark, 1999], 717-21).

[15] This was the (once-popular) view of T. W. Manson, "St. Paul's Letter to the Romans—and Others," in T. W. Manson, *Studies in the Gospels and Epistles*, ed. Matthew Black (Manchester: Manchester University Press, 1962), 225-41.

[16] See, especially, Harry Y. Gamble, *The Textual History of the Letter to the Romans: A Study in Textual and Literary Criticism* (Grand Rapids, MI: Eerdmans, 1977), 36-55, 89.

in writing to a community he had never visited, he would want to establish as many points of contact as possible. He need not have met all those whose names he mentions; some might be leaders in the Roman community about whom he had learned from Prisca and Aquila. In any case, it is not at all unlikely that a number of people whom Paul had met in his travels now found themselves in Rome. Prisca and Aquila would merely have returned to the city from which they had been driven (Acts 18:1-2); the same might be true of others as well.

Our focus here is confined to those of whom something is said betokening friendship with the apostle. Paul allowed himself to address the community of Roman believers as "beloved," even though he had not met most of them (Rom 12:19); it seems likely, however, that he enjoyed a warm relationship with the *individuals* whom he calls "my beloved": so Epaenetus (16:5), Ampliatus (v. 8), and Stachys (v. 9). The latter two are, for us, only names; Epaenetus, Paul informs us, was his first convert in Asia. Persis, in v. 12, represents an interesting case: she is referred to as "beloved"— but not "*my* beloved." Is Paul simply referring to her as one of whom everyone spoke highly? Or does propriety prevent him from speaking of a woman as "my beloved"?[17] More interesting still is the reference to Rufus's mother—"and my mother, too" (v. 13). Presumably, Rufus and his mother, like Gaius (v. 23) and, probably, Phoebe (a "patron" [προστάτις] of Paul [v. 2]), had hosted Paul in their home, and Paul had enjoyed the maternal solicitude he received![18]

Paul has good things to say about Andronicus and Junia; but although he refers to them as his "kin" (συγγενεῖς) and "fellow-prisoners" (cf. Col 4:10; Phlm 23), a personal relationship need not be implied (Rom 16:7). On the other hand, he could hardly speak more warmly of Prisca and Aquila, who, like Epaphroditus (Phil 2:25-30), had—in some unknown way, in unknown circumstances—"risked their necks" for his sake (Rom 16:3-4).

In short, without setting out to cultivate friendships, or even valuing friendship as such, Paul became a friend of many, particularly of those who cooperated with, or in some way supported, his mission. Friendship in such cases represented a (no doubt unconscious, but by no means inevitable) development that grew out of shared commitments and endeavors.[19]

---

[17] If the latter, Paul's language in v. 1 may display a similar sensitivity: Phoebe is referred to as "*our* sister"—although Paul has no hesitancy about referring to Titus and Epaphroditus as "*my* brother" (2 Cor 2:13; Phil 2:25).

[18] In a sermon ("When the Roll Is Called Down Here"), Fred Craddock imagines a background to the greeting Paul sends to Rufus's mother: "He probably stayed in their home. She was a rather large woman, always wore an apron. A lot of things stuffed in the pocket of the apron. Hair pulled back in a bun. Fixed a good breakfast. Paul said, 'I'm sorry. I can't stay. I have to be on my way.' 'Sit down and eat your breakfast. I don't care if you are an apostle. You've got to eat.'" Cf. Fred Craddock, sermon excerpted in *Christian History* 132 (2019): 9.

[19] Fitzgerald ("Paul and Friendship," 343) notes how, for Greco-Roman authors, those different in social status and wealth might nonetheless become "affectionate collaborators within their shared sphere of aspirations, activities, and values."

9

"As to the Law—a Pharisee" (Phil 3:5c): Do We Have a Friend in Paul?

Kathy Ehrensperger

Phil 3:5-6 is one of the passages where Paul clearly identifies himself with Jewish tradition of the first century CE. However, together with Gal 1:13 ("You have heard, no doubt, of my earlier life in Ἰουδαϊσμός" NRSV), the passage has been interpreted as expressing that he had actually left Jewish tradition behind upon his calling experience, which had led to his conviction that Jesus was the Christ. If this was the case, Paul would have set Jewish tradition and being in Christ in opposition to each other and could hardly be seen as friend and even less as part of Jewish tradition. However, Paul does not refer to something that was relevant for him only in the past; he here states that he is a torah observant Pharisee—at the moment of writing the letter to the Philippians—meaning that he did not cut his ties to his people nor cease to be concerned about them, despite debates between them that were triggered by the messianic claims of Christ-followers. The implications of this perception of Paul for Jewish–Christian relations need to be further explored. Do they render Paul a friend to be trusted when it comes to the overcoming of anti-Judaism in Christian tradition—or does he stay at the margins, contributing to the ongoing problems? These are aspects I wish to explore in this contribution dedicated to Adele Reinhartz, a dear colleague, trustworthy and inspiring as well as challenging in the sharpness of her analyses of trajectories of anti-Judaism in Christian traditions.[1] By not holding back critical questions where necessary, especially to the Christian partners in the conversation, she proves to be a true friend, trusting that critical debates should not alienate colleagues concerned with overcoming anti-Judaism and antisemitism wherever and in whatever form it presents itself. Although through her long research journey with the Beloved Disciple she has come to the conclusion that John is not a true friend, I would like to explore in this contribution whether Paul might qualify.

Paul is the only Jew of antiquity who self-identifies (at least, as far as we are aware) as a Pharisee and the only one who has written texts that have been transmitted until today.[2] This self-identification is not something of the past, since the other credentials

---

[1] See, for example, Adele Reinhartz and Paula Fredriksen, eds., *Jesus, Judaism, and Christian Anti-Judaism: Reading the New Testament after the Holocaust* (Louisville, KY: Westminster, 2002).
[2] Josephus followed the Pharisaic tradition but nowhere self-identifies as a Pharisee. Steve Mason has demonstrated that the claim that Josephus was a Pharisee rests upon one sentence (*Life* 12b)

he claims for himself, except his pursuing the assemblies, clearly refer to his present identity. Some of these identity references are also found in 2 Cor 11:22 (Hebrew, Israelite, σπέρμα Abraham) and Rom 11:1 (Israelite, of the tribe of Benjamin, σπέρμα Abraham), whereas in Gal 2:15 he identifies together with Peter as φύσει Ἰουδαῖος. Possibly the identifier σπέρμα Abraham is replaced in Phil 3:5b with reference to eighth day circumcision. All of these are aspects of Paul's Jewish identity in the present, after his call, and there is no reason to assume that the Pharisaic aspect of his identity has been left behind in his call experience.[3] Therefore, Paul was evidently a Christ-following Pharisee.

Although apart from New Testament texts, Josephus and rabbinical texts refer to Pharisees, which provide some information about them, there is very little historically reliable to go by when trying to understand what Paul could have meant with this statement, "as to the νόμος—a Φαρισαῖος" in Phil 3:5b. The statement clearly sets the self-identification in relation to the νόμος. Thus, νόμος and Φαρισαῖος are presented as being linked in some way.

The conundrum with Paul's statement is the combination of a group, Pharisees, about which little can be historically ascertained,[4] and a term, νόμος, about which little consensus has emerged as to its meaning in past and recent Pauline scholarship. Hence, the challenge is to come to some conclusion about two entities whose meaning is unclear and surrounded by a cluster of controversial debates. This means that other clues in Paul's letters are needed to come to some potential understanding of what he might have meant.

Before trying to unravel aspects of the identity of a Pharisee, the term νόμος needs to be considered, since Paul indicates an intrinsic connection between νόμος and being a Pharisee. This coheres in some sense with the image Josephus depicts of Pharisees (*J.W.* 1.110–112, 2.162, *Ant.* 13.297, *Life* 191) as highly knowledgeable in the νόμος and also concerned with traditions in relation to, but beyond, the νόμος, labeled as "traditions of the ancestors." Shayna Sheinfeld has drawn specific attention to the fact that in *J.W.* 2.162 Josephus refers to the Pharisees as "most skillful in the exact explanation of their νόμιμα," which she translates as "customs/legalities" rather than "laws." This differentiation is to be welcomed, as it coheres with Josephus's presentation of diverse Jewish groups who all approach the torah/law in different ways, the Pharisees thus being one of these.[5]

---

but finds that Josephus nowhere states that he is a Pharisee. Mason's analysis of Josephus's wording indicates that Josephus followed the Pharisaic tradition in his public life. See Steve Mason, "Josephus's Pharisees," in *The Pharisees*, ed. Amy-Jill Levine and Jospeh Sievers (Grand Rapids, MI: Eerdmans, 2021), 80–111.

[3] This was Alan Segal's assumption, although he did not argue that Paul, by ceasing to be a Pharisee, left his Jewish tradition but rather that he identified with a different strand within his tradition, that is, apocalyptic Judaism. See Alan F. Segal, *Paul the Convert: The Apostolate and Apostasy of Saul the Pharisee* (New Haven, CT: Yale University Press, 1992), especially 34–73.

[4] Cf. Vasile Babota, "In Search of the Origins of the Pharisees," in *The Pharisees*, ed. Amy-Jill Levine and Jospeh Sievers (Grand Rapids, MI: Eerdmans, 2021), 23–40.

[5] The article by Shayna Sheinfeld presents a discussion of further writers' presentation of "*nomos*"; cf. "From *Nomos* to *Logos*: Torah in First-Century Jewish Texts," in *The Message of Paul the Apostle within Second Temple Judaism*, ed. František Abel (Lanham, MD: Lexington/Fortress Academic, 2020), 61–74, here 66. I would like to thank Meredith Warren for reminding me of this excellent

Phil 3:5c is actually one of the few passages where Paul says something about the νόμος in relation to Jewish identity. Although he refers to νόμος frequently in his letters, most passages provide little or no insight to its relation to Jewish self-understanding in general or Paul's in particular. Paul, as apostle to the nations, addresses non-Jewish Christ-followers[6] in his letters, and therefore most of his discussions of the νόμος concern the relation and status of non-Jews apart from Christ or in Christ to the Jewish νόμος and have thus nothing to say about the meaning of the νόμος for Jews. This includes Romans 7 as well as ἔργα νόμου in Romans and Galatians. These passages have non-Jews in view in relation to the νόμος rather than Jews.

The only other passage where νόμος is mentioned in relation to Jews is Rom 9:4 (νομοθεσία), and possibly Rom 3:1 and 3:19, significantly with positive connotations throughout. Even in the passages where the function of the νόμος in relation to non-Jews is in view, it is seen as holy and good (Rom 7:12). The problem in these passages is thus not the νόμος per se, but the effect it has on non-Jews, who try to be ὑπὸ νόμου and do ἔργα νόμου, trying to achieve δικαιοσύνη apart from or in Christ.[7]

That the νόμος is relevant for Jews is taken for granted in the few references found in the Pauline letters. The question is in what ways. It is taken self-evidently by Paul as the gift of God (νομοθεσία) for guiding his people Israel (Rom 9:4). It can be assumed that Paul means the Torah here, or possibly more widely the Scriptures. Certainly, it is the tradition that is considered authoritative by Jews of the Second Temple period, and Paul lives by it, as he asserts in Phil 3:5c. However, the implications of the authoritative function of the νόμος for everyday life in different contexts was a matter of contention and debate. This is evident in the traces of discussions that can be discerned in the Qumran literature, in Josephus, partially in Philo, in the early rabbinic literature as well as in Gospel narratives.

Paul specifies that as far as the νόμος is concerned he is a Pharisee. This implies that he follows in his daily life and under specific circumstances the Pharisaic interpretation and application of the νόμος. This reference to himself as a Pharisee actually coheres with his claim that he exceeded his peers in his education/knowledge of "the traditions of the ancestors." It needs to be noted that he does not claim that he exceeded them in his knowledge of the νόμος, but in "the traditions of the ancestors."

In Josephus and Philo such traditions are attributed to Pharisees, referring to nonwritten traditions. Josephus here sees a fundamental distinction between Pharisees and Sadducees, a distinction also found in later rabbinical sources. Thus, Josephus

---

article. Cf. also Karl-Wilhelm Niebuhr's article "Jesus, Paul, and the Pharisees. Observations on Their Commonalities and Their Understanding of Torah," in the same volume, 109–41.

[6] Thus, already Stanley K. Stowers, *A Rereading of Romans: Justice, Jews and Gentiles* (New Haven, CT: Yale University Press, 1994); Mark D. Nanos, *The Mystery of Romans: The Jewish Context of Paul's Letter* (Minneapolis, MN: Fortress, 1996); now William S. Campbell, *Romans: A Social Identity Commentary* (London: T&T Clark, 2023); also Kathy Ehrensperger, *Searching Paul: Conversations with the Jewish Apostle to the Nations*, WUNT 429 (Tübingen: Mohr Siebeck, 2019), 3–18.

[7] Kathy Ehrensperger, "Imagine—No 'Works of Law'! Struggling with Ἔργα νόμου' in Changing Times and Places" (paper presented at the Annual Meeting of the SBL, San Diego, November 20, 2019). Also Mark D. Nanos, "Re-framing Paul's Opposition to *Erga Nomou* as 'Rites of a Custom' for Proselyte Conversion Completed by the Synecdoche 'Circumcision,'" *The Journal of the Jesus Movement in Its Jewish Setting* 8 (2021): 75–115.

notes that "the Pharisees had passed on to people certain regulations handed down by former generations and not recorded in the laws of Moses, for which reason they are rejected by the Sadducean group who hold that only those regulations should be considered valid which were written down, and those handed down by the fathers need not be observed" (*Ant.* 13.297 [Marcus, LCL]). Josephus attributes to the Pharisees popularity among the population and asserts that Pharisaic traditions were widespread, a perception also found in the Gospel of Mark.[8] It can hardly be doubted that they considered the traditions of the fathers as authoritative, a stance that seems to rely on a positive perception of popular practices. The notion of unwritten law (νόμος ἄγραφος) is also found in Philo. He advocated that the Scriptures needed to be complemented by ancestral traditions. He argues:

> For customs are unwritten laws, the decisions approved by men of old, not inscribed on monuments nor on leaves of paper which moth destroys, but on the souls of those who are partners in the same citizenship. For children ought to inherit from their parents, besides their property, ancestral customs which they were reared in and have lived with even from the cradle, and not despise them because they have been handed down without written record. (*Spec. Laws* 4.149-50 [Colson, LCL])[9]

Philo's stance is reliant on Greek philosophical approaches, but he adapts it for his purpose to Jewish tradition. The note above is actually part of a discussion of Deut 19:14, "the landmark set by the former ones," which Philo interprets as applying not only to physical landmarks but also to ancestral traditions. Both Philo and the Pharisees thus considered these unwritten traditions as relevant for communal life. This is confirmed by polemic found in some Qumran manuscripts, targeting those who "seek smooth things," generally understood to refer to the Pharisees. Thus, in the Damascus Document (4QD[a] I, 14-16) they are accused of "neglecting the original divine laws by moving the ancient borders and decreeing other human laws instead."[10] It seems that the Pharisees were seen in this Qumran text as those who shift borders, whereas the Qumran sectarians see their adherence to the tradition as guarding these borders. Both Qumran texts as well as Philo refer to traditions beyond the written ones, although assessing these differently. In the Qumran texts, this is seen as problematic, whereas Philo considers this a necessary aspect of being true to tradition. The critical stance found in Qumran texts against "those who seek smooth things" and Philo's emphasizing of the importance of ancestral traditions are evidence, although in different ways, confirming Josephus's image of the Pharisees as promoting and encouraging these traditions. It appears, especially from the accusations found in Qumran texts, that the Pharisees in their legal rulings tended toward leniency, as also noted by Josephus: "indeed the Pharisees are not apt to be severe in punishments"

---

[8] Yair Fürstenberg, "The Shared Image of Pharisaic Law in the Gospels and Rabbinic Tradition," in *The Pharisees*, ed. Amy-Jill Levine and Joseph Sievers (Grand Rapids, MI: Eerdmans, 2021), 199–219, here 205.

[9] Naomi Cohen, "The Jewish Dimension of Philo's Judaism: An Elucidation of *de. Spec. Leg.* IV 132–150," *JJS* 38 (1987): 165–87.

[10] Fürstenberg, "Shared Image," 209.

(*Ant.* 13.294).[11] The aim of the Pharisees seems to have been to interpret the rules of the νόμος in such a way as to make it possible for people to participate in ritual activities in the temple and beyond. It was a pragmatic approach, working with traditions as they possibly had emerged over a long period of time, advocating compromise, and a form of observance that took into account the circumstances of everyday life rather than advocating a rigid literal application of the νόμος. Whether these "customs" or "traditions" are a precursor of rabbinical oral torah, or whether the Pharisees rather embodied practices that had been handed down over the generations is controversially debated and cannot conclusively be decided, as there is not sufficient historical information available.[12] But from Josephus as well as Qumran texts it emerges that they were attributed with a pragmatist approach to living according to the torah, one that accommodates the observance of the torah to everyday life needs and conditions. This "leniency" is the aspect that interests me most when trying to understand what Paul might mean when he affirms that "as to the νόμος—a Pharisee" (Phil 3:5c). For this it is useful to look beyond Philippians.

An indication of "ancestral customs" is evident in Gal 1:14. Paul mentions what he calls Ἰουδαϊσμος in the same sentence as his passionate engagement for the "traditions of the ancestors," in what appears to be an educational setting. The terminology undoubtedly resonates with what Josephus describes also as "traditions of the ancestors," attributed by him especially to stances affirmed by Pharisees. Paul then refers to his take on these traditions as something in which he was very involved, more than others. This indicates that he is aware of different perceptions and stances in relation to these "ancestral traditions," whether others were less passionate than Paul, or less educated in these is unclear. That Ἰουδαϊσμος clearly is not what we refer to as Judaism today has been clearly demonstrated in recent research, and I will not repeat the respective arguments here.[13] Whether this Ἰουδαϊσμος is linked to the "ancestral traditions" and thus the Pharisaic aspect of Paul's identity is open. Paul mentions both in Gal 1:13-14 in close proximity but does not link them directly. In Phil 3:5-6 Ἰουδαϊσμος is not mentioned, and his going after the ἐκκλησία is not linked to him as a Pharisee. The only linking term in both texts is ζῆλος—which in Galatians refers to the "traditions of the ancestors" and in Philippians to the going after the ἐκκλησία. The use of ζῆλος in both instances has actually been seen as an indication that Paul's zeal for the "ancestral

---

[11] Fürstenberg, "Shared Image," 213; cf. also Vered Noam, "Pharisaic Halakha as Emerging from 4QMMT," in *The Pharisees*, ed. Amy-Jill Levine and Joseph Sievers (Grand Rapids, MI: Eerdmans, 2021), 55–79. Fürstenberg notes that in this respect there are similarities to later rabbinic avoidance of corporal punishment, evident, for example, in a rabbinic tradition attributed to the Sadducees's literal interpretation of "an eye for an eye," with the Pharisees opting for financial compensation (214).

[12] Martin Goodman, "A Note on Josephus, the Pharisees and Ancestral Traditions," in *Judaism in the Roman World. Collected Essays* (Leiden: Brill, 2007), 117–21; also Yael Fisch, "The Origins of Oral Torah," *JSJ* 51 (2020): 43–66.

[13] Steve Mason, "Jews, Judeans, Judaizing, Judaism: Problem of Categorization in Ancient History," *JSJ* 38 (2007): 457–512; and Adele Reinhartz's excellent critique of Mason's proposal to replace Jew with Judean in "The Vanishing Jews of Antiquity," in *Jew and Judean: A Marginalia Forum on Politics and Historiography in the Translation of Ancient Texts*, ed. Timothy Michael Law and Charles Halton, *Marginalia/Los Angeles Review of Books* (June 24, 2014), 10–23, https://themarginaliareview.com/response-jew-judean-forum-adele-reinhartz (checked March 19, 2022). Also Daniel Boyarin, *Judaism: The Genealogy of a Modern Notion* (New Brunswick, NJ: Rutgers University Press, 2019), 3–59.

traditions," understood as referring to the νόμος, was the reason for his pursuing the ἐκκλησία. Thus, for James D. G. Dunn, zeal and law are intrinsically connected and lead to an ethnocentrism in Paul's Jewish self-understanding that eventually will be overcome in Christ. Zeal, law, and ethnocentrism are seen as intrinsically linked not only in the individual Paul but also in some strands of Second Temple Judaism generally, which for some interpreters is embodied by the Pharisaic movement.[14]

However, neither in Phil 3:5-6 nor in Gal 1:13-14 is there such an obvious link. In Phil 3:5-6 there is no causal link between "zeal" and the previous statements, where Paul relates his adherence to the law with being a Pharisee, nor is there a link to the following statement that concerning righteousness emerging through the νόμος he was blameless. To argue that because the persecuting activity is mentioned between two statements concerning the νόμος, it must have had something to do with the νόμος, and then to conclude that the zeal of the persecution must have something to do with zeal for the νόμος[15] is a mere hypothesis with only a slight support in the text, if any at all. The note in Phil 3:6 states that Paul had directed his ζῆλος in activities against the ἐκκλησία. The issue in this statement is not ζῆλος but rather the activity, that is, persecution, following from it. There is no indication that this ζῆλος had anything to do with the νόμος.[16]

The situation is even more problematic when we consider Gal 1:13-14. Paul here talks about two different items: his persecuting activity before his call and his commitment to the "traditions of the ancestors." Paul does not make a causal link, nor is there any indication in these two verses that such a link should be made.[17] Thus, he first indicates that prior to his call, his life as a Jew led him to persecute the ἐκκλησία with some intensity and with the aim to destroy it. This is a factual statement and no reason for this activity is given. In a second statement, Paul then emphasizes his commitment to "the traditions of the ancestors," not "zeal for the νόμος." He does not say that this ζῆλος was the reason for his persecuting activity. What Paul might emphasize here is that the focus of this ζῆλος, his commitment to the traditions of his ancestors, does not render him the most obvious candidate for a mission to the gentiles.

In neither of these two texts nor anywhere else in the Pauline letters is there a link between zeal, persecution, and "traditions of the ancestors" or the νόμος. There is a link between ζῆλος and persecution and ζῆλος and "traditions of the ancestors." But these are two different activities that Paul himself does not relate to each other. The assumed link emerges possibly through the parallelization of the term ζῆλος/ζηλωτής used in both texts; thus, the ζῆλος of the persecuting activity of Phil 3:6 is combined with having become ζηλωτής for the "traditions of the ancestors" in Gal 1:13-14 and

---

[14] Martin Hengel, *The Pre-Christian Paul* (London: SCM, 1991), 65-70.
[15] See, for example, Carolyn Osiek, *Philippians, Philemon* (Nashville, TN: Abingdon, 2000), 89.
[16] Contra James D. G. Dunn, *The Theology of Paul the Apostle* (Grand Rapids, MI: Eerdmans, 1998), 351.
[17] Contra, for example, Hengel, who argues that persecution happened because of "Paul's zeal for the law and the consciousness of his own flawlessness." See Martin Hengel, "The Stance of the Apostle Paul toward the Law in the Unknown Years between Damascus and Antioch," in *The Paradoxes of Paul*, vol. 2 of *Justification and Variegated Nomism*, ed. D. A. Carson, Peter O'Brien, and Mark A. Seifried (Grand Rapids, MI: Baker, 2004), 75-103, here 84. A similar argument substantiated by a supposed inherent link with the zeal of Phinehas and Elijah as part of "the ideal of radical groups since the time of the Maccabees" is presented in Hengel, *Pre-Christian Paul*, 70.

interpreted in a cause and effect vein. The link is neither the νόμος nor the "traditions of the ancestors," but seen in the qualifying term ζῆλος/ζηλωτής in both passages. In addition, the interpretation of "zeal for the traditions of the ancestors" as "zeal for the law" is introduced via parallelization with 1 Macc 2:26-27 ("Thus, he burned with zeal for the law, just as Phinehas did against Zimri son of Salu. Then Mattathias cried out in the town with a loud voice, saying: 'Let everyone who is ζῆλος for the *nomos* and supports the covenant come out with me!'"); 1 Macc 2:50 ("Now, my children, show zeal for the law, and give your lives for the covenant of our ancestors"); and 1 Macc 2:58 ("Elijah, because of great zeal for the law, was taken up into heaven").[18] Rather than being self-evident, the link between Paul's persecuting activity against the ἐκκλησία and his commitment to the νόμος or "traditions of the ancestors" before his call is actually imported into the respective texts.

The assumption of a link between zeal, the νόμος, and Paul's persecuting activity against the ἐκκλησία provides interpreters with a seemingly clear rationale for this activity. The key focus is in the defense of the boundaries of the law to safeguard Jewish identity, or as Dane C. Ortlund argues, "Paul's zeal is intense devotion to living out the way of life prescribed by Torah."[19] Paul's assumed "zeal" for the law is considered to be the wrongly understood, ethnocentric or nationalistic misunderstanding of the law by Jews (cf., e.g., James D. G. Dunn, N. T. Wright), or the "religious" misunderstanding of obedience to the law as the means of salvation (cf., e.g., Martin Hengel, Dane C. Ortlund, J. Louis Martyn).[20] Zeal, the law, Pharisees, and persecution are combined via a cause and effect link and thus lead to an interpretation where Judaism one way or another serves as the negative foil for Paul's actions before his call.[21] The solution Paul found in his call then is matched against this problem: the ethnocentric, nationalistic, or theological misunderstanding of Judaism is overcome in Christ, and access to God is freed from these particularistic or self-centered distorted constraints.

But, as mentioned above, the links between the terms thus combined are inferred rather than actually present in the text. Although there are passages in Paul where ζῆλος has negative connotations, this is in passages where the term appears alongside other characteristics that the addressees should avoid, like ἔρις, and so on. In these

---

[18] Thus Martin Hengel, *The Zealots: Investigations into the Jewish Freedom Movement in the Period from Herod I until 70 A.D.*, trans. David Smith (Edinburgh: T&T Clark, 1989), especially 177–83; Dane C. Ortlund, "Phinehan Zeal: A Consideration of James Dunn's Proposal," *JSP* 20 (2011): 299–315. Dunn also concludes that the impact of Paul's conversion was a reaction against his previous zeal for the law, though not as normally understood. In Dunn's understanding, this zeal "was an unconditional commitment to maintain Israel's distinctiveness, to prevent the purity of its covenant set-apartness to God from being adulterated or defiled, to defend its religious and national boundaries." See Dunn, *Theology*, 346–54, here 351.

[19] Dane C. Ortlund, *Zeal without Knowledge: The Concept of Zeal in Romans 10, Galatians 1, and Philippians 3* (London: Bloomsbury, 2014), 148.

[20] Dunn, *Theology*, 352–3; N. T. Wright, *What Saint Paul Really Said: Was Paul of Tarsus the Real Founder of Christianity?* (Grand Rapids, MI: Eerdmans, 1997), 25–37; Hengel, *Pre-Christian Paul*, 45; Ortlund, *Zeal without Knowledge*, esp. 166–76; J. Louis Martyn, *Galatians: A New Translation with Introduction and Commentary* (New York: Doubleday, 1997), 154–5.

[21] Zeal is often considered problematic in itself, in that it is a wrong emotion or attitude that inherently leads to problematic actions (Robert Jewett, *Romans* [Minneapolis, MN: Fortress, 2007], 616; Dunn, *Theology*, 351; Vincent M. Smiles, "The Concept of 'Zeal' in Second Temple Judaism and Paul's Critique of It in Romans 10:2," *CBQ* 64 [2002]: 282–99).

contexts, translations such as "jealous" make sense. However, in other passages it clearly has positive connotations. Thus, the persecuting activity of Paul renders zeal in this case rather negative; however, to then link this negative view with his zeal for the traditions of the ancestors is not warranted, since the context does not lend itself to such a negative interpretation linked to these traditions or the law. If other passages are considered, it is evident that here also, in relation to ancestral traditions, the connotation is positive. Thus, in 1 Cor 14:12 he notes that they were ζῆλος, or as the NRSV translates this passage, "they were eager for things spiritual": οὕτως καὶ ὑμεῖς, ἐπεὶ ζηλωταί ἐστε πνευμάτων πρὸς τὴν οἰκοδομὴν τῆς ἐκκλησίας ζητεῖτε ἵνα περισσεύητε. This is the only use of the term ζηλωταί apart from Gal 1:14 clearly with a positive connotation. However, "zeal" is not something with an inherently negative connotation. It is a term used for a number of attitudes and emotions, and Paul more than once admonishes his communities to have, or commends them for, "zeal" (Rom 12:11; 2 Cor 7:7, 12; 9:2).

Hence also in Gal 1:14, zeal for the ancestral traditions is not negatively connoted but indicates his passion for his own tradition, which he lives according to the widespread popular customs handed down through generations. The implications of him being a Pharisee are further highlighted by his sharing of the trust in God's intervention at the final consummation in the resurrection and thus vindication of the dead. All of these aspects of his Pharisaic identity do not come to an end or are thrown overboard when he is called to proclaim Messiah Jesus to the nations. All of this is still part of who he is and is not in opposition to his conviction that in Christ the messianic age was beginning to dawn in anticipation of the world to come.

Paul is thus a Pharisee, passionate for the traditions of the ancestors, that is, one of those who lived a torah observant life pragmatically applied to everyday life, when in the land of Israel, according to the conditions there, when in the diaspora, according to the conditions there.[22] This Pharisaic way was considered by some as lenient and inappropriate, but as noted above, seems to have been widely accepted based on popular traditions. Thus, with regard to his way of life Paul does not seem to have been different from other Jews of his time who lived their Jewishness in different ways. What does distinguish him is the fact that he teaches non-Jews how they can relate to the one God of Israel at the dawning of the messianic time without beginning a process of becoming Jews, that is, members of the people of Israel. Part of this teaching consists in working out and explaining how the νόμος is relevant for non-Jews in Christ. This teaching might orient itself precisely on his "advancing in the traditions of the ancestors," that is, the Pharisaic way of applying the torah to everyday life, based on ancestral customs—only that these customs now needed to be adjusted to the status of non-Jews in Christ.

It is evident that Paul nowhere argues that the torah/νόμος is not relevant for non-Jews in Christ. All he argues is that by ἔργα νόμου they cannot arrive at a status of δικαιοσύνη. This status and the holiness associated with it is granted to them graciously

---

[22] This may shed light on the puzzling assertion that he καὶ ἐγενόμην τοῖς Ἰουδαίοις ὡς Ἰουδαῖος (1 Cor 9:20), if *Ioudaios* is taken as a geographical indicator, meaning that when in Judea Paul would live according to the rules that apply when in the land.

by God through Christ, and as such they have now come near. But for living a life conforming to being in Christ, to exclusively relate to the one God and "giving their body as living sacrifice," they need orientation, and this orientation comes mainly from the torah, interpreted and applied—pragmatically in Pharisaic style to them as non-Jews. No Pauline guidance for his addressees is not torah/νόμος oriented. Rom 12:9-21 reads like an exposition of the νόμος, as does Rom 13:8-10 explicitly, although of course not exclusively, for non-Jews.

It has also been argued that Paul's Judaism, and more specifically his Pharisaism, may also have been decisive for his advice concerning the question what Christ-followers should do "when married to an unbeliever" (1 Cor 7:12-16). Tal Ilan has argued that this resonates with similar guidance in t. Demai 3.17, which she interprets as referring to Pharisees.[23] Here it is asserted that "a daughter of a *haver* married to an *am-ha-aretz*, the wife of a *haver* married to an *am-ha-aretz* ... they remain trustworthy unless they become suspect." Ilan identifies the "*haver*" as a Pharisee, a view that has been contested, but whoever the "*haver*" precisely is, there is here actually an argument very similar to Paul's advice to those members of the Christ-movement who are "married to an unbeliever." The status of the *am-ha-aretz* in the case of the Tosefta text does not affect the status of the member of the movement of the *haverim* or of Christ, respectively, as long as the members retains their own life according to the way of life of the *haverim* or messianic community. Paul's guidance resonates with guidance found elsewhere in Jewish interpretive tradition, now creatively applied to non-Jews in Christ.[24]

If Paul was and remained a Pharisee, a Pharisee of the kind described by Josephus and opposed by members of the Qumran community, he had hardly any similarity with the image depicted of Pharisees in Christian tradition as legalistic, narrow-minded, exclusivist, or zealous adherents of the torah. An alternative image of Pharisees emerges from recent research, which also sheds a very different light on Paul the Pharisee. No need then to argue that he had left behind or converted from a supposedly narrow perception of his own tradition. Quite the opposite: this lenient negotiation of torah observance, accurate for everyday life, is precisely what renders Paul well prepared for finding ways to creatively negotiate guidance for everyday life for these newcomers to the God of Israel, these non-Jews who in Christ now as non-Jews also belonged to this God and thus were an associate movement to the people Israel.[25] His informed way of arguing from Scriptures and traditions and his hope for the resurrection are not the only evidence for this.

Another important aspect is Paul's high concern for the well-being of others, supporting each other, and avoiding as far as they are concerned quarrel also with outsiders (Rom 12:17-21). Thus, also in Phil 2:1-4 he expresses the hope that the

---

[23] Tal Ilan, *Silencing the Queen: The Literary History of Shelamzion and Other Jewish Women* (Tübingen: Mohr Siebeck, 2006), 98–105.

[24] Ilan, *Silencing the Queen*, 107–10. Cf. also Caroline E. Johnson Hodge's article, which focuses on the dimension of holiness in this passage, "Married to an Unbeliever: Households, Hierarchies, and Holiness in 1 Corinthians 7:12–16," *HTR* 103 (2010): 1–25.

[25] William S. Campbell, *The Nations in the Divine Economy: Paul's Covenantal Hermeneutics and Participation in Christ* (Lanham, MD: Lexington/Fortress Academic, 2018), 225–54.

Philippians will be able to look after each other in the spirit of the one they follow. He is concerned above all that there be no ἔρις among them. This coheres with the admonition later in that letter that Euodia and Syntyche be of one mind and should be supported (Phil 4:2-3). Whatever the reason for this admonition here in particular, Paul is concerned that they live in harmony, promoting reconciliation where there is potential conflict. This is a concern of course not only in Philippians, but also one that appears throughout Paul's letters for diverse reasons. It may cohere with an aspect in his self-understanding as a leader, which he mentions briefly in 2 Cor 11:6. Although not being a skilled or learned rhetorician, he emphasizes that he is not unskilled when it comes to knowledge. Maybe this is an allusion to the image of the wise, knowledgeable man, an image of course that would resonate with philosophers of his day.[26] Above all, however, when considered from the perspective of Paul's primary context, that is, Jewish tradition, this might include his education in the traditions of his ancestors, as a Pharisee. He would thus fall into a category of men who, according to Josephus, are held in highest regard among the Jews who "give credit for wisdom to those alone who have an exact knowledge of the law and who are capable of interpreting the meaning of the holy scriptures" (*Ant.* 20.264). There is a further aspect mentioned in Josephus that could also have impacted Paul's self-understanding. Josephus maintains that "the Pharisees are friendly among each other and cultivate harmonious relations with the community" (*J.W.* 2.166). Albert Baumgarten interprets this passage as "meaning that the Pharisees worked to achieve reconciliation among members of the larger public."[27] If there is any hint of historical accuracy here, this may highlight a further aspect of Paul the Pharisee. If Paul sees himself as embodying the traditions of his ancestors as a man of knowledge and wisdom, then this role would have encompassed the notion that it was his task to settle disputes, to mediate reconciliation, to advocate communal care, and to build up a sense of communal belonging. If there were conflicts, it would thus be his task—not just since he had become convinced that Jesus was the Messiah but already before that—to promote peace and reconciliation, now among the Christ-followers in a given place. Baumgarten sees a trajectory between this perception of Pharisaic leadership roles and what can be found in later rabbinical literature without claiming a direct lineage. Whatever the trajectories, most likely rhizomatic rather than linear,[28] there is one known Pharisee of the first century CE who seems to fit the description of Josephus quite well.

Paul's activity among the nations distinguishes him from other Pharisees; there certainly were disputes going on about this, but it does not set him in opposition to other Pharisees or other Jews generally. It does not render him less Jewish, but it

---

[26] Catherine Hezser, "The Rule of the Wise as an Alternative to Kingdom and Democracy in Ancient Rabbinic and Philosophical Thought" (lecture given at the University of Zurich, Zürich, September 23, 2019).

[27] Albert I. Baumgarten, "'Sages Increase Peace in the World': Reconciliation and Power," in *The Faces of Torah: Studies in Texts and Contexts of Ancient Judaism in Honor of Steven Fraade*, ed. Michal Bar-Asher Siegal, Tzvi Novick, and Christine Hayes (Göttingen: Vandenhoeck & Ruprecht, 2017), 221–36, here 235.

[28] Gilles Deleuze and Félix Guattari, *Das Rhizom* (Berlin: Merve, 1977).

sets him on a trajectory to reach out to others who remain different so that in their difference they join with the Jewish people to rejoice in the one God. Thus, there is a difference between Paul the Pharisee and other Pharisees of his time. But difference is not inherently antagonistic, nor does it render those who are different enemies. Paul was a self-declared Pharisee. He was a teacher of the nations, passionate for the traditions of his ancestors, and possibly at least trying to be true to these traditions in embodying a role as a broker of reconciliation. In this Paul we could well have a friend, possibly a conversation partner, in our attempts to respect each other in difference.

10

The Wet Nurse as a Model for Communal Relationships in 1 Thessalonians

Margaret Y. MacDonald

This essay brings together the themes of nursing and work.[1] In the midst of various projects on Paul's letters, early Christian families, and childhood in the biblical world, I have on a few occasions been startled by the presence of nursing metaphors in unexpected places. One such place is 1 Thess 2:5-8. In this text, Paul offers a surprising comparison of his own leadership to that of a "nurse," raising the obvious question of why Paul would employ a metaphor so infused with female associations as part of his rhetorical strategy to settle and comfort the fragile Thessalonian community—though perhaps the obvious need to soothe is part of the answer. Nevertheless, a more comprehensive response requires attention regarding points of convergence in recent scholarship on the Thessalonian correspondence, childhood and family life in the Roman world, slavery, and the linkages of the world of work with ancient associations. It will be argued here that rather than being understood as an anomaly, Paul's reference to himself as a nurse in 1 Thess 2:5-8 is part of his broader attempt to establish a rapport with the community as a person who works.[2]

---

[1] This combination of themes seems especially appropriate for my contribution to this festschrift to honor the career of Adele Reinhartz. As someone who combined the labor of biblical scholarship with the labor of nurturing children, Adele offered me a model for what was possible when one was willing to challenge some expectations and boundaries, while being faithfully dedicated to one's multifaceted work.

[2] This essay builds upon my earlier work with Carolyn Osiek and has been informed especially by studies by Beverly Gaventa and Jennifer Houston McNeel, who discusses how nursing metaphors serve Paul's rhetorical goals in 1 Thess 2:5-8. It complements these earlier studies, however, by examining the connection between nursing metaphors and the spaces, activities, and cultural norms associated with women's work. See Carolyn Osiek and Margaret Y. MacDonald (with Janet Tulloch), *A Woman's Place: House Churches in Earliest Christianity* (Minneapolis, MN: Fortress, 2006); Beverly Roberts Gaventa, *Our Mother St. Paul* (Louisville, KY: Westminster John Knox, 2007); Jennifer Houston McNeel, *Paul as Infant and Nursing Mother: Metaphor, Rhetoric and Identity in 1 Thessalonians 2:5–8*, ECL 12 (Atlanta, GA: SBL Press, 2014).

The Familial Context of 1 Thess 2:5-8

In 1 Thessalonians, as elsewhere in his letters, Paul employs a rich array of images and metaphors that draw upon the experiences of family life, including parenting, childhood, marriage (if the vessel of 1 Thess 4:4 refers to a wife), and even the experiences of slaves within the family if one accepts that 1 Thess 2:7 refers primarily to the circumstances of a slave wet nurse.[3] It must be acknowledged, however, that interpreters have been puzzled by Paul's apparent use of mixed metaphors in 1 Thess 2:7, where he apparently refers to himself simultaneously as an infant and as a wet nurse caring for children. Translations have varied, with many opting for the weaker manuscript evidence (e.g., RSV, NRSV, NABR, NCB, NKJV) for ἤπιοι ("gentle") instead of the seemingly less logical (and introducing a mixed metaphor) νήπιοι ("infants"). But despite what at first glance might appear as contradictory, both the references to infancy and to the nurse place Paul in a position of vulnerability in relation to the community, which, as will be argued later in the text, highlights his solidarity with those who labor and suffer.[4]

In casting himself as a nurse caring for children, Paul acknowledges his need to build bridges across social gulfs. Paul's use of the mixed metaphor to describe himself as a nurse and as an infant allows him to join the community of children on a metaphorical plane. A similar move occurs in 1 Thess 2:17, where Paul seems to describe his situation in relation to the Thessalonians as being like that of a helpless orphan.[5] The living conditions of slaves are not far from the surface, as abandoned children were a source of foundlings for the slave market. Such a demeaning vulnerability is not what one would expect for a leader and calls to mind Paul's rather shocking reference to his apostolic status in 1 Cor 15:8 using the term ἔκτρωμα for his identity as one untimely or prematurely born, "or possibly born with some type of physical defect."[6]

With respect to parenting metaphors, Paul's reference to himself as fatherly in 1 Thess 2:11-12 (almost immediately following the references to his identity as both infant and nurse) is far more conventional. Fathers were recognized generally for their

---

[3] Technically wet nurses could be slaves, freed persons, or freeborn, though it is likely that freeborn women would be those of modest means. An inscription commemorating the nurse of Julia, daughter of Germanicus, indicates that Prima was a freedwoman held in high esteem (*CIL* 6.4352). Numerous contracts have been discovered indicating that wet nursing was paid work, but these might often have involved the paying of an owner for the use of a slave (Tacitus, *Dial.* 28). Dio Chrysostom indicates that the work, though honorable, was often undertaken because of poverty on the part of freeborn women (*Ven.* 7.114). See Susan E. Hylen, *Women in the New Testament World*, Essentials of Biblical Studies (Oxford: Oxford University Press, 2019), 116–17. On nursing as work, see also Keith R. Bradley, "Wet-Nursing at Rome: A Study in Social Relations," in *The Family in Ancient Rome*, ed. Beryl Rawson (Ithaca, NY: Cornell University Press, 1986), 201–29.
[4] For full discussion of the manuscript evidence and issues of translation, see McNeel, *Paul as Infant*, 35–43. On the issue of Paul's use of mixed metaphors, see Gaventa, *Our Mother*, 19–20. To alleviate the problem of contradiction, McNeel challenges the traditional punctuation of the passage (as in NRSV), offering instead the following translation of v. 7: "(though we could have insisted on our own importance as apostles of Christ), but we were infants in your midst. Like a nurse tenderly caring for her own children." See McNeel, *Paul as Infant*, 60.
[5] Reidar Aasgaard, "Like a Child: Paul's Rhetorical Uses of Childhood," in *The Child in the Bible*, ed. Marcia J. Bunge (Grand Rapids, MI: Eerdmans, 2008), 249–77, here 257–8.
[6] Aasgaard, "Like a Child," 258.

teaching authority. But even more directly relevant for the figure of Paul is the standard representation of teachers as surrogate fathers, which stands out especially clearly in the depiction of Paul's relationship with his son Timothy (e.g., Phil 2:19-23; 2 Tim 1:2; 2 Tim 1:13-14).[7] In 1 Thess, Paul asserts an intimate individualized relationship as a family member, as a loving father to his children (1 Thess 2:8). More than serving elementary rhetorical purposes, the familial terminology seems designed to instill an emotional response of social solidarity and love to be given in return to the Apostle and his fellow workers. Paul's unusual comparison of himself to a nursing mother emerges as even more striking within the broader matrix of familial metaphors and associations, including the conventional roles of fathers.

We should pause to ponder the unusual nature of the "nurse" metaphor applied to Paul. With the exception of Gal 4:19 (cf. Rom 8:22-25), where he places himself in the position of a mother giving birth to children (i.e., community members), no other self-description of Paul is so overtly feminized. Tied so closely to infant care, it resembles Philo's description of the creator as both mother and nurse, whose natural sustenance of the animal world resembles the capacity for women to "well up springs of milk" as delivery approaches.[8] An even greater emphasis on nurturing surfaces in Tertullian's comparison of the mother who offers her "bountiful breasts" to the sustenance offered by the church-community to prisoners in need.[9] Similarly, Paul presents his own communal intervention as tender, using the verb θάλπω, which literally means "to cherish or comfort," and carries connotations of keeping warm.[10] The association of the terminology with intimacy, love, and basic human needs for life can be seen in the use of the term in Eph 5:28-29, where a husband's love for his wife is associated with the nourishment and tender care he must give to his own body. In keeping with this emphasis on physicality, the impact of nursing metaphors, which also appear in 1 Cor 3:1-2 and 1 Pet 2:1-3 (but not personalized in the same way as in 1 Thess 2:7), is based on the widely recognized reality in the ancient world of the nursing mother's ability to provide a commodity required for life.[11] While it is possible that the word simply refers to a mother who nurses, the much more common and widely accepted translation of "nurse," τροφός in this case is that it refers to a wet nurse who is hired or charged out (in the case of a slave wet nurse) to provide nourishment and care.[12] In light of this probability, commentators have reflected on the significance of the reference to the nurse who cares for her own children τὰ ἑαυτῆς τέκνα. It has been noted that the use of ἑαυτῆς did not always retain its reflexive quality in this era and, therefore, the

---

[7] On representation of teachers as fathers, see Robert A. Kaster, *Guardians of Language: The Grammarian and Society in Late Antiquity* (Berkeley: University of California Press, 1997), 68. On the symbolic association of the teaching with parenting, see Teresa Morgan, "Ethos: The Socialization of Children in Education and Beyond," in *A Companion to Families in the Greek and Roman Worlds*, ed. Beryl Rawson (Oxford: Blackwell, 2011), 504–20.

[8] See Philo, *Concerning Noah's Work as Planter* 4.14-16 (Colson and Whitaker, LCL).

[9] See Tertullian, *To the Martyrs* (ANF 3.693).

[10] See BDAG, s.v. θάλπω, 442, and McNeel, *Paul as Infant*, 56, where she offers example from the LXX where the terminology is associated with providing warmth.

[11] As reported by Aulus Gellius, the second-century CE philosopher, Favorinus associated human milk with sperm, with both having a similar ability to form the body and mind (*Noct. att.* 12.14-15).

[12] For relevant ancient sources, see n. 3.

phrase could be translated simply as "her children." But comparison to usages in 1 Thess 4:4 and especially 2:8 supports the reflexive use of ἑαυτῆς given the continuing emphasis on intimacy.[13] As discussed later, this reading also strengthens the argument for understanding Paul's self-reference in light of an attempt to establish greater social solidarity with the recipients of the letter.

The Work of Wet Nurses and Wet Nurses as Workers

Assessment of Paul's nursing metaphor must take account of what wet nurses were expected to do. Broadly speaking, this involved not only lactation, but childcare and even preliminary education.[14] Wet nursing was certainly recognized as hard work, which women across history and into the modern day can certainly attest. Satirists, moralists, and even ancient physicians associated avoidance of nursing with the laziness of elite women. The philosopher, Favorinus, for example, purportedly condemned women in the strongest possible terms who did not nurse their own babies as failing to provide products of their own blood with "natural nourishment."[15] On the other hand, women—probably from the wealthier families—who nursed their own children and made painful sacrifices to do so were lauded in a culture that viewed the practice as lamentably on the decline.[16] These ancient commentaries reveal unspoken recognition of fatigue and hard work. Even the physician writing in the early second century, Soranus of Ephesus, who favored the nourishment of mother's milk in theory, stressed that suckling could lead to premature aging.[17] Writing about the same time, Aulus Gellius, the Latin author and grammarian, offers a window into the kind of debate that might have occurred in more well-to-do circles about whether mothers should nurse their own children. Bolstered by a group of philosophically inclined friends, a father entered into an argument with a young woman's mother following a particularly difficult labor and delivery. The grandmother's voice of advocacy in favor of the hiring of a wet nurse is strong and not far removed from the leadership of older women in relation to younger women expected by the author of Tit 2:3-5.[18]

The link between wet nursing and education is also grounded in work. Wet nurses were often kept on as the nannies and "tutors" of very young children—a fact not to be dismissed in discussion of the expansion of Christ-groups.[19] On the one hand, this expansion of the role was related to the domains and sometimes drudgery of childcare—including the challenges of keeping infants alive, illustrated poignantly by one scholar who points to "the impossibility of keeping a swaddled baby clean on the

---

[13] For further discussion of issues of translation and interpretation, including the reflexive use of ἑαυτῆς, see McNeel, *Paul as Infant*, 55–7.
[14] See, for example, (Pseudo)-Plutarch, *Mor.* 3E, *On the Education of Children*.
[15] See Aulus Gellius, *Noc. att.* 12.1.8-9. For satirical commentary on the laziness of upper-class women who do not nurse their own children, see Juvenal, *Satire* 6.592-601.
[16] See, for example, Tacitus, *Dial.* 28.4-5; Plutarch, *Cons. ux.* 5.
[17] See, for example, Soranus, *Gynecology* 2.18-20.
[18] Aulus Gellius, *Noc. att.* 12.1.1-5.
[19] Beryl Rawson, *Children and Childhood in Roman Italy* (Oxford: Oxford University Press, 2003), 123.

fourth floor of a tenement with the water supply at the end of the street."[20] On the other hand, the educational nanny was recognized as key to the proper development of the child. Reflecting elite preoccupations, but also shedding light on the ascription of value to some lower-class individuals and slave women, physicians and philosophers offered striking advice about how to choose a wet nurse. For the physician Soranus, physical qualities (e.g., size of breasts), history (e.g., preference for one who had previously born children), nationality (Greek for the best speech), and religious inclinations (superstitions to be avoided) were all important criteria.[21] The latter is especially suggestive of the risks taken by early Christian wet nurses and of environments where they may have been under considerable scrutiny. Beyond speech, which is typically viewed as highly significant, some texts focus upon the educational role of wet nurses, highlighting their characters, the quality of the early lessons they could provide, and even extending to the careful selection of slave children to be brought up alongside free children to form the correct educational environment.[22] An understanding of this historical context adds another layer of meaning to Paul's reference to himself as a "nurse" in 1 Thess 2:7: as "nurse" Paul has a formative influence on the Thessalonian community, since he expands the conventional educational associations of his role as their father/apostle articulated a few verses later in 1 Thess 2:11-12 (as discussed earlier). If the community is the child, Paul represents the gamut of care and educational–familial influence.

In this composite metaphorical framework, however, the status of wet nurses requires attention. Free women could be hired as wet nurses based on a contract, but they were very often slaves, either for the children of the household (slave and free) or could even be contracted out to other households by their owners. Slave children could be born within the family either as the offspring of household slaves or even as the offspring of the head of the household and slaves, which he used for sexual gratification.[23] Slave children born to slaves were not legally the children of the slaves but were in every sense the property of their owners. Slaves could also enter households from the outside sometimes as infants picked up as foundlings and reared by the slaves of house. Paul's self-description as both an infant and an orphan displays an awareness of extreme vulnerability and a sense of separation from parental love (1 Thess 2:7, 17). The wet nurse would be charged with filling that void, but as a slave her own life would be marked by vulnerability, lack of control, and cycles of separation from the children she nourished and reared, sometimes including her own children.[24] This state of affairs was based on the complete lack of reproductive choice for slave women, with the sale of their bodies as girls or in their childbearing years based on their potential to

---

[20] Gillian Clark, "Roman Women," *GR* (Ser. 2) 28 (1981): 193–212, here 198.
[21] Soranus, *Gynecology* 2.18-20.
[22] See, for example, Pseudo-Plutarch, *Mor.* 3E, *On the Education of Children*; Quintilian, *Inst.* 1.1.4-20. Quintilian pays remarkable attention to what today we would call child development. See the discussion in Osiek and MacDonald, *A Woman's Place*, 84–5.
[23] See, for example, Seneca's description of the presence of slaves at dinner parties in *Ep.* 47.8.
[24] Plautus, for example, implies that there is a recognized figure to suckle the household slaves, freeing slave mothers for other work and thereby preventing slave mothers from nursing their own children. See *Miles gloriosus* 697.

give birth to other slaves or to offer a supply of life-giving milk.[25] Female slaves were a lucrative commodity for their owners because they were a source of a type of physical work and production, as was recognized by Columella in granting exceptions from work to female slaves who had born three children and even freedom to those who had born more.[26]

The Nature of the Bond and the Realities of Separation

An understanding of this context allows Paul's self-description as a "nurse tenderly caring for her own children" to emerge in a new light. It seems to have been common practice for one slave to have been chosen to nurse the children of the household, as implied by Plautus in his reference to "the nurse who suckles the *vernas*."[27] It was also common practice for a slave wet nurse to care for the freeborn children of the household, acting as a type of foster mother—freeing their mother from the labor of nursing and caring for very young children.[28] No doubt the same woman often did both tasks, combining care of young toddlers with the nursing of infants. An outgrowth of this approach to childminding was that free and enslaved children would often play together and share the same spaces.[29] The commitment of the wet nurse to her charges was reinforced by contractual regulations that prohibited the women from becoming pregnant.[30] Bonding presumably occurred, and scholars have pointed to situations where the wet nurse became a type of pseudo-parent, having an influence on the child and becoming a potential companion that extended well beyond the weaning period.[31] The role of the wet nurse is an important element of the expanded notion of family in antiquity, involving nonkin relations as central to the experience of childhood—in this case attachment was created very clearly by milk and not by blood.[32]

---

[25] See Osiek and MacDonald, *A Woman's Place*, 99. The reproductive potential of female slaves in their reproductive years is revealed by sale records from Egypt, with a noticeable decline as women age. There is also some indication that prices for girls sometimes exceeded prices for boys on account of reproductive potential. See also Keith R. Bradley, *Slaves and Masters in the Roman Empire: A Study in Social Control* (New York: Oxford University Press, 1987), 159.

[26] See Columella, *On Agriculture* 1.8.19. This is related to the freedom from *tutela* granted to freeborn women who had born three children and freedwomen who had four in the *lex Papia Poppaea* of Emperor Augustus in 9 CE. See discussion in Osiek and MacDonald, *A Woman's Place*, 99–100.

[27] Plautus, *Miles gloriosus* 697. See Suzanne Dixon, *The Roman Mother* (London: Croom Helm, 1988), 17–18, 70–1. See also Osiek and MacDonald, *A Woman's Place*, 100–1.

[28] Dixon, *Roman Mother*, 146.

[29] With a focus specifically on education Quintilian, for example, went so far as to suggest that care should be taken in selecting the slaves that should be brought up with the child as playmates. See *Inst.* 1.1.4–5, 8. See also Rawson, *Children and Childhood*, 216.

[30] Osiek and MacDonald, *A Woman's Place*, 100. Wet-nursing contracts extended from six months to three years, stipulating that the wet nurse should not become pregnant or engage in intercourse. For more information about nursing contracts, see n. 3.

[31] See, for example, Rawson, *Children and Childhood*, 123; Hylen, *Women in the New Testament World*, 117–18.

[32] Véronique Dasen, "Childbirth and Infancy in the Greek and Roman Worlds," in *A Companion to Families in the Greek and Roman Worlds*, ed. Beryl Rawson (Oxford: Blackwell, 2011), 291–314, here 309. See also Rawson, *Children and Childhood*, 123.

In drawing attention to the wet nurse who tenderly cares for her own children, Paul displays awareness of a type of bond that typically exceeds the connection between the wet nurse and her charges, since this bond refers to attachment that is created by *both* milk and by blood. The metaphorical language only makes sense, however, in light of an implied differentiation between the intimacy shared with one's own infant and the care provided to other children. The situation of slave women deserves special attention, and it seems highly likely that Paul has the circumstances of these women in mind.[33] Behind Paul's metaphorical reference to tender care is the alternate scenario of lesser attachment to the free children of the household, the children of other slaves, and the unspoken reality of the nurse who has no access to her own children.

Despite the pervasive evidence of intimate and long-lasting relations between wet nurses and their nurslings in the ancient world (albeit heavily influenced by elite perspectives), comparative analysis with the situation of slave nannies from the American South—especially accounts of behavior with respect to the advance of the Union Army—suggests that attitudes of wet nurses toward their charges may well have been more complex and ambivalent than this evidence would suggest.[34] It is impossible to know how slave caregivers in the ancient world actually felt, but it is not difficult to construe the very real scenarios of domination and familial separation inherent in circumstances where women's bodies are owned and women's lactation induced/commodified for economic purposes. We may perhaps detect a sigh of relief encoded in Paul's metaphorical description of the wet nurse feeding her own children, since this was an event that could be interrupted or prevented altogether by a slave owner or the householder (male or female), who had arranged for a nursing contract or simply decided to make use of the slave for other purposes (not to mention, perhaps selling the slave altogether). Such tender care might only be a fraction more nurturing than the care the wet nurse would give to her charges, but it was notable, perhaps because it was known to be longed for and rare. For the wet nurse with the ready supply of milk produced by childbirth, much would conspire against her to conceive another child, whom she could nurse herself. Once again recalling the terminology of the American South, Margaret Aymer compares Paul's metaphor to "the mammy back in the slave quarters who *finally* gets to nurse her own children."[35]

Early Christian literature offers perhaps a hint of this isolation and loss of control in the depiction of the slave Felicitas's birthing experience while imprisoned, according to *The Martyrdom of Perpetua and Felicitas*. No father is mentioned, and Felicitas's orphaned daughter is said to have been raised by a believing woman. Enhancing the tragedy of the situation, Felicitas is presented as facing death as a mother ready to

---

[33] On the low status of wet nurses as women of meagre means and very often slaves, see McNeel, *Paul as Infant*, 138–9.

[34] See, especially, Sandra R. Joshel, "Nurturing the Master's Child: Slavery and the Roman Child-Nurse," *Signs* 12 (1986): 3–22. See also discussion in McNeel, *Paul as Infant*, 79.

[35] Margaret Aymer, "'Mother Knows Best': The Story of Mother Paul Revisited," in *Mother Goose, Mother Jones, Mommie Dearest: Biblical Mothers and Their Children*, ed. Cheryl A. Kirk-Duggan and Tina Pippin, SemeiaSt 61 (Atlanta, GA: SBL Press, 2008), 187–98, here 194. Cited in McNeel, *Paul as Infant*, 139.

nurse her child with milk dripping from her breasts.³⁶ The drama of a martyrdom account is absent from 1 Thessalonians, but some of these same familial realities of isolation and loss of the ability to nurture and be nurtured are reflected in Paul's metaphorical mosaic, combining images of infants, orphans, wet nurses, and fathers. His relationship with the Thessalonians is emotionally charged, and he recounts both his past dealings and longing to be with the community again. Distance, separation, comfort in the form of his envoy Timothy (1 Thess 3:1-2), and longing are all part of the picture of Paul's absence (cf. also 1 Thess 2:17-20). The forces separating him from his "children" (1 Thess 2:11) are strong and oppressive. The experience of repeatedly being thwarted from coming to them is likened to the experience of being orphaned (1 Thess 2:17), bringing to mind the later circumstances of the slave Felicitas and her newborn infant.

Childcare Spaces and the Workshop Setting of 1 Thessalonians

The depth of emotion expressed in 1 Thessalonians is one of the letter's most notable features and quite obviously functions to align Paul's own suffering (e.g., 1 Thess 2:2) and estrangement with the suffering and persecution (1 Thess 1:6-7) experienced by the Thessalonians.³⁷ Familial metaphors play a central role in Paul's warm and sometimes even passionate communication. As noted above, the use of the feminine metaphor of the wet nurse remains striking even within this broader framework of familial concepts and is rendered even more remarkable by the observation that unlike most of the other Pauline letters (with 1 Corinthian offering an obvious example), there are no explicit references to female members of the Thessalonian assembly. Building upon the emphasis on labor and working with one's hands (1 Thess 4:11), it has even been suggested that this was an all-male group possibly composed of an occupational guild (these tended to be all-male or all-female), perhaps of curtain makers, leather cutters, or goldsmiths.³⁸ But even if one accepts this hypothesis, one must explain why

---

³⁶ See *The Martyrdom of Perpetua and Felicitas*, 20, trans. H. Musurillo in *The Acts of the Christian Martyrs: Introduction, Texts, and Translations*, OECT (Oxford: Oxford University Press, 1972), 106–31, here 123–4. See also Osiek and MacDonald, *A Woman's Place*, 60–1.

³⁷ For a recent study that highlights the significance of emotion for understanding Paul's interaction with his communities, see Ryan S. Schellenberg, *Abject Joy: Paul, Prison, and the Arts of Making Do* (Oxford: Oxford University Press, 2021). On the circumstances of the Thessalonian community involving suffering see John M. G. Barclay, "Thessalonica and Corinth: Social Contrasts in Pauline Christianity," *JSNT* 47 (1992): 49–74.

³⁸ Offering some interesting comparative evidence, this has recently been argued by John S. Kloppenborg. However, the lack of explicit reference to women in 1 Thessalonians in my view does not warrant the conclusion that no women were present, especially given the ample references to women in other Pauline letters. I would argue that we should assume that women were present without explicit evidence within the text to support their exclusion. Kloppenborg notes that Acts 17:4 offers evidence in the opposite direction, but he associates it with Luke's particular agenda. Furthermore, against those who would point to 1 Thess 4:4 as offering evidence for wives (if that translation is accepted), he notes that the perspective is clearly androcentric. See John S. Kloppenborg, *Christ's Associations: Connecting and Belonging in the Ancient City* (New Haven, CT: Yale University Press, 2019), 89–90, 371. For a different perspective, which focuses on female

such feminized language, complete with associated references to infants and orphans, would be an appropriate choice to address such a group. In this instance, it is useful to consider the workshop setting, which is increasingly being understood as key to understanding the context of the Thessalonian correspondence.[39]

In recent years, scholars have called for a greater openness to possibilities for spaces where Christ-followers chose to gather, rather than limit these communities to gatherings in houses (e.g., 1 Cor 16:19).[40] For example, in the Thessalonian correspondence, there are no references to "house churches," and the probable presence of artisans and laborers (1 Thess 4:11; cf. also 5:12) in the group suggests that the workshop may have offered a more typical meeting place. But the association of living quarters with shops must be borne in mind for members who were less economically secure than those who owned a *domus*—a residence shared with an extended household, which was probably the case for a figure like Stephanas (1 Cor 1:16; 16:15). Instead, in Thessalonica, the members may well have lived in more cramped apartment buildings (*insulae*) with workshops on the ground floor that might have served as a gathering place. In fact, 2 Thess 3:6-13 has been interpreted as offering a window into situations where subsistence was a present need and laborious manual work was accepted as a necessity for survival.[41]

This is the context where Paul's wet nurse metaphor becomes especially applicable. The membership of the Thessalonian community has been identified as a fairly homogeneous group composed of "slave, free handworkers, and perhaps some freedmen."[42] Even if the group included few women, the members would be immediately familiar with the circumstances of slave women whose bodies bore the burden of reproductive work. If not community members themselves, they were the daughters, partners, and former caregivers of community members. If we expand the circle to consider who may have entered the meeting spaces—bearing in mind Paul's interrelated references to fatherhood, infancy, and the state of orphans—the role of the wet nurse caregiver becomes even more pertinent. We must remember that the presence of children in the Roman world was ubiquitous—they seemingly wandered in from everywhere, from the most auspicious of settings, to the humble shop and place of trade.[43] Slave nannies were likely often part of the entourage, minding the children and trying to keep track of them. In describing the behavior of troublesome early Christians, the second-century critic Celsus points to children escaping the surveillance of the legitimate figures of authority, such as schoolteachers and fathers, and going along with Christian leaders to workshops where slaves would

---

converts, see Florence Morgan Gillman, "Paul, His Nurse Metaphor (1 Thessalonians 2:7) and the Thessalonian Women Who Turned Against Idols," *CBQ* 84 (2022): 279–94.

[39] See, for example, Richard S. Ascough, *1 & 2 Thessalonians, An Introduction and Study Guide: Encountering the Christ Group at Thessalonike* (London: Bloomfield, 2017).

[40] See, for example, Edward Adams, *The Earliest Christian Meeting Places: Almost Exclusively Houses* (London: Bloomsbury T&T Clark, 2016).

[41] See Robert Jewett, "Tenement Churches and Communal Meals in the Early Church," *BR* 38 (1994): 23–43.

[42] Kloppenborg, *Christ's Associations*, 90.

[43] See, for example, Christian Laes, *Children in the Roman Empire: Outsiders Within* (Cambridge: Cambridge University Press, 2011), 37.

have worked. According to Roman historian of the family, Beryl Rawson, despite the polemical quality of Celsus's remarks, the description of physical spaces reflecting the intermingling of freeborn children, slave children, women, and slaves are completely believable.[44]

Conclusion

Long before the tensions of the second century CE, the Thessalonian community seems to have experienced social harassment (1 Thess 1:6).[45] We have no explicit details, but the repeated emphasis on labor and work highlights the fact that life in the workshop might well have played a role. An examination of the relation between nursing and work allows for a fuller appreciation of Paul's attempt to bring comfort to the community by comparing his own action to that of a wet nurse. Paul associates himself with the social experience and suffering of the community. Recognition of the strong association of nursing with work adds new intensity to the fact that Paul draws on images from his work as an artisan (e.g., 1 Thess 2:9) to address his great efforts on behalf of the community, which are intertwined with a mosaic of familial images. Any references to parenting and children in the Roman world are tied to the involvement of slaves caring for children. Both the appeals to manual labor and to the work of a wet nurse (most often a slave) are part of a rhetorical strategy where Paul reverses the values of elite society, which found such efforts taxing and even increasingly demeaning. Overtly feminized symbolism places Paul in the role of servant to his community and presents a standard of nurturing that would be recognized as rare and longed for, like a wet nurse tenderly caring for her own children. Ultimately, Paul's language becomes meaningful in this context, as it is steeped with the ideals of love and intimacy that characterized the relationship between a mother and her infant. Such immeasurable warmth becomes the model for relationships in a community in need of great comfort.

---

[44] Rawson, *Children and Childhood*, 216, referring to Origen, *Against Celsus* 3.55.
[45] For more detailed discussion, see Margaret Y. MacDonald, "The Thessalonian and the Corinthian Letters," in *The New Cambridge Companion to St. Paul*, ed. Bruce W. Longenecker (Cambridge: Cambridge University Press, 2020), 56–91.

Part 3

Further Texts and Contexts in Jewish Antiquity

11

Wine, Dine, and Bind: Sacrificial Food and Community Formation in Asia Minor

Shayna Sheinfeld and Meredith J. C. Warren

Introduction

Meals are just as closely associated with friendship now as they were two thousand years ago; as Plutarch wrote, "A guest comes to share not only meat, wine and dessert, but conversation, fun and the amiability that leads to friendship" (Plutarch, *Mor.* 660b [Clement Hoffleit, LCL]). We, Shayna Sheinfeld and Meredith Warren, have been fast friends for over a decade, and Adele has been a mentor to both of us during that time. Meredith completed a portion of her book, *Food and Transformation in Ancient Mediterranean Literature*,[1] while she was a postdoctoral researcher at the University of Ottawa under Reinhartz's guidance. Shayna first got to know Adele after inviting her to give a lecture at Colgate University in 2015, and the two have subsequently shared bread, wine, and conversation at several Enoch Seminars. It seemed fitting to contribute to this volume in honor of Adele Reinhartz, whose overarching theme is friendship, by writing a piece together. This piece touches on both aspects of our work: on commensality around food and on the formation of community relationships.

The title of this piece, "Wine, Dine, and Bind," makes explicit the third, unspoken element of the more common phrase "wine and dine"—the implication being that once wined and dined, the relationship between host and guest is deepened. Wining and dining can connote a tactic used to forge or deepen interpersonal relationships, including romantic ones, or relationships between (potential) business partners, where special expense and effort are undertaken in order to strengthen those relationships. It is sometimes implied in the phrase that a sense of obligation to the host is instilled in the guest by the host's generosity. As such, it is often taken for granted that wining and dining implies a special connection between the host and the diner. The phrase implies the creation or reinforcing of a bond between host and guest(s), and therefore the decision to share a meal can be a significant identity-creating decision—you should choose your friends and dining companions carefully.

---

[1] Meredith J. C. Warren, *Food and Transformation in Ancient Mediterranean Literature* (Atlanta, GA: SBL Press, 2019).

The question of what role meal practices play in the formation and maintenance of relationships among the early Christ-worshipers was broached by some of the writings that were later compiled into the canonical New Testament. Although none of the undisputed letters of Paul overlap geographically with any of the seven assemblies to which the author of Revelation addressed his letters, both Paul and John write concerning community bonding in Asia Minor vis-à-vis sacrificed food. Moreover, it is likely that John writes directly against "Pauline and neo-Pauline proselytes to the Jesus movement who were not, in John's eyes (and many others' in the first century), halakhically pure enough to merit this term in its practical sense."[2] Read together, these two writers' focus on meals illuminates how ancient communities used rituals around meals to establish community relationships and to distinguish between themselves and outsiders.

Virtually all meals in Greek and Roman antiquity would have included some connection to sacrifice, honoring various gods, at some point during the dinner, whether that be meat purchased from temple butchers or libations.[3] Sacrificial elements at meals reinforced social relationships not only among diners but also between gods and diners.[4] As such, they were bound up in an important and very real way, as was just about everything else, in the honor-shame economy of the ancient world. Honor could be bestowed on a god by making an offering and likewise on the person making the offering. Participating in a meal, including its libations and consumption of sacrificed meat, fostered and maintained business relationships as well as friendships, and nonparticipation could have financial and social ramifications. No wonder both Paul and John's communities wrestled so intensely with how to hold their dinner parties. The choice to offer a libation to the *genius* of the emperor, for example,[5] is a choice made about one's friendliness with the emperor and therefore with the empire, and eating meat offered to idols could look like the eater was participating in the worship of those gods. This produced some anxiety for Christ-worshiping groups, including those affiliated with Paul and with John the Seer, given that such gatherings followed a similar pattern to other group meetings in antiquity, which generally met for a meal, drink,

---

[2] David Frankfurter, "Jews or Not? Reconstructing the Other in Rev 2:9 and 3:9," *HTR* 94 (2001): 403–25, here 403. Sarah Emanuel (*Humor, Resistance, and Jewish Cultural Persistence in the Book of Revelation: Roasting Rome* [Cambridge: Cambridge University Press, 2020], 33–4 and n. 32) suggests that John is writing to ethnically Jewish groups in the epistles but agrees that Revelation prioritizes "halakhically oriented Christ-followers" in his hierarchy of eschatological rewards and that John excludes any gentile Christ worshipers who did not follow (his interpretation of) Jewish law.

[3] Dennis E. Smith, *From Symposium to Eucharist: The Banquet in the Early Christian World* (Minneapolis, MN: Fortress, 2003); E. P. Sanders, "Jewish Association with Gentiles and Galatians 2:11–14," in *The Conversation Continues: Studies in Paul and John in Honor of J. Louis Martyn*, ed. Robert T. Fortna and Beverly R. Gaventa (Nashville, TN: Abingdon, 1990), 170–88, here 178.

[4] Margaret Froelich, "Sacrificed Meat in Corinth and Jesus Worship as a Cult among Cults," *Journal of Early Christian History* 10 (2020): 44–56. This is important when understanding how Revelation uses libation imagery since the divine genius of the emperor was one such recipient of wine offerings. Moreover, since the Emperor Augustus's defeat of Egypt, all meals were technically obliged to include a libation to the *genius* of the emperor. See Hal Taussig, *In the Beginning Was the Meal: Social Experimentation & Early Christian Identity* (Minneapolis, MN: Fortress, 2009), 78.

[5] The worship of the *genius* of a person is not identical to worship of that person; the *genius*, whether of the head of household (*paterfamilias*) or of the emperor, is the deified personification of the qualities of that person.

and discussion. Indeed, in 1 Corinthians, Paul highlights the import of commensality by limiting the eating of sacrificial meat based on how it may encourage members of weaker conscience to participate in the worship of other gods, in other words, to forego what might have been their normal civic practice as residents of Roman cities.[6] We argue that it is perception, what is later called *mar'it 'ayin* (literally: what appears to the eye), that Paul argues should guide the choice of whether or when to eat such foods. Revelation's use of wine imagery sheds light on how some early communities in Asia Minor seem to have constructed their community relationships. It is our contention that John of Patmos condemns all wine use by the assemblies as participating in wrong ritual practice: wine is a drink that indicates friendly tolerance, or even enthusiastic support of the empire, not of community with Christ. Both authors are concerned with the ways in which commensality constructs and enforces the boundaries that protect their communities from the dangers of outsiders. Even the appearance of meal-related behaviors,[7] they claim, is enough to forge friendships with the wrong sorts of allies.

In 1 Corinthians 8 and 10, Paul discusses how disruption to the social cohesion of the group can occur when it appears that members are partaking of foods offered to idols because this perception can lead to an actual participation in idol worship by weaker members of the community. For Paul, the possible misinterpretation of the meal event can destabilize the relationship of the community and its relationship with Christ and reinforce relationships with other gods or supernatural beings. In Revelation, John of Patmos is particularly concerned with meal practice, condemning those assemblies that tolerate "eating food sacrificed to idols" and associating wrong meal practice with immorality and idolatry (e.g., Rev 2:15). For John, doing community meals in the wrong way demonstrates the closest kind of relationship—that is, sexual intimacy or fornication—with Babylon[8] rather than a relationship with Christ. Like Paul earlier, John also finds himself in competition with other "apostles" who promoted different definitions of what it meant to be a follower of Christ. This essay will consider the ways that wining and dining binds people to each other and how some meals create dangerous liaisons with perceived enemies.

1 Corinthians 8:1-13; 10:23–11:1

Communities all over the ancient Mediterranean shared meals that created and maintained social cohesion, and at the core of these communities was a set of understandings about what these meals meant. For Paul's communities, the interpretation of various meal practices played a crucial role in identifying who belongs

---

[6] Froelich, "Sacrificed Meat," 54.
[7] We are not alone in arguing for the importance of appearances in ancient communities. Paula Fredriksen writes, "Cult focused on actions, on showing and (no less important) on being seen to show respect for the gods" ("Judaizing the Nations: The Ritual Demands of Paul's Gospel," *NTS* 56 [2010]: 232–52, here 235).
[8] For John, Babylon is convenient shorthand for all that he sees as wrong with the Roman Empire. See Sara Parks, Shayna Sheinfeld, and Meredith J. C. Warren, *Jewish and Christian Women in the Ancient Mediterranean* (London: Routledge, 2022), 227–32.

to the group. Disagreement about what food is appropriate for consumption was therefore a point of contention, causing confusion in the participants' relationships to one another and creating discord among the assembly.[9] Within the Corinthian congregation, eating is understood by Paul to be an activity of belonging, community, and friendship, even if this understanding is not as clear to his intended audience. In 1 Corinthians 8 and 10, Paul highlights the importance of the commensality of the assembly by critiquing just such a lack of understanding.[10] In these chapters, Paul is addressing whether members of the assembly may partake of food that has been sacrificed to idols. As Margaret Mitchell notes, "Paul's overriding concern here is not merely idol meats in themselves but the impact of conflicts over idol meats on the concord of the church community."[11] In other words, what Paul is arguing in chs. 8 and 10 is that the actions of individual members should first be guided by what is good for the assembly as a whole. In the case of food sacrificed to idols (εἰδωλόθυτον), we argue that Paul's concern is about what the later rabbis call *mar'it 'ayin* (מראית עין), or the appearance of impropriety, that should guide a member's choice of whether and/or when to eat food that may have been sacrificed to idols.

While the term *mar'it 'ayin* is not used until much later, the idea is present in texts as early as 2 Maccabees.[12] Under the religious persecution of Antiochus IV, many Jews were forced to choose between eating sacrificial meat or being killed (2 Macc 6–7). One ninety-year-old man, Eleazar, was offered an out: rather than eating meat sacrificed to Dionysus, he was told that he could bring his own meat, and as long as he pretended that he was following the instructions of eating the sacrificial meat, he would not be killed. Eleazar refused, noting that younger Jews might think that the respected Eleazar had eaten of the improper meat and thus they might be led astray to do the same (2 Macc 6:24-25). Eleazar refused to play this game because he recognized that it would appear that he was eating sacrificial meat. As a result, others might be encouraged to actually eat the sacrificial meat under the illusion that it was permitted because (it looked like) Eleazar had done it first.[13]

In 1 Corinthians 8, the issues around *mar'it 'ayin* are at play in the disagreement over whether or not food sacrificed to idols is permissible for consumption by the assembly.

---

[9] Froelich, "Sacrificed Meat," 53.
[10] Most scholars generally agree that 1 Cor 8:1–11:1 is meant to be read as a cohesive unit. While we focus here on 1 Cor 8:1–13 and 10:23–11:1, this reading fits into the narrative address of the larger unit, which focuses on Paul's argument to the Corinthians to set aside factionalism and place the good of the group before what may be advantageous for the individual, as he himself has done. Margaret M. Mitchell, *Paul and the Rhetoric of Reconciliation: An Exegetical Investigation of the Language and Composition of 1 Corinthians* (Louisville, KY: Westminster John Knox, 1991), 126–49.
[11] Mitchell, *Paul and the Rhetoric of Reconciliation*, 238.
[12] Which is dated to the mid- to late second-century BCE.
[13] Examples of *mar'it 'ayin* in rabbinic literature include m. Šeqal. 3:2, where officials who entered the temple treasury must not have clothes with pockets or hems so that people cannot say that the official took anything from the treasury, and in the Babylonian Talmud, where the question of whether it is permitted to hang wet clothes to dry on the Sabbath, as it may appear they were laundered that day, which is not permissible (b. Šabb. 65a). A more contemporary example would be that some Jews do not eat rice, corn, legumes, or seeds (*kitniyot*) on Passover as they could be mistaken for one of the five grains forbidden on Passover, and thus it would look like they were breaking the holiday laws by eating these foods or their derivatives.

Paul reaffirms that there is no god but the one God (8:4) and that these so-called gods worshiped are not, in fact, gods at all.[14] Therefore, this food should not be forbidden, since it is not actually sacrificed to any god. Thus, the issue of eating food sacrificed to "pagan" gods is not the issue per se. Instead, Paul is concerned with *perception*: when members who have a weak conscience witness a member who possesses knowledge (γνῶσις) eat food sacrificed to idols, they may still believe that this sacrifice creates a potent connection to the "pagan" gods. As a result, weak-of-conscience members may worship "pagan" gods when they mimic the knowledgeable members in eating such food; in doing so, they align themselves with those other gods.[15]

This issue is an example of *mar'it 'ayin*.[16] According to Paul, if a Christ-worshiper— one who knows that there is no god but God and therefore that so-called idols are in fact not representative of gods—is eating food sacrificed to one of these idols, it is fine; there is no harm done in the eating of the sacrifice (τὸ τὰ εἰδωλόθυτα ἐσθίειν). But, Paul says, not every member of the assembly has yet digested this knowledge (8:10). If a member is watching another Christ-worshiper eat meat sacrificed to an idol, it might *look like* the eater is participating in the worship of other gods. This is because the member watching is under the impression that the god-as-idol is real, whereas the eater is confident that the god-as-idol does not exist.[17] And since the weak member in this scenario knows that the eater possesses the knowledge of Christ, they too will consider it acceptable to eat this food that they believe is an offering to a very real other god (8:11). In this example, the weak member will be reinforced in their conviction that other gods exist and are worthy of worship by emulating a knowledgeable member of the Christ assembly. Moreover, in participating in sacrificial food offerings to that deity, the weak worshiper forges a bond between themselves and that particular deity.

This instance of *mar'it 'ayin* highlights how food sharing can bind an individual to a community. In this example, a weak member of the assembly can be bound back up in the worship of other gods through what appears to be the example of a member who possesses knowledge, disrupting the weak member's relationship to the Christ assembly. At a fundamental level, Paul's letter here is suggesting that for some the eating of sacrificed foods serves as the act of worshiping these other gods, while the eating of the same food by others would not constitute a participation in the worship of these gods.[18] The solution, Paul argues, is that the assembly has a responsibility to

---

[14] Although participating in the consumption of this food may lead to consorting with demons, see 1 Cor 8:5; 10:20-21; see also Paula Fredriksen, "Philo, Herod, Paul, and the Many Gods of Ancient Jewish 'Monotheism,'" *HTR* 115 (2022): 23–45, here 37–8.

[15] Thus those "weak in conscience" should be identified as members of the Christ-worshipers who still retain some internalized acceptance of polytheistic gods. See Gregory W. Dawes, "The Danger of Idolatry: First Corinthians 8:7–13," *CBQ* 58 (1996): 82–98, here 88–90, who notes that these "weak" are different from those addressed in Paul's letter to the Romans.

[16] Appearing to worship correctly was also important in Greek and Roman ritual practice. See Fredriksen, "Judaizing the Nations," 235.

[17] This is not to deny the existence of other gods and supernatural beings but rather the efficacy of idols as representing these gods; Fredriksen, "Philo," 37–8.

[18] This is similar to how the eating (or not eating) of pork in early Jewish and rabbinic texts serves as a metonym for participating in the foreign domination of Jews. Jordan Rosenblum notes examples from 1, 2, and 4 Macc, Josephus, Philo, Targumim, the Palestinian and the Babylonian Talmud, Avot of Rabbi Nathan, and in Midrash Rabbah (Jordan Rosenblum, "'Why Do You Refuse to Eat Pork?' Jews, Food, and Identity in Roman Palestine," *JQR* 100 [2010]: 95–110).

act in a manner that is in line with what reinforces commensality even if what they would like to do is not expressly forbidden. This is because an individual could lead others from the assembly to incorrect practice and, therefore, lead them to sin (8:12). Leading one another into sin is the opposite of promoting social cohesion and could result in (and in the case of Corinth, seems to have already resulted in) the breakdown of community relationships.

This topic is explicitly picked back up a little further into the letter. Paul argues that members of the assembly can eat whatever is sold in the meat market (μάκελλον), without concern for its origin, whether originally sacrificial meat or not (10:25-26).[19] Likewise, Paul encourages Christ-worshipers to eat with an "unbeliever" (ἄπιστος)[20] if they are so disposed without questioning the origin of the food set before them (10:27). However, if it becomes known that the meat in question is sacrificial meat, then the believer should not eat the meat. While these directions seem to conflict with those given in chapter 8 in that in some instances the meat may be allowed, the principle of *mar'it 'ayin* is still in practice. As long as it is not explicitly known or stated that the meat is sacrificial meat—in other words, as long as it appears to be nonsacrificial meat—it is fine to consume it. Once it is known outright, then the concept of *mar'it 'ayin* applies, and one should not partake. Paul notes that one should follow this for "the other's conscience," not "your own" (10:29 NRSV). As with the discussion of eating foods sacrificed to idols in chapter 8, what is at stake (and at steak) here is how the act of eating this food could affect the larger assembly. As Philip Tite has noted, "Paul is less concerned with *what* is eaten and more with the act of eating. In other words, Paul's concern is the impact of commensal relations upon the community."[21]

Paul places the blame for the fall of the "weak" community members solidly on the members who know better. The act of eating in 1 Corinthians 8 and 10—in this case, eating meat sacrificed in a ritual to an idol—becomes, just like the ritual meal, an act that defines the relationships within the community and among community members and other gods,[22] because of how the eater interprets and understands the act. This is important to bear in mind when attempting to rectify the apparently contradictory discussion earlier in the chapter (10:14-22), where Paul's concern is that the *assumption* that a person is participating in a meal with demons is equivalent to *actually* participating in a meal with demons, even though that person only intends to worship the God of Israel. Because the interpretation of meal events lies at the core of how shared meals create and reinforce community boundaries, Christ-worshipers who misinterpret what eating food sacrificed to idols means destabilize their relationships

---

[19] Laura Nasrallah, "1 Corinthians," in *The Letters and Legacy of Paul: Fortress Commentary on the Bible Study Edition*, ed. Margaret Aymer, Cynthia Briggs Kittredge, and David A. Sanchez (Minneapolis, MN: Augsburg Fortress, 2016), 427–71, here 446–7.

[20] T. J. Lang argues effectively that the ἄπιστος in 1 Corinthians is a developed category of people who have social and political ties to the Corinthian assembly but who are themselves not members of the assembly. T. J. Lang, "Trouble with Insiders: The Social Profile of the ἄπιστοι in Paul's Corinthian Correspondence," *JBL* 137 (2018): 981–1001.

[21] Philip L. Tite, "Roman Diet and Meat Consumption: Reassessing Elite Access to Meat in 1 Corinthians 8 and 10," *JSNT* 42 (2019): 185–222, here 210. Italics added.

[22] Gods who are, in effect, part of that community and perhaps seen as among its patrons.

with members of their community and instead forge relationships with the gods associated with those idols.

While Paul's discussions of dining behaviors in 1 Corinthians 8 and 10 can seem discordant when taken as a whole, what he is ultimately highlighting is that the commensality of the assembly has implications for the entire community, whether taken together for the Lord's Supper, eating at the home of one's "unbelieving" neighbor, or as individuals buying food at the meat market.[23] In 1 Corinthians 8, Paul encourages congregants to consider the potential outcomes if a member of weaker conscience were to see a member who possesses knowledge eat food sacrificed to idols. In chapter 10, Paul returns to the question of eating food potentially sacrificed to idols, whether purchased from the market or provided as part of a meal with an unbelieving neighbor. In each of these situations, Paul is focused on how commensality is affected by the appearance of improper eating behavior. The concern is not the eating of sacrificial meat per se but the disruption to the social cohesion of the community and its relationship with God through Christ.

Revelation

The Book of Revelation,[24] too, shows how its concern for the appearance of right meal practice is crucial for creating and maintaining strong community relationships as well as for avoiding alignment with the wrong cosmic forces.[25] Revelation couches its discussion of correct performance in the language of biblical Israelite idolatry. Especially of note are the letters to the seven assemblies in Revelation 2–3 that condemn those assemblies that tolerate "eating food sacrificed to idols." Those communities are friendly with the wrong sort of dining companions, according to Revelation. Using language of "love" and "hate" (e.g., Rev 2:4, 6), the text indicates just how important maintaining the right sorts of friendships is and how wine-drinking allows the wrong sort of guest into the party. Jesus, writing to the messenger of the assembly in Laodicea, announces to the community, "Listen! I am standing at the door, knocking; if you hear my voice and open the door, I will come in to you and eat with you, and you with me" (3:20 NRSV). Those who do right by John dine with Jesus; those who do not might be said to dine with Satan. The letters clearly associate wrong meal practice with immorality and idolatry and use commensality to speak about the kind of relationships necessary for righteousness. For John, consuming sacrificial food breaks down the community partition that distinguishes Jew from worshiper of the empire.

---

[23] Tite, "Roman Diet," 213.
[24] For a discussion of the ongoing debate about the dating of Revelation, see Emanuel, *Humor*, 9–10; Brian Blount, *Revelation: A Commentary* (Louisville, KY: Westminster John Knox, 2009), 8; and Elisabeth Schüssler Fiorenza, *The Book of Revelation: Justice and Judgment* (Minneapolis, MN: Fortress, 1998), 20. For a discussion of the text's Jewishness vis-à-vis nascent Christianity, see Emanuel, *Humor*, 26–35.
[25] Portions of the Revelation section of this essay were originally published by Meredith J. C. Warren as "The Cup of God's Wrath: Libation and Early Christian Meal Practice in Revelation," *Religions* 9, 413 (2018): 1–13.

For Paul, the appearance of right meal practice depends on context: what is known about the origins of the meat and what effect might a community member who possesses knowledge have on a weak-of-conscience member. Revelation presents a characteristically dualistic approach to partaking of comestibles associated with "pagan" ritual. As noted above,[26] for Paul, participating in the consumption of sacrificial food may lead to consorting with demons (e.g., 1 Cor 8:5; 10:20-22), but Paul's view of the risks of inappropriate dining is more nuanced than John's. Where Paul seems to differentiate between Satan and the crowds of other divine beings roaming the ancient Mediterranean,[27] John has his sights set on connecting Rome with Satanic power. Paul suggests that something like later rabbinic discussions of *mar'it a'yin* are a way to understand the problems of eating sacrificed meat. In many cases, for Paul, there is a way to eat such meat neutrally, in a "don't ask, don't tell" kind of way.[28] For Revelation, however, even private, in-group consumption of ritually associated items, in this case wine, risks inviting Satan to dine among the group: the appearance of drinking wine *is* the participation in the ritual.

While Revelation's epistolary section is vague about what practices are frowned upon, there are clues in the rest of the text to suggest that it is wine in particular that the author condemns. Wine is closely associated with libation and with the emperor cult.[29] Wine was certainly not a neutral beverage in Asia Minor, perhaps because of this association between wine and empire for early communities that might have made up Revelation's earliest hearers. We know that meals were one way that groups created relationships and also established boundaries against deviant groups, and wine was a significant means of distinguishing friend from foe. So it is not surprising that we have evidence of communities in Asia Minor who were careful not to include wine at their eucharistic meals, including at Smyrna.[30]

In the *Martyrdom of Pionius* 3.1, in the context of being asked to make "pagan" sacrifices in the city of Smyrna, Pionius takes bread and water (rather than wine) and offers the eucharist to his companions. The text does not remark on the choice of liquid. Laodicean evidence also suggests some groups avoided using wine in their meals: in an inscription Laodicean Christ-worshipers refer disparagingly to "wine-drinkers" (οἰνοπόται), other Christ-worshiping groups whose wine use the Laodiceans disagreed with.[31] In this context, the disagreements in the letters to the assemblies may more readily refer to wine use as specifically inappropriate, rather than sacrificial foods generally. John identifies especially the Nicolaitans.[32] While the heavily coded fictional

---

[26] See n. 13.
[27] See Fredriksen, "Philo," 37–8.
[28] Fredriksen, "Judaizing the Nations," 237.
[29] Warren, "The Cup of God's Wrath," 6, 9–10.
[30] Andrew McGowan, *Ascetic Eucharists: Food and Drink in Early Christian Ritual Meals* (Oxford: Clarendon, 1999), 164–5.
[31] McGowan, *Ascetic Eucharists*, 215; see Paul Lebeau, *Le Vin Nouveau du Royaume: Étude Exégétique et Patristique sur la Parole Eschatologique de Jésus à la Céne* (Paris: Desclée de Brouwer, 1966), 147, n. 6, who records the inscription. McGowan briefly posits a connection between Revelation and the Asian tendency to ascetic Eucharists (*Ascetic Eucharists*, 237).
[32] Irenaeus is of little help in narrowing down the characteristics of the Nicolaitans, since he gathers his information from Revelation as well; Irenaeus, *Haer.* 1.26.33. See also Kenneth A. Fox, "The Nicolaitans, Nicolaus, and the Early Church," *SR* 23 (1994): 485–96.

epistle mentions food from sacrifices, the Asian context suggests that wine use is the real target of the seer's ire. He identifies allies among the Ephesians (2:6), whom he praises for also being against the Nicolaitans, but the Pergamian community appears divided. Some side with "the teaching of Balaam, who taught Balak to put a stumbling block before the people of Israel, so that they would eat food sacrificed to idols and practice fornication" (Rev 2:14 NRSV). Balaam appears in Num 24; 25:1–6; and 31:16, where there is clear reference to eating food offered to other gods (25:2).[33] Sarah Emanuel discusses this reference as evidence of John's "halakhically oriented theology" in which the kind of behavior that is exhibited in 1 Corinthians 8 is unthinkable, since consuming sacrificial offerings to idols is equivalent to sexual intimacy, fornication, with those gods.[34]

It is curious, however, that Revelation does not explicitly point to meat or food sacrifice elsewhere; rather, wine use comes up again and again as associated with judgment and wrong behavior, indicative of Roman corruption. Perhaps, then, John uses the Balaam reference to criticize the Pergamians for some of them finding the use of wine acceptable. Finally, and perhaps most vividly, Thyatira is implicated in John's venom against those whose practices differ from his ideals. There, a figure called Jezebel "is teaching and beguiling my servants to practice immorality and to eat food sacrificed to idols" (2:20).[35] In 1 and 2 Kings, where the biblical Jezebel appears, there is no explicit mention of eating food sacrificed to other gods. This suggests that John does use "eating food sacrificed to idols" metonymically to stand in for some other practice he finds abhorrent. It alludes to wrong religious practice generally rather than food or eating specifically. Thus, the struggle within communities mentioned in Revelation may not be one of *eating* at non-Christ-worshiping ritual events but of an internal debate about *drinking* within their *own* meals.

This debate resides in the relationships forged by dining and drinking. Wine is dangerous because it strengthens friendly ties between the drinker and Babylon, even if that is not the intention of the drinker. Just as in Paul's epistles, although with less nuance, what matters is the appearance of the act. In the vision portion of the text, John uses wine explicitly to point to its connection to the empire. This confirms that the recipients of John's letters may be tolerating wine at their meals, and in doing so are inviting not Jesus but Satan to dine with them. Revelation repurposes libation imagery to stand in for what its author perceives as wrong community practice.

Despite the apparent importance of wine in many other early Christ-worshipers' ritual practice and meal practice, libation bowls (φιάλαι), pouring out wine (ἐκχέω), and wine itself are used to paint a vivid picture of what the author of Revelation finds abhorrent. This is in contrast, for example, to the use of wine and viticulture imagery

---

[33] For more on Balaam, see Emanuel, *Humor*, 99–103; Jan Willem van Henten, "Balaam in Revelation 2:14" in *The Prestige of the Pagan Prophet Balaam in Judaism, Early Christianity and Islam*, ed. George H. van Kooten and Jacques van Ruiten (Leiden: Brill, 2008), 247–63.

[34] Emanuel, *Humor*, 22.

[35] Emanuel, *Humor*, 104–18; in that discussion, Emanuel suggests that Jezebel's description of a woman may be just one more insult the Seer heaps upon his enemy and does not denote a gender for a historical Jezebel at all. For the biblical Jezebel, see 1 Kings 16:31; 18:4-19; 19:1, 2; 21:5-25; 2 Kings 9.

in 2 Baruch 29, where plentiful grape harvest results in unfathomable bounty in wine production as part of the coming joy of the messianic age. In Revelation, however, each instance where wine, cups, or pouring out occurs in the text points to the wrath of God against those who have worshiped incorrectly, rather than denoting community celebration.[36]

While libations would have persisted at the temple in Jerusalem until its destruction in 70 CE,[37] for John's communities, a more prominent example of libations would be those offered at private meals and banquets or during the public imperial worship.[38] For John, the appearance of drinking wine is enough to link the consumer to the imperial cult. Revelation's concern with libation may then reflect concerns about private behavior among members of his communities rather than with their participation at public festivals. John's concerns are intimate, at the scale of households and their relationships to one another, not large scale.

The libation bowl plagues of chapter 16, for example, represent a concentrated and intentional example of this pervasive allusion to cult with which Revelation both critiques and subverts normative ritual behavior in its struggle to articulate what right worship entails for John's community of Christ worshipers. True worship reveres the Lamb and the one who truly sits on the imperial throne (Rev 4:9-10; 22:3-4). The ubiquity of libation, in particular in emperor worship, allows John to subvert a familiar ritual and turn it into a symbol associated with violence and death, rather than with appropriate commensality.[39] The choice is to fraternize either with Babylon through the use of wine or with God who rejects wine in associating it with abomination. Even if communal diners are careful to avoid direct worship of Rome, for John, the appearance of taking a wine cup in one's hand is equivalent to the worship of the Beast.

---

[36] Revelation uses music for this purpose.

[37] There is no convincing evidence that worship at the Jerusalem temple declined in the lead up to that event (see Maria-Zoe Petropoulou, *Animal Sacrifice in Ancient Greek Religion, Judaism, and Christianity, 100 BC to AD 200* [Oxford: Oxford University Press, 2008], 127–8). Philo indicates that worship at the temple during festive times created new friendships through the "reciprocity of feeling" engendered by "sacrifices and libations" (θυσιῶν καὶ σπονδῶν). See Philo, *Spec. Laws* 69–70. Multiple sources from Jewish antiquity confirm the continued practice of pouring out wine offerings: Josephus, *Ant.* 3.9.4 refers to libations of wine being poured out around the altar; 11QT 21.9-10 (Yadin, *Temple Scroll* 2.95) associates pouring out drink offerings on the altar with rejoicing; Jubilees 2:68-69 describes Noah's wine offering; and later, m. Sukkah includes the wine and water offering at Sukkot.

[38] Price's discussion of the cultic worship of the emperors notes that libations were a common element in this kind of sacrifice but that in public festivals incense and animal sacrifice were more prevalent; Simon Price, *Rituals and Power: The Roman Imperial Cult in Asia Minor* (Cambridge: Cambridge University Press, 1984), 208–9. Revelation also alludes to the imperial cult, with its call to "ecumenical" or worldwide worship of the beast—that is, Babylon, that is, Rome (13:3). See also Jörg Frey, "The Relevance of the Roman Imperial Cult for the Book of Revelation: Exegetical and Hermeneutical Reflections on the Relation between the Seven Letters and the Visionary Main Part of the Book," in *The New Testament and Early Christian Literature in Greco-Roman Context: Studies in Honor of David E. Aune*, ed. John Fotopoulos, NovTSup 122 (Leiden: Brill, 2006), 224–50, here 238–9.

[39] See Warren, "Cup of God's Wrath." For a discussion of the wine imagery in Isaiah, see Rebekah Welton, "Yahweh the Wrathful Vintner: Blood and Wine-Making Metaphors in Isaiah 49.26a and 63.6," *Journal for Interdisciplinary Biblical Studies* 4 (2022): 19–41.

Conclusion

The way that meals create and maintain bonds within communities and individuals plays a role in how drinking and eating are understood in Paul and in Revelation. Each element of the meal has deep symbolic importance to insiders and outsiders; even, or perhaps especially, the appearance of the meal and its elements has real significance. The meaning behind certain foods and drinks, like meat sacrificed to other deities or the close association of wine with both libation to the imperial cult and the wrath of God, determines the relationships forged when those sharing a table break bread or raise a glass. Will they be among insiders, strengthening the community and its relationship with God, or will the relationship be with dangerous outsiders, such as Babylon or idols? It is the appearance of these elements of the meal, even more than their substance, that is crucial in these first-century discussions of meal practice in Asia Minor.

Disagreements within and among communities potentially destabilize the boundaries between group insiders and group outsiders; friendship with the wrong group has significant, eternal consequences. That is why both Paul and John are so concerned to reaffirm the boundaries they have established and to remind their audiences about the imbued meaning of these important symbols and symbolic actions. Both John of Patmos and Paul are concerned with the appearance of meal-related behaviors. Where Paul errs on the side of caution, recommending that community members refrain from doing what is permitted by avoiding foods offered to idols, Revelation presents the issue with no nuance at all: the appearance of participating in the worship of Rome *is* participating in the worship of Rome. While social pressure from friends or neighbors not part of the believer's community might not present as much of a problem for a Corinthian, for one of John's assemblies, dining with outsiders would be fraught. Social isolation would surely result from such an extreme view of dining practice.

That meals can create and solidify bonds of friendship is clear to us, too. It is with fond memories that we remember eating each meal together with Adele in Camaldoli, Italy, at the "John the Jew" Enoch Seminar in June 2016. Initially Shayna sat with Adele because of their mutual dietary restrictions, with Meredith joining out of friendship. Our table fellowship strengthened the bonds of our friendship and of collegiality, while Adele served—and continues to serve—as a mentor and model for us both.

12

Socializing with the Impure (or Not): Interactions and Impurity in Late Second Temple Judaism

Cecilia Wassén

Introduction

How impurity affected social interaction between Jews in late Second Temple Judaism is a difficult and highly debated question but a critical question for the discussion of friendships and relationships in that period.[1] The diversity of opinions on this matter can be illustrated by two different comments on Mark 5:24-43, the story about the woman with a hemorrhage—a *zavah* (Lev 15:19-30)—who is healed by Jesus when she touches him. In *The Women's Bible Commentary*, Elizabeth Struthers Malbon claims that she had been "isolated" from her community due to her illness.[2] In contrast, a note by Lawrence M. Wills in *The Jewish Annotated New Testament* explains, "whether such ritual impurity—an issue not mentioned in the text—would have mattered in a local village, where access to the Temple is not an issue, is not clear."[3] I will discuss these very different views about whether and in what ways different categories of ritually impure people would typically be restricted in their interaction with others. I will also examine if purity mattered far from the sanctuary as Wills doubts, something also important for questions of social interaction.

---

[1] I'm delighted to contribute to a volume in honor of my dear friend and former professor, Adele Reinhartz, from whom I learned immensely and by whom I have been greatly inspired.

[2] Elizabeth Struthers Malbon, "Gospel of Mark," in *The Women's Bible Commentary: Revised and Expanded Edition*, ed. Carol A. Newsom, Sharon H. Ringe, and Jacqueline E. Lapsey (London: SPCK, 2012), 478–92, here 483.

[3] Lawrence M. Wills, "The Gospel according to Mark," in *Jewish Annotated New Testament*, ed. Amy-Jill Levine and Marc Zvi Brettler, 2nd ed. (New York: Oxford University Press, 2017), 67–106, here 80. For a detailed analysis, see Susan Haber, *They Shall Purify Themselves: Essays on Purity in Early Judaism*, ed. Adele Reinhartz (Atlanta, GA: SBL Press, 2008), 125–41.

Concerns about Impurity in the Land

The opinion that purity primarily concerned the sacred sphere, as expressed by Wills, is understandable given the importance of purity in relation to the temple and its personnel, the priests, and the Levites. Nevertheless, there is reason to doubt that purity was ever limited to items, persons, or food connected to the sanctuary. On a basic level, categories of impurity stem from ancient taboos concerning bodily fluids, corpses, skin diseases, and eating certain animals. Many scholars have suggested different symbolic, structuralist, or ideological reasons behind conceptions of impurity. The work of Jacob Milgrom, who linked impurity to notions of death, and Mary Douglas, who described uncleanness as "matter out of place," have been particularly influential.[4] In contrast, Thomas Kazen highlights the cross-cultural phenomenon of categorizing certain things as impure and offers a convincing explanation based on evolutionary biology and psychology that traces the underlying reasons to the primary emotion of disgust.[5] Evidently, customs surrounding notions of purity and impurity have evolved throughout history and left imprints on biblical legislation in different contexts.

If the general background to conceptions of impurity is found in basic human emotions, then it also makes sense that purity mattered anywhere. Mark, for one, claims that the Pharisees and Jews in general were careful to wash their hands before meals, as well as washing products from the market and various vessels (Mark 7:3-4). Clearly, these washings are made for ritual purification. John Poirier makes a strong case for the view that purity practices were deeply ingrained in the general Israelite and Jewish society and never restricted to the sacred sphere.[6] He notes that the key sections on purity laws in Leviticus infrequently refer to the tabernacle (e.g., Lev 7:19-21; 15:31; 16:16; but see Lev 22:1-16, which belongs to the Holiness Code).[7] Certainly, the requirement to purify after sexual intercourse (Lev 15:18) and burial (Num 19) imply that purity mattered everywhere. In addition, Poirier points to purity practices in the diaspora (e.g., Tobit 2:9; Philo, *Spec. Laws* 3.206) as well as to archaeological evidence indicating the spread of stone vessels and stepped pools in both Judea and Galilee.[8] While pushing for a broad impact of purity in society in general, Poirier endorses a rather limited explanation for the reasons for practicing purity like the majority of biblical scholars. Accordingly, he claims that "purity is connected to holiness, which is enjoined upon all of Israel."[9] Certainly, purity practices are part of a desire to attain or maintain holiness, as we see, for example, in the sectarian literature from the Dead Sea

---

[4] Jacob Milgrom, *Leviticus 1-16: A New Translation with Introduction and Commentary*, AB 3 (New York: Doubleday, 1991), 766-8, 1000-4; Mary Douglas, *Purity and Danger: An Analysis of Concepts of Pollution and Taboo* (London, Routledge, 1966), 41.
[5] Thomas Kazen, "Evolution, Emotion and Exegesis: Disgust and Empathy in Biblical Texts on Moral and Ritual Issues," in *Linnaeus and Homo Religiosus: Biological Roots of Religious Awareness and Human Identity*, ed. Carl R. Bråkenhielm (Uppsala: Acta Universitatis Upsaliensis, 2009), 191-218.
[6] John C. Poirier, "Purity beyond the Temple in the Second Temple Era," *JBL* 122 (2003): 247-65.
[7] Poirier, "Purity beyond the Temple," 253.
[8] See also Thomas Kazen, "Purity as Popular Practice: Erasing the Anachronistic Divide between Household and Cult," in Thomas Kazen, *Impurity and Purification in Early Judaism and the Jesus Tradition*, RBS 98 (Atlanta, GA: SBL Press, 2021), 277-302.
[9] Poirier, "Purity beyond the Temple," 255.

Scrolls, and this may well have been one reason for people in general to practice purity.[10] Still, we should not assume that this was always the case. People may have purified because they preferred to be pure, as E. P. Sanders has argued, or simply because they followed customs without reflecting much on underlying reasons.[11] I would argue that whether or not purity is linked to holiness depends on the context. Kazen explains the development behind biblical purity laws well: "They ... reflect customary everyday behavior, codified as socioreligious law, interpreted theologically as holiness, and therefore particularly applicable in relation to the sanctuary."[12]

The widespread use of stone vessels and stepped pools are usually taken as strong evidence for a general concern about purity. Nevertheless, there is no clear textual evidence that vessels made out of stone would have been impervious to impurity.[13] I will therefore not take stone vessels into account for evaluating the interest in purity. When it comes to stepped pools, we are on somewhat firmer ground. Over 850 stepped pools, mostly built in the first century BCE until early second century CE, have been discovered in Jewish towns and villages in Judea and Galilee, with fewer than seventy such pools in Galilee.[14] Their large concentration near the Jerusalem temple demonstrates ritual purification use. Presence close to wine and oil installations as well as cemeteries similarly points to their use in ritual washing.[15] I have elsewhere argued that people purified in different ways and that the practice of *immersing* in water developed as the standard form of purification in early Roman time, likely influenced by the Roman bathing practices.[16] Importantly, the general term for "washing" רחץ has a wide range of meaning in the Hebrew Bible: washing, bathing, dousing with water, and rinsing off. In other words, we should not assume that all people necessarily immersed when they purified themselves. Instead, as we will see later, there were

---

[10] That stringent purity rituals are connected to a drive for holiness is evident in metaphors of the community as a sanctuary; see Cecilia Wassén, "Do You Have to Be Pure in a Metaphorical Temple? Sanctuary Metaphors and Construction of Sacred Space in the Dead Sea Scrolls and Paul's Letters," in *Purity, Holiness, and Identity in Judaism and Christianity: Essays in Memory of Susan Haber*, ed. Carl S. Ehrlich, Anders Runesson, and Eileen Schuller, WUNT 305 (Tübingen: Mohr Siebeck, 2013), 55–86.

[11] E. P. Sanders, *Jewish Law from Jesus to the Mishnah: Five Studies* (Philadelphia, PA: Trinity Press international, 1990), 218.

[12] Kazen, *Impurity and Purification in Early Judaism*, 291.

[13] See Stuart S. Miller, *At the Intersection of Texts and Material Finds: Stepped Pools, Stone Vessels, and Ritual Purity among the Jews of Roman Galilee* (Göttingen: Vandenhoeck & Ruprecht, 2015), 153–83; Cecilia Wassén, "The Connection between Purity Practices and the Jerusalem Temple (the House of God) around the Turn of the Area," in *La Maison de Dieu / Das Haus Gottes*, ed. Christian Grappe, WUNT 471 (Tübingen: Mohr Siebeck, 2021), 167–90.

[14] Yonatan Adler, "Religion, Judaism: Purity in the Roman Period," in *The Oxford Encyclopedia of the Bible and Archaeology*, ed. Daniel M. Master (Oxford: Oxford University Press, 2013), 240–9.

[15] Yonatan Adler, "Second Temple Period Ritual Baths Adjacent to Agricultural Installations: The Archaeological Evidence in Light of the Halakhic Sources," *JJS* 59 (2008): 62–72; Mordechai Viam, "Yodefat—Jotapata," in *The Archaeological Record from Cities, Towns, and Villages*, vol. 2 of *Galilee in the Late Second Temple and Mishnaic Periods*, ed. David A. Fiensy and James Riley Strange (Minneapolis, MN: Fortress, 2015), 109–26, here 122; Rick Bonnie, "Pure Stale Water: Experiencing Jewish Purification Rituals in Early Roman Palestine," in *The Routledge Handbook of the Senses in the Ancient Near East*, ed. Kiersten Neumann and Allison Thomason (London: Routledge, 2022), 234–53.

[16] Cecilia Wassén, "Stepped Pools and Stone Vessels: Rethinking Jewish Purity Practices in Palestine," *BAR* 45 (2019): 53–8.

various practices of purification. Consequently, the spread of stepped pools demonstrates the emerging practice of *immersing* when purifying, not a heightened concern about ritual purity in general, contrary to the claims by Yonatan Adler, among others.[17] Still, stepped pools in Galilee indicate that people practiced ritual purification far from the sanctuary. Turning back to the different opinions about the impure woman touching Jesus, we can conclude that people in both Galilee and Jerusalem would have cared about purity.

Avoidance of Impurity

Let us then turn to the question of limitations of social interactions for impure people like the woman in Mark 5:24-34. The key question is whether people in general actively avoided incurring impurity. The most common form of impurities would have been sexual intercourse and menstruation, for which Leviticus provides systematic regulations. According to Lev 15:18, a couple should wash themselves after having sex, but they would still be unclean until the evening. The same prescription applies to the semen emitter, indicating that it is the semen that renders a couple impure. A menstruating woman is impure for seven days and she transmits impurity to everything she sits or lies upon. People touching her or furniture she has defiled will also be unclean. Hence, menstruation is a more severe form of impurity than contact with semen, since it easily transmits impurity to others. A woman having given birth to a child transmits impurity in the same way as a menstruant for varying durations depending on the sex of the baby (Lev 12:2-5). These impurities were unavoidable, but people would have known how to deal with them. It is safe to say that people did not avoid having sex or having children because it rendered them impure; nevertheless, priests would have been careful to time sexual intimacy in order to be ritually pure when serving in the temple and eating sacred food.

Another common cause of impurity is corpse impurity. According to Numbers 19, touching a dead person or entering the tent where there is a corpse renders a person impure for seven days. In order to purify, one should be sprinkled with purification water that contains ashes of the red heifer on the third and seventh day, as well as washing oneself and one's clothes on the seventh day. Priests are prohibited from incurring corpse impurity except when close relatives have died (Lev 21:1-4), which implies that other people would commonly be defiled when friends and distant relatives passed away. The parable in Luke 10:29-37 about the Good Samaritan also presumes that priests and Levites would try to avoid incurring corpse impurity. Taking care of dead relatives was of course customary, as it is in all societies. That common people did incur impurity by visiting grieving families and taking part in mourning

---

[17] Yonatan Adler, "Tosefta Shabbat 1:14—'Come and See the Extent to Which Purity Had Spread': An Archaeological Perspective on the Historical Background to a Late Tannaitic Passage," in *Talmuda De-Eretz Israel: Archaeology and the Rabbis in Late Antique Palestine*, ed. Steven Fine and Aaron Koller, vol. 73 of *Studia Judaica; Forschungen Zur Wissenschaft Des Judentums*, ed. Günter Stemberger et al. (Berlin: de Gruyter, 2014), 63–82.

rituals and funerals is attested by Mark 5:38-41, where the author takes for granted that the whole house would be full of people from the village when the little girl had died.[18] In this case they would have contracted impurity by standing under one roof (Num 19:14). Josephus paints a similar picture of people joining a funeral procession when it passed by (*Ag. Ap.* 2.205). The wording in Num 19:20 emphasizes the importance of purification after contact with a corpse: "Any who are unclean but do not purify themselves, those persons shall be cut off from the assembly, for they have defiled the sanctuary of the Lord." In these cases, impurity was a regular part of ordinary life and—if Torah laws were followed—so was purification. Other kinds of impurities were less frequent.

The purity laws concerning people suffering from pathological discharges (the *zav* and *zavah*; Lev 15:19-30), as well as for a woman who has given birth (Lev 12), are similar to those of a menstruant concerning transmission of impurity. But after childbirth, a woman is not to "touch any holy thing, or come into the sanctuary, until the days of her purification are completed" (Lev 12:4-5).[19] The *zav* transmits impurity by touch unless he has washed his hands (Lev 15:11), presumably after urinating. Furthermore, the purification in these cases ends with sacrifices (Lev 12:6-8; 15:14-15, 29-30). In quite neutral terms the Torah explains how impurity is transmitted and prescribes how to perform purifications. Yet, the implied message is to avoid impurity if possible. This is made explicit in the general command at the end of the section on purity laws: "Thus you shall keep the people of Israel separate from their uncleanness, so that they do not die in their uncleanness by defiling my tabernacle that is in their midst" (Lev 15:31). How exactly they would defile the sanctuary is not evident, but purifications are undoubtedly essential.

Isolation of the Impure

To what extent were impure people isolated? The texts discussed earlier do not prescribe quarantine for any of them. On the contrary, the purity laws in Leviticus 15 assume that the ritually impure people are around people at home, since other people can contract impurity by sitting on chairs and so on. People suffering from skin disease ("lepers"[20]), on the other hand, should be expelled according to Lev 13:46: "he shall live alone; his dwelling shall be outside the camp." In contrast, Num 5:1-3 also requires those impure from corpse impurity and discharges to stay outside of the camp. In comparison, the Temple Scroll, which in general imposes more stringent purity regulations than the Torah, differentiates between the purity levels of the temple city (Jerusalem) and regular cities. Accordingly, lepers, dischargers, menstruants, and women after childbirth are to stay in special places outside of ordinary cities (11QT

---

[18] Cecilia Wassén, "The Jewishness of Jesus and Ritual Purity," *SIDA* 27 (2016): 11–36.
[19] All translations of biblical texts are from the NRSV.
[20] See Milgrom, *Leviticus 1–16*, 775, 816–20. The exact nature of the skin disease is unknown. Milgrom states unequivocally with reference to the condition, "One thing, however, is certain; it is not leprosy (Hansen's disease)" (816). I will still refer to this group as "lepers" for lack of a better term.

XLVIII, 14-17) and the same applies to lepers, dischargers, and "men who have had a (nocturnal) emission" (XLVI, 16-18) in the temple city. Evidently, no married couples or young women are assumed to live in the holy city (cf. XLV, 11-12). Overall, these regulations appear quite utopian. Nevertheless, when Josephus summarizes the laws of Moses in *Ant.* 3.261-2, he gives the impression that at least two categories of impure people were banned from Jerusalem:

> He [Moses] expelled (ἀπήλασε) from the city both those whose bodies were attacked by leprosy and those with discharge (τοὺς περὶ τὴν γονὴν ῥεομένους). He segregated (μετέστησε) until the seventh day women whose secretion occurs for them in accordance with nature, after which he permitted them, as already pure, to associate with the community. Similarly, it is prescribed by law for those who have buried the dead to associate with the community after as many days.[21]

Josephus clearly distinguished the degree of separation between lepers and dischargers (a *zav* and *zavah*) who are expelled from that of menstruants and the corpse impure who are restricted somehow.[22] To what extent this was actually practiced is hard to tell. According to Sanders, the regulations for menstruants and the corpse impure mainly reflect the praxis of priestly aristocrats of Josephus's kind. He disagrees with those such as Gedalyahu Alon who, referring to m. Niddah 7:4, claim that menstruants had separate houses. He also dismisses Jacob Neusner's argument that people made special arrangements within the household, particularly for changing beds and chairs. Instead, Sanders points to the impracticality and cost involved in having separate lodging or extra furniture for impure women and the inability of a small household to do without women's work during their periods.[23] I would add that it would have been extremely difficult to take care of the (often numerous) children in a household without the mother present. In addition to general laws in the Mishnah that presume that menstruants live at home, Sanders points to Josephus's description of the temple cult: "Persons afflicted with gonorrhea [dischargers] or leprosy were excluded from the city altogether; the temple was closed to women during their menstruation" (*J. W.* 5.227 [Thackeray, LCL]).[24] This description implies that menstruating women were able to move around in the city in contrast to the other two categories. Since Josephus is not referring to the Mosaic laws in this context, it may be that his description is closer to actual practice than in *Ant.* 3.261.[25] Kazen, on the other hand, argues that seclusion for menstruating women is a reasonable reconstruction. He points out that women did not menstruate as frequently as today (due to childbirth and nursing) and that households would typically include many women who could help out with the women's jobs. More important for his argument is his claim that other groups

---

[21] Translation based on Steve Mason and Louis H. Feldman, eds., *Judean Antiquities 1-4*, Flavius Josephus: Translation and Commentary 3 (Leiden: Brill, 2000).
[22] Sanders, *Jewish Law from Jesus to the Mishnah*, 157.
[23] Sanders, *Jewish Law from Jesus to the Mishnah*, 155-62; 351, n. 20.
[24] Similar instructions appear in m. Kelim 1:7-8.
[25] Sanders, *Jewish Law from Jesus to the Mishnah*, 158.

in society did practice separation and seclusion of menstruants for which he points to "the Qumranites, Samaritans, Karaites, and Falashas."[26] He states, "The rabbinic evidence of m. Nid. 7:4, suggesting the existence of a special place for seclusion, should not be too easily disregarded, especially in view of evidence from Num 5 and from the Dead Sea texts."[27] Nevertheless, the textual evidence for the complete isolation of menstruating women is quite slim. Apart from the late date and the uncertain meaning of the passage in the Mishnah, Leviticus 15 takes for granted that those impure from discharge, menstruation, and semen emission were around other people at home. Josephus implies that menstruating women were able to move around in Jerusalem but were not to enter the sanctuary. It is questionable whether even the Qumran sectarians lived according to the stringent regulations concerning expulsion of the impure in the Temple Scroll, a document likely not composed within the sect. The sectarian purity regulations in 4QTohorot A elicit a different impression. Here the menstruant is admonished not to mingle with pure individuals: "She shall with all her effort not mingle (with others) during her seven days so as not to contaminate the ca[m]ps of the sanct[ities of] Israel" (4Q274 1 l. 5-6 [Allegro]). The passage gives the impression that her mingling should be circumspect but not that she is isolated.

We should not lose sight of the basic fear of vaginal blood and the actual flux of male dischargers that underlies the regulations concerning furniture and riding animals in Leviticus. It was not that easy to contain vaginal blood in a premodern society. The reason for why only menstruating women and not corpse-impure people, for example, were prohibited from entering the outer court was likely because of the fear of blood getting on the ground that people in turn could step on, thus unknowingly becoming impure before proceeding into the holy area (see m. Nid. 7:4, 8).

On the basis of these very limited clues, I think it is reasonable that many people would make arrangements within the households to limit the spread of impurity, for example, by having special seats and bedding for women who were menstruating. Possibly these women would not have participated in common meals, since transmission of impurity at meals was a particular concern, as evidenced in the sectarian literature from Qumran (e.g., 4QTohorot A [4Q274] and 1QS VI, 13–VII, 25).[28] At the same time, of course, practices would vary between households. Priestly families, who frequently ate meals from offerings, would have been more careful than others.

When it comes to a *zav* and *zavah*, Josephus places them on the same level as lepers, that is, that they were not allowed in the city (*Ant.* 3.261; *J.W.* 5.227). While Mark does not comment on the impurity status of the *zavah* nor that she moved around in the crowd, he does emphasize her feelings of fear (7:33) that may point to remorse for touching Jesus's cloak given her impurity. Kazen argues that the *zavah* would have been the most vulnerable category of all dischargers since, in contrast to the *zav*, she could

---

[26] Kazen, *Impurity and Purification in Early Judaism*, 186.
[27] Kazen, *Impurity and Purification in Early Judaism*, 204.
[28] See Cecilia Wassén, "The (Im)Purity Levels of Communal Meals within the Qumran Movement," *JAJ* 7 (2016): 102–22.

not lessen the potency of contamination by washing hands (Lev 15:11). He concludes that "she was certainly subject to restrictions, in many instances probably isolated."[29] At the same time, we should note that Josephus does not distinguish between men and women in this regard but treats them as the same category. Whereas I find it reasonable to assume that female chronic dischargers would have been subject to restrictions in the households, I would not dismiss the possibility that a *zavah* could also wash her hands and thereby minimize the contagion. Susan Haber argues that the prescriptions for the *zav* in Lev 15 apply to all dischargers, which is quite plausible: "Since the more abbreviated law concerning the female is modeled on that of the male, this detail [i.e., rinsing hands] is assumed rather than repeated."[30] This conclusion fits well with the popularity of the practice of washing hands at this time, to which I will return later.

There is stronger evidence that lepers were indeed kept isolated. Lev 13:45-46 demands that a leper shows his or her status by physical appearance and by calling out "unclean, unclean" (cf. Num 5:1-4; 4QMMT B64-72). This stringency is understandable given the fear of contamination from the actual disease. There are no biblical laws concerning purifying from contact with the leper. In other words, they were not supposed to have physical contact with others. Luke's account of a group of lepers approaching Jesus indicates they would be staying together with each other rather than with their families as well as keeping at a distance from others (Luke 17:11-19).

As noted earlier, Josephus does not include the corpse impure among the categories of impure people expelled from the sacred city; instead, he compares their impurity status with that of menstruants who were secluded in some ways (*Ant.* 3.261). Conspicuously, not even the Temple Scroll demands that the corpse impure need to dwell outside of regular cities or the temple city. Several scholars have highlighted the common practice of first day ablutions for *purifying persons* (not people in their primary impurity, such as a *zavah*), attested in several documents from Qumran, including the Temple Scroll. In contrast to Numbers 19, whereby a corpse impure person should be sprinkled on the third and seventh day as well as washing themselves and their clothes on the seventh day, 11QT adds a first day of washing like the seventh (11QT XLIX, 16-21; L, 4-9, 13-16). This would decrease the level of impurity and mitigate the transference of impurity. Such a practice may explain why corpse impurity appears to be a less serious impurity than the others. Interestingly enough, the book of Tobit also describes how Tobit washes immediately after carrying and later burying a corpse (Tob 2:5, 9). Similarly, Jews washed themselves and their clothes immediately after contracting corpse impurity according to Philo (*Spec. Laws* 3.205-206).

The practice of washing hands prior to meals is also not attested in biblical law. Martin Goodman reminds us of how religious praxis functions on a fundamental level: "Religion is caught through imitation of parental customs, rather than taught, whether through writings or verbal instruction."[31] He highlights that both Josephus

---

[29] Thomas Kazen, *Issues of Impurity in Early Judaism*, ConBNT 45 (Winona Lake, IN: Eisenbrauns, 2010), 109–11.
[30] Haber, *They Shall Purify Themselves*, 128.
[31] Martin Goodman, "A Note on Josephus, the Pharisees and Ancestral Tradition," *JJS* 1 (1999): 17–20, here 18.

and Philo often describe Jewish traditions as ancestral customs without referring to the Torah (cf. Gal 1:14). Philo also clarifies the distinction in *Spec.Laws* 4.149-150 (Colson, LCL), explaining that "customs are unwritten laws, the decisions approved by men of old, not inscribed on monuments nor on leaves of paper." Josephus famously characterizes the Pharisees as a group who keep "regulations handed down by former generations and not recorded in the Laws of Moses" (*Ant.* 13.297-298 [Marcus, LCL]; cf. 13.408; 17.41). Accordingly, Goodman submits that the Pharisees had the support of the masses simply because they upheld common customs. Thereby, the Pharisees were the traditionalists, while the Sadducees (and similarly the Qumran sectarians) who rejected some common customs were more radical. Along similar lines, Adiel Schremer distinguishes between text-based and tradition-based observance and argues that the effort to establish authority of halakah in the texts, as we see among the Qumran sectarians, represented a shift from tradition to the book.[32]

From this perspective, the practice of handwashing to mitigate spread of impurity was not a new Pharisaic invention but a common, traditional practice. This explains why the Pharisees wonder why the disciples do not wash their hands (Mark 7:1-8). Washing hands is not required in sectarian laws from Qumran, which is logical in light of their emphasis on Torah studies. Handwashing, then, was a common way of dealing with impurities. We know of additional purity practices not recorded in the Torah. For example, some texts attest to washing before prayer from the early second century BCE forward (Jdt 12:6-10; Sib. Or. 3:591-593; 4:162-166; Let. Aris. 305-306; cf. *Ant.* 14.258; Acts 16:13). Mosaic laws reflect customs, but there is no reason to assume that the Torah laws include all the customs or that the laws were followed by the majority of Jews in every case. Indeed, sometimes the laws were written to correct popular practice.

Conclusion

We have seen that Jews cared about purity all over the land and not only in relation to the sancta. Thereby they also had different ways of dealing with impurity regardless of where they were living, as we see, for example, in the writings of Philo from Alexandria. It is impossible to know which precautions they actually took in order to limit the spread of impurity; evidence allows very general ideas. While people suffering from "leprosy" were isolated from others by different means, common impurities, such as corpse impurity, sexual intercourse, and semen emission, did not seem to have had much of an impact on everyday life. The praxis of a first-day washing, which appears to have been common, would have mitigated the spread of impurity and enabled the corpse impure to live as usual. Josephus indicates that menstruating women did in

---

[32] Adiel Schremer, "'[T]He[y] Did Not Read the Sealed Book'; Qumran Halakhic Revolution and the Emergence of Torah Study in the Second Temple Judaism," in *Historical Perspectives: From the Hasmoneans to Bar Kokhba in Light of the Dead Sea Scrolls. Proceedings of the Fourth International Symposium of the Orion Center for the Study of the Dead Sea Scrolls and Associated Literature, January 27-31, 1999*, ed. David M. Goodblatt, Avital Pinnick, and Daniel R. Schwartz, STDJ 37 (Leiden: Brill, 2001), 105-25.

fact move around in Jerusalem but were banned from the outer temple court. Possibly, many people would also wash after having sex, as Philo and his peers did. Mark 5 indicates that a *zavah* did move around other people, but that touching another person was likely unacceptable. Nevertheless, the widespread practice of handwashing may have helped all kinds of dischargers to be able to do their daily chores.

When it comes to accommodating the impure in the households, we can only offer qualified guesses. What we do know is that the practices would have differed between families and villages according to their particular traditions. It is reasonable to assume that dischargers, including menstruants, would commonly have had special seats and beddings and possibly did not partake of the common meals in an ordinary way. So whereas there would have been some restrictions in place, it is unlikely that they would have been isolated. This general reconstruction indicates that when discussing the nature of relationships within Second Temple Judaism, we acknowledge that people would have been very conscious of their purity status and out of respect for each other would have taken steps to contain that impurity. It also indicates that they would have created means by which that impurity did not unduly limit social interactions.

13

How to Be Better Neighbors: Rewriting the Conquest in Greek Terms

Albert I. Baumgarten

The Problem Posed by the Conquest

The conquest of Canaan and the extermination of the Canaanites were an opportunity for criticism by ancient enemies of the Jews.[1] For example, Lysimachus, a Greco-Egyptian writer whose date is unknown, but who probably lived in the second or first century BCE, asserted that Moses led the Israelites who were expelled from Egypt to Judea, where they maltreated the population and plundered and set fire to local temples. They built the city called Hierosyla, "destroyer of sacred things." This name was an expression of their sacrilegious propensities. Later, embarrassed by that disgraceful name, they called the city Hierosylyma (Jerusalem).[2]

In another version of this accusation, centuries later, the Byzantine historian Procopius (c. 500–570 CE) cited two pillars erected by the Phoenician exiles in North Africa, written in Phoenician letters and in the Phoenician language, which proclaimed, "We are the people who fled (here) before the thief Joshua, son of Nun." Alternately, the inscription on the pillars read, "We are the Canaanites who were pursued by the thief Joshua."[3]

It would be one thing to respond to these charges in terms of the common theology of the Near East, as Jephthah did to the King of Ammon, "It is for you to possess

---

[1] It is a happy circumstance, indicative of reaching a certain stage of life, to be writing an essay in honor of a student. Professor Adele Reinhartz came to McMaster, where I taught, in 1974. She was one of several outstanding students, who made my years at McMaster a memory I treasure. Her achievements since are at the highest level. The ties that bind us have remained over the years, even if I left Canada and now live in Israel. Adele Reinhartz and her family have been frequent visitors, and we have enjoyed staying in touch whenever possible.

[2] Menahem Stern, *Greek and Latin Authors on Jews and Judaism*, 3 vols. (Jerusalem: The Israel Academy of Sciences and Humanities, 1976–84), #158, 1:386. Following the lead of many scholars, Stern interpreted these remarks not as a response to the biblical past, but rather in the context of the indignation caused by the territorial expansion of the Hasmonean state during the time of Lysimachus.

[3] Hans Lewy, "Ein Rechtsstreit um den Boden Palästinas," *MGWJ* 77 (1933): 84–99, 172–80. This article was then translated into Hebrew in the collection of Lewy's works published after his untimely death; cf. Hans Lewy, *Studies in Jewish Hellenism* (Jerusalem: Bialik Institute, 1960), 60–78 [Hebrew]. My summary that follows and page references are based on the Hebrew version. Here: Lewy, *Studies*, 61.

whatever Chemosh your god gives you; and all that the Lord our God gave us as we advanced is ours" (Judg 11:24). Simon Maccabee offered a similar response but based on history, not theology. Simon was charged by Antiochus VII with occupying Joppa and Gazzara, making his house master of many places in the Seleucid Kingdom. Simon replied, "We have not occupied other people's land or taken other people's property, but only the inheritance of our ancestors, unjustly seized for a time by our enemies. We have grasped the opportunity and have claimed our patrimony" (1 Macc 15:33-34).[4]

But did Jews who lived in the Land of Israel during the first centuries CE— often in conflict with their non-Jewish neighbors—sense that the conquest posed a problem in relations with their neighbors, that it had a sting that needed to be removed?

As might be expected, the evidence is mixed. Ben Sira offered a portrait of Joshua that faithfully reflected the biblical account. He reveled in Joshua's military achievements and miraculous deeds:

> Joshua the son of Nun was a mighty warrior,
> who succeeded Moses in the prophetic office.
> He lived up to his name
> as a great liberator of the Lord's chosen people,
> able to take reprisals on the enemies who attacked them,
> and to put Israel in possession of their territory.
> How glorious he was when he raised his hand
> and brandished his sword against cities!
> Never before had a man made such a stand,
> for he was fighting the Lord's battles.
> Was it not through him that the sun stood still
> and made one day last as long as two?
> He called on the Most High, the Mighty One,
> when the enemy was pressing him on every side,
> and the great Lord answered his prayer
> with a violent storm of hail.
> He overwhelmed that nation in battle
> and crushed his assailants as they fled down the pass,
> to make the nations recognize his strength in arms
> and teach them that he fought under the very eyes of the Lord,
> for he followed the lead of the Mighty One. (Sir 46:1-6 NEB)

Josephus, by contrast, toned down accounts of slaughter in the Book of Joshua or insisted that these actions were necessary for national security. He had recourse to the accepted

---

[4] Versions of the theological or historical arguments just noted are remembered in contemporary Middle Eastern political life. I do not mean to draw any inferences from antiquity to the current discourse. My interest is in efforts that showed ancient Jewish sensitivity concerning the biblical record and that recognized the dilemma it created in relationship with neighbors, to be discussed more fully later. For a historical analysis of this passage, see Katell Berthelot, "Reclaiming the Land (1 Maccabees 15:28–36): Hasmonean Discourse between Biblical Tradition and Seleucid Rhetoric," *JBL* 133 (2014): 539–59.

formula in relating miracles that "everyone is welcome to his own opinion." He can find a natural explanation for some miracles, such as that God diminished the waters of the Jordan so that it was passable for Joshua and his army. When Joshua commanded the sun not to set at Gibeon, the Bible adds that there never was or will be a day like that in human experience. For Josephus, the prolonged day "surpassed the customary measure," no more or no less.[5]

Scholars debate just how immersed Ben Sira was in the culture of the Greco-Roman world, but there is less doubt concerning Josephus. At the risk of oversimplifying, Josephus suggested that Jews in the Land of Israel who participated in the larger cultural world were troubled by the conquest account, especially the extermination of the inhabitants by Joshua. What sort of neighbors could they be, even if only in their own minds, when their tradition consecrated a slaughter of the ancient locals? To paraphrase Erich Gruen on the issue of the conquest, how could Jews, thoroughly at home in the Greco-Roman world, reassert the character of their heritage within it?[6] This was their predicament in dealing with the biblical account of the conquest of Canaan.

Following Gruen's suggestion, I want to show that ancient Jews in the Land of Israel who were immersed in the Greco-Roman world felt that the conquest narratives had a sting in relations with neighbors that they wanted to remove. Josephus was not alone. However, significantly, the tools these Jews utilized to remove that sting were based on arguments derived from the Greco-Roman world. How convincing were these arguments for non-Jews on the other side? Did their formulation in Greco-Roman terms make them more effective? Did this sort of narrative help promote friendship or, if not, at best modulate gentile accusation? Did it make Jews seem less offensive? Perhaps the most we can say is that the texts to be discussed later show that a problem in relations with neighbors was recognized by Jews in the Land of Israel, and the solutions proposed were meaningful for them as participants in the larger culture. As suggested by Katell Berthelot, the explanations in these texts may have made ancient Jews feel that they were better neighbors, but did they have any real impact on actual non-Jewish neighbors?[7] In my view, it is very likely that the sources to be analyzed in this essay were "preaching to the converted."

Hans Lewy: The Trial before Alexander

Hans (Yohanan) Lewy,[8] Menahem Kister,[9] and Katell Berthelot[10] have each devoted studies to the relevant sources. Lewy was the pioneer in the analysis of this material

---

[5] Louis H. Feldman, "Josephus's Portrait of Joshua," *HTR* 82 (1989): 351–76.
[6] Erich S. Gruen, *Heritage and Hellenism: The Reinvention of Jewish Tradition*, HCS 30 (Berkeley: University of California Press, 1998), xiv.
[7] Katell Berthelot, "The Canaanites Who 'Trusted in God': An Original Interpretation of the Fate of the Canaanites in Rabbinic Literature," *JJS* 62 (2011): 233–61, here 253.
[8] See n. 3.
[9] Menahem Kister, "The Fate of the Canaanites and the Despoliation of the Egyptians: Polemics among Jews, Pagans, Christians and Gnostics: Motifs and Motives," in *The Gift of the Land and the Fate of the Canaanites in Jewish Thought*, ed. Katell Berthelot, Joseph E. David, and Marc Hirshman (Oxford: Oxford University Press, 2014), 66–111. For an earlier discussion of some of these sources, see Saul Lieberman, *Tosefta Ki-Fshuta: Part III, Oder Moed, Shabbat-Eruvin* (New York: Jewish Theological Seminary of America, 1962), 105.
[10] See n. 7.

from the perspective that I find most interesting. Lewy (1901–1945) was a classicist trained to the highest international level in the Weimar years at the Institut für Altertumskunde in Berlin.[11] Lewy began by citing Procopius, who related the North African tradition already noted earlier that considered Joshua a robber. Lewy then connected this tradition with an account in the Babylonian Talmud (b. Sanh. 91a) and Gen. Rab. 666 (Theodor-Albeck) of a trial held before Alexander the Great at which the "Africans" claimed title to the Land of Israel, based on the verse in Num 34:2, "This is the land assigned to you as a perpetual patrimony, the Land of Canaan, thus defined by its borders," and Canaan is "our" father. Geviha ben Pesisa undertook the defense of the Jews, citing Gen 9:25, "Cursed shall be Canaan, slave of slave shall he be to his brothers." Geviha insisted on the legal principle that just as the slave belonged to the master, so do any goods acquired by the slave belong to his master. Thus, even if the Land of Israel once belonged to Canaan, the slave, the real title was his master's.

Lewy noted one key point common to both sides of the dispute: both were citing biblical verses as a secular legal argument. Of course, the "trial" before Alexander the Great was imaginary, but Lewy dated the origin of the story to the Maccabean era and to a real confrontation between Hellenized Phoenicians and Jews. The source of the tension between the parties was the expansion of the Maccabean state at the expense of non-Jewish groups living in the Land of Israel.[12] What was particularly important to Lewy was that in the rabbinic imagination both sides were applying Hellenistic legal arguments to the Bible, much as the Greeks were doing to Homer, particularly to the "Catalogue of Ships" in the *Iliad* (2.494-759). As one well-known example of this exploitation of Homer for legal purposes, in the dispute between Athens and Megara over the title to Salamis, Solon added a verse to the "Catalogue of Ships" specifying that Ajax of Salamis brought twelve ships, which he ranged on the beach alongside the Athenian forces (Plutarch, *Solon* 10:2-3). This supposedly clinched the legal argument over Salamis in favor of Athens.[13] In short, according to Lewy, Jews were learning legal and rhetorical ways of arguing from the Greeks and then deploying them to defend sensitive points in their tradition. Whether the opponents were real, as Lewy thought, or only imagined in the minds of ancient Jews, Jews were saying: you "Africans" want to base a legal argument on our texts. Well, if that is the basis for your claim then we will show that the claim is invalid based on those same texts. Canaan was a slave and "everyone" knows that a slave has no independent legal status, other than as walking and talking property of the master.

Menahem Kister: Rabbinic Responses

Almost eighty years after Lewy wrote, his topic was discussed at length in parallel articles by Katell Berthelot[14] and Menahem Kister.[15] Kister's article is exhaustive, extensively

---

[11] On Lewy, see Albert I. Baumgarten, "Elias Bickerman and Hans (Yohanan) Lewy: The Story of a Friendship," *Anabases* 13 (2011): 95–118.
[12] Lewy, *Studies*, 67–72.
[13] Lewy, *Studies*, 72–8.
[14] See n. 7.
[15] See n. 9.

researched, and heavily annotated. The bulk of the paper is based on Gen. Rab., 4Q252, The Genesis Apocryphon, Jubilees, Josephus, Mekilta, Sifra, the *Hypothetica*, hereafter [*H*], which Kister attributed to Philo (more on [*H*] later),[16] and a late midrash. Kister admitted at the outset that these texts raised important questions for which he did not presume to offer a definitive solution. Rather, his goal was a survey of the data, bringing forth the insights that the various sources might shed on each other. Nevertheless, one of Kister's tentative conclusions touches tangentially on the particular aspect of Lewy's article that is central to my paper.

For Kister, Jubilees occupied an unusual place in this survey. While Kister understood most of the other sources as apologetic responses to charges by non-Jews, Kister apparently excluded Jubilees from this class. He disagreed with Lewy that Hasmonean expansion evoked an unfavorable response among the local nations to which Jubilees was responding with its own version of the original title to the land.[17] The dispossession of the Canaanites from their land, according to Jubilees, as understood by Kister, was a consequence of the curse of Canaan in Genesis compounded by Canaan's violation of the oath taken by the descendants of Noah not to dwell in each other's territory. Canaan was warned by his brothers not to settle in Lebanon, the land deeded to Shem (Jub. 10:31). Dire consequences followed this transgression.

Kister asked what might have been the motivation for apologetic arguments concerning the ownership of the land in these sources? He thought Lewy's solution that the issue became acute thanks to Hasmonean conquests unlikely: "There is no evidence of such a connection in the passages in which these accusations appear. Rather, the context in which this motif appears—in Philo, rabbinic literature, and possibly also Procopius—leads us in a different direction: the defamation of the Jews as taking hold of what had not been theirs."[18]

While Kister rejected Lewy as proposing a context unattested in the sources, he followed Lewy in recognizing that the legal arguments of both sides were based on the Bible and had to concede as follows:

> Anti-Jewish polemics based on the Bible are quite atypical before the emergence of Christianity; I suggest, however, that the existence of such arguments may be inferred from Philo's writings. Yet, it might be argued that not only the title "the land of Canaan" but also the biblical description of the despoilation of Egypt could be known to Gentiles not by any access to the Bible itself, but rather by consulting Jewish informants.[19]

---

[16] Despite the extensive annotation in Kister's article, he did not discuss or mention Barclay's attribution of [*H*] to an anonymous author in the land of Israel (see n. 26) first published in 2007, four years before Kister's article, and considered Philo as the author.

[17] While James C. VanderKam (*Jubilees 1: A Commentary on the Book of Jubilees Chapters 1–21*, Hermeneia [Minneapolis, MN: Fortress, 2018], 420, n. 101) included Jubilees among the texts responding to the charges of non-Jews, he nevertheless noted the odd place of Jubilees among those sources: "Jubilees seems to be a much earlier witness to the debate about Joshua's conquest of Canaan."

[18] Kister, "Fate of the Canaanites," 89–90.

[19] Kister, "Fate of the Canaanites," 90.

This series of arguments allowed Kister to conclude with the following words: "Philo's evidence proves that the Rabbinic material is not the product of the post-70 CE period."[20]

Katell Berthelot: Philo's Response

Berthelot took up these sources in two articles, the first in 2007,[21] the second in 2011 (above, n. 7).[22] The first article was written to disagree with Louis Feldman,[23] who claimed that Philo ignored the biblical passages that mention the commandment to eradicate the Canaanites, "perhaps because he [Philo] found it inconsistent with his tolerance towards non-Jewish religions."[24] In reply, Berthelot presented four strategies employed by Philo for dealing with the discomfort posed by the biblical conquest, of which one, based on [H], is of interest here:

> 5. So much for the story of the migration. But when they came to this land the holy records show clearly how they established themselves there and occupied the country. Yet in discussing the probable facts of this occupation I think it better to go not so much by the historical narrative (καθ' ἱστορίαν) as by what our reason (κατά τινα λογισμόν) tells us about them. 6. Which alternative do you prefer? Were they still superior in the number of their fighting men though they had fared so ill to the end, still strong and with weapons in their hand, and did they then take the land by force, defeating the combined Syrians and Phoenicians when fighting in their own country? Or shall we suppose that they were unwarlike and feeble, quite few in numbers and destitute of warlike equipment, but won the respect of their opponents who voluntarily surrendered their land to them and that as a direct consequence they shortly afterwards built their temple and established everything else needed for religion and worship? 7. This would clearly show that they were acknowledged as dearly beloved of God even by their enemies. For those whose land they suddenly invaded with the intention of taking it from them were necessarily their enemies. (*Hypothetica* 6.5-7 [Colson, LCL])

Berthelot attributed [H] to Philo, as was usual in 2007, and interpreted its rewriting of the Book of Joshua in the context of Philo's other works. She understood that [H] wanted its reader to disregard the historical narrative (the Bible) and prefer a rational explanation, namely, that the Israelites won the respect of their opponents, who voluntarily surrendered their land. Even the people whose land was invaded

---

[20] Kister, "Fate of the Canaanites," 78.
[21] Katell Berthelot, "Philo of Alexandria and the Conquest of Canaan," *JSJ* 38 (2007): 39–56.
[22] See n. 7.
[23] Cf. Louis Feldman, *"Remember Amalek!": Vengeance, Zealotry, and Group Destruction in the Bible according to Philo, Pseudo-Philo, and Josephus*, HUCM 31 (Cincinnati, OH: Hebrew Union College, 2004).
[24] Feldman, ap. Berthelot, "Conquest," 40.

with the intent of conquest acknowledged that the Israelites were beloved by God and responded appropriately (*Hypothetica* 6.7).

Berthelot found corroboration for this interpretation of the conquest in *QE* on Exod 23:27, which notes "the surpassing virtue of the nation in that it would convert not only its own (members) but also its enemies and by 'enemies' I mean not only those who commit acts of war but also those who are heterodox." Another possible source reaching the conclusion of voluntary Canaanite submission, Berthelot argued, was Strabo, who wrote of Moses that "the people all round, one and all, came over to [Moses] because of his dealings with them and the prospects he held out to them" (*Geographica*, XVI, 2, 36 = Stern, *GLAJJ*, #115, 1:300).

The analysis of the sources in Berthelot's 2011 article is more pertinent to my topic and more directly parallel to Kister. The list of sources there duplicates Kister's (i.e., Jubilees, 4Q252, Mekilta de R. Ishmael, Sifra, t. Šabbat, Genesis Rabbah, y. Šebi'it, b. Sanhedrin, and Procopius). Berthelot had a special interest in these sources, beginning with Mekhilta de R. Ishmael, Pesaḥim 18 (Horovitz-Rabin 69-70), which reported that there were Canaanites who "trusted in God," recognized the right of Israel to the land and voluntarily left their homeland for Africa, actions for which they were rewarded by God. Given the range of sources—which are especially wide for Berthelot, since, unlike Kister, she included Jubilees in this tradition—she concluded that "it remains difficult to formulate more than guesses about the historical context in which the positive tradition about the Canaanites who left the Land developed, but it looks decidedly Tannaitic."[25] Whatever the date and context, a more accommodating explanation of how the Israelites came to occupy Canaan can hardly be conceived: the Canaanites were blessed by God with Africa for recognizing the divine right of Israel to Canaan!

Berthelot introduced [H] as her final source. She attributed the work to Philo, despite knowing that Barclay had argued that the work was by an unknown author from the Land of Israel,[26] but insisted that this point did not really matter, since [H] was a Jewish Hellenistic text dating no later than the first century CE, in any case.[27]

Considering [H] as a text written by Philo, Berthelot was concerned to argue that its audience included non-Jews. She also noted differences between the rabbinic sources and [H], such as that the latter does not present the Canaanites as having faith in God, but only as respecting or admiring the newcomers. Philo, in a word, was "less concerned to prove that the Jews were the legitimate owners of the Land."[28]

But are matters quite this simple? Can Barclay be dismissed so easily? While I will not rehearse Barclay's arguments in detail here, having done so elsewhere,[29] I note that they are substantial, and I find them convincing. Barclay pointed to the exceptional un-Philonic

---

[25] Berthelot, "Canaanites Who Trusted," 253.
[26] John M. G. Barclay, *Flavius Josephus: Translation and Commentary, vol. 10: Against Apion*, ed. Steve Mason (Leiden: Brill, 2007; repr., Leiden/Boston: Brill, 2013), 352–61.
[27] Berthelot, "Canaanites Who Trusted," 254, n. 62.
[28] Berthelot, "Canaanites Who Trusted," 260.
[29] Albert I. Baumgarten, "The 'Hypothetica'—A Jewish Rationalist in the Land of Israel," in *History, Historians and Historiography*, ed. Meron M. Piotrkowski, Robert A. Brody, Noah Hacham, and Jan Willem van Henten (forthcoming).

vocabulary of these passages on topics close to Philo's heart and central to his thought, to which I would now add Berthelot's observation of the use of *historia*, referring to the biblical text.[30] Barclay suggested that this was a case of what Robert Merton called the Matthew Effect: "The world is peculiar in this matter of how it gives credit: It tends to give the credit to already famous people."[31] Eusebius or his sources attributed an unknown text to Philo, a well-known ancient Jewish author. Indeed, [H] is not the only example of Eusebius or his source misleading by the Matthew Effect. Eusebius attributed 4 Maccabees to Josephus (*Hist. eccl.* 3.10.6). The vague parallel between [H] and the passage from QE on Exod 23:27 cited by Berthelot is insufficient to tie the work to Philo's other writings and to overcome the force of Barclay's other arguments for an anonymous author.

Following Barclay, what makes [H] special are two points: first, this anonymous author lived in the Land of Israel. He referred to the Israelites who left Egypt as coming to "this land" (τὴν γῆν ταύτην; 6.5). The best and simplest explanation of τὴν γῆν ταύτην here, an unattested term for Philo, on a topic for which he showed little or no concern, is that it marked the anonymous author's location in "this" land, the Land of Israel.[32]

Next, what makes [H] truly distinctive in comparison with the rabbinic texts cited by Kister and Berthelot was the author's willingness to dismiss the written account in the Bible in favor of what the author believed was a more rational explanation. Ben Sira and Josephus illuminate what disturbed [H] so exceedingly in the biblical account of the conquest and what made his rejection of the biblical account so special. However, all the strategies Josephus deployed for dealing with awkward biblical aspects of the conquest named earlier stop short of baldly rejecting the biblical account in favor of a more rational one, as [H] did.

These two points together concerning [H] indicate the lengths to which a Jew from the Land of Israel was willing to go to take the sting out of the account of the conquest. Perhaps, as indicated at the outset of this essay, he was preaching to the converted, soothing their conscience, and had no intention or hope of convincing non-Jews. But even so, the need [H] felt and the means he employed to meet that need show a level of interaction and familiarity with the larger cultural world and the desire to stay on better terms with it. Whether or not his non-Jewish neighbors would have welcomed him with his tradition of conquest, he wanted to be a better neighbor in the Land of Israel, at least in his own mind.

Hypothetica

The friendlier, less offensive, more neighborly, and more rational version of the conquest proposed by [H] was based on offering two alternatives, either one of which

---

[30] Berthelot, "Canaanites Who Trusted," 255.
[31] Robert K. Merton, "The Matthew Effect, II," in *On Social Structure and Science*, ed. Piotr Sztompka (Chicago, IL: University of Chicago Press, 1996), 318.
[32] There is therefore no need to stretch and twist the meaning of the phrase in Hebrew, to somehow preserve an Alexandrian provenance of the text, as done by David Rokeah, "Hypothetica," in *Historical Writings, Apologetic Writings*, vol. 1 of *Philo of Alexandria*, ed. S. D. Nataf (Jerusalem: Bialik Institute, 1986) [Hebrew], 158, rendering the phrase אל הארץ ההיא.

had to be true. This approach was apparently a favorite of [H], as he dealt with the question of the origin of the laws of Moses in a similar manner, also proposing two alternatives.[33]

The first possibility [H] considered for the Israelites in Canaan was as follows:

> Were they still superior in the number of their fighting men though they had fared so ill to the end, still strong and with weapons in their hand, and did they then take the land by force, defeating the combined Syrians and Phoenicians when fighting in their own country? (6.6 [Colson, LCL])

Demetrius the Chronographer, in the third century BCE, had already asked and answered a similar awkward question concerning consistency in the Exodus story. If the Israelites left Egypt suddenly as fleeing slaves, saying that they were going for a three-day journey to offer sacrifice, where did they get the weapons to fight the subsequent battles, narrated in the Pentateuch? Demetrius's answer was that those who did not drown in the Reed Sea appropriated the weapons of those who did (frag. 5). [H] was troubled by a similar question, at the time of Joshua. However, his answer was different. He thought it unlikely that Joshua and his men had the military means to conquer by force. In effect, this was his reason for rejecting the biblical account as implausible. Instead, [H] preferred the second option, the one that echoes points in the rabbinic sources analyzed by Kister and Berthelot:

> Or shall we suppose that they were unwarlike and feeble, quite few in numbers and destitute of warlike equipment, but won the respect of their opponents who voluntarily surrendered their land to them and that as a direct consequence they shortly afterwards built their temple and established everything else needed for religion and worship? 7. This would clearly show that they were acknowledged as dearly beloved of God even by their enemies. For those whose land they suddenly invaded with the intention of taking it from them were necessarily their enemies. (6.6-7 [Colson, LCL])

For [H] this was the only way left to explain the occupation of Canaan: if/since the Israelites were weak, they could never have conquered by force. They only came to occupy the land because their enemies recognized that they were "dearly beloved of God" (6.7 [Colson, LCL]).

As Sterling noted, this style of arguing, with only two alternatives from which to choose, had a Stoic veneer.[34] Or, as Carlos Lévy wrote to me:

---

[33] See further Baumgarten, "The 'Hypothetica' – A Jewish Rationalist."

[34] Gregory E. Sterling, "*Hypothetica*," in *Outside the Bible: Ancient Jewish Writings Related to Scripture*, ed. Louis H. Feldman, James L. Kugel, and Lawrence H. Schiffman (Philadelphia, PA: Jewish Publication Society, 2013), 2503. However, since I accept Barclay's identification of [H], I do not follow Sterling's suggestion that this veneer made it likely that Philo wrote the *Hypothetica* in preparation for his role in the embassy to Rome, where one of his opponents was Chaeremon, an Egyptian priest who embraced Stoic thought. See also Berthelot, "Canaanites Who Trusted," 255, n. 66.

en ce qui concerne le stoïcisme, son succès fut tel qu'il devint une sorte de koinè intellectuelle et linguistique, influençant beaucoup de gens qui n'étaient pas à proprement parler des stoïciens, et notamment des historiens.[35]

The success of Stoicisms was so great that it became an intellectual and linguistic commonplace, which influenced many authors who, strictly speaking, were not Stoics, especially historians.

This Stoic veneer in the style of arguing makes [H] unique among the sources analyzed by Kister and Berthelot. It indicates the extent to which a Jew from the Land of Israel had picked up Greco-Roman thought and utilized it to question the tradition and pose a more acceptable answer, which would take the sting out of the tradition, if understood in its literal sense as narrated in the Bible. Perhaps this Jew from the Land of Israel imagined or hoped that relations with the local non-Jews could be ameliorated by means of an argument whose style was learned from the Greeks. The similarity to the conclusions drawn by Hans Lewy concerning the proof for Israelite ownership of the Land of Israel based on a tactic of analysis learned from Greek practice with Homer is impressive. To return to Gruen, in both cases, Jews at home in the Greco-Roman world reasserted the character of their heritage, dealt with a problematic aspect of that heritage, and tried to appear as better neighbors, perhaps only in their own minds, based on knowledge and techniques learned in that Greco-Roman world.

---

[35] Letter from January 25, 2020. I thank Prof. Lévy for his friendship and the extended conversations concerning [H] over several years.

14

Negotiating National and Sectarian Identities in the Dead Sea Scrolls: The Case of Words of the Luminaries and the Yaḥad's Covenant Ceremony

Esther G. Chazon

I am thrilled to write in honor of my dear friend and colleague, Adele Reinhartz. I am constantly amazed by Adele's ability to adroitly fulfill many demanding roles, juggle competing responsibilities, and assume multiple personal and social identities—scholar, teacher, journal editor, film critic, society volunteer, mother, daughter, grandmother, spouse, friend, Torah reader, and choir singer, to mention only a few. So inspired, I have chosen the topic of identity for Adele's festschrift, and I take this opportunity to wish Adele continued fulfillment in all her undertakings in good health עד מאה ועשרים.

Ancient communities often had to negotiate discordant beliefs, perspectives, customs, relationships, and identities underlying divergent texts that they preserved. A sect restricted to insiders and self-segregating from outsiders would have had to find ways to appropriate the outsiders' texts that it adopted and negotiate them with its own sectarian social identity.[1] Such negotiations plausibly informed the sect's social identity but, at the same time, might have enabled some kinds of relationships with the world outside the confines of the sectarian community. To illustrate this phenomenon, I will provide a comparison between the Yaḥad's annual covenant ceremony prescribed by the Community Rule (Serekh ha-Yaḥad) and the nonsectarian collection of prayers for the days of the week entitled the Words of the Luminaries (4Q504–506).[2] I will suggest

---

[1] For social identity theory and its application to sectarian social identity, see Jutta Jokiranta, *Social Identity and Sectarianism in the Qumran Movement*, STDJ 105 (Leiden: Brill, 2013), 1–3, 77–92. Jokiranta adopts Tajfel's landmark definition of social identity: "that part of an individual's self-concept which derives from his knowledge of his membership of a social group (or groups) together with the value and emotional significance attached to that membership." Henri Tajfel, *Differentiation between Social Groups: Studies in Social Psychology of Intergroup Relations* (London: Academic Press, 1978), 63.

[2] The 4Q504 manuscript (*c*. 150 BCE), which predates the earliest archaeological evidence for the Qumran sectarian settlement (*c*. 100 BCE), provides strong evidence for the text's nonsectarian origin. This text also lacks distinctive sectarian markers and employs a pan-Israelite rhetoric dissonant with sectarian discourse. See later and Esther G. Chazon, "Sectarian or Not: What Is the Question," in *Emerging Sectarianism in the Dead Sea Scrolls: Continuity, Separation, and Conflict*, ed. Ananda Geyser-Fouché and John J. Collins, STDJ (Leiden: Brill, 2022), 13–32.

that the common foundational narratives, scriptural sources, and liturgical traditions prominent in both texts would have enabled the Yaḥad to negotiate the dissonant chords in the Words of the Luminaries and read these prayers in consonance with its sectarian identity. Although the actual performance of these two liturgical texts cannot be verified, it is reasonable to assume the Yaḥad's familiarity with them, both of which were preserved in multiple copies at Qumran.[3]

The first section of this study will demonstrate how the Community Rule constructs Yaḥad identity through its sectarian accentuation of biblical texts in the covenant ceremony, especially in the blessing to "God's lot" and cursing of "Belial's lot." Reading the nonsectarian prayers in the Words of the Luminaries through a sectarian lens and in harmony with sectarian identity will be considered in this context.

The second section will examine national themes in other recitations of the Rule's covenant ceremony and expose a tension between national and sectarian perspectives *within* this Yaḥad ceremony. Considering how these different perspectives might have functioned together in the sectarian covenant ceremony can provide a paradigm for imagining the reception of nonsectarian texts like the Words of the Luminaries that take a decidedly "all-Israel" stance and engender a national identity.

The Annual Covenant Ceremony in the Community Rule (Serekh ha-Yaḥad)

The powerful role of the Community Rule's covenant ceremony in constructing Yaḥad sectarian identity has been universally recognized since the pioneering study by Carol Newsom.[4] The sectarian adaptation of biblical models and scriptural quotations plays a major role in priming this ceremony for constructing sectarian identity, promoting in-group cohesiveness "together" (*yaḥad*), and ensuring separation from "all the people in Belial's lot."

The instructions for the ceremony begin with the words, "And all those entering the organization of the community (lit. the Yaḥad) shall gain admittance into (יעבורו lit. "pass into," Deut 29:11) the covenant before God to act according to all that He

---

[3] The covenant ceremony in 1QS 1:16–2:25a is partially preserved in three more copies (4Q256, 4Q257, 5Q11); 4Q255, 4Q257, and 4Q262 have parallels with 1QS 2:25b–3:12a, which some scholars consider additional instructions for this ceremony. See Charlotte Hempel, *The Community Rules from Qumran: A Commentary*, TSAJ 183 (Tübingen: Mohr Siebeck, 2020), 67–93; the English translation of 1QS in this article is based on that by Hempel. The Words of the Luminaries is extant in two or three copies from Qumran that range in date from c. 150 BCE (4Q504) to c. 50 CE (4Q506); 4Q505 (c. 70–60 BCE) is considered another copy by some scholars—for example, Maurice Baillet, *Qumrân Grotte 4.III (4Q482–4Q520)*, DJD 7 (Oxford: Clarendon, 1982), 168; and Esther G. Chazon, "The Classification of 4Q505: Daily or Festival Prayers?" in *'Go Out and Study the Land' (Judges 18:2): Archaeological, Historical and Textual Studies in Honor of Hanan Eshel*, ed. Aren M. Maeir, Jodi Magness, and Lawrence H. Schiffman, JSJSup 148 (Leiden: Brill, 2012), 23–34—but not by everyone—see Florentino García Martínez, review of *Discoveries in the Judaean Desert VII. Qumrân Grotte 4 III [4Q482–4Q520]* by Maurice Baillet, *JSJ* 15 (1984): 157–64; and Daniel K. Falk, *Daily, Sabbath, and Festival Prayers in the Dead Sea Scrolls*, STDJ 27 (Leiden: Brill, 1998), 59–61.

[4] Carol A. Newsom, *The Self as Symbolic Space: Constructing Identity and Community at Qumran*, STDJ 52 (Leiden: Brill, 2004), 1–190; her sustained analysis of the covenant ceremony is at 117–27.

has commanded and not to turn (לשוב) their back on Him" (1QS 1:16-17 // 4Q256 II 1; cf. Deut 30:2). The instructions surely extend to those for the annual procession (lit. "passing") by rank (1QS 2:19-25a); some scholars see the unit extending to the rule for the "one who (initially) refuses to enter the covenant" (1QS 2:25b–3:12a).[5] The liturgical text for the ceremony comprises four sets of recitations by priestly and levitical officiants, each followed by a response by "all those passing into the covenant":

> I. Priests and Levites bless the God of salvation and all his true deeds.
> Response: Amen Amen. (1QS 1:18b-20 // 4Q256 II:3)
>
> II. Priests recount God's righteous, powerful, and merciful deeds toward Israel.
> Levites recount Israel's sins during Belial's dominion.
> Response: Confession of "our" sins and the sins of "our" fathers; Proclamation of divine judgment for "our" sins and the sins of "our" fathers. (1QS 1:21–2:1a // 4Q256 II:5-6)
>
> III. Priests bless the people of God's lot.
> Levites curse the people of Belial's lot.
> Response: Amen Amen. (1QS 2:1b–10 // 4Q256 II:12–III:3 // 4Q257 II:1-7 // 5Q11 i 2-5)
>
> IV. Priests and Levites curse those who enter the covenant insincerely.
> Response: Amen Amen. (1QS 2:11-18 // 4Q256 III:4)

The Deuteronomic account of the covenant undertaken in Moab (Deut 27–29), which also stipulates the blessings and curses to be recited on Mt. Gerizim and Mt. Ebal, respectively (Deut 27:11-26, cf. Josh 8:30-35), served as a model for the Rule's covenant ceremony.[6] This is evident in many features: the division between two groups for reciting the blessings and the curses; the priestly and levitical officiants; the responsorial Amen; the nearly verbatim curse of an insincere participant who, "when he hears the terms of covenant, he will bless himself in his heart saying, 'May I enjoy happiness even though I walk with a hardened heart'" (1QS 2:12b-17 // Deut 29:18-20); and the frequently cited Deuteronomic collocation "to pass into the covenant" (Deut 29:11 // 1QS 1:16, 18, 20, 24; 2:10; 1:16-17a also seems to echo Deut 30:2).

---

[5] Sarianna Metso, *The Serekh Texts*, LSTS 62 (London: T&T Clark, 2007), 8; Hempel, *Community Rules*, 72-4; and Charlotte Hempel, "The Long Text of the *Serekh* as Crisis Literature," *RevQ* 27 (2015): 3–23. See n. 3.

[6] Jacob Licht, *The Rule Scroll: A Scroll from the Wilderness of Judaea* (Jerusalem: Bialik Institute, 1965), 54–5, 64–73 (Hebrew), identified the ceremony's biblical sources, its use of interpretative traditions, and its principal sectarian adaptations. See also Bilhah Nitzan, *Qumran Prayer and Religious Poetry*, trans. Jonathan Chipman, STDJ 12 (Leiden: Brill, 1994), 121–35, 148–54; Falk, *Daily, Sabbath and Festival*, 219–25; Russell C. D. Arnold, "Repentance and the Qumran Covenant Ceremony," in *The Development and Impact of Penitential Prayer in Second Temple Judaism*, vol. 2 of *Seeking the Favor of God*, ed. Mark J. Boda, Daniel F. Falk, and Rodney A. Werline, EJL 22 (Atlanta, GA: SBL Press, 2007), 159–75; Newsom, *Self as Symbolic Space*, 119–21; Shani Tzoref, "The Use of Scripture in the Community Rule," in *A Companion to Biblical Interpretation in Early Judaism*, ed. Matthias Henze (Grand Rapids, MI: Eerdmans, 2012), 203–34.

The sectarian accentuation of this biblical model is most pronounced in the third set of recitations—the blessing to "God's lot" and the curse to "Belial's lot."[7] Unlike the Deuteronomic covenant in which the blessings and curses are extended to all the people and are conditional upon their choice of Torah observance or nonobservance, the Rule's blessing and curse are in-group or out-group specific and reflect a sectarian, dualistic-deterministic ideology. Another significant difference from Deut 27-29 is the choice of the priestly blessing (Num 6:23-26) and its inversion to formulate the blessing to "God's lot" and curse to "Belial's lot," respectively. The Rule expands the biblical priestly blessing with promises of all good things, knowledge, God's loving kindness, and protection from evil for "all the people of God's lot who walk perfectly in all His ways" (1QS 2:1b-4a). It thereby builds sectarian social identity as the blessed, knowledgeable, "perfect" elite group, while shoring up members' adherence to the covenant lest they incur the frightening curses pronounced to "the people of Belial's lot" and to insincere participants (1QS 2:4b-18).[8]

Reading the Words of the Luminaries in Nonsectarian and Sectarian Contexts

The Words of the Luminaries is conspicuously devoid of distinctive, sectarian markers. Accordingly, its use of some of the same key biblical texts as the Community Rule lacks all sectarian accentuations. Notably, the prayer for the fifth day cites the Deuteronomic covenant curses in its petition for healing "from madness, blindness, and bewilderment" (4Q504 XV 15 [1-2 ii 14], Deut 28:27-28) and in its historical recollections, which stress that God caused the curses to "cleave to us" as "discipline" because he chose Israel as his "firstborn son" from among the nations (4Q504 XVI 6b-15 [1-2 iii 5-14]; cf. Exod 4:22; Deut 8:5; 28:21, 60).[9] These historical recollections exemplify the pan-Israelite stance of the "we" speakers in the Words of the Luminaries and the identification of their "Other" as "all the nations" (e.g., 4Q504 XVI 3-6a [1-2 iii 2-5]).

The divine promises in Lev 26:40-45 and Deut 30:1-10 affixed to the covenant curses in both biblical books figure prominently in the prayer for the sixth day. They follow one upon the other in this prayer's historical prologue, recounting that, despite Israel's idolatry and punishment, God did not utterly reject or destroy them but rather took them out "in the nations' sight" and enabled their "return" (לשוב) to Him[10] (4Q504

---

[7] Note also the words "cut off from all the children of light" added to the rewriting of Deut 29:20 in the curse to the insincere participant in 1QS 2:16.

[8] On such functions of the blessing and curses and for the covenant ceremony's conferring of sectarian identity, see Newsom, *Self as Symbolic Space*, 117–27, 188–9.

[9] The Arabic numerals are the fragment numbers as in the *editio princeps* (DJD 7); I arranged the 4Q504 fragments in columns, numbered by Roman numerals, in their original order in the reconstructed scroll. Consult Maurice Baillet and Esther G. Chazon, eds., "4Q504 (4QDibHamᵃ)," in *The Dead Sea Scrolls Reader, part 5, Poetic and Liturgical Texts*, ed. Donald W. Parry and Emanuel Tov (Leiden: Brill, 2005), 240–60; repr. in 2nd ed. (Leiden: Brill, 2014), 2:490–507.

[10] Returning (לשוב) to God and the Torah is a central sectarian principle, as evident in the covenant ceremony's preamble (1QS 1:16-17, see above) and the initiation of novices (e.g., 1QS 5:1, 8; 6:15). For this central, Yaḥad group belief and the function of group beliefs in forming social identity, see Jokiranta, *Social Identity*, 90–6, and Esther G. Chazon, "Prayer and Identity in Varying Contexts: The Case of the Words of the Luminaries," *JSJ* 46 (2015): 484–511, esp. 485–6, 505–8.

XVIII 7-15 [1-2 v 6-14]). Lev 26:40-45 is requoted at the end of this historical prologue in the "we" speaker's admission of guilt, their paying for sin through suffering, and their disclaimer of any abhorrence toward God for their suffering (4Q504 XIX 6-9 [1-2 vi 5-8]). Deut 30:1-4 is echoed again in this prayer's petition for deliverance of "Your people Isra[el from all] the lands, near and far, to whi[ch You banished them]" (4Q504 XIX 13-15 [1-2 vi 12-14]). The national perspective, identity, and concern is evident throughout these passages.

The Words of the Luminaries' liturgical adaptation of Deut 28–30:4 and Lev 26:40-45 thus differs markedly from the Rule's appropriation of these biblical passages in the covenant curses to the "people of Belial's lot" and to insincere participants in its covenant ceremony.[11] Nevertheless, the fact that this sectarian ceremony is deeply rooted in the same foundational, covenantal biblical passages could have enabled the Yaḥad's reception of the Words of the Luminaries and facilitated its reading of this nonsectarian liturgical text through the lens of their sectarian identity as the true, repentant keepers and beneficiaries of God's covenant with Israel. The covenant and giving of the Torah at Sinai (Exod 19:3-8; Deut 5:1-5), which ultimately lie behind the shared biblical covenantal passages and both liturgical appropriations—implicitly in the Rule's ceremony and explicitly in the Words of the Luminaries (4Q504 V 8-10 [4 8-10], XI 10-19, [3 ii 7-16])—could have contributed to such a sectarian reading.[12]

National Perspectives in the Covenant Ceremony and the Words of the Luminaries

Paradoxically, the features of the Words of the Luminaries that would have facilitated its reception by the Yaḥad and enabled its reading with a sectarian lens and in consonance with sectarian identity, could also have kept a sense of national identity in view. Such a national perspective underlies the second set of recitations in the Rule's covenant ceremony (1QS 1:21–2:1), which precedes the blessing to "God's lot" and curse to "Belial's lot":

> II.a ²¹Then the priests shall enumerate God's righteous deeds as reflected in His powerful acts ²²and they shall proclaim all His loving acts of kindness towards Israel.
>
> II.b And the levites shall enumerate ²³the trespasses of the children of Israel and all their guilty wrongdoings and their sins during the rule of ²⁴Belial.
>
> II.c [And al]l those entering the covenant shall confess after them saying, "We have trespassed, ²⁵we have committed [wr]ongdoings, [sin]ned and acted wickedly,

---

[11] Notably, both sectarian curses call for the complete destruction of those cursed (1QS 2:6-8, 15), inverting Lev 26:44's promise not to annihilate the exiled Israelites. For the Rule's use of Deut 27:11–30:2 in its covenant ceremony, see the previous section.

[12] For more examples of the pan-Israelite perspective and themes in the Words of the Luminaries, their dissonance with those of the Yaḥad, and possibilities for negotiating that dissonance, see Chazon, "Prayer and Identity."

we [and] our [fa]thers before us by walking ²⁶[*contrarily,*] truth and righteous is [Go]d ... His judgment is upon us and upon [our] fathers. ²·¹ªBut He has favoured us with His kind love from eternity to eternity."¹³

The first recitation recalls God's mighty deeds and merciful acts toward the nation, Israel; the second recalls Israel's sins. Apparently, the model for these recitations and for the historical prologues in the weekday prayers of the Words of the Luminaries is the prayer in Neh 9:6-36, which consists almost entirely of historical recollections contrasting Israel's past sins with God's mercies and precedes the covenant-making account in Nehemiah 10.¹⁴ Although the Rule does not record the words of these recitations, we can surmise that, apart from the reference to the era of Belial's dominion, they were in tune not only with Neh 9:6-36 but also with the historical recollections in the Words of the Luminaries. The main theme of the recollections in the Words of the Luminaries is remembering and recounting God's past wonders (נפלאות) and mighty deeds (גבורות, 4Q504 IX 19 [5 i 4], XIX 10 [1-2 vi 9]; similarly, גבורתום in 1QS 1:21). The divine acts recalled in these weekly prayers include God's guidance of His people in the wilderness, giving of the Torah, forgiveness of the people's sins in the wilderness, bringing covenant curses upon the Israelite idolaters who sinned in the land, and not abandoning the diaspora (for the last phrase, לוא עזבתנו בגוים in XVIII 11-12 [1-2 v 10-11], see Ezra 9:9; Neh 9:30-31). Israel's sins during the course of its history and, in contrast, God's acts of mercy and loving-kindness toward Israel are clearly an important component of these remembrances (compare רחמיכה in 4Q504 XII 13 [7 11] and [חסד]כה in XV 11 [1-2 ii 10] with חסדי רחמיו/רחמי חסדו in 1QS 1:22; 2:1; the terms for sin are discussed later in this chapter).

By explicitly including "our fathers" in their confession and proclamation of divine justice that constitute their response in this second set of recitations, the covenanters in the Rule's ceremony assume the mantle of national responsibility.¹⁵ The use of traditional formulae for the confession (e.g., 1 Kgs 8:47 // 2 Chr 6:37; Ps 106:6; Dan 9:5; Neh 9:33)¹⁶

---

¹³ The translation is by Hempel, *Community Rules*, 70. The itemizing of the subsections is my own.
¹⁴ Psalm 106 may also be in the background of either or both scrolls. Psalm 106 features long historical remembrances contrasting Israel's sins with God's saving acts, a confessional ("We have sinned with our fathers, we have committed iniquity, we have acted wickedly," 106:6) and, like the Words of the Luminaries, a final petition for deliverance from the nations (106:47). However, the covenant context of Nehemiah 9–10 resonates more with the Rule's covenant ceremony.
¹⁵ The Yaḥad's mission to "expiate iniquity" and "atone for the Land" (1QS 8:3, 6; 9:4) also seems to bespeak a sense of national responsibility.
¹⁶ The order of the verbs in 1QS 1:23-25 and inclusion of the verb [פ]שׁענו ("we have committed [wr]ongdoings") resemble Lev 16:21 and the confessionals recited by the high priest in the temple on the Day of Atonement according to m. Yoma 3:8; 4:2; 6:2. But, 1QS 1:25 also includes the verb, הרשענו ("we have acted wickedly"), which appears in the late biblical prayers cited parenthetically above. Note also the acknowledgment of God's mercy and loving-kindness as well as the confession and proclamation of divine justice in Dan 9:5-9 and Neh 9:31-33. For a confessional juxtaposed with a proclamation of divine justice in apocryphal prayers, see, for example, Bar 1:15-17, 2:6-12; Esth 14:6-7 LXX; Pr Azar 4-8; Tob 3:2-6, and the next note. Falk (*Daily, Festival, and Sabbath*, 221–7) suggested that although "there is nothing exclusive" about the Rule's confession, the lack of a petition for forgiveness and mercy reflects the Yaḥad's unique adaptation of an existing prayer pattern.

and proclamation of divine justice (e.g., Lam 1:18; Dan 9:14; Ezra 9:15; Neh 9:33)[17] positioned the Yaḥad covenanters in a line of received tradition from the scriptural exemplars to the present that could have enlivened a sense of continuity with the common heritage, Israel's past, and national identity. Reading the comparable—albeit not identically formulated—confession of sin and proclamation of divine justice in the Words of the Luminaries could have had the same effect. Several of the weekday prayers in the Words of the Luminaries preserve a confession of sin by the "we" speakers that also acknowledges their forefathers' sins. To illustrate, I quote two excerpts from the prayers for the fifth and sixth days; the latter includes a standard proclamation of divine justice:[18]

> Please, Lord, act as Yourself, as the greatness of Your power, as You [fo]rgave our fathers when they rebelled against Your command (Num 14:17–19, Deut 9:23) … Let Your anger and rage turn back from Your people Israel for all [their] sin[s] (cf. Dan 9:16) … [cause] us to [re]turn with all our heart and all our soul (cf. Deut 4:29–30, 1 Kgs 8:48) … we were sold [in] our [in]iquity, yet despite our transgression, You called us. (Isa 50:1b–2) … Save us from sinning against You (4Q504 XV 8–17 [1–2 ii 7–16], from the fifth day's petition).
>
> We have come into difficult straits, [and blo]ws, and trials through the rage of the oppressor (Isa 51:13) for we too (i.e., like those exiled for idolatry) [wea]ried God with our iniquity, burdened the Rock with [our] si[n] (Isa 43:24) … [You have cas]t all ou[r] transgressions fro[m] us, and pu[ri]fied us from our sin for Your sake. To You, Lord, is righteousness, for You have done all these things.[19] And now, on this day, when our heart is humbled, we have repaid the debt of our iniquity and the iniquity of our fathers (that accrued) for our rebellion against You in that we walked contrarily (Lev 26:40)[20] … Let Your anger and Your rage turn back from us (4Q504 XVIII 18–XIX 12 [1–2 v 17–vi 11], from the sixth day's historical prologue and petition).

---

[17] 1QS 1:26 reads צדי֯ק [א]ל, translated as "righteous is [Go]d." For the Greek equivalent of this formula in apocryphal prayers, see, for example, Bar 2:9; Esth 14:7 LXX; Pr Azar 4; Tob 3:2; cf. Ps 51:6; Pss Sol. 9:2. (Tob 3:2 is not extant in the Qumran Hebrew and Aramaic manuscripts.) For the adaptation of this formula and the alternate formula, "To you, Lord, is righteousness" (לך אדני הצדקה), see Dan 9:7) in the Yaḥad's *hodayot*, and the use of both formulas in the later synagogue liturgy, see Esther G. Chazon, "Tradition and Innovation in Sectarian Religious Poetry," in *Prayer and Poetry in the Dead Sea Scrolls and Related Literature: Essays in Honor of Eileen Schuller on the Occasion of Her 65th Birthday*, ed. Jeremy Penner, Ken M. Penner, and Cecilia Wassén, STDJ 98 (Leiden: Brill, 2012), 55–67. For "To you, Lord, is righteousness" in the Words of the Luminaries, see later in chapter.

[18] For additional examples, see 4Q504 V 6-7 (4 6-7, from the prayer for the first day), X 19-20 (5 ii 5-6 from the third day's prayer), XII 15-18 (7 13-16, from the fourth day's prayer), and "You are/were just" (ותצדק) later in the fifth day's prayer (XVI 21 [1-2 iii 20]). The text and translation for the Words of the Luminaries follow Baillet and Chazon, *DSSR 5*, 240–55.

[19] The Hebrew of this proclamation of divine justice reads: לכה אתה אדוני הצדקה כיא אתה עשיתה את כול אלה 4)Q504 XIX 4-5 [frg. 1-2 vi 3-4]). The first part of the formula לך אדני הצדקה is attested in Dan 9:7, and the second part has a close but not exact parallel in the continuation of the "God is just" formula in Dan 9:14; cf. Neh 9:33; Jer 14:22; the closest parallel to 4Q504 XIX 4-5 is 1QHª 8:27 (Chazon, "Tradition and Innovation," 58–61). See n. 17.

[20] See the next note for reconstructing the same Leviticus 26 expression in 1QS 1:25-26.

These selections use the same standard terms for sin (חטא), iniquity (עוון), and transgression (פשע) as the confession in 1QS 1:24-26[21] but couch them in nominal forms and in the prose style typical of these weekday prayers. These and other passages in the Words of the Luminaries that recall God's mighty deeds and merciful acts toward Israel could have been read seamlessly with the opening parts of the Rule's covenant ceremony.

In sum, unlike the subsequent blessing to "God's lot" and curse to "Belial's lot," the opening recitations in the Rule's covenant ceremony cultivate a sense of continuity with Israel's national history and responsibility for the sins of "our fathers."[22] Consequently, it is possible to imagine how sectarians reciting or otherwise reading the covenant ceremony's script and the prayers in the Words of the Luminaries could have maintained a sense of historic Israelite identity as a component of their sectarian identity. Indeed, claiming rightful, privileged ownership of the shared heritage from which it distinguished itself is an important strategy in sectarian identity formation.[23]

Conclusion

The question that I would like to pose in conclusion is this: What was the effect of the national perspective in the opening recitations of the Rule's covenant ceremony that might have been enhanced by reading texts like the Words of the Luminaries in the Yaḥad context? Surely, this national perspective worked to confirm Yaḥad sectarian identity as the elect "Congregation of God"[24] and inheritors of God's covenant with Israel. But, might it also have served additional functions such as arming the polemics against Jewish opponents or, conversely, enabling an alignment with other Israelites against the common foreign enemy or a hope for growth in the Yaḥad's ranks prior to the eschatological war against Belial's forces?[25] For any of these functions, it would have

---

[21] The fourth term in 1QS 1:25, הרשענו ("we acted wickedly"), is not extant in the Words of the Luminaries. But, the Rule's confessional would contain a fourth parallel with the passage quoted from the sixth day's prayer if the reconstruction of the Levitical expression [קרי] בלכתנו ("in our walking [contrarily]") in 1QS 1:25-26 is correct. See Lev 26:21-28, 40-41, and Licht, *Rule*, 68.

[22] Jacob Licht, "The Plant Eternal and the People of Divine Deliverance," in *Essays on the Dead Sea Scrolls in Memory of E. L. Sukenik*, ed. Chaim Rabin and Yigael Yadin (Jerusalem: Shrine of the Book, 1961), 49–75 (Hebrew), observed the juxtaposition and tension between these two tendencies in Yaḥad writings, including in the Rule's covenant ceremony—the connection with the people of Israel in the ceremony's introduction as contrasted with the ensuing sectarian blessing and curse. But he admitted that he could not fully explain why the sect kept the national connection (62–3). Advanced theories of social identity, discourse, and sectarianism and their application to the Scrolls, as in Newsom, *Self as Symbolic Space*, and Jokiranta, *Social Identity*, better equip us to address this issue.

[23] See Maxine L. Grossman, "Cultivating Identity: Textual Virtuosity and 'Insider' Status," in *Defining Identities: We, You, and the Other in the Dead Sea Scrolls, Proceedings of the Fifth Meeting of the IOQS in Groningen*, ed. Florentino García Martínez and Mladen Popović, STDJ 70 (Leiden: Brill, 2008), 1–11; Newsom, *Self as Symbolic Space*, 3, 193–5, and Jokiranta, *Social Identity*, 2, 205.

[24] For this Yaḥad self-designation, see 1QS 1:8; 1QSb 4:24; 4Q511 48-49 + 51 ii 1 (עצת אל) and 1QM 4:9; 4QH[a] 8i10 (עדת אל).

[25] The sectarian halakic letter, *Miqṣat Ma'aśê ha-Torah*, ("Some Precepts of the Torah"), which appeals to "You" addressees concerning the halakic disagreements between "us" and "them," attests the Yaḥad's polemical engagement, at least rhetorically, with Jewish outsiders. The Roman "Kittim" enemy are highlighted in Pesher Habbakuk and the War Scroll. Some passages in the War Scroll

been important for the Yaḥad to lay claim to the common cultural heritage, a claim staked so effectively in the Rule's annual covenant ceremony that would have garnered support in repeated readings of nonsectarian texts like the weekly prayers in the Words of the Luminaries. Thus, maintaining continuity with Israelite identity would have been important principally in the construction of the Yaḥad's salient sectarian identity but, at the same time, could have enabled the Yaḥad to negotiate different perspectives reflected in their "library" and to navigate their fraught relationships, expedient as well as adversarial, with the outside world.

---

seem to envision a broader "people of God's redemption" (עם פדות אל, 1 QM 1:12, 14:4-5), whereas elsewhere this expression can be exclusivist (e.g., the expulsion ceremony in 4QD^a 11:13; note also 1QpHab 5:3-6). CD 4:10-12 implies that people will be able to join the sect until "the completion of the time of these years" when "each must stand on his fortress." Some scholars understand the Rule of the Congregation (1QSa) as legislation for a large eschatological community. See Licht, "Eternal Plant," 67–8; Lawrence H. Schiffman, *The Eschatological Community of the Dead Sea Scrolls: A Study of the Rule of the Congregation*, SBLMS 38 (Atlanta, GA: Scholars Press, 1989), 12, 68; and the new edition with a review of research by Yigal Bloch, Jonathan Ben-Dov, and Daniel Stökl Ben Ezra, "The Rule of the Congregation from Cave 1 of Qumran: A New Annotated Edition," *REJ* 178 (2019): 1–46. Many passages in Yaḥad works potentially bear on this issue (for a maximalist survey, see Gudrun Holtz, "Inclusivism at Qumran," *DSD* 16 [2009]: 22–54), but they are piecemeal and often nuanced differently, sometimes contradictorily; each warrants its own analysis and consideration for how it might have been negotiated—but not homogenized—with other sectarian texts and readings. Such a task is beyond the scope of the present article and is a suggested direction for future research.

Part 4

Scriptures on the Silver Screen 2.0

15

Lovers or (Just) Friends? Jesus and Mary Magdalene in the Gospel of John and in Film

Caroline Vander Stichele

In an article entitled "To Love the Lord: An Intertextual Reading of John 20" (1999), Adele Reinhartz presents two different readings of the relationship between Mary Magdalene and Jesus. One reading focuses on the issue of discipleship, the other on issues of physicality and sensuality. As far as the first reading is concerned, Reinhartz notes that Mary Magdalene can be considered a disciple in the broad sense of the word as someone who follows Jesus and believes he is the Messiah, but not in the narrow sense of someone who shared his life and traveled with him. In John 20:18 she serves as messenger between the risen Christ and his disciples, but "the words of Mary Magdalene have no discernable effect on their audience within the narrative."[1]

A different picture emerges in the second reading. In this case, the starting point is Mary's preoccupation with the absent body of Jesus and his reply in 20:17 that she should not touch him. Reinhartz chooses to read these features against the background of other biblical texts in which similar concerns appear. She draws attention to the garden setting in which the encounter takes place, a highly symbolic location in light of the creation story in Genesis 2–3 where the first couple meets. Equally relevant is Song of Songs, which features another garden representing the female lover, who is moreover depicted as searching for her beloved (3:1-14). This intertextual reading makes it possible to understand Mary Magdalene and Jesus as lovers. Even though the Gospel itself is silent about their relationship, such a reading is still available to the reader.

While Reinhartz herself refers in passing to Martin Scorcese's film *The Last Temptation of Christ* (1988) as an example of such a reading, in what follows I first explore the relationship between Jesus and Mary Magdalene as depicted in the more recent film *Mary Magdalene* (2018). In the second section of this essay, I compare the representation of their relationship with that in other films, taking Reinhartz's discussion of Mary Magdalene in *Jesus of Hollywood* (2007)[2] as my starting point. In

---

[1] Adele Reinhartz, "To Love the Lord: An Intertextual Reading of John 20," in *The Labour of Reading: Desire, Alienation, and Biblical Interpretation*, ed. Fiona C. Black, Roland Boer, and Erin Runions (Atlanta, GA: SBL Press, 1999), 53–69.
[2] Adele Reinhartz, *Jesus of Hollywood* (Oxford: Oxford University Press, 2007).

my conclusion I suggest that the interpretation of John 20 in *Mary Magdalene* makes it possible to see the relationship between Jesus and Mary Magdalene in a different light.

Mary Magdalene in *Mary Magdalene* (2018)

The film entitled *Mary Magdalene* was released internationally in 2018, but only came out a year later in Canada and the United States due to the scandals related to Harvey Weinstein, the producer of the film.[3] Its director was Garth Davis, who received the Academy Award for Outstanding Directorial Achievement for a First-Time Feature Film Director for his film *Lion* (2016). Major roles are played by well-known actors, such as Rooney Mara (Mary Magdalene), Joaquin Phoenix (Jesus), Chiwetel Ejiofor (Peter), and Tahar Rahim (Judas). The film was awarded twice for its music score by Hildur Guðnadóttir and Jóhann Jóhannsson. Notable also is that the script for the film was written by two women, Helen Edmundson and Philippa Goslett.[4] Notwithstanding this impressive lineup, the film was not successful.[5]

In what follows, I first give a general outline of the film before discussing the representation of Mary Magdalene and how she relates to Jesus. I focus more specifically on two scenes that frame their relationship, that is, their first encounter in the beginning of the film and their final encounter at the empty tomb.

Outline of the Film

The film starts with underwater shots of a woman who is swimming upward toward the surface, while a female voice-over tells, "And she asked him, 'What will it be like? The Kingdom?' And he said, 'It is like a grain of mustard seed, which a woman took and sowed in her garden. And it grew and it grew. And the birds of the air made nests in its branches.'"[6] Next, the viewer is informed (text on screen) that the following narrative plays out in Judea, 33 CE, where Herod Antipas governs the Jewish people. They look forward to the Messiah, who will deliver them from the Romans and initiate the kingdom of God.

---

[3] See, for instance, the attention that *Time Magazine* devoted to the issue in 2017: https://time.com/magazine/us/4979222/october-23rd-2017-vol-190-no-16-u-s/ and https://time.com/time-person-of-the-year-2017-silence-breakers/ (checked June 20, 2022).

[4] Goslett expressed the hope that *Mary Magdalene* "goes some way to restoring her spiritual authority." Quote from Nick Hasted, "Mary Magdalene and Christian Cinema's Resurrection," *The Independent* (March 15, 2018), https://www.independent.co.uk/arts-entertainment/films/features/mary-magdalene-film-rooney-mara-joaquin-phoenix-religion-a8258036.html.

[5] It was rated a meager 5.9/10 by 10,000 reviewers on the IMDB website: https://www.imdb.com/title/tt5360996/?ref_=nv_sr_srsg_0 (checked April 30, 2022), or as Fletcher notes, "Indeed, its place within a capitalistic society is one of total failure, if profits are the judge." See Michelle Fletcher, "Seeing Differently with *Mary Magdalene*," in *The T&T Clark Handbook of Jesus and Film*, ed. Richard Walsh (London: T&T Clark, 2021), 55–65, here 62.

[6] The parable of the mustard seed appears in the canonical Gospels (Mark 4:30-32; Matt 13:31-32; Luke 13:19) and in the Gospel of Thomas 20. Only Luke identifies the place as a garden. Unique to the film is that the sower is a woman.

After this introduction, the first characters we learn about are not Jesus and his followers, but Mary Magdalene and her family. Because she refuses to marry, an exorcism is performed to free her from the demon that they believe is the cause of her unnatural behavior. This interaction does not have the wished-for result and another healer is called in to cure her. The healer in question appears to be Jesus. This encounter changes her, but not in the direction that her family wants.

Instead of marrying, Mary Magdalene decides to leave her family and follow Jesus. She joins the group of his (exclusively male) disciples. In this group, two disciples stand out in terms of how they relate to her at several points in the story. One is Judas, who welcomes her. The other one is Peter, who sees her as an intruder. Another important, in this case female, character is Jesus's mother. What she has in common with Mary Magdalene is her love for Jesus. On the journey to Jerusalem, she asks, "You love my son, don't you?" Mary Magdalene remains silent. His mother continues, "Then you must prepare yourself like me." "For what?" asks Mary Magdalene. "To lose him."

After sharing the Last Supper, Jesus is taken captive in the garden of Gethsemane. Mary Magdalene is knocked unconscious by a Roman soldier. When she wakes up, Jesus has already been sentenced to death and is on his way to Golgotha. She catches a glimpse of him bearing his cross. She is present again when he dies on the cross and when he is buried. She is the only one who stays at the tomb and sees the risen Christ when she wakes up in the morning. She then goes to the other disciples, who are staying in a room together. Here a final confrontation with Peter takes place. He tells her, "It's not right that you come here now to tell us he has chosen you before us, that he has brought you some special message." She replies, "He gathered us for what was inside. We were all precious to him. We were all his apostles." He answers, "Every man in this room is his rock, his church, upon which he will build his glorious new world with *one* purpose and *one* message." She responds, "Your message. Not his." Peter sighs and says, "You have weakened us, Mary. You weakened him." She leaves them with the words, "You are all my brothers and I thank you. But I will not stay and be silent. I will be heard."

She returns to the tomb, where she meets Jesus one more time. After this meeting, we see her walk. She is joined by other women, while a voice-over repeats the lines from the opening: "It is like a seed ... ." An underwater scene follows that mirrors the beginning of the film, but in this case with multiple women swimming to the surface. After this underwater scene, the following statement appears in white on a black background, worth quoting in full:

> According to Christian Gospels, Mary of Magdala was present at both Jesus' death and burial; and is identified as the first witness to the resurrected Jesus. In 591, Pope Gregory claimed that Mary of Magdala was a prostitute, a misconception which remains to this day. In 2016, Mary of Magdala was formally identified by the Vatican as Apostle of the Apostles—their equal—and the first messenger of the resurrected Jesus. This film is inspired by the story of Mary Magdalene. While artistic license has been taken, we believe that the film is true to the essence, values and integrity of Mary and her story. The biblical story of Mary Magdalene can be found in the Gospels.

Mary Magdalene and Jesus

Mary Magdalene is introduced at the Sea of Galilee, busy with fishing nets. She has a pale, delicate skin; regular features; long, black hair; and a slender body. She is a beauty according to white Western standards. She is usually dressed in sober, earth-colored garments, and most often appears with her head covered. Jesus has a more tanned, weathered skin and disheveled, brown hair. Gray hairs appear in his beard, making him look older than her. At first sight, this representation of both Mary Magdalene and Jesus conforms to gendered stereotypes. However, as Emmett (2020) argues, the picture looks different when their respective behavior is considered. In leaving her family, Mary breaks away from traditional gender roles, while Jesus's body language and voice tend to problematize dominant perceptions of masculinity.[7]

The following scenes are important for what they tell us about the relationship that is established between Mary and Jesus throughout the story: Mary Magdalene meets Jesus the healer; she hears him preach and sees him heal the sick in Magdala; she decides to follow him; Jesus baptizes her; they have a private conversation; he asks her advice on what to preach to the women of Cana; she comforts him after the raising of Lazarus; she washes his feet before the Last Supper and he anoints her eyes; she sees him on the road to Golgotha; she is present when he dies on the cross; she meets the risen Christ at the empty tomb (twice). Since I cannot discuss all these scenes in detail here, I will focus on the first and last meetings of Mary and Jesus and make some general observations about the way in which Mary and Jesus relate to each other throughout the film.

The scene in which they first meet takes place the morning after the exorcism. Mary Magdalene and her father are lying fully dressed together on the floor in an otherwise empty room. She has her back turned to him. Her brother Joseph comes in and says, "Father, please, let me bring the healer." He nods, goes outside, and says off-screen, "She won't talk to me. I don't know who she is anymore." Mary tears up. The presumed healer replies off-screen, "I'll see her alone." We hear the door open and close. Still off-screen the healer says, "Your family says you grapple with the demon." Without turning around, Mary replies, "If there's a demon in me, it's always been there. I wish there was a demon." Healer (still off-screen): "Why? What is it that you fear in yourself?" Mary: "My thoughts. My longings, my unhappiness. I fear that I shame my family. I do shame them. I'm not as I'm supposed to be." Healer: "What is it you long for?" Mary: "I'm not sure. To know God."

For the first time, the camera turns to the healer who is sitting/kneeled and looking down at her, saying, "And yet you've felt God's presence." At this point, Mary turns

---

[7] More problematic is the way in which gender and ethnicity intersect in the film. As Greydanus observes, "Only Mara's white heroine understands Phoenix's divine white man; Ejiofor's black patriarchal leader rejects the truth, while Arabic actor Tahar Rahim's naïve Judas betrays Jesus and commits suicide." See Steven D. Greydanus, "Through Other Eyes: Point of View and Defamiliarization in Jesus Films," in *The T&T Clark Handbook of Jesus and Film*, ed. Richard Walsh (London: T&T Clark, 2021), 77–88, here 86. On the issue of Jesus's whiteness and ethnicity, see also Adele Reinhartz, *Bible and Cinema: An Introduction* (London: Routledge, 2013), 62; Grace Emmett, "'You Weakened Him': Jesus's Masculinity in *Mary Magdalene*," *Religion and Gender* 10 (2020): 97–117, here 102, and Fletcher, "Seeing Differently," 61.

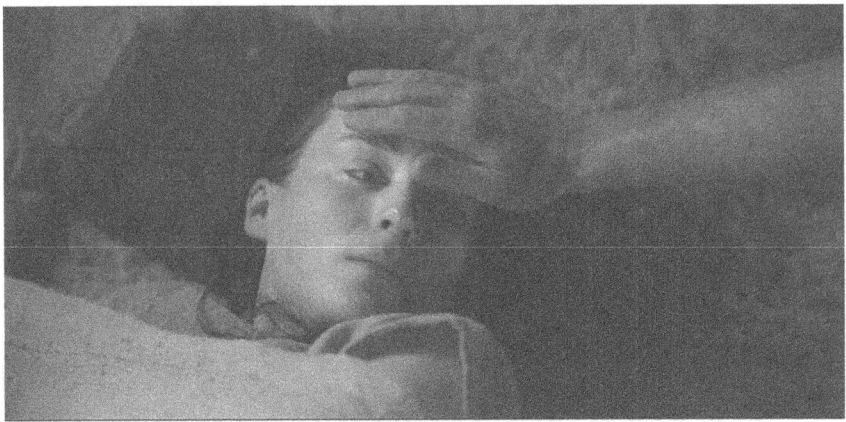

Figure 15.1 Jesus blesses Mary, *Mary Magdalene* (Film4 et al., 2018).

around and looks at him. She replies, "Sometimes, in the stillness, I think I feel it." The healer/Jesus says, "It's always been there. All it needs is your faith." They look at each other. Jesus smiles and says, "There are no demons here." He holds a hand over her forehead without touching it and adds, "Rest now. Rest in the light." In the next shot, we see her look through the window while he leaves the house and goes away with his disciples.

This scene is highly relevant both in terms of what we see and also what we hear in the conversations. The position of the father at the beginning of the scene is ambiguous. It can be interpreted as an expression not only of paternal care and concern but also of paternalistic control. In any case, Mary lies literally turned away from him and refuses to talk. The healer is called in to do what the failed exorcism could not. He kneels/sits down on the floor. Initially, Mary stays in the same position on the floor, turned away from him. Verbal contact is established first. Only halfway through the conversation does she turn her head to face him. At that point, eye contact is made as well. Mary is still lying on the floor looking up at him, while he is sitting on the floor looking down on her. He declares that there is no demon. This diagnosis replaces that of her father/family. The result is that a transfer of authority takes place from the father to Jesus as healer, marked by the gesture he makes with his hand and his final blessing (see Figure 15.1).

Because Jesus is framed as superior, his interpretation is validated over against that of her family. In both cases Mary Magdalene appears as the object of competing interpretations. As Walsh and Staley note, "Despite the film's feminist concern for Mary's POV and experience, this camerawork reflects a decidedly 'orthodox Christian' predisposition about Jesus's identity, and a 'paternalistic' leading of the viewer to 'confess' Jesus as 'God,' before Mary herself is capable of such a confession."[8]

---

[8] Richard Walsh and Jeffrey L. Staley, *Jesus, the Gospels, and Cinematic Imagination: Introducing Jesus Movies, Christ Films, and the Messiah in Motion* (London: T&T Clark, 2022), 315. On the

Figure 15.2 Mary greets the resurrected Jesus, *Mary Magdalene* (Film4 et al., 2018).

Nevertheless, it is worth noting at this point that Jesus dismisses the dominant interpretation of Mary Magdalene as someone "from whom seven demons had gone out" (Luke 8:3), because he denies here that she was really possessed to begin with. Instead, he recognizes and affirms her spiritual aspiration "to know God," over against the expectation that she would marry and bear children. In the process, however, this framing of the conflict reinscribes the opposition between the flesh and the spirit, which we also find in *The Last Temptation of Christ*, where it is the ultimate inner struggle of Jesus himself.

The final meeting of Jesus and Mary at the end of the film is also highly relevant to understand how their relationship is portrayed in the film. This meeting consists of two parts that bracket Mary's visit to the disciples in the room. In the first part, Mary wakes up at the tomb in the morning when she hears a voice whisper "Mary." She looks up and sees Jesus sitting at a distance looking out over the mountains, with his back turned to her. He is dressed in white. She gets up, walks over, sits down next to him, and looks at him. They do not say a word. When she returns from her visit to the disciples, Jesus still sits in the same place. When she stands next to him, he looks up at her. They make eye contact. She sits down and turns to him. He says, "You do not lose heart. Even now. Didn't you ask, 'What will it be like? The Kingdom?'" He smiles, she smiles back, and they both start laughing. Important visual features of these scenes at the tomb are that she does not cover her hair, as most often is the case throughout the film (see Figure 15.2), and that she sits down next to him.[9]

These scenes are reminiscent of the story in John 20. They have the following elements in common: Mary stays at the tomb weeping (20:11); the tomb is open the

---

importance of POV in the film, see also Fletcher, "Seeing Differently," and Greydanus, "Through Other Eyes."

[9] Mary and Jesus also had a private conversation earlier in the film. In that case too, Mary joins Jesus, who is sitting alone outside at a distance. She sits down next to him, but in this instance, she keeps her hair covered.

next morning (20:1); Jesus calls her by her name (20:16); she sees him (20:14) and goes to the disciples to tell them (20:18). There are, however, notable differences as well: no other people are present at the tomb; she does not enter the tomb; there are no messengers/angels; she does not address Jesus; she does not receive a message for the disciples from him.

More in general, the following observations can be made about their relationship in the film. She is the only female disciple in the inner circle.[10] She addresses him with 'Rabbi' like the other disciples but relates to him in a way that other disciples do not. Jesus and Mary often make eye contact. They have private conversations. Besides their first and last meetings, this is also the case after the raising of Lazarus and before the Last Supper. Moreover, they have physical contact. Mary grasps his head when he is overwhelmed by the sick in Magdala. After the raising of Lazarus, Jesus puts his head in her lap, and she caresses it. She washes his feet before the Last Supper, he anoints her eyes. In sum, there is a certain degree of physical intimacy. Finally, she is the only one to meet the resurrected Jesus. As a result, their relationship is presented as both unique and exclusive.

This representation of Mary Magdalene is strikingly different when compared with the two intertextual readings of John 20 that Reinhartz presents in the article mentioned at the beginning of this essay. On the one hand, in the film she is clearly portrayed as his disciple who not only follows Jesus but also travels with him and shares his life. Moreover, her message to the disciples does have a clear impact, especially on Peter. On the other hand, Jesus and Mary are not portrayed as lovers. Jesus is the object of Mary's affection and devotion. She touches him. He allows her to do so, and, in a few cases, he also touches her.[11] They get together outside on a mountain, but not in a garden setting (apart from Gethsemane, where they are not alone). However, as Walsh and Staley note, considering the many references to the Gospel of John, "one might argue that the film's Mary is the 'Beloved Disciple,' and even the Johannine tradition's source."[12]

Comparison with Other Films

In her book *Jesus of Hollywood* (2007), Reinhartz discusses the way in which Mary Magdalene appears and relates to Jesus in earlier movies.[13] She notes that filmmakers

---

[10] As Greydanus rightly notes with reference to Luke 8:1-3 where more women are mentioned, this is a missed opportunity "for a genuinely novel feminist contribution to the world of Jesus," but "it runs counter to the wish to highlight Mary's uniqueness." Greydanus, "Through Other Eyes," 86.

[11] This is the case when she is baptized by Jesus and when he anoints her eyes after she washed his feet. In both these cases, the touching is related to a ritual.

[12] Walsh and Staley, *Jesus, the Gospels, and Cinematic Imagination*, 319, n. 25. That Mary Magdalene may have been the Beloved Disciple in the Gospel of John has been suggested by Esther de Boer, *The Gospel of Mary: Beyond a Gnostic and a Biblical Mary Magdalene*, JSNTSup 260 (London: T&T Clark, 2004), 183-90.

[13] See also the shorter discussion in Reinhartz, *Bible and Cinema*, 66-7, 72-4, and Caroline Vander Stichele, "Mary Magdalene Portrayed on the Silver Screen," in *Mary Magdalene: Chief Witness, Sinner, Feminist* (Utrecht: Museum Catharijneconvent, 2021), 26-31.

address four issues related to her character: Mary's life before Jesus, Mary among the apostles, Mary as apostle to the apostles, and Mary and Jesus. These issues are a useful starting point for my comparison with *Mary Magdalene*.

As far as Mary's life before she meets Jesus is concerned, Reinhartz notes that the dominant interpretation of Mary as a prostitute or adulteress is reproduced from the silent film era onward. *The Last Temptation of Christ* (1988) is a notable example here. This reputation is reflected in the way she appears: her clothes, hairdo, jewelry, and makeup. Reinhartz notes that more recently a shift has taken place in that Mary no longer is a troublesome woman but rather a troubled one. The result being that "Magdalene still needs redemption."[14] *Mary Magdalene* distances itself explicitly from the view that Mary was a prostitute. It is called a "misconception" in the statement quoted earlier that appears on screen at the end of the film. There is also nothing in her appearance that hints in that direction. More interesting is the fact that the film also distances itself from the perception that she was somehow "possessed." In the first scene, discussed earlier, Jesus himself declares that "there are no demons here." In doing so, he also distances himself from the view reflected in Luke 8:3 that seven demons had gone out from her. Some progress has thus been made in leaving behind these traditional interpretations, which are nevertheless reproduced in other films until the present day.[15]

This brings us to the second issue that Reinhartz mentions: Mary among the apostles. She notes that Mary Magdalene is often represented as traveling along with Jesus and his disciples. This is also the case in *Mary Magdalene*, where she receives a mixed response. Of special interest is the presence of Mary at the Last Supper in some films.[16] In *Mary Magdalene*, Jesus and Mary are the last ones to arrive at the table and Mary is seated at his right-hand side (see Figure 15.3).

This is the place of honor, occupied in other cases by the apostle John.[17] Another observation concerns her relationship with Jesus's mother, equally a recurring element in Jesus films.[18] In Gibson's *The Passion of the Christ* (2004), for instance, she appears as Mary's younger double, as they are dressed alike and following Jesus around together.[19] This is not the case in *Mary Magdalene*. Although they meet on several occasions, they

---

[14] Reinhartz, *Jesus of Hollywood*, 135.

[15] A recent example is the first episode of the series *The Chosen* (2017–), which features a demonically possessed Mary Magdalene. In *Son of Man* (2006), the woman caught in adultery from John 8:1-11 is lumped together with the sinner from Luke 7:36-50 and identified as Mary Magdalene in the credits. In a similar vein, the woman from John 8 is played by a former sex worker and identified in the credits as Mary Magdalene in *Das Neue Evangelium* (2020).

[16] Reinhartz refers to *The Last Temptation*, *Jesus* (1999), and *The Gospel of John* (2003) in this respect. See Reinhartz, *Jesus of Hollywood*, 136.

[17] This is, for instance, the case in Leonardo Da Vinci's famous fresco. In Dan Brown's, *The Da Vinci Code* (New York: Doubleday, 2003) and the film based on this novel, John is identified as Mary Magdalene.

[18] As, for instance, is the case in *The Greatest Story Ever Told* (1965) and Zeffirelli's *Jesus of Nazareth* (1977). See Reinhartz, *Jesus of Hollywood*, 136-7.

[19] See my analysis of *The Passion* in Caroline Vander Stichele, "Mary Magdalene in Motion," in *Recent Releases: The Bible in Contemporary Cinema*, ed. Geert Hallbäck and Annika Hvithamar (Sheffield: Sheffield Phoenix, 2008), 93–114, here 94–9.

Figure 15.3 Mary's place at the Last Supper, *Mary Magdalene* (Film4 et al., 2018).

do not have a close relationship. Nevertheless, what they have in common is their love for Jesus.

The third issue that Reinhartz discusses relates to the representation of Mary as apostle to the apostles, a view that is largely based on the story about Mary's visit to the tomb in John 20. This scene is often included in Jesus biopics, but Mary's role in the resurrection narrative is frequently overshadowed by that of other characters, especially Peter.[20] As already noted, Mary does not even leave the tomb in *Mary Magdalene*. When she sees Jesus the next morning, she goes to the disciples to report it, but she does not receive a message from Jesus. Nevertheless, she is identified at the end of the film as "first messenger of the resurrected Jesus" and as "apostle of the apostles" with reference to the Vatican decree that was issued in 2016.[21] She is moreover identified as "their equal," an addition that does not appear in the Vatican decree.

The fourth issue is the relationship between Mary and Jesus. Reinhartz notes that in most films a romance develops between the two, but that the passionate potential of their relationship, as expressed in their gazes, is never consummated. A notable exception is *The Last Temptation* in which Jesus and Mary are portrayed as lovers, but this scene is later unmasked as a trick from the devil to lead Jesus astray and as part of the last temptation referred to in the title. So even in this film, Jesus and Mary were "not really" lovers. In *Jesus Christ Superstar* (1973), Mary is portrayed as loving Jesus and she expresses this in the comfort and care she seeks to give him. Much to Judas's frustration, Jesus does not refuse her attention. This is also very much the case in *Mary Magdalene*. Here too, Mary expresses her love and care for Jesus, who accepts

---

[20] The response of the disciples to her message is one of unbelief in Zeffirelli's film, but she is taken seriously in Young's *Jesus* (Reinhartz, *Jesus of Hollywood*, 139). See also Schaberg's analysis of Zeffirelli's Magdalene in Jane Schaberg, "Fast Forwarding to the Magdalene," in *Biblical Glamour and Hollywood Glitz*, ed. Alice Bach, Semeia 74 (Atlanta, GA: SBL Press, 1996), 33–45, here 38–43.

[21] See https://www.vatican.va/roman_curia/congregations/ccdds/documents/sanctae-m-magdalenae-decretum_en.pdf (checked April 30, 2022).

her attention. If a special bond develops between the two, it is clearly on a spiritual, not a physical level.

In her conclusion, Reinhartz observes that the relationship between Jesus and Mary is usually hierarchical in film (148). She identifies more specifically three ways in which Jesus relates to Mary. The first is the *asexual Jesus* who loves all of humankind. She identifies *Jesus of Montreal* (1989) as a film in which this is the case. The second is the *conflicted Jesus*, who is torn between the spirit and the flesh, including sexual desire. Examples are Young's *Jesus* and Scorcese's *Last Temptation*. The third is the *sexual Jesus*, as portrayed in the final part of *The Last Temptation* and to some degree in *Jesus Christ Superstar*, but also suggested in *The Da Vinci Code* (2006) in which Mary Magdalene is identified as Jesus's wife.

Where does *Mary Magdalene* fit in then? Although Mary's gender is very much an issue in this film, it is not an issue in her relationship with Jesus, but with Peter. From their very first encounter Mary and Jesus connect on a spiritual level and that remains the case throughout the film. As in other films, their relationship is asymmetrical as well as asexual.[22] He accepts her as one of his disciples when he baptizes her, and she addresses him as Rabbi. She offers him (physical) comfort and care, as is also the case in *Jesus Christ Superstar*. The traditional anointing scene is, however, strikingly missing and "replaced" by her washing his feet before the Last Supper, a gesture that is attributed to Jesus himself during Last Supper in the Gospel of John (13:1-20), and by his anointing her eyes, a reversal of the anointing scenes in the different Gospels in which a woman anoints Jesus's head or feet (Mark 14:3-9; Matthew 26:6-13; Luke 7:36-50; and John 12:1-8).

The relationship between Mary and Jesus is exclusive and unique in that he relates to her in a different way than with the other disciples. This does not go unnoticed by the others, especially Peter, who has an antagonistic relationship with her from the beginning. This issue reaches its climax when Mary visits them after seeing the resurrected Jesus and Peter accuses her of weakening both Jesus and them. She is perceived as a bad influence, distracting him from his mission. This conflict does not appear in the canonical Gospels, but in the Gospel of Mary.[23] Both *Mary Magdalene* and also other films (*The Da Vinci Code* and *Mary* [2005]) draw on material from this document in their plot.[24]

---

[22] So also Rindge, who notes that "Jesus and Mary form an intimate, *asexual* bond. In contrast to most depictions, Mary is not sexual with anyone." Matthew S. Rindge, *Bible and Film: The Basics* (London: Routledge, 2022), 114 (italics in original).

[23] Especially Gospel of Mary 17:10–18:21, where not only Peter, but also Andrew and Levi play a role in the discussion. See Christopher Tuckett, ed., *The Gospel of Mary* (Oxford: Oxford University Press, 2007), 99–101. In "Mary Magdalene and Christian Cinema's Resurrection," Hasted mentions that Edmundson consulted the Gospel of Mary. Peter also takes on an antagonistic attitude toward Mary at the end of the Gospel of Thomas 114. Moreover, in both the canonical Gospels and extracanonical literature (the Epistle of the Apostles and the Gospel of Mary), the disciples express their doubts about the message of the women returning from the tomb; see Caroline Vander Stichele, "Talking Nonsense? The Disciples' Response to the Women in Luke 24:1-22 and Other Early Christian Texts," in *Themes and Texts in Luke-Acts: Essays in Honour of Bart J. Koet*, ed. Bert Jan Lietaert Peerbolte, Caroline Vander Stichele, and Archibald L. H. M. van Wieringen (Leiden: Brill, forthcoming).

[24] See my discussion of both films in Vander Stichele, "Mary Magdalene in Motion," 99–109.

Conclusion

Mary Magdalene presents the empty tomb story of John 20 with a twist. After her initial meeting with the resurrected Jesus, Mary visits the disciples to tell them. She did not receive a message for them from Jesus, as is the case in John 20:17, but her words do have an impact on the disciples. When she returns to the tomb, Jesus is still seated in the same place. She sits down next to him, happy to see him again, with "all his pain gone from him," as she tells Peter. This representation differs from traditional iconography in which the resurrected Jesus, sometimes disguised as gardener, is standing while Mary is on her knees.[25] It opens the possibility of still another reading of their relationship than that of lovers and seeing them in a refreshing new light: looking and laughing just like friends.

---

[25] See Ann-Sophie Lehmann, "Maria Magdalena und die feministische Kunstgeschichte," in *Doing Gender in Medien-, Kunst- und Kulturwissenschaften: Eine Einführung*, ed. Rosemarie Buikema and Kathrin Thiele (Berlin: LIT, 2017), 159–77, here 165. An example is Rembrandt's depiction of this famous scene, known as *Noli me tangere* (*c.* 1645). See https://www.rijksmuseum.nl/en/collection/RP-T-1961-80 (checked May 9, 2022). See also Tizian (*c.* 1514): https://www.nationalgallery.org.uk/paintings/titian-noli-me-tangere (checked May 9, 2022).

16

What a Friend We Have in Jesus: A Consideration of Jesus as Friend in Jesus Films

Richard Walsh

Looking for Friends (in All the Wrong Places)

In her influential *Jesus of Hollywood*, Adele Reinhartz explores Jesus films as biopics and demonstrates that the genre's template overrides the films' historical claims. In the template, the biopic hero/heroine pursues a new idea invariably bringing him/her into conflict with the surrounding culture. A friend and a romantic interest sustain the hero/heroine. A judicial trial "provides the occasion for an impassioned summation of the hero's primary message."[1] Reinhartz, however, detects peculiarities in the Jesus biopics: (1) Jesus is a celibate, not a romantic figure (with infamous exceptions). (2) Jesus is an individualistic loner, with an ambiguous attitude to his own ethnic group. He is a universal, spiritual savior, not a Jew living under Roman domination. (3) The Hollywood Jesus fails to liberate his people, a failure the biopics bypass without comment. Further, the final judicial trial ladles blame onto Jesus's opponents rather than providing a final statement of his message.[2] These deviations suggest Jesus films' failure as biopics.

The last two peculiarities raise the specter of anti-Semitism or anti-Judaism,[3] a matter to which Reinhartz has often attended;[4] but it is her search for the biopic Jesus's

---

[1] Adele Reinhartz, *Jesus of Hollywood* (Oxford: Oxford University Press, 2007), 5. Reinhartz relies on George F. Custen, *Bio/Pics: How Hollywood Constructed Public History* (New Brunswick, NJ: Rutgers University Press, 1992), who himself built upon Leo Lowenthal, "Biographies in Popular Magazines," in *Radio Research: 1942–43*, ed. Paul Lazarsfeld and Frank Stanton (New York: Duell, Sloan, and Pearce, 1944), 507–48.

[2] Reinhartz, *Jesus of Hollywood*, 44, 63, 126, 249–50, 252–6. The last peculiarity understates, while devastatingly criticizing, the passion tradition's persistent ad hominem rhetoric.

[3] On the implicit supersessionism in Jesus films' tropes/themes, see Richard Walsh, "'My Kingdom Is Not of This World': Johannine Jesus Films and Christian Supersessionism," in *The Gospel of John and Jewish-Christian Relations*, ed. Adele Reinhartz (Lanham, MD: Lexington Books/Fortress Academic, 2018), 165–83. On "anti-Judaism" as a foundational concept utilized to construe Western "worldviews," see David Nirenberg, *Anti-Judaism: The Western Tradition* (New York: Norton, 2013).

[4] In addition to *Jesus of Hollywood* and her *Bible and Cinema: An Introduction* (New York: Routledge, 2013), see, for example, her "Violence against the Jews: Anti-Judaism in the Jesus Movies," in *Religion und Gewalt im Bibelfilm, Film und Theologie* 20, ed. Reinhold Zwick (Marburg: Schüren, 2012), 99–126; "Judaism and Antisemitism in Bible Movies," in *The Bible in Motion: A Handbook of*

friends that captures my attention here. The quest leads her to Mary Magdalene and Judas, but Jesus's aloof distance, which is intensified, if not created, by the Jesus biopics' peculiarities, typically undercuts his potential as friend.[5] While interpreters (since the Gospel of Mark) have routinely pointed to Jesus's friends' failure (e.g., through misunderstandings or betrayals), Reinhartz's analysis points toward the cinematic Jesus's own failure as friend.[6] Or, at the very least, her work invites one to consider, in the words of a famous Protestant hymn, "What a Friend We Have in (the Cinematic) Jesus."

Reinhartz asks a similar question in her *Befriending the Beloved Disciple*. Instead of Jesus, however, she looks to the Fourth Gospel's implied author (or the text's narrative standards) as a potential friend and asks what kind of friend this implied author is and what this friend asks the reader to become.[7] The Gospel of John's alienation of "the Jews" as Other makes it impossible for Reinhartz to accept the implied author/text's offer of friendship.[8] Accordingly, she moves beyond a complimentary reading, which would install the implied author as mentor, to three other readings: (1) a resistant reading that rejects the implied author as opponent, but which simply reverses the text's Othering (binary oppositions); (2) a sympathetic reading that sees the implied author as colleague, ignoring difference and celebrating similarities, but which lacks the openness and reciprocity of true friendship; and finally (3) an engaged reading that retains the Jewish identity the text threatens while striving to maintain a relationship and conversation with the implied author as Other (as well as with those who adopt the Gospel's message). Adopting a critical pluralism, Reinhartz appeals for a dialogue between, if not final adjudication of, different interpretations in light of ethical/

---

the Bible and Its Reception in Film, Part 2, ed. Rhonda Burnette-Bletsch (Berlin: de Gruyter, 2016), 777–91.

[5] The distant Jesus in Pasolini's *Il vangelo secondo Matteo* (1964) is not atypical. The film that embeds Jesus in community most successfully is Rossellini's *Il messia* (1975). *Godspell* (1973) and *Son of Man* (2006) also emphasize community, but with less success.

[6] Aristotle's three types of friendship (utility, pleasure, and shared values; *Eth. nic.* 8.2.4) loom large in the background of most discussions of "friend." The last relies on a reciprocity and equality (and a respect of common excellence) lacking in the cinematic Jesus's relationships. In *Befriending the Beloved Disciple: A Jewish Reading of the Gospel of John* (New York: Continuum, 2005), 157, Reinhartz says similarly that friendship includes engagement, reciprocity, and acceptance of the Other. See further David Konstan, *Friendship in the Classical World* (Cambridge: Cambridge University Press, 1997). Speaking of biopics, Custen notes similar "friendship" failings: the hero/heroine is often an idiot savant, the price of whose fame is estrangement; the hero/heroine takes from friends, rather than giving; friends are mirrors reflecting the hero/heroine's glory; and they are surrogates for the audience (*Bio/Pics*, 163–5). The statements apply well to Jesus films.

[7] Reinhartz, *Befriending the Beloved Disciple*, 30–1, 156–67. In conceiving a book as a friend, Reinhartz follows Wayne Booth, *The Company We Keep: An Ethics of Fiction* (Berkeley: University of California Press, 1988). My focus on the Jesus of film, rather than film's implied filmmaker, differs theoretically from Reinhartz's implied author-focus but is still arguably a site to consider film's (narrative) standards.

[8] She also rejects the Gospel's claims about Jesus's divinity, its failure to acknowledge that Jesus's virtues are Jewish, and its assertion of an atoning death's necessity (Reinhartz, *Befriending the Beloved Disciple*, 134–6, 141). Here, she follows Samuel Sandmel, *We Jews and Jesus* (New York: Oxford University Press, 1965), vii, 44–7. In addition to her own Jewish and feminist experiences/studies, she relies, in the move to and beyond a resistant reading, on Judith Fetterley, *The Resisting Reader: A Feminist Approach to American Fiction* (Bloomington: Indiana University Press, 1978).

political desiderata. Given the inherent certainties and dangers of monomyths, she is understandably uncertain of the outcome.[9]

In what follows, I celebrate Reinhartz's quest for unlikely friends with this brief footnote to her work, considering the typical kind of friends on offer in cinematic Jesuses. I begin by dismissing what appears to be rosy evidence for friend Jesus, and then look briefly at two moments in Jesus cinema to make some comments on the kind of friend Jesus typically is in Jesus cinema.

Pray without Ceasing: Can We Have a Friend in Jesus?

Some recent appraisals of the US Jesus suggest US religiosity and popular culture have moved steadily toward what one might call friend Jesus. Thus, Steven Prothero traces a move from a focus on God to one on the loving Son, including the gradual liberation of Jesus from Calvinism, creed, the Bible, and Christianity. For Prothero, this trend Americanizes Jesus.[10] US optimism and a move toward an increasingly personal Jesus are undeniable; nevertheless, Jesus remains, with some exceptions, loftily above potential friends. He is dubbed an icon, in Prothero's subtitle, and a savior and cultural hero in the subtitle of Richard Wightman Fox's similar work.[11] Jesus simply does not become the reciprocal, engaged friend that Reinhartz (and Aristotle) desires.

Even the popular hymn "What a Friend We Have in Jesus" tells this tale. The hymn began as a poem in the 1850s by Joseph M. Scriven.[12] He had a difficult, subsistence life, lost two fiancées to death, and became estranged from his family because of his attraction to the Plymouth Brethren. Reportedly, Scriven wrote the poem for his mother when he learned either of her illness or of his father's death. The highly sentimental poem appeals to pathos, rather than logos or ethos, and its imagery relies heavily on pain/pleasure, rather than evil/good.

The poem became a hymn around 1870. Charles Converse wrote the music and gave the hymn its well-known title. The poem's original title, "Pray Without Ceasing" (1 Thess 5:17), rightly depicts both poem and hymn as calls to prayer. Therefore, the poem/hymn instructs devotees or clients, not friends, to entreat Jesus as God, Lord, and Savior.[13] If he is "friend," he is above all other friends in the poem/hymn's final stanza. He is a benevolent deity or patron, bearing his underlings' burdens, rather than

---

[9] Reinhartz, *Befriending the Beloved Disciple*, 156–67.
[10] Stephen Prothero, *American Jesus: How the Son of God Became a National Icon* (New York: Farrar, Straus and Giroux, 2003), 10–16.
[11] Richard Wightman, *Jesus in America: Personal Savior, Cultural Hero, National Obsession* (San Francisco, CA: HarperSanFrancisco, 2004).
[12] For the hymn's history and interpretation, see Chris Fenner, "What a Friend We Have in Jesus," *Hymnology Archive*, March 22, 2021, https://www.hymnologyarchive.com/what-a-friend-we-have-in-jesus. Fenner includes the lyrics. Ira Sankey popularized the hymn by including it in the first and subsequent editions of his *Gospel Hymns and Sacred Songs* (Chicago, IL: Biglow & Main, 1875).
[13] Perhaps Jesus is not the God and/or Lord of later lines, but a disjoint worthy of note seems unlikely given the hymn's evangelical Protestantism.

calling companions to their work (John 15:15) or to his yoke (Matt 11:28-30).[14] His followers are weak, not Aristotle's excellent friends.

Jesus hagiography is at work here. Jesus is hallowed and, almost always, deified. Can such a figure be "friend"? As the sacred is normally defined (at least in biblical religions) as the source of power and meaning upon which worshipers rely (like the branches on the Johannine vine), it is hard to imagine. Accordingly, in biblical passages where friends of God are in view, the aura is still worship, obedience, and faith. For example, Abraham is God's friend in James 2:23, but because of the belief he expressed in following God's demand to sacrifice Isaac. The Johannine Jesus's followers are friends, but only because they are branches dwelling in the Jesus-vine and because they follow Jesus's commandments, which separates them from the world (John 15:12-15). The reference to Moses in Exod 33:11 might be an exception, but it occurs in a simile, and even there Moses receives commands from the sacred Other.

Typically, matters are similar in Jesus cinema. When Jesus addresses his disciples as friends in *The Gospel of John* (2003), he is mentoring them (in a visualization of John 15:12-16). He is doing something like what Reinhartz imagines the Gospel's implied author doing in her complimentary reading of John or exercising what Michel Foucault pithily termed "pastoral power."[15] The cinematic Jesus leads from above. Notably, a similar aloofness is in play when Jesus addresses the betraying Judas as friend (Matt 26:50)—even in the comic *Godspell*.

Sacred figures make unlikely friends. Accordingly, one of Reinhartz's most significant moves in her quest to befriend the Beloved Disciple is to shift away from a quest for a hardly conceivable friendship with the theological/metaphysical Other, or with one who claims to speak for this Other, to an attempt to imagine the more human, post-structural or postcolonial Other as friend.[16] Even Prothero finally seems to agree that friend Jesus is unlikely or, perhaps, undesirable. Although he is remarkably tolerant of diverse Jesuses, he wonders in his conclusion if any Jesus is "over the top" and cites as possibilities Ralph Kozak's "The Laughing Christ," *Dogma*'s Buddy Christ, and, one might add, the protagonist of *Monty Python's Life of Brian*.[17] Significantly, the last two amuse only if the viewer reads them as parodies of a divine/epic Christ.[18] They are funny only because they are "wrong" or incongruous.[19]

---

[14] These passages are often cited by hymnal editors, but the Jesus of these passages is much more demanding than that of the hymn. Proverbs 18:24 or Psalm 55:22, cited by some hymnal editors, may be nearer the hymn's aura. See Fenner, "What a Friend."

[15] See Michel Foucault, "The Subject and Power," in *Michel Foucault: Beyond Structuralism and Hermeneutics*, ed. Hubert L. Dreyfus and Paul Rabinow (Chicago, IL: University of Chicago Press, 1982), 208–26. Pastoral power is one of Foucault's many examples of the surveilling, normalizing interventions of biopolitics. For an application to biblical texts, see Elizabeth A. Castelli, *Imitating Paul: A Discourse of Power* (Louisville, KY: Westminster John Knox, 1991).

[16] Reinhartz, *Befriending the Beloved Disciple*, 54–80.

[17] Prothero, *American Jesus*, 291–6. Prothero also makes various disparaging comments about the Jesuses of the so-called Jesus Seminar.

[18] See Richard Walsh and Jeffrey L. Staley, *Jesus, the Gospels, and Cinematic Imagination: Introducing Jesus Movies, Christ Films, and the Messiah in Motion* (London: T&T Clark, 2022), 184–96.

[19] On the incongruity between comedy and the Bible, see George Aichele, "Comedic Films in the Bible," in *T&T Clark Companion to the Bible and Film*, ed. Richard Walsh (London: T&T Clark, 2018), 73–8.

Too Good: Jesus as "Friend" in *The Greatest Story Ever Told*

Despite deploying the notion of "friend Jesus" more than any other film, *The Greatest Story Ever Told* (1965) ultimately affirms the cinematic Jesus's typical (divine) unfriendliness.[20] Jesus appears in the film from a supernatural world above in a church apse as light for a dark world and departs, larger-than-life, into the heavens before adoring worshipers. He does not belong to this world or to mere humans. The following discussion of the film's trajectory of "friend moments" and two key moments where characters remark on Jesus's eerie, off-putting, hagiographic "goodness" explores Jesus's lofty remoteness.

The film's first fifty minutes or so continues the prologue's establishment of Jesus as the light for a dark world and also sets up a conflict between (wilderness) prophecy and the Herodian/Roman politics of fortress Jerusalem. In the wilderness, the Dark Hermit offers "friend Jesus" an easy life, rather than the harder semiascetic "trust God" message with which Jesus soon gathers disciples. Clearly, Jesus rejects the Dark Hermit's friendship, which leads immediately to an almost-apocalyptic triumph in majestic Western scenery before Jesus embarks on his ministry.

As Jesus tramps on to Galilee, the film cuts repeatedly to shots of fortress Jerusalem where authorities discuss the Baptist and Jesus. Outside the fortress, the disciples marvel at the city, but Jesus describes it as prophet-murderer. An unidentified Lazarus sees these "pilgrims" from within his country estate, just outside the fortress, and offers hospitality to his "good friend" Jesus. Only the Dark Hermit has called Jesus "friend" previously. Meanwhile, Pilate tells Caiaphas to work with Antipas to deal with the Baptist and "anyone like him."

Jesus sits in a veranda, slightly above his host Lazarus, proclaiming his semiascetic "trust God" message (e.g., Mark 12:29-34). Lazarus's agreement leads Jesus to remark that Lazarus, finally identified, is not far from the kingdom. Unfortunately, Lazarus is also not far from—in fact, just outside—fortress Jerusalem. When Lazarus asks permission to follow Jesus, Jesus focuses on discipleship's difficulty for the rich (Mark 10:25). Defending her brother, Mary says Lazarus is a good man who will go to heaven. Jesus remains firm: one cannot serve two masters (Matt 6:21-24). When Lazarus mentions his magnanimity, Jesus reports a widow's gift of all she had (cf. Mark 12:41-44) and asks Lazarus to do the same (cf. Mark 10:21-22). Shocked, Lazarus wonders, "Who could do such a thing?" In a last effort to befriend Jesus, Lazarus invites Jesus's group to stay the night, but Jesus moves on, telling Lazarus he will not be forgotten. As the pilgrims depart, Mary tells Lazarus she is frightened for Jesus because "he is too good" (for his "own good" [and for her not quite so "good" brother]).

A composite figure drawn from John's Lazarus, the interested scribe (Mark 12:28b-34), and the anonymous rich man (Mark 10:17-25), this Lazarus befriends Jesus but cannot follow him. Lazarus lives at ease, just outside the city walls in his comfortable

---

[20] Jesus is friendliest in *Godspell* and *Jesus* (1999) and has a single, special friend in *The Last Temptation of Christ* (1988) and *Mary Magdalene* (2018), but he also stands aloofly apart in each film.

country estate. He is too close to Jesus's foes—the Dark Hermit and the fortress. By contrast, Jesus is too good, too ethically or religiously demanding, to be this wealthy man's friend.

Lazarus, however, does not quit easily. After Jesus's triumph in Capernaum and the Baptist's execution, Antipas sends troops after Jesus as well. A very ill Lazarus travels to Nazareth to warn his "good friend." Soon thereafter, Jesus learns of Lazarus's death and travels to Lazarus's home for the funeral, as Martha notes caustically.[21] At the resurrection, in a dramatic shot influencing the visuals of the later cinematic tradition, the audience sees Jesus from within Lazarus's tomb. After Lazarus comes forth, from darkness into the light, the duo is so far away that their identities are indistinguishable. The camera focuses instead on the crowd's worshipful awe and the witnesses who race to fortress Jerusalem to declare that the messiah has come. Friendship between Jesus and Lazarus is less important than the miraculous creation of life in the dark tomb and the subsequent revelatory message.

After an intermission, Jesus is in Lazarus's house for his anointing. Lazarus is briefly in the background, but his sisters lead him away, so he does not interact with Jesus. After the women wrap Jesus in grave clothes, Jesus emerges out of the shadows (like Lazarus before him) and sets out for his Jerusalem triumph. Lazarus may be in Jesus's adoring throng, but he is unimportant, as he is, relatively speaking, when the disciples later loiter in his home before the resurrection message comes to them.

In the passion, the focus shifts to Judas as the prominent would-be friend. The film pairs Judas with the Dark Hermit, that earlier would-be friend, in the dark streets as Judas makes his way to arrange Jesus's betrayal. Introducing himself to Sorak and Caiaphas as Jesus's friend, Judas still surprisingly offers to give Jesus to them, if they promise no harm will come to "the purest, kindest man I have ever known. I have never seen him do anything but good. His heart ... his heart is gentle. Old people worship him; children adore him; I love him." Is Jesus's goodness again "too much," as Mary prophesies when Jesus first visits Lazarus's house? Does Judas find Jesus's superiority belittling? Can he not bear the light Jesus shines upon his darkness? Is Jesus's "goodness" the reason Judas betrays?

While the film also includes Jesus's Johannine supper reference to friends, the film's intriguing friend-trajectory, traced briefly here, is that from the Dark Hermit through Lazarus to Judas. One opposes Jesus's hard life and tempts Jesus to an easier path; one cannot follow; one betrays the best man he knows. With respect to these friends, the film suggests that the implicit issue is Jesus's call to something beyond ordinary life.[22] Like the mentoring beloved disciple Reinhartz finds in John, this Jesus can only be worshiped or rejected; he is no friend.

---

[21] As Jesus tarries before going to Lazarus's rescue, various Jesus-cinema characters wonder how much "friend" Lazarus means to Jesus. Other than this Martha, Tamar in *The Miracle Maker* (2000) may be most dismissive of Jesus's so-called friendship. On these sisters' striking lack of faith in *Greatest Story*, in contrast to other cinematic renderings, see Jeffrey L. Staley, "One Hundred Years of Cinematic Attempts at Raising a Stiff (John 11:1–46)," in *The T&T Clark Handbook of Jesus Film*, ed. Richard Walsh (London: T&T Clark, 2021), 45–7.

[22] Of course, in multiple tales, "friends" betray heroes/heroines for just this reason. The friends cannot rise to the hero/heroine's stature.

While Christian supersessionism undergirds *Greatest Story*, Lazarus's depiction is not obviously anti-Semitic. He is not, however, very Jewish. Instead, he is an analog for the film's audience—for a wealthy modern (predominantly US) audience with a glimmering sense that Jesus's message/mission is incongruous with their comfortable status.[23] Who can do such a thing, that is, follow the semiascetic Jesus? The Jesus epic that could successfully lift its audience to "Jesus" (and consequently deify them as the inevitable end of the Jesus tradition) belongs to the past.[24] For many in the audience, Jesus is an impossible demand.

Friend of the Romans: Jesus as a Friend in *Jesus of Nazareth*

Franco Zeffirelli's *Jesus of Nazareth* (1975) deploys friend Jesus differently. The most dramatic moment comes when Barabbas rejects Jesus in Jerusalem. After Jesus's triumph and temple cleansing, he settles down to teaching in the temple under the watchful eye of the Jewish authorities, notably Zerah, and the curious, like Barabbas and Nicodemus. Sensing the day of revenge at hand, Barabbas demands Jesus lead the battle against the Romans. For Jesus, however, the day of forgiveness is here. An angry Barabbas stalks away, but returns to listen, albeit in disbelief, to Jesus's "love your enemies" message. When Jesus grants a Roman centurion's request for his servant's healing (at a distance; cf. Matt 8:5-13), Barabbas sees Jesus as a quisling, a "friend of the Romans," and plots insurrection more urgently.

After Jesus's healing of the blind man, a tumult breaks out over Jesus's blasphemous words (John 10:30). As some prepare to stone Jesus, Barabbas tries to seize the momentum, killing a Roman soldier, taking a Roman standard, and calling for the crowd to stone Jesus as a friend of the Romans and false prophet. Roman soldiers quickly quiet the unrest and arrest Barabbas. Barabbas's words linger, however, first as the Jewish authorities take up the question of whether Jesus is messiah or false prophet and then as Judas "betrays" Jesus to Zerah so the Sanhedrin can decide this question.

Over against Zerah, Judas, Barabbas, and the (divided) Sanhedrin's political scheming, Jesus articulates the film's religion of the heart, rather than a religion deliberately, rationally involved in political machinations. The issue comes up not just in Jesus's "born of the spirit" conversation with Nicodemus after the attempted stoning but also in conversations with Judas that bookend the temple sequence described earlier. In the first, Judas arranges a meeting between Jesus and Zerah, hoping that Zerah can bring about the Sanhedrin's acclamation of Jesus as messiah, but Jesus

---

[23] Reinhartz has repeatedly noted—most notably in *Jesus of Hollywood* and *Bible and Cinema*—that Jesus cinema and other biblical films participate "in a 'then as now' discursive field" (*Bible and Cinema*, 9). Her point is that biblical films present the past anachronistically, turning the past into a drama reflecting present concerns.

[24] Jesus, the Baptist, and the film belong to the sacred wilderness (the West). Lazarus is never quite ready for that wilderness. See further Richard Walsh, *Reading the Gospels in the Dark: Portrayals of Jesus in Film* (Harrisburg, PA: Trinity, 2003), 147-71; and Walsh and Staley, *Cinematic Imagination*, 105-20.

rudely dismisses Zerah and dashes Judas's hopes. When Judas chastises Jesus for this missed opportunity, Jesus lectures Judas to open his heart (not his mind). The second conversation is during Judas's betrayal, which opens—strangely enough— with Judas muttering bewilderedly that Jesus claims the heart is more important than political ideas.

This common Jesus film trope of touting the spirit over politics (or the flesh) deifies/heroizes Jesus and his followers and vilifies Jesus's foes, depicting them as wrong-headed about Jesus's apolitical, privatized religious message.[25] From this perspective, cinematic Judases configured *à la* Thomas DeQuincey and the Zealots, as often constructed by both historians and filmmakers, are all guilty of politicizing and thus misunderstanding Jesus's message.[26] What Zeffirelli's Barabbas knows—and critics and artists often overlook—is that this depoliticized Jesus, with his attendant universal message of love, is indeed a "friend of the Romans." His pacifist message supports keeping the empire in place—either Roman or, in a Reinhartzian "then and now" interpretation, the later US (or modern capitalist) empire.

Zeffirelli's film is one of the most blatantly supersessionist Jesus films. Despite its elaborate, sympathetic portrayal of Jewish village life, the village rabbi's repeated message is relentlessly messianic, and *Jesus of Nazareth*'s overarching trajectory moves from the almost "Christian" messianism of this village to the embryonic, soon-to-be Roman church (the film's final third establishes both Peter as community leader and the community's resurrection message). The Last Supper scene, which writes Christian institution language over that of the Jewish Passover, is emblematic of the film's overall structure. This plotting also enables Zeffirelli to move Christianity's "victory" over Rome back in time. The Christian epics had already charted Roman conversions to Christianity in the generation after Jesus (e.g., *The Sign of the Cross* [1932]; *Quo Vadis* [1951]; or *The Robe* [1953]), moving Christianity's triumph over Rome backward in time by centuries. Zeffirelli moves it even earlier by making it part of his supersessionist structure of Jesus's life and by merging the film's embryonic Roman church with the later imperial victory over Rome. Barabbas is the prophet who sees this inevitability and thus sees who Jesus is—the friend of the Romans (or of later empires).[27]

How could Jesus be universal love if he did not hitch a ride on the empire's universal reach or, at least, pretensions?[28] And, how could he be the contemporary audience's

---

[25] In the 1999 *Jesus*, a similar scene occurs. Barabbas and his men slaughter tax-collecting Romans, with Barabbas violently slapping the "turn the other cheek" Jesus twice. When Jesus weeps over the fallen Romans, Judas rejects Jesus's offer of friendship.

[26] On the De Quincey Judas as Jesus's cinematic foil, see Richard Walsh, *Three Versions of Judas* (London: Equinox, 2010). On the similar use of the Zealots, see Richard Walsh, "The Zealots in the Jesus Film Tradition," in *Religion und Gewalt im Bibelfilm, Film und Theologie* 20, ed. Reinhold Zwick (Marburg: Schüren, 2012), 99–126.

[27] Pilate is not as astute, but he articulates the film's fundamental question at Jesus's trial: Whose Jesus is this? The film answers by giving Jesus to empire and to the modern, consuming television audience. See Walsh and Staley, *Cinematic Imagination*, 164–83. The cinematic hallowing of Pilate also configures Jesus as a friend of the Romans. See, particularly, the Pilate in *The Passion of the Christ*, who is one of that film's rare "human" characters. See Walsh and Staley, *Cinematic Imagination*, 280–97.

[28] For a more conscious struggle with the disjoint between empire and Jesus, see Nicholas Ray's *King of Kings* (1961), whose centurion Lucius is almost, but, significantly, not quite converted. See Walsh and Staley, *Cinematic Imagination*, 74–89.

friend without supporting, if not deifying, the audience's cultural identity (whether imperial or righteously sectarian) so that they can finally stand shoulder to shoulder with the lofty Christ at, and as, the end of history (or, at least, of the Jesus tradition)? The deifying (ennobling or saving) of the otherwise weak audience is, of course, exactly the mechanics at work in "What a Friend We Have in Jesus" and that which Reinhartz rejects in the Gospel of John in her "complimentary" reading. As a friend of the empire, the cinematic Jesus does not make a very good friend for those mortals left outside the empire.[29]

Befriending Jesus Cinema

The cinematic Jesus is not very friendly. He is not collegial, but loftily above even his followers. As in the hymn, he is God, Lord, Savior or, as in Reinhartz's complimentary reading of John, he is mentor. One becomes a mentee/worshiper to the extent that one accepts his commands and his (imperial) deification, without demur.

Facing this cinematic Jesus, it is exceedingly helpful to befriend Reinhartz and her readings of Jesus cinema. Like *Greatest Story*'s Lazarus, she wonders who could follow the divinely unfriendly Jesus. Like *Jesus of Nazareth*'s Barabbas, she recognizes that the cinematic Jesus befriends someone else. In addition to her excellent scholarly record in biblical film, she is important to the field precisely because she abandons a compliant reading of Jesus cinema, with its seductive call to deification, as she does when reading the Gospel of John, in favor of a reading that leads toward the ideal of reciprocal, critical, engaged conversation.[30] That she is Jewish, Canadian, and feminist—and that she loves *Jésus de Montréal* (1989) above all other Jesus films—enables her resistance to the films' allure. To follow her lead in befriending Jesus cinema in such an open and involved fashion, one would need to share her love of fiction and cinema. One would need to follow her careful amassing of detail on exactly how biblical material—and particularly the Jews and Judaism (or any of those Othered by empire)—appears in film. Finally, one would have to abandon Jesus cinema's seductive imperial, deifying offer by recognizing this offer as those films' attempts to create modern (imperial or sectarian) identities ("then as now") under the guise/ruse of presenting history or truth. Therein, may lie truly reciprocal conversations—and unlikely friends.

---

[29] Some Jesus films try to reject imperial deification for these others. See, for example, *Il vangelo secondo Matteo*; *Jésus de Montréal*; *Son of Man*.

[30] Compare the search for parabolic Jesus films in Walsh, *Reading the Gospels in the Dark*, 173–85.

17

Dividing the Red Soup: An Antimodel in *Bruce Almighty*

Jan Willem van Henten

Dividing the Red Soup is the name I conveniently give to one of my favorite movie scenes. Although the scene takes only two minutes and fifteen seconds, it deserves a brief case study because there are so many fascinating things to observe for scholars interested in Bible and film. I do hope that Adele, who is not only a great "connoisseur" of movies and TV series but also the most important author in the field of Bible and film, will have at least some fun rewatching this scene and reading my musings about it.

The *Red Soup* scene is part of *Bruce Almighty*, a light-hearted Hollywood comedy, which has a serious undertone and an explicit religious subtext.[1] In this film, Bruce Nolan, a self-centered local TV reporter, played by Jim Carrey, temporarily takes over God's job. After Bruce becomes aware of his newly acquired divine powers, he soon abuses them, which affects his relationship with his girlfriend Grace, a character played by Jennifer Aniston. Grace ends their relationship, and Bruce painfully realizes in this way that he cannot get around people's free will, as God previously explained to him during a walk on the lake in front of the city of Buffalo.[2] Ultimately, Bruce's failed performance as God leads to a serious accident and a radical turn. A conversation with God right after the accident—in heaven?—leads him to repent. This is the start

---

[1] *Bruce Almighty*. Directed by Tom Shadyac, screenplay by Steve Koren, Mark O'Keefe, and Steve Oedekerk, Spyglass Entertainment/Universal, 2003. Discussions of this movie include Jan Willem van Henten, "Playing God in the Movies: *Bruce Almighty* and the Preposterous History of Genesis 1:26-27," in *Creation and Creativity: From Genesis to Genetics and Back*, ed. Alastair Hunter and Caroline Vander Stichele, Amsterdam Studies in the Bible and Religion 1 (Sheffield: Sheffield Phoenix, 2006), 125-41. About interconnections with the book of Job, see Reinhold Zwick, "The Book of Job in the Movies: On Cinema's Exploration of Theodicy and the Hiddenness of God," in *The Bible in Motion: A Handbook of the Bible and Its Reception in Film*, ed. Rhonda Burnett-Bletsch (Berlin: de Gruyter, 2016), 355-77 (esp. 362-3), and about representations of God in film including *Bruce Almighty*, see Rhonda Burnett-Bletsch, "God at the Movies," in *The Bible in Motion*, 299-326, who characterizes *Bruce Almighty* as "a loose modern retelling of the biblical book of Job, where Bruce's 'suffering' is characteristic of upper-middle class America" (314).

[2] For the claim that love requires free will as expressed in *Bruce Almighty* and other Hollywood movies, such as *Frailty* (David Kirschner Productions, 2002) and *The Adjustment Bureau* (Universal, 2011), see Thaddeus J. Williams, *Love, Freedom and Evil: Does Authentic Love Require Free Will* (Amsterdam: Rodopi, 2011).

of a spiritual journey in which Bruce quickly learns how to become a responsible human being. In this contribution, I will first describe the *Dividing the Red Soup* scene, then discuss the interconnections with Exodus 14 and Cecille B. DeMille's *The Ten Commandments* (1956) on which the scene also builds, and finally deal with the meaning of the scene in the larger context of Bruce's relations with humans as well as God.

The *Red Soup* Scene

The *Red Soup* scene takes place just after Bruce takes on God's job at the Omni Presents warehouse. He leaves the warehouse in disbelief ("I am not God, I don't have his powers. If I was God I would be Clint Eastwood ..."), but during a short and wild drive in his damaged car he realizes that something has changed. He takes a break at the Grand Avenue diner, which only has a few customers at that time. He decides to have the special of the day, which is tomato soup. After he has been given coffee, he carefully tries out his new powers, assuming that he is unobserved. By simply putting forward his intention, he manages to manipulate the milk and sugar and get them in his hands. He is also capable of creating a spoon by just thinking about it and retrieving it from his mouth. His body language still expresses some surprise about these miracles. Then he gets his bowl of tomato soup and thinks for a moment of eating it, but next decides to try out his divine powers on the soup, this time using his hands. He holds his hands above the bowl while the music swells and the pace of the film slows down. A huge wind starts blowing, papers fly around, and the guest who is sneakily observing Bruce is horrified. Bruce extends his hands more and more, with his palms up. The soup is gradually divided into two halves, being separated from each other by the pounding wind, so that a clear space in between is formed. Bruce is thrilled by this success, and the music confirms his triumph over nature, which is suddenly interrupted by God (played by Morgan Freeman), who asks Bruce, "Having fun?" This interruption forms the transition to the next scene in which God explains what it means to perform his job. Not long afterward, Bruce is fully convinced of his divine powers and in a theophanic shot at night, with lightning flashing across the sky, he shouts from the top of one of Buffalo's skyscrapers, "I am Bruce Almighty, My Will Be Done."

Allusions to the Bible

Viewers of the *Dividing the Red Soup* scene who are well-versed in the Bible cannot miss the allusions to Exodus 14, the famous story of the crossing of the Red Sea by the Israelites. The scene offers a creative and funny short reinterpretation of this episode, in which Bruce plays the roles of God and Moses at the same time.

During the Exodus from Egypt narrated in Exod 12:33–40:38, God gives the Israelites instructions to turn back and camp in front of Pi-hahiroth in anticipation of Pharaoh's pursuit of them (Exod 14:1-4). God acts as the guide of the Israelites through Moses as his messenger (14:31) and directs the unfolding of the events in this story.³ God creates, in fact, a trap for the Egyptians, which is partly explained to Moses and the readers, but not to the Israelites: "I will harden Pharaoh's heart,⁴ and he will pursue them, so that I will gain glory for myself over Pharaoh and all his army;⁵ and the Egyptians shall know that I am the LORD" (14:4).⁶ The Israelites panic because of their pursuit by Pharaoh and his army, and they cry out in great fear to God and complain to Moses (14:10-12). Moses responds that God will bring deliverance that very day (14:13-14). He receives instructions from God to lift up his staff and stretch out his hand over the sea and divide it, so that the Israelites can safely cross the sea on dry ground (14:16). God also explains that he will harden the hearts of the Egyptians so that they will go after the Israelites through the sea so that "I [God] will gain glory for myself over Pharaoh and all his army" (14:17).⁷ And so it happens. Moses stretches out his arm over the sea, and God blows a strong east wind, which drives the sea back so that the waters are divided and a passageway over dry land is formed (14:21-22; also 14:29). God's pillar of cloud⁸ creates panic among the Egyptians, and Moses's second act of stretching his hand, commanded by God, causes the sea to return so that Pharaoh and his army are drowned (14:26-29).⁹

The deliverance of Israel and the punishment of the Egyptians are attributed to God (14:30-31), and the flashbacks of the crossing in Moses and Miriam's songs in Exod 15:1-21 consistently present the Red Sea miracle as a triumph of God over Pharaoh and his army, and praise God for Israel's deliverance and defeat of the enemy (e.g., 15:1-2, 21). Moses emphasizes that God showed his power during the crossing and shattered the enemy through his right hand (15:6, 9, 12, 16).¹⁰ The fate of Pharaoh and his beautiful chariots implies that all power and authority belong to God, who also rules over the forces of nature. The implication of the story is clearly that all should obey God and that the Israelites should fear and trust God, as the concluding verse states (14:31). Moses's role in the story is mainly that of God's messenger and facilitator (e.g., 14:27, 31).¹¹ Although Moses renders all honor to God, as we have seen (15:1 etc.), Exod 14:31 attributes some credit to him as well, since it ends with "they [the Israelites] put their trust in¹² the Lord *and in his servant Moses* (ויאמינו ביהוה ובמושה עבדו) [my emphasis])."¹³

---

³ Cees Houtman, *Exodus. Volume 2 Chapters 7:14–19:25*, HCOT (Peeters: Leuven, 1996), 225.
⁴ About this motif, see Matthew McAfee, "The Heart of Pharaoh in Exodus 4–15," *BBR* 20 (2010): 331–53.
⁵ Similarly, Exod 14:17-18.
⁶ Unless indicated otherwise, all Bible translations given are taken from the NRSV.
⁷ The motif of God's glory is repeated in Exod 14:18.
⁸ See Exod 13:17-22.
⁹ As several commentators explain, a rational reading of the miracle that takes the data given in the context into account implies that it could never have happened. Josephus's elaborate retelling of the story leaves the judgment about it ultimately to the readers (*Ant.* 2.315-348). Further discussion and references in Houtman, *Exodus*, 237–8.
¹⁰ For example, Exod 15:6: "Your right hand, O LORD/glorious in power—/your right hand, O LORD/shattered the enemy."
¹¹ Houtman, *Exodus*, 229–30. Exod 14:15 presupposes a role as intercessor as well, George W. Coats, *Moses: Heroic Man, Man of God*, JSOTSup 57 (Sheffield: JSOT Press, 1998), 117.
¹² NRSV: "believed in."
¹³ See also Exod 4:1-9 and 19:9 and Heinrich Gross, "Der Glaube an Mose nach Exodus (4. 14. 19)," in *Wort—Gebot—Glaube: Beiträge zur Theologie des Alten Testaments. Walter Eichrodt zum*

The similarities between the text of Exodus and the *Red Soup* scene in *Bruce Almighty* are unmistakable. Although the name of the sea is transmitted as Sea of Reeds in the Masoretic Text (יָם סוּף; Exod 13:18),[14] it was already associated with the color red and identified with the Red Sea in the Septuagint (εἰς τὴν ἐρυθρὰν θάλασσαν) and the Vulgate (*mare Rubrum*).[15] The strong wind that helps to divide the soup or the waters of the sea (Exod 14:21) is an important point of contact between the events, together with Bruce's hands and Moses's hand raised over the sea (Exod 14:16, 21, 26). That Bruce performs both Moses and God's roles in comparison to Exodus is confirmed by the focus on the hands. The miracle in *Bruce Almighty* displays both of Bruce's hands, but Exodus refers to "the hand" of Moses as well as God's right hand (Exod 15:6 etc., discussed earlier). The hands of Bruce may evoke still other associations with biblical passages because they also have a creative effect, which is more prominent in other parts of the movie. The creative function of hands is reminiscent of Jewish interpretations of the creation story as well as Michelangelo's depiction of the creation of Adam on the ceiling of the Sistine Chapel in which God's hand plays a prominent role.[16] The position of Bruce's hands changes during the miracle, first he spreads his hands over the soup with his palms down, and the soup soon starts to stir. While the soup is parting, he spreads his arms and moves his hands up, with his palms half open to heaven. His posture at the end of the miracle depicts him as being triumphant and ecstatic about his powers over the soup. The implication of both miracles, therefore, is similar: they demonstrate God and Bruce's (newly acquired) powers.

Of course, there are also differences between the biblical passage and the film, which may be even more interesting than the similarities. Moses's staff (Exod 14:16) is absent in the film. The crossing of the Red Sea is a massive event, with the drowning of Pharaoh's army as the horrific ending. As a matter of fact, the defeat of the enemy, which is the second part of the miracle in Exodus, is entirely missing in *Bruce Almighty*. Bruce's experiment is relatively innocent, and there is hardly any audience present (discussed later in this chapter). But although Bruce is basically on his own, he clearly displays his power and visibly enjoys the act. Interconnecting the *Red Soup* scene with the Exodus story clearly strengthens the associations of Bruce with God and suggests that the scene is the first and relatively harmless theophany of Bruce as Almighty.

---

80. *Geburtstag*, ed. Johann J. Stamm, Ernst Jenni, and Hans Joachim Stoebe (Zürich: Zwingli, 1970), 57–65.

[14] Cf. Exod 2:3, 5, and see Ludwig Koehler, Walter Baumgartner, Benedikt Hartmann, and Edward Y. Kutscher, *Hebräisches und Aramäisches Lexikon zum Alten Testament*, 4 vols, 3rd ed. (Leiden: Brill, 1967–1990), s.v. 1 2.394-396 יָם 3d.

[15] Also Josephus, *Ant.* 2.315. William Johnstone, *Exodus*, OTGu (Sheffield: Sheffield Academic, 1990), 28, 35.

[16] See in particular Rashi's commentary on Gen 1:27, who comments that everything apart from humankind was created "by hand," referring to Ps 139:5; see https://www.sefaria.org/Rashi_on_Genesis.1.27.1?lang=bi&with=all&lang2=en (checked June 20, 2022).

Nods to DeMille

Bruce Almighty's soup miracle interconnects not only with the story in Exodus 14 but also with the classic cinematic re-creation of the Red Sea crossing in Cecil B. DeMille's magnum opus *The Ten Commandments*.[17] In fact, while God parted the Red Sea only once, DeMille did it twice,[18] first in his silent movie in 1923 and then again in the much longer 1956 version in which the Exodus story is reinterpreted from the perspective of the United States in the situation of the Cold War, as DeMille himself indicates in the unusual preface to the movie.[19] DeMille visualizes the miracle of the Red Sea episode by following the biblical text quite closely.[20] That the movie was filmed on location in Egypt and at Mount Sinai gives the representation of the events told in Exodus an authentic flavor.[21] The Red Sea episode starts with close-ups of Moses (played by Charlton Heston), who states that "the Lord of hosts will do battle for us" (cf. Exod 14:14) and refers in this connection to God's mighty hand. He then spreads out his hands—both hands, similar to Bruce—with his staff. The point of view changes; the audience now sees the backside of Moses and the Israelites looking at the sea. There is a crescendo of the music, the wind is blowing, and next there is another close-up of Moses with his hands spread, followed by another view upon the sea, which divides into two so that a pathway appears in front of Moses and the Israelites, between two walls of water, just as the biblical text indicates (Exod 14:22).[22] Next, we see in detail how the Israelites enter the sea with their cattle and belongings. The admiration for God's miracle is expressed in a few shots of small groups of Israelites.

The audiovisual allusions to DeMille's 1956 movie *The Ten Commandments* in *Bruce Almighty* are unmistakable. First of all, there is the obvious analogy between the Red Sea and the red tomato soup, which are both divided into two. Moreover, the alternation of the close-ups of Bruce and the shots of the tomato soup, which is slowly

---

[17] *The Ten Commandments*. Director: Cecil B. De Mille. Paramount, 1956.
[18] As noted by Robert S. Birchard, *Cecil B. DeMille's Hollywood* (Lexington, KY: University of Kentucky Press, 2004), 361.
[19] There are many discussions of this movie: for example, Katherine Orrison, *Written in Stone: Making Cecil B. DeMille's Epic, the Ten Commandments* (Lanham, MD: Vestal, 1999); Melanie J. Wright, *Moses in America: The Cultural Uses of Biblical Narrative* (Oxford: Oxford University Press, 2003), 89–127; Simon Louvish, *Cecil B. DeMille and the Golden Calf* (London: Faber and Faber, 2007); Anton Karl Kozlovic, "The Ten Commandments," in *The Bible and Cinema: Fifty Key Films*, ed. Adele Reinhartz (London: Routledge, 2013), 252–8; Adele Reinhartz, "Holy Words in Hollywood: DeMille's *The Ten Commandments* (1956) and American Identity," in *The Bible in the Public Square: Its Enduring Influence in American Life*, ed. Mark A. Chancey, Carol Meyers, and Eric M. Meyers (Atlanta, GA: SBL Press, 2014), 123–35; and Adele Reinhartz, "The Bible Epic," in *The Bible in Motion*, 175–92 (esp. 178–82 and 186–90). Discussions of both the 1923 and the 1956 versions are in Birchard, *Cecil B. DeMille's Hollywood*, 178–89, 351–63.
[20] The movie had its own researcher, who also consulted extrabiblical sources like Josephus and the *midrashim*. He wrote a book about his task; cf. Henry S. Noerdlinger, *Moses and Egypt: The Documentation of the Motion Picture* The Ten Commandments (Los Angeles: University of Southern California Press, 1956).
[21] Robert Ridinger, "From Moses to DeMille: Adapting the Bible to the Big Screen," *JRTI* 19 (2020): 129–47, here 134.
[22] Detailed discussion of the music by Elmer Bernstein in *The Ten Commandments* in Stephen C. Meyer, *Epic Sound: Music in Postwar Hollywood Biblical Films* (Bloomington: Indiana University Press, 2015), 114–41.

but steadily divided into two halves, is reminiscent of the alternation of the close-ups of Moses and the shots of the sea during which the audience, as it were, looks at the sea together with the Israelites. The way Bruce is holding his hands and is looking at the soup is rather similar to Moses's behavior in *The Ten Commandments*. Bruce first holds his hands above the soup and then spreads his arms like Moses until the soup is divided into two, with a straight line in between, very similar to the Red Sea scene, although the scale is, of course, very different. The reminiscences of the scene in *The Ten Commandments* are strengthened by the noise of the wind and the use of the music, which first crescendos and is then triumphant. Thus, there seem to be visual as well as auditive allusions to *The Ten Commandments* in the *Red Soup* scene.

Of course, there are also differences between the two scenes. Bruce combines the roles of Moses and God in contrast to Exodus 14 and *The Ten Commandments*. Another difference, which is not explicit but clear for the careful observer, is that Bruce's deed is physically impossible and therefore a miracle indeed: to successfully split the soup in the full bowl into two and open a considerable space in the middle would only be possible after taking out a considerable part of the soup, otherwise the bowl would overflow. An important difference concerns the other persons beside God and Moses or Bruce involved in the miracle. In *Bruce Almighty*, there is one customer whose responses to Bruce's behavior are shown time and again. This reminds one of the shots of the Israelites or the Egyptians during the performance of the miracle in *The Ten Commandments*. But the role of this customer is very different from those of the Israelites and the Egyptians: he remains intrigued by Bruce, but he feels uneasy and moves away from Bruce after the "creation" of the coffee spoon. In the end, he protects himself from the papers that are flying around him when Bruce has succeeded in dividing the soup. Bruce's miracle is, therefore, mostly a relatively harmless individual performance, and others hardly play a role in it. This is very different from the deliverance of the Israelites and the death of Pharaoh and his army in *The Ten Commandments*. The difference is also apparent from the exchange of shots at this point in *Bruce Almighty*: the camera moves back and forth from Bruce's face to the soup and the scene ends with a shot in which the audience looks up from the vacant space in the bowl right into Bruce's face above the bowl at the moment of his triumph. The parting of the red soup focuses on Bruce alone. This brings us to the final section of this contribution.

Character Development

The *Dividing the Red Soup* scene in *Bruce Almighty* is all about Bruce, which matches Bruce's characterization in the first half of the movie. Bruce acts in this part as a self-centered person who does not care about others. He ridicules his girlfriend Grace when he brings her to a blood drive to donate blood, and he does not give blood himself, as he does later on after he has learned his lesson. He is good at making people laugh and that makes him a valuable field reporter for WKBW TV/Eyewitness News, but he despises his job and aspires to get the vacant anchor position at the company. In a complex scene presented simultaneously from three different locations, Bruce learns that someone else got the anchor position while he is giving a live report at Niagara

Falls. He is very disappointed, and although he is "live," he first remains silent for a long time and then heads for a terrible climax in which he ridicules all of his colleagues in an unforgivably rude way. Those present in the studio, as well as Grace, who see all of this, are shocked. Another example of his selfish behavior takes place after Bruce has lost his job and had a car accident. Out of frustration he throws away the set of prayer beads that he received from Grace, which were made by the children at the Small Wonders nursery where she works.

One would assume that Bruce's attitude changes after receiving God's job, but that is not at all the case. Bruce uses his divine powers to create his own stunning news. In this way, he gets his job back and even takes over the news anchor position, but his manipulations of nature and humans cause casualties and considerable damage. He has no idea what to do with the countless prayers that he receives. He deeply disappoints Grace during dinner in a famous restaurant; she thinks that Bruce is going to propose while he invited her only to tell her that he received the anchor position. In short, the experiment ends in total desperation for Bruce, who learns the hard way what it means to take over God's job and that God too has to reckon with human beings' free will. Becoming aware of this leads to a dramatic turn in Bruce's life when he submits to God's will. Another conversation with God forms the beginning of a radically different attitude in Bruce. From the perspective of this plot development, the *Red Soup* scene can be seen as the middle of the movie's first half in which Bruce's self-glorification functions as the negative contrast to the main message of the movie's second half, which is in a nutshell about becoming a responsible person by acting as a partner of God by helping other humans.

Submitting to God's will is the turning point in Bruce's life, after which Bruce learns how to read the signs from God, how to repent, and how to become a better person. That this works for him is apparent from the fact that he is able to restore his relationship with Grace. The second half of the movie presents a coherent and optimistic message by suggesting that it is worthwhile to act according to the important values of justice, mercy, and love; to hear people's prayers; and to offer concrete help, by, for example, donating blood—one of the motifs that occurs in both halves of the movie. These points are articulated by all kinds of auditive and visual allusions to both the Old and the New Testaments. The wealth of biblical references and the ways in which they are presented imply that the movie is not so much building on traditions and practices from various religions, as director Tom Shadyac states in one of his comments, but that it mainly conveys an optimistic, middle-of-the-road Christian worldview, which ignores important ongoing debates in current society.[23]

The symbolism of God as cleaner in two scenes is a case in point. Its message is positive and practical—"whatever mess you create, you clean up"—but the movie does not do anything with the fact that it is the Black actor Morgan Freeman who presents this message as a friendly, elderly, African American man. One could say that the movie is basically color-blind by not paying any attention to the problems of

---

[23] In the scene about the job offer, God is a janitor, electrician, and boss at the same time, as Bruce acknowledges. The association of these three roles of God with the Christian Trinity can hardly be missed. Further discussion in van Henten, "Playing God," 135–6.

racism.[24] Its view on gender relations remains conventional, and the attitude toward animals and nature expressed in the movie is clichéd, although the optimistic message of the movie could have been an impetus to include more progressive perspectives.

Nevertheless, the movie does make an important point about God's powers, because Bruce's learning process implies that God cannot do without humans for the fulfillment of the divine plan. The associations with the biblical creation narrative and more specifically the creation of humans as God's image in Gen 1:26-27 are relevant here. The movie demonstrates that God's powers are limited because humans are created with a free will. It emphasizes, therefore, that humans have an important role to play in order to realize God's intention with the world. It suggests a role for humans as God's partners, which matches significant Jewish as well as Christian interpretations of the Genesis passage.[25] The movie calls upon humans with an optimistic incitement to act, more specifically to act as God's image: "be the miracle," and "you have the power … ." This implies, with an eye on Gen 1:26-27, a radical interpretation of the biblical passage: by doing the right thing and exploiting their unique talents, humans can become "divine." And indeed, God explains to Bruce after the fatal accident that he has a divine spark: his gift to make people laugh.

Conclusion

The argument of my analysis of the *Dividing the Red Soup* scene in *Bruce Almighty* implies that the movie re-creates the Red Sea miracle as it is depicted in Exod 14 and reinterpreted in Cecil B. DeMille's *The Ten Commandments*. The character of Bruce combines the roles of God and Moses in the miracle. Although the scale and purpose of the miracles in Exodus and *Bruce Almighty* are very different, there is a clear analogy by the corresponding motifs—the color red, the acts of Moses and Bruce who perform the miracle, and, finally, the parting of the sea and the soup as a result. The camera work with its alternation of shots of the performer, the parting liquid as well as the onlookers, and the use of sound, not only the music but also the wind, suggest that *Bruce Almighty* also builds on *The Ten Commandments*. The comparison of *Bruce Almighty* with Exodus 14 and DeMille's movie points to important differences as well, which imply, among other things, that the miracle in *Bruce Almighty* is all about Bruce. The *Dividing the Red Soup* scene functions in the broader context of the movie as a counterpoint to the positive perspective on human relations that is elaborated in the second part of the film.

---

[24] As observed by Michele Aaron, *Death and the Moving Image: Ideology, Iconography and I* (Edinburgh: Edinburgh University Press, 2014), 138 and 141. For Morgan Freeman playing God in *Bruce Almighty* and *Evan Almighty* (2007), see Robert Eberwein, "Clint Eastwood and Morgan Freeman: Million Dollar Seniors," in *Shining in Shadows: Movie Stars of the 2000s*, ed. Murray Pomerance (New Brunswick, NJ: Rutgers University Press, 2012), 32–49, here 43–4.

[25] For example, Abraham J. Heschel, "What Is Man?" in *Between God and Man: An Interpretation of Judaism from the Writings of Abraham J. Heschel*, selected, edited and introduced by F. A. Rothschild (New York: Free Press, 1997), 233–41, here 236; Abraham J. Heschel, *God in Search of Man: A Philosophy of Judaism* (New York: The Jewish Publication Society of America, 1959), 289–92, 411–13; Louise Schottroff, "The Creation Narrative: Genesis 1.1–2.4a," in *A Feminist Companion to Genesis*, ed. Athalya Brenner (Sheffield: Sheffield Academic Press, 1993), 24–38; van Henten, "Playing God," 136–7.

18

The Quick and the Dead in Film Treatments of the Raising of Lazarus

Jo-Ann A. Brant

Human societies tend to manage the relationship between the living and the dead with care to ensure that the living give the dead their due—proper disposition of remains and commemoration—and that their death does not prevent the living from getting on with their lives.[1] In the Gospel of John, this is not the case, because Jesus and Lazarus violate the confines of death and life, and the Gospel redefines the relationship between the biologically alive and the biologically dead. In its polemic against Jesus's Jewish opponents, those who trust in Jesus are the living and never die, even if they are dead (1:12; 5:24; 8:52; 10:10-11). Those who do not trust in him have no life in them (6:53). In the following analysis, we will look at two significant patterns in Jesus films in which the redefinition of relationships focuses on either the Johannine emphasis of the establishment of a new community or the pivotal role that Lazarus's resurrection plays in the Johannine plot in which Jesus joins Lazarus in death's snare.[2] As we shall see, early films tend to favor the former with joy as the primary consequence of the disruption of death. Later films often play with this disruption to explore not only the unsettling of the relationship between the living and the dead but also tensions in the relationship between Christian dogmas and the realities of Jesus's death.

Scholars of ritual studies Arnold van Gennep and Victor Turner provide a framework to map out the rites of passage for the dead in different cultures.[3] Between death or significant markers that indicate that the afflicted is dying, both the dying or dead and their family and/or community slip out of the classifications that define cultural positions and relationships and enter into a liminal state. The rites of passage serve to deliver the dead to the realm of the dead and restore the living to the realm of the living, albeit some with the new status of widow, widower, or orphan. By resurrecting

---

[1] Without the challenging and inspiring gift of Adele Reinhartz's scholarship, I would not have looked at the films that I examine in this paper with as critical an eye to their representation of Judaism and their exploitation of silence and ambiguities in the Gospel of John.

[2] For a broader treatment of the Lazarus episodes, see Jeffrey L. Staley, "One Hundred Years of Cinematic Attempts at Raising a Stiff (Jn 11:1-46)," in *T&T Clark Handbook of Jesus and Film*, ed. Richard Walsh (London: Bloomsbury, 2021), 41-54.

[3] Arnold van Gennep, *The Rites of Passage* (London: Routledge, 1960), 146-65. Victor Turner, "Liminality and Communitas," in *The Ritual Process: Structure and Anti-Structure* (Chicago: Aldine, 1969), 359-74.

Lazarus without reintegration into the society of the living from which he has come, he and those with whom he has contact remain in a liminal state somewhere between life and death. Whereas the Gospel's narrative only hints at the nature of Lazarus's post-resurrection relationships, film treatments often dramatize the social consequences.

Lazarus's Resurrection as Life

The raising of Lazarus appears in most of the silent Jesus films and follows the pattern in which his resurrection serves as a sort of baptism into a redeemed community.[4] *From the Manger to Cross* (1912; directed by Sidney Olcott; 38:45–40:58) stands out among the early films for its clear demarcation between the living and the dead. The mourners stand to the far left of the tomb opening with heads covered in dark prayer shawls, bowing deeply downward in gestures of grief that mirror the *Shuckling* one sees when orthodox Jews recite the Torah in study or worship.[5] Jesus's actions are oriented upward. He and the disciples, who spill over the right margin of the frame, are clad in white robes and the disciples' heads are uncovered. While not a dogma, Western art tends to place objects and people with a positive value on the right side of a frame.[6] Meanwhile, Martha stands between Jesus and the mourners and Mary kneels in front of Jesus, both beseeching Jesus in gestures to do something. When Jesus orders the stone to be removed, the lead mourner seems to object but then moves in front of the stone to participate in rolling it away. After Jesus gestures a prayer and points to the tomb with the intertitle "Lazarus come forth," the mourners peer into the darkness of the tomb. As Lazarus, shrouded in white, slowly walks out of the darkness, they lurch to the left horrified as Lazarus drops his shroud, removes his own veil, and then reaches out to them with a shuddering grasp (see Figure 18.1).

The action suggests that Lazarus still thinks he participates in the liminal state of the mourners, who belong to the darkness of blindness and death. Audiences tend to view characters who move from right to left negatively and characters who move from left to right positively.[7] When Lazarus turns to the right of the frame, his eyes fix on Jesus and his shuddering shifts subtly from horror to excitement, at which point he falls before Jesus's feet. When he stands again, he recognizes his sisters and embraces them in apparent joy.[8] The action paints a near-perfect Johannine picture of the complete

---

[4] See Bernhard Lang, "The Baptismal Raising of Lazarus: A New Interpretation of John 11," *NovT* 58 (2016): 301–17. Lazarus's resurrection is the central plot of *La résurrection de Lazare* (1910, dir. Victorin-Hippolyte Jasset, Georges Hatot).

[5] Adele Reinhartz, "The Bible Epic," in *The Bible in Motion: A Handbook of the Bible and Its Reception in Film Part 2*, ed. Rhonda Burnette-Bletsch (Berlin: de Gruyter, 2016), 179–93, here 180, notes "the tendency of films to portray Jewish liturgical practices in ways that would be familiar to modern audiences."

[6] Peter Ward, *Picture Composition for Film and Television*, 2nd ed. (Oxford: Focal Press, 2003), 66.

[7] Confirmed through quantitative analysis by Matthew L. Egizii, Kimberly A Neuendorf, James Denny, Paul D. Skalski, and Rachel Campbell, "Which Way Did He Go? Directionality of Film Character and Camera Movement and Subsequent Spectator Interpretation," *Visual Communication* 17 (2017): 221–43.

[8] Films in this category support Philip F. Esler and Ronald Piper's thesis that Lazarus, Mary, and Martha, the Bethany trio, serve as a prototype of those whom Jesus loves (Minneapolis: Fortress, 2006), 21–2.

Figure 18.1 *From the Manger to Cross* (Kalem, 1912).

joy of life everlasting. Meanwhile the mourners move closer to the left of the frame, clinging to each other in fear.[9]

Cecille B. DeMille's *King of Kings* (1927) uses advancements in film acting and editing to support the impression that Lazarus's resurrection (44:50–49:50) signifies a severing of relationship with some of the Jewish mourners. Jesus, who appears to be the source of illumination, descends from left to right into a very deep tomb, where Lazarus's body lies within a solitary stone sarcophagus. Jesus and his followers position themselves to the right of the sarcophagus. DeMille inserts reaction shots of Caiaphas's spies described in an early intertitle as "Pharisee, scribe and temple guard—driven by the fury of religious hatred" and dressed expensively in dark fabric.[10] These then are the Jews from Jerusalem for whom mourning serves as a disguise.[11] DeMille stages the scene so that the spies appear in the upper left near the door, as far away as possible from Jesus, signifying a reluctance to participate. After he gestures to the disciples to remove the lid and they obey, Jesus pronounces "I am the Resurrection and the Life: he

---

[9] The various versions of the Pathé Frères's *La Vie et Passion de Notre Seigneur Jésus-Christ* released between 1902 and 1914 depict only the joy of Jesus's followers.

[10] Caiaphas's motivation is money, an antisemitic trope as Adele Reinhartz points out in "The Bible Epic," 188.

[11] The notion that the party from Jerusalem is insincere and even paid to mourn continues to be perpetuated without warrant in many commentaries.

Figure 18.2 *King of Kings* (DeMille Pictures, 1927).

that believeth in Me, though he were dead, yet shall live" over Lazarus's motionless shrouded corpse. The camera then cuts to the Jerusalem Jews looking down and sneering upon the action from the top of the stairs (see Figure 18.2).[12]

When Lazarus moves his arm and grasps the edge of the sarcophagus and slowly sits up, DeMille inserts a series of reaction shots. The witnesses standing on the floor of the tomb turn away slightly in fear, but their eyes remain riveted upon Lazarus. The Jerusalem trio's horror causes them to cover their eyes and then flee the scene, moving necessarily from right to left. The focus returns to Lazarus, who sits motionless gripping the edges of the sarcophagus as Martha slowly unwraps his bindings. When she unwraps his eyes, he gazes blankly ahead until he recognizes Jesus and draws in a deep breath of life. He then looks down and sees that he is in a sarcophagus and realizes that he has been dead. The witnesses who remain, with the exception of Judas, express the transformation of their fear into joy. The scene ends with expressions of thanks to God and adoration of Jesus.

---

[12] David J. Shepherd, *The Bible on Silent Film: Spectacle, Story and Scripture in the Early Cinema* (Cambridge: Cambridge University Press, 2013), 262–6, explains how in DeMille's first cut the anti-Jewishness was more pronounced. Bowing to pressure from Jewish criticism, DeMille inserted intertitles to place the blame upon Caiaphas alone for persecution of Jesus and to reduce the emphasis upon Caiaphas's monetary motivation. But as Shepherd points out, the *mise en scène* continues to depict Jesus's Jewish opponents stereotypically as money-grubbers.

Despite his avowed intention of representing Jesus as a Jew and to represent Judaism positively, Franco Zeffirelli's depiction of Lazarus's resurrection and its aftermath in his *Jesus of Nazareth* 1977 television series contains signifiers that perpetuate the distinction between life in Christ and death in Judaism.[13] The mourners remain at the rim of a dry quarry, the floor of which is dotted with smaller, deeper pits, and watch as Jesus descends, followed by the few disciples who obey his command to take away the stone. Just in case the audience does not get the visual allusion to Sheol, Peter recites a version of Jonah 2:6, "I went down into the countries underneath the earth to the peoples of the past but you lifted my life from the pit, Lord my God."

Zeffirelli then positions the camera first in the tomb so that the audience enjoys the privileged vantage point of seeing a brilliantly sunlit Jesus and then looking down from a divine perspective at the scene in which only the long shadows of the mourners are visible. Bathed in light, Jesus prays before the tomb's darkness, "Those who believe in me shall never die" (John 11:26). As Lazarus emerges, he pronounces, "He that believes in me but he were dead yet shall he live" (John 11:25). Lazarus is brilliantly white, the picture of transfiguration or sanctification. This is the last we see of Lazarus, who seems to have crossed over into the realm of the transcendent. The temple and Last Supper scenes imply that any relationship with a Jewish community has been severed.[14]

Lazarus's Resurrection as Death

A number of subsequent Jesus films continue the pattern of depicting Lazarus's resurrection as a quick jump from death to a life in Christ by treating the event as equivalent to baptism.[15] Beginning in the 1960s, some films adopt a distinctly different representation of the process. The emergence of Lazarus from the grave pulls Jesus into the liminal zone of the walking dead. This new plotline marks a shift from emphasis upon the Johannine ontology of belief to the Johannine narrative with its emphasis upon Lazarus's resurrection as a signifier of Jesus's death or kenosis.

In *The Greatest Story Ever Told* (1965), director George Stevens exploits the grandeur of settings, such as Canyonlands National Park in Utah, as a backdrop for

---

[13] Franco Zeffirelli, *Zeffirelli's Jesus: A Spiritual Diary*, trans. Willis J. Egan, S.J. (San Francisco: Harper & Row, 1984 [Italian original, 1977]), 59. Cited by Adele Reinhartz, "Jesus in Film: Hollywood Perspectives on the Jewishness of Jesus," *Journal of Religion & Film* 2 (1998), article 2, 10, https://digitalcommons.unomaha.edu/jrf/vol2/iss2/2 (checked 26 Aug 2022).

[14] Richard C. Stern, Clayton N. Jefford, and Buerric Debona, O.S.B., *Savior on the Silver Screen* (New York: Paulist Press, 1999), 207–8, observe that while Zeffirelli attempts to situate Jesus within a Jewish world, "He has read Judaism as a Christian!" and consequently represents the coming of Jesus as the fulfillment of Judaism. Adele Reinhartz, *Jesus of Hollywood* (Oxford: Oxford University Press, 2007), 50–51, exposes the supersessionist theology evident in the Last Supper scene.

[15] *Jesus* (1999, dir. Roger Young), which perhaps makes the best attempt at being historical and respectful in portraying Jewish mourning; *The Miracle Maker* (1999, dir. Derek W. Hayes and Stanislav Sokolov); *Son of God* (2014, dir. Christopher Spenser) in which Jesus kisses Lazarus on the head. *Son of Man* (2007, dir. Dornford-May) falls into its own category by juxtaposing black and white video footage of the resurrection used by tyranny to indict Jesus with a shot of a man painting a colorful mural depicting the event as a liberation.

a story that pits human achievement against God's sovereignty over creation.[16] His dramatization of the raising of Lazarus participates in this conflict by first providing Lazarus with a backstory largely based upon Christian tradition.[17] In the first Bethany scene (52:00–56:06), Lazarus speaks the lines of the rich young man from Matt 19:16-22 while Jesus spouts all of his teachings about the problems of wealth. Stephenson Humphries-Brooks contends that Lazarus's wealth is not so much a signifier of his Judaism but rather what he describes as middle-class American suburbanite faith.[18]

Stevens draws a sharp distinction between two groups in Bethany by draping the mourning women in black and the men and disciples, including Mary Magdalene, in homespun garments that blend into the landscape. There is no overt polemic against Jewish ritual or insincerity in his account, but there is a startling contrast between the expense of Lazarus's mountainside, rock-cut tomb, and the grave of someone buried in the earth to which a group of black-garbed female mourners cling, glimpsed as three witnesses run through a graveyard. Gone is also the villanization of the Jerusalem mourners. The informants from earlier films, such as *King of Kings*, become faith-filled witnesses. Stevens draws his line between the joyful anticipation of the witnesses to the film's three miracles and the gloomy prescience of Jesus, his disciples, and the Bethany family about the consequences of Lazarus's restoration.

After a series of close-up shots taken from inside the tomb looking out at an unblinking Jesus praying with arms stretched heavenward and calling for Lazarus to come forth, Stevens films Lazarus walking out of the tomb from the perspective of witnesses who remain at the bottom of the mountain. The film alternates between long shots looking up the mountain and close-ups of the witnesses' reactions. The audience must, for the most part, infer what is happening from the expressions of powerful emotions of awe and tearful joy. Lazarus appears only briefly alongside Jesus in the background of a single frame in which Uriah, whose strength of limbs has been restored by Jesus, is seen running as he makes his way along with two other witnesses toward Jerusalem. The scene ends with three witnesses staring up at Roman soldiers standing atop a city gate proclaiming in turn, "The Messiah has come! A man was dead and now he lives. I was crippled and now I walk! I was blind, and now I see!" followed by an intertitle announcing an intermission.

Stevens creates continuity between the two halves of his film by opening the second half with a shot of the temple gate with figures clothed in white blowing trumpets to summon the people to Jerusalem (2:03:00). In a very brief scene (2:03:20), Caiaphas learns of the report of the Lazarus miracle, but the news does not become a critical factor in Jesus's eventual arrest. The setting shifts back to Bethany (2:03:44), where a crowd has gathered. The shot fades to a close-up taken from outside a latticed window through which Lazarus peers, presumably at the crowd. He appears to be trapped in a

---

[16] Tatum, W. Barnes, *Jesus at the Movies: A Guide to the First Hundred Years* (Santa Rosa: Polebridge, 1977), 97–8, calls this an anti-worldliness critique of the comfortable life.

[17] The depiction of Lazarus as a wealthy man fits into an exegetical tradition that struggles with the absence of an account of Lazarus's faith. For Augustine (*In Evangelium Ioannis - Tractatus XLIX*), Lazarus's death and stench represents his habitual sin leading to his death.

[18] Stephenson Humphries-Brooks, *Cinematic Savior: Hollywood's Making of the American Christ* (Westport, CT: Praeger, 2006), 44.

Figure 18.3 *The Greatest Story Ever Told* (1965, George Stevens Productions).

net. His resurrection transforms what had been his comfortable villa into a prison. His sisters approach from behind and lead him into the dark room past Jesus, who gazes pensively down at the floor. The disciples somberly intone a version of Psalm 118, repeating the refrain, "his mercies endure forever" throughout the scene. The lighting casts shadows of bars across the disciples' faces and bodies and one large cross pattern on the floor upon which Jesus gazes (see Figure 18.3), thereby capturing the Johannine treatment of the Lazarus episode as the catalyst for Jesus's arrest and death.

Following Jesus's death, after a montage of shots of the witnesses and the temple enveloped in a rainstorm, the action returns to Bethany (3:09:50), where Lazarus is standing in a dark room facing the camera. When he turns his head to his left, the camera pans to show that he is looking at the empty chair where Jesus had sat. Lazarus slowly kneels and embraces it in penitent grief. He next reappears standing beside Joseph of Arimathea when the tomb is sealed (3:11:14). The resurrection of Lazarus does not participate in the joy of eternal life but keeps Jesus's followers in the shadowy realm of the vigil in which one waits for death or mourns the dead.

While Steven's reverent and orderly orchestration of the Lazarus resurrection scene stands in sharp contrast with Martin Scorcese's chaotic action in *The Last Temptation of Christ* (1988) in which Jesus seems doubtful and hesitant, the two films both treat Lazarus's resurrection as something other than a joyful transition to eternal life in Christ. Scorcese's dramatization fits into a pattern that runs throughout the film in which Jesus does not understand what his mission entails but nevertheless is continually drawn toward his death. For example, in an early scene set in Jesus's carpentry workshop where the principal products are crosses, Judas comes to assassinate Jesus.

The Bethany scene begins with a shot of a cluster of women draped completely in homespun garments ululating in grief. As in the scenes of the wedding at Cana and the Last Supper, Scorsese chooses to draw from Arab culture. Lloyd Baugh describes it as "exotic orientalism" and is harsh in his critique of the Last Supper that ignores the Jewish ritual Seder and includes a song based on the Muslim call to prayer.[19] When Jesus passes by a group of elderly men wearing prayer shawls and phylacteries, he tells them, "You think God belongs only to you? God is not an Israelite. He belongs to everybody." The de-Judaizing of Jesus participates in the agenda of demythologizing Christ and in doing so reduces Lazarus's resurrection to a disruption of the rhythms of what Mary of Bethany calls a "real life."

The dialogue is sparse. Mary and Martha say little. Jesus asks only when Lazarus was buried and commands the disciples to roll away the stone. As they do so, Jesus and the other onlookers cover their mouths and noses, gagging at the stench of death. After Jesus slowly approaches the opening, the camera's perspective shifts back and forth from Jesus to the tomb's perspective. With the camera positioned in the tomb, Jesus peers in and then makes a sudden quick gesture with his arms briefly piercing the threshold of the tomb. The camera then returns to the exterior, capturing Jesus's profile as he says in a quiet, slow voice, "Lazarus, in the name of the prophet, in the name of Jeremiah and my father, in the name of the most holy God, I call you here." He then repeats "I call you here" as a loud command. The camera then shifts its perspective back to the interior looking out at Jesus, who stands with his hands braced against the entrance of the tomb, emphasizing the threshold that divides the living and the dead. After he crouches down and quietly begins repeating Lazarus's name, the camera returns to the exterior looking over Jesus's shoulder and slowly limits the shot to the darkness of the tomb before flipping back to the interior looking out. The action is slow and hesitant with only the sound of buzzing flies. Then suddenly, Lazarus's hand shoots out toward a startled Jesus. When Jesus cautiously reaches in to take Lazarus's decomposing hand (see Figure 18.4), Lazarus pulls Jesus into the tomb before Jesus can forcefully pull him out. After Lazarus pulls back his head cloth, he leans forward and embraces Jesus, to which Jesus responds with a silent prayer, "God help me." Jesus can no longer doubt that he is the Son of God.

As in Steven's film, the resurrection of Lazarus is not to the fullness of life but to a half-life in a partially dead body that is never fully animated. Later in the film, Saul asks an ashened-faced Lazarus what death is like and which is better, life or death, to which Lazarus responds, "I was a little surprised. There wasn't that much difference." In this undifferentiated state, he shows no resistance to the dagger with which Saul then kills him. In the context of a story in which Jesus is tempted to avoid death by climbing down from the cross, Lazarus's subplot seems to underscore the importance of the living respecting the dead and leaving them to rest in peace. Just as Lazarus must die, so Jesus's thirty-one-minute daydream while on the cross about having a long and quiet life must be brought to its conclusion with his voluntary death.

In *Mary Magdalene* (2018, directed by Garth Davis), Jesus's story is told primarily through the eyes of the title character, with Jesus's dialogue and action pared down to produce a Jesus who is an esoteric sage with divine powers yet extremely vulnerable in his humanity. As such, he stands in contrast to the dominant understanding of power

---

[19] Lloyd Baugh, *Imagining the Divine: Jesus and Christ-Figures in Film* (Kansas City: Sheed & Ward, 1997), 54, 59–60.

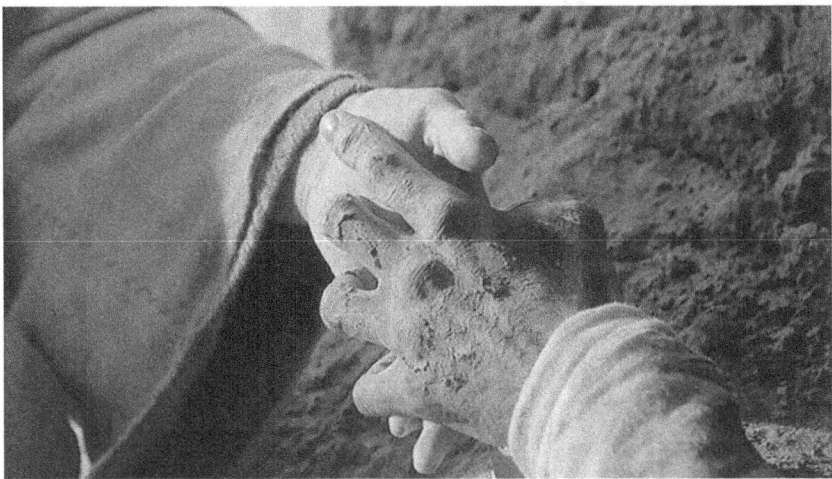

Figure 18.4 *The Last Temptation of Christ* (Cineplex Odeon, 1988).

as male authority exercised over others and teaches women that God's authority over them supersedes that of husbands and fathers. The film juxtaposes Mary's response to Jesus's ministry to those who suffer with that of the male disciples, led by Peter, who are preoccupied with the coming kingdom.

The framing and action of Jesus within the scene's setting point to Lazarus's resurrection as a sort of kenosis that Jesus undergoes: as Lazarus is filled with life, Jesus appears drained of it. The scene (0:52–0:56) begins with a visual metaphor. Shot through a doorway, Jesus crosses the threshold (*limen*) between the light of day into the darkness that leads to a valley of rock-cut tombs. The camera then shoots up from the ground upon which Lazarus has been laid, surrounded by a small group of mourners clad in dark homespun garments, toward Jesus and the disciples draped in lighter material. At this point, the audience must infer that this is Lazarus's family, for no names are given and only one woman speaks, saying, "You're the healer. I prayed for you to come, but it's too late." Jesus kneels down beside Lazarus and places his hand on the corpse's chest and then slowly lies down on his side gently embracing it. The camera is positioned close to the two figures' heads as Jesus draws in a deep breath, speaks inaudibly, and breathes life into Lazarus. A series of even more extreme close-ups edited without music amplify the emotion of the scene.[20] Lazarus and Jesus lock eyes. Jesus's eyes tear and then he grimaces (see Figure 18.5)

When Lazarus breaks his hold on Jesus by turning away, Jesus rolls over on his back exhausted while Lazarus sits up and turns to embrace a young boy. There is no new community for Lazarus. He seems simply to resume his former life. Peter, in contrast, follows the trajectory of earlier Jesus films and sees the resurrection of Lazarus as a

---

[20] Observations contributed by Lilly Summhammer (2021), Tisch School of the Arts student.

Figure 18.5 Jesus in *Mary Magdalene* (Film4 et al., 2018).

sign of the establishment of God's kingdom: "Now I know that you are the Son of God. And the people will shout it from the rooftops." Mary, in contrast, is privy to the narrative turn toward death when she reaches out to Jesus in the aftermath of Lazarus's resurrection:

> Jesus: I saw it so clearly. I know it is slipping away.
> Mary: What is?
> Jesus: This life.
> Mary: I can feel the blood running through your veins. I can see light in your eyes. You're here now. I'm here. Be here with me.
> Jesus: But the path, it goes into darkness.
> Mary: And I will walk it with you.
> Jesus: Jerusalem.

The new relationship that forms around Jesus is one defined by two Marys—Mary Magdalene and Mary, the mother of Jesus—who both recognize that they are in the liminal space between life and death.

At the conclusion of the story, after Mary has reported that she has seen Jesus resurrected, she recognizes that the kingdom is within, saying, "It grows with us, with every act of love and care, with our forgiveness. We have the power to lift the people, just as he did, and then we will be free, just as he is." Peter, on the other hand, proclaims his appearance as a sign that Jesus will return and bring the kingdom and the male disciples are the rocks upon which Jesus will build his church, "with one purpose and one message." He describes an institution and doctrinal orthodoxy. While Jesus criticizes temple sacrifice when he visits Jerusalem, the polemic of the film is aimed squarely at male authority, be it that of the synagogue, the temple, or the church. Seen through the lens of Victor Turner, the male disciples choose a "model" for "human relatedness" in which society is "a structured, differentiated, and often hierarchical system" that separates people "in terms of 'more' or 'less.' "[21] Peter exploits the fluidity of the liminal space, proclaiming himself a sort of master of ceremony, thereby robbing the liminal moment of its egalitarian potential and replacing it with a rivalry.[22] Mary follows the second of Turner's two models established in the liminal period, a society of "undifferentiated comitatus … or even communion of equal individuals who submit together to the general authority of the ritual elders," in this case, Jesus and God.[23]

Conclusion

This analysis focuses on what is seen on screen. A longer analysis should say something about the cultural climate in which these films were first screened. Early filmmakers were subject to stricter censorship that called for a pious representation of Jesus and marketed these films to a Christian audience. No censor objected to the use of the signifiers of Judaism as signifiers of death or sin to dramatize a quick transition from death to a blissful eternal life in Christ. While many filmmakers since the Second World War may be more cautious about treating anything Jewish in a negative light, the shift from dramatizing Johannine ontology to capturing the significance of Lazarus's resurrection to the Johannine plot reflects more than an avoidance of anti-Judaism or anti-Semitism. By focusing the camera's lens on the transgression of boundaries between the living and the dead, these films dramatize the dangers and anxieties of Lazarus's restored relationship with the living. Suspense supplants comfortable familiarity. They open up a prolonged liminal space in which to explore tensions within the religion of Christianity and the life of Jesus. The raising of Lazarus becomes a transformative experience for the film audience's relationship to the Jesus narrative.

---

[21] "Liminality and Communitas," 360.
[22] Bjørn Thomassen, "The Uses and Meanings of Liminality," *International Political Anthropology* 2 (2009): 5–28, here 22, describes this potential danger within liminal space.
[23] "Liminality and Communitas," 360.

Bibliography

Ancient Author Translations

Aristotle. *Nicomachean Ethics*. Translated by H. Rackham. LCL 73. Cambridge, MA: Harvard University Press, 1926.
Athenaeus. *Deipnosophistae*. Translated by C. D. Yonge. LCL 345. Cambridge, MA: Harvard University Press, 1941.
Babylonian Talmud: Shabbath. Translated by H. Freedman. New York: Rebecca Bennet, 1959. https://halakhah.com/shabbath/index.html.
Cicero. *Letters to Atticus*. Vol. 1. Edited and translated by D. R. Shackleton Bailey. LCL 7. Cambridge, MA: Harvard University Press, 1999.
Cicero. *On Old Age. On Friendship. On Divination*. Translated by W. A. Falconer. LCL 154. Cambridge, MA: Harvard University Press, 1923.
Epictetus. *Discourses*. Vol. 1. Translated by W. A. Oldfather. LCL 131. Cambridge, MA: Harvard University Press, 1925.
Epistle of Barnabas. Papias and Quadratus. Epistle to Diognetus. The Shepherd of Hermas. Vol. 2 of *The Apostolic Fathers*. Edited and translated by Bart D. Ehrman. LCL 25. Cambridge, MA: Harvard University Press, 2003.
Homeric Hymns. Homeric Apocrypha. Lives of Homer. Edited and translated by Martin L. West. LCL 496. Cambridge, MA: Harvard University Press, 2003.
Josephus. *Jewish Antiquities. Books XII–XIV*. Translated by Ralph Marcus. LCL 365. Cambridge, MA: Harvard University Press, 1978.
Josephus. *The Jewish War. Books I–III*. Translated by H. St. J. Thackeray. LCL 203. Cambridge, MA: Harvard University Press, 1927.
Laertius, Diogenes. *Lives of Eminent Philosophers*. Vol. 4. Translated by R. D. Hicks. LCL 185. Cambridge: Cambridge University Press, 1925.
Lucian. Translated by A. M. Harmon. 8 vols. LCL. Cambridge, MA: Harvard University Press, 1962.
The Martyrdom of Perpetua and Felicitas. Translated by H. Musurillo. Pages 106–31 in *The Acts of the Christian Martyrs: Introduction, Texts, and Translations*. OECT. Oxford: Oxford University Press, 1972.
The Pentateuch with Rashi's Commentary. Translated and annotated by M. Rosenbaum and A. M. Silbermann. 5 vols. London: Shapiro, Valentine & Co., 1929–34.
Philo. Translated by F. H. Colston and G. H. Whitaker. 10 vols. LCL. Cambridge, MA: Harvard University Press, 1966–71.
Phlegon of Tralles' Book of Marvels. Translated with an Introduction and Commentary by William Hansen. Exeter: University of Exeter Press, 1996.
Plato. *Euthyphro. Apology. Crito. Phaedo*. Edited and translated by Christopher Emlyn-Jones and William Preddy. LCL 36. Cambridge, MA: Harvard University Press, 2017.
Plato. *Lysis. Symposium. Gorgias*. Translated by W. R. M. Lamb. LCL 166. Cambridge, MA: Harvard University Press, 1925.

Plutarch. *The Education of Children. How the Young Man Should Study Poetry. On Listening to Lectures. How to Tell a Flatterer from a Friend. How a Man May Become Aware of His Progress in Virtue.* Vol. 1 of *Moralia.* Translated by Frank Cole Babbitt. LCL 197. Cambridge, MA: Harvard University Press, 1927.

Plutarch. *Table Talk.* Vol. 8 of *Moralia.* Translated by P. A. Clement and H. B. Hoffleit. LCL 424. Cambridge, MA: Harvard University Press, 1969.

Suetonius. *The Lives of the Twelve Caesars.* Translated by Alexander Thomson. London: George Bell, 1909.

Theophrastus, Herodas, and Sophron. Characters. Herodas: Mimes. Sophron and Other Mime Fragments. Edited and translated by Jeffrey Rusten and I. C. Cunningham. LCL 225. Cambridge, MA: Harvard University Press, 2003.

Tyrtaeus, Solon, Theognis, and Mimnermus. Greek Elegiac Poetry: From the Seventh to the Fifth Centuries BC. Edited and translated by Douglas E. Gerber. LCL 258. Cambridge, MA: Harvard University Press, 1999.

Modern Scholars

Aaron, Michele. *Death and the Moving Image: Ideology, Iconography and I.* Edinburgh: Edinburgh University Press, 2014.

Aasgaard, Reidar. "Like a Child: Paul's Rhetorical Uses of Childhood." Pages 249–77 in *The Child in the Bible.* Edited by Marcia J. Bunge. Grand Rapids, MI: Eerdmans, 2008.

Adams, Edward. *The Earliest Christian Meeting Places: Almost Exclusively Houses.* London: Bloomsbury T&T Clark, 2016.

Adler, Yonatan. "Religion, Judaism: Purity in the Roman Period." Pages 240–9 in *The Oxford Encyclopedia of the Bible and Archaeology.* Edited by Daniel M. Master. Oxford: Oxford University Press, 2013.

Adler, Yonatan. "Second Temple Period Ritual Baths Adjacent to Agricultural Installations: The Archaeological Evidence in Light of the Halakhic Sources." *JJS* 59 (2008): 62–72.

Adler, Yonatan. "Tosefta Shabbat 1:14—'Come and See the Extent to Which Purity Had Spread': An Archaeological Perspective on the Historical Background to a Late Tannaitic Passage." Pages 63–82 in *Talmuda De-Eretz Israel: Archaeology and the Rabbis in Late Antique Palestine.* Edited by Steven Fine and Aaron Koller. SJ 73. Berlin: de Gruyter, 2014.

Aichele, George. "Comedic Films in the Bible." Pages 73–8 in *T&T Clark Companion to the Bible and Film.* Edited by Richard Walsh. London: T&T Clark, 2018.

Alföldy, Géza. "Pontius Pilatus und das Tiberieum von Caesarea Maritima." *SCI* 18 (1999): 85–108.

Allegro, John Marco. *Qumrân Cave 4.* Vol. 35. Oxford: Clarendon, 1968.

Allison, Dale C., Jr. *A Critical and Exegetical Commentary on the Epistle of James.* New York: Bloomsbury T&T Clark, 2013.

Ameling, Walther, Hannah M. Cotton, and Werner Eck. *Caesarea and the Middle Coast 1121–2160.* Vol. 2 of *Corpus Inscriptionum Iudaeae/Palestine: A Multi-lingual Corpus of the Inscriptions from Alexander to Muhammad.* Berlin: de Gruyter, 2011.

Ando, Clifford. *The Matter of the Gods.* Los Angeles: University of California Press, 2008.

Arnold, Russell C. D. "Repentance and the Qumran Covenant Ceremony." Pages 159–75 in *The Development of Penitential Prayer in Second Temple Judaism.* Vol. 2 of *Seeking the Favor of God.* Edited by Mark J. Boda, Daniel K. Falk, and Rodney A. Werline. SBLEJL 22. Atlanta, GA: SBL Press, 2007.

Ascough, Richard S. *1 & 2 Thessalonians. An Introduction and Study Guide: Encountering the Christ Group at Thessalonike.* London: T&T Clark, 2017.

Ascough, Richard S. *Paul's Macedonian Associations: The Social Context of Philippians and 1 Thessalonians.* WUNT 2/161. Tübingen: Mohr Siebeck, 2003.

Aymer, Margaret. "'Mother Knows Best': The Story of Mother Paul Revisited." Pages 187–98 in *Mother Goose, Mother Jones, Mommie Dearest: Biblical Mothers and Their Children.* Edited by Cheryl A. Kirk-Duggan and Tina Pippin. SemeiaSt 61. Atlanta, GA: SBL Press, 2008.

Babota, Vasile. "In Search of the Origins of the Pharisees." Pages 23–40 in *The Pharisees.* Edited by Amy-Jill Levine and Joseph Sievers. Grand Rapids, MI: Eerdmans, 2021.

Badian, Ernst. "Amicitia." *BNP* 1 (1996): 590–1.

Baillet, Maurice. *Qumrân Grotte 4.III (4Q482–4Q520).* DJD 7. Oxford: Clarendon, 1982.

Baillet, Maurice, and Esther G. Chazon, eds. "4Q504 (4QDibHam^a)." Pages 490–507 in *Poetic and Liturgical Texts. Part 5 of The Dead Sea Scrolls Reader.* Edited by Donald W. Parry and Emanuel Tov. Leiden: Brill, 2005. Reprinted in pages 490–507 of vol. 2. 2nd ed. Leiden: Brill, 2014.

Bammel, Ernst. "Φίλος τοῦ Καίσαρος." *TLZ* 77 (1952): 205–10.

Barclay, John M. G. *Against Apion.* Vol. 10 of *Flavius Josephus: Translation and Commentary.* Edited by Steve Mason. Leiden: Brill, 2007. Repr., Leiden: Brill, 2013.

Barclay, John M. G. "'Am I Not a Man and a Brother?' The Bible and the British Antislavery Campaign." *ExpTim* 119 (2007): 3–14.

Barclay, John M. G. *Jews in the Western Mediterranean Diaspora, from Alexander to Trajan (323 BCE To 117 CE).* Berkeley: University of California Press, 1996.

Barclay, John M. G. "Paul, Philemon and the Dilemma of Christian Slave-Ownership." *NTS* 37 (1991): 161–86.

Barclay, John M. G. "Thessalonica and Corinth: Social Contrasts in Pauline Christianity." *JSNT* 47 (1992): 49–74.

Baugh, Lloyd. *Imagining the Divine: Jesus and Christ-Figures in Film.* Kansas City, MO: Sheed & Ward, 1997.

Baumgarten, Albert I. "The 'Hypothetica'—A Jewish Rationalist in the Land of Israel." In *History, Historians and Historiography.* Edited by Meron M. Piotrkowski, Robert A. Brody, Noah Hacham, and J. W. van Henten. Forthcoming.

Baumgarten, Albert I. "Elias Bickerman and Hans (Yohanan) Lewy: The Story of a Friendship." *Anabases* 13 (2011): 95–118.

Baumgarten, Albert I. "'Sages Increase Peace in the World': Reconciliation and Power." Pages 221–36 in *The Faces of Torah: Studies in Texts and Contexts of Ancient Judaism in Honor of Steven Fraade.* Edited by Michal Bar-Asher Siegal, Tzvi Novick, and Christine Hayes. Göttingen: Vandenhoeck & Ruprecht, 2017.

Beckwith, Christopher I. *Empires of the Silk Road. A History of Central Eurasia from the Bronze Age to the Present.* Princeton, NJ: Princeton University Press, 2009.

Bernier, Jonathan. *Aposynagōgos and the Historical Jesus in John: Rethinking the Historicity of the Johannine Expulsion Passages.* BibInt 122. Leiden: Brill, 2013.

Berry, Ken L. "The Function of Friendship Language in Philippians 4:10–20." Pages 107–24 in *Friendship, Flattery, and Frankness of Speech: Studies on Friendship in the New Testament World.* Edited by John T. Fitzgerald. Leiden: Brill, 1996.

Berthelot, Katell. "The Canaanites Who 'Trusted in God': An Original Interpretation of the Fate of the Canaanites in Rabbinic Literature." *JJS* 62 (2011): 234–61.

Berthelot, Katell. "Philo of Alexandria and the Conquest of Canaan." *JSJ* 38 (2007): 39–56.
Berthelot, Katell. "Reclaiming the Land (1 Maccabees 15:28–36): Hasmonean Discourse between Biblical Tradition and Seleucid Rhetoric." *JBL* 133 (2014): 539–59.
Bieberstein, Sabine. "Der Brief an Philemon: Brieflektüre unter den kritischen Augen Aphias." Pages 676–82 in *Kompendium Feministische Bibelauslegung*. Edited by Luise Schottroff and Claudia Janssen. Gütersloh: Gütersloher Verlagshaus, 1998.
Bieberstein, Sabine. "Disrupting the Normal Reality of Slavery: A Feminist Reading of the Letter to Philemon." *JSNT* 23 (2001): 105–16.
Bieringer, Reimund, Didier Pollefeyt, and Frederique Vandecasteele-Vanneuville, eds. *Anti-Judaism and the Fourth Gospel*. Louisville, KY: Westminster John Knox, 2001.
Binder, Donald D. *Into the Temple Courts: The Place of the Synagogues in the Second Temple Period*. Atlanta, GA: SBL Press, 1999.
Birchard, Robert S. *Cecil B. DeMille's Hollywood*. Lexington: University of Kentucky Press, 2004.
Bloch, Yigal, Jonathan Ben-Dov, and Daniel Stökl Ben Ezra. "The Rule of the Congregation from Cave 1 of Qumran: A New Annotated Edition." *REJ* 178 (2019): 1–46.
Blount, Brian. *Revelation: A Commentary*. Louisville, KY: Westminster John Knox, 2009.
Boeckhius, Augustus. *Corpus Inscriptionum Graecarum*. Vol. 2. Berlin: Akademie der Wissenschaften zu Berlin, 1843. Repr., Hildesheim: Olms, 1977.
Boer, Esther de. *The Gospel of Mary: Beyond a Gnostic and a Biblical Mary Magdalene*. JSNTSup 60. London: T&T Clark, 2004.
Boer, Martinus C. de. "The Johannine Community under Attack in Recent Scholarship." Pages 211–41 in *The Ways That Often Parted: Essays in Honor of Joel Marcus*. Edited by Lori Baron, Jill Hicks-Keeton, and Matthew Thiessen. Atlanta, GA: SBL Press, 2018.
Bond, Helen K. "The Coins of Pontius Pilate. Part of an Attempt to Provoke the People or to Integrate Them into the Empire?" *JSJ* 27 (1996): 241–62.
Bond, Helen K. *Pontius Pilate in History and Interpretation*. Cambridge: Cambridge University Press, 1998.
Bonnie, Rick. "Pure Stale Water: Experiencing Jewish Purification Rituals in Early Roman Palestine." Pages 234–53 in *The Routledge Handbook of the Senses in the Ancient Near East*. Edited by Kiersten Neumann and Allison Thomason. London: Routledge, 2022.
Booth, Wayne. *The Company We Keep: An Ethics of Fiction*. Berkeley: University of California Press, 1988.
Boyarin, Daniel. *Judaism. The Genealogy of a Modern Notion*. New Brunswick, NJ: Rutgers University Press, 2019.
Bradley, Keith R. *Slaves and Masters in the Roman Empire: A Study in Social Control*. New York: Oxford University Press, 1987.
Bradley, Keith R. "Wet-Nursing at Rome: A Study in Social Relations." Pages 201–29 in *The Family in Ancient Rome*. Edited by Beryl Rawson. Ithaca, NY: Cornell University Press, 1986.
Brant, Jo-Ann A. "Husband Hunting. Characterization and Narrative Art in the Gospel of John." *BibInt* 4 (1996): 205–23.
Brant, Jo-Ann A. *John. Paideia: Commentaries on the NT*. Grand Rapids, MI: Baker Academic, 2011.
Braund, David C. *Rome and the Friendly King: The Character of Client Kingship*. New York: St. Martin's, 1984.
Brooten, Bernadette. *Women Leaders in the Synagogue: Inscriptional Evidence and Background Issues*. Providence, RI: Brown Judaic Studies, 1982.

Brown, Dan. *The Da Vinci Code*. New York: Doubleday, 2003.
Brown, Raymond E. *The Death of the Messiah*. 2 vols. ABRL. New York: Doubleday, 1994.
Bruce, F. F. *The Pauline Circle*. Grand Rapids, MI: Eerdmans, 1985.
Burnett, Andrew, Michel Amandry, Ripollés Alegre P. P., Ian Carradice, Jerome Mairat, Marguerite Spoerri Butcher, Antony Hostein, William E. Metcalf, Laurent Bricault, and Maryse Blet-Lemarquand, eds. *From the Death of Caesar to the Death of Vitellius (44 BC–AD 69)*. Vol 1 of *Roman Provincial Coinage*. London: British Museum, 1992.
Burnett-Bletsch, Rhonda. "God at the Movies." Pages 299–326 in *The Bible in Motion: A Handbook of the Bible and Its Reception in Film*. Edited by Rhonda Burnett-Bletsch. Berlin: de Gruyter, 2016.
Campbell, William S. *The Nations in the Divine Economy: Paul's Covenantal Hermeneutics and Participation in Christ*. Lanham, MD: Lexington Books, 2018.
Campbell, William S. *Romans: A Social Identity Commentary*. London: T&T Clark, 2023.
Caragounis, Chrys. "'Abide in Me.' The New Mode of Relationship between Jesus and His Followers as a Basis for Christian Ethics (John 15)." Pages 250–63 in *Rethinking the Ethics of John: "Implicit Ethics" in the Johannine Writings*. Vol. 3 of *Contexts and Norms of New Testament Ethics*. Edited by Jan G. van der Watt and Ruben Zimmermann. WUNT 291. Tübingen: Mohr Siebeck, 2012.
Carey, Greg. "Looking for White in the Synoptic Problem." *Political Theology Network* (2020). https://politicaltheology.com/looking-for-white-in-the-synoptic-problem/.
Carter, Warren. *John and Empire: Initial Explorations*. New York: T&T Clark, 2008.
Carter, Warren. *John: Storyteller, Interpreter, Evangelist*. Grand Rapids, MI: Baker Academic, 2006.
Castelli, Elizabeth A. *Imitating Paul: A Discourse of Power*. Louisville, KY: Westminster John Knox, 1991.
Chazon, Esther G. "The Classification of 4Q505: Daily or Festival Prayers?" Pages 23–34 in *"Go Out and Study the Land" (Judges 18:2): Archaeological, Historical and Textual Studies in Honor of Hanan Eshel*. Edited by Aren M. Maeir, Jodi Magness, and Lawrence H. Schiffman. JSJSup 148. Leiden: Brill, 2012.
Chazon, Esther G. "Prayer and Identity in Varying Contexts: The Case of the *Words of the Luminaries*." *JSJ* 46 (2015): 484–511.
Chazon, Esther G. "Sectarian or Not: What Is the Question?" Pages 13–32 in *Emerging Sectarianism in the Dead Sea Scrolls: Continuity, Separation, and Conflict*. Edited by Ananda Geyser-Fouché and John J. Collins. STDJ. Leiden: Brill, 2022.
Chazon, Esther G. "Tradition and Innovation in Sectarian Religious Poetry." Pages 55–67 in *Prayer and Poetry in the Dead Sea Scrolls and Related Literature: Essays in Honor of Eileen Schuller on the Occasion of Her 65th Birthday*. Edited by Jeremy Penner, Ken M. Penner, and Cecilia Wassén. STDJ 98. Leiden: Brill, 2012.
Cirafesi, Wally V. *John within Judaism: Religion, Ethnicity, and the Shaping of Jesus-Oriented Jewishness in the Fourth Gospel*. AJEC 112. Leiden: Brill, 2021.
Clark, Gillian. "Roman Women." *GR* (Ser. 2) 28 (1981): 193–212.
Coats, George W. *Moses: Heroic Man, Man of God*. JSOTSup 57. Sheffield: JSOT Press, 1998.
Cohen, Naomi. "The Jewish Dimension of Philo's Judaism: An Elucidation of *de Spec. Leg.* IV 132–150." *JJS* 38 (1987): 165–87.
Cohen, Shaye J. D. *The Beginnings of Jewishness: Boundaries, Varieties, Uncertainties*. HCS 31. Berkeley: University of California Press, 1999.
Collins, Adela Yarbro. "'How on Earth Did Jesus Become a God?' A Reply." Pages 55–66 in *Israel's God and Rebecca's Children*. Edited by David B. Capes, April D. DeConick, Helen K. Bond, and Troy A. Miller. Waco, TX: Baylor University Press, 2007.

Coloe, Mary. *John 1–10. Wisdom Commentary 44A*. Collegeville, MN: Liturgical Press, 2021.
Craddock, Fred. "When the Roll Is Called Down Here." *Christian History* 132 (2019): 9.
Culpepper, R. Alan. *Anatomy of the Fourth Gospel*. Philadelphia, PA: Fortress, 1983.
Culpepper, R. Alan. *The Johannine School: An Evaluation of the Johannine School Hypothesis Based on an Investigation of the Nature of Ancient Schools*. SBLDS 26. Missoula, MT: Scholars Press, 1975. Repr., 2007.
Culpepper, R. Alan. *Matthew*. NTL. Louisville, KY: Westminster John Knox, 2021.
Culy, Martin M. *Echoes of Friendship in the Gospel of John*. NTM 30. Sheffield: Sheffield Phoenix, 2010.
Custen, George F. *Bio/Pics: How Hollywood Constructed Public History*. New Brunswick, NJ: Rutgers University Press, 1992.
Danker, Frederick W., Walter Bauer, William F. Arndt, and F. Wilbur Gingrich. *Greek-English Lexicon of the New Testament and Other Early Christian Literature*. 3rd ed. Chicago, IL: University of Chicago Press, 2000.
Dasen, Véronique. "Childbirth and Infancy in the Greek and Roman Worlds." Pages 291–314 in *A Companion to Families in the Greek and Roman Worlds*. Edited by Beryl Rawson. Oxford: Blackwell, 2011.
Davies, W. D., and Dale C. Allison, Jr. *The Gospel according to Saint Matthew*. Vol. 3. ICC. London: Bloomsbury, 1997.
Dawes, Gregory W. "The Danger of Idolatry: First Corinthians 8:7–13." *CBQ* 58 (1996): 82–98.
Deines, Roland. "Jesus the Galilean: Questioning the Function of Galilee in Recent Jesus Research." Pages 53–93 in *Acts of God in History: Studies towards Recovering a Theological Historiography*. Edited by Christoph Ochs and Peter Watts. WUNT 317. Tübingen: Mohr Siebeck, 2013.
Deissmann, Gustav Adolf. *Licht vom Osten: Das Neue Testament und die neu entdeckten Texte der hellenistisch-römischen Welt*. 4th ed. Tübingen: J. C. B. Mohr (Paul Siebeck), 1923.
Deissmann, Gustav Adolf. *Light from the Ancient East: The New Testament Illustrated by Recently Discovered Texts from the Graeco-Roman World*. 2nd ed. London: Hodder & Stoughton, 1927. Repr., Grand Rapids, MI: Baker, 1978.
Deleuze, Gilles and Félix Guattari. *Das Rhizom*. Berlin: Merve, 1977.
Demandt, Alexander. *Pontius Pilatus*. München: Beck, 2012.
Dixon, Suzanne. *The Roman Mother*. London: Croom Helm, 1988.
Douglas, Mary. *Purity and Danger: An Analysis of Concepts of Pollution and Taboo*. London: Routledge, 1966.
Dunn, James D. G. *The Theology of Paul the Apostle*. Grand Rapids, MI: Eerdmans, 1998.
Eberwein, Robert. "Clint Eastwood and Morgan Freeman: Million Dollar Seniors." Pages 32–49 in *Shining in Shadows: Movie Stars of the 2000s*. Edited by Murray Pomerance. New Brunswick, NJ: Rutgers University Press, 2012.
Eck, Werner. "Der Kaiser und seine Ratgeber." Pages 67–78 in *Herrschaftsstrukturen und Herrschaftspraxis. Konzepte, Prinzipien und Strategien der Administration im römischen Kaiserreich*. Edited by Anne Kolb. Berlin: Akademie, 2006.
Egizii, Matthew L., Kimberly A. Neuendorf, James Denny, Paul D. Skalski, and Rachel Campbell. "Which Way Did He Go? Directionality of Film Character and Camera Movement and Subsequent Spectator Interpretation." *Visual Communication* 17 (2017): 221–43.

Ehrensperger, Kathy. "Imagine—No 'Works of Law'! Struggling with Ἔργα νόμου' in Changing Times and Places." Paper presented at the Annual Meeting of the SBL. San Diego, November 20, 2019.

Ehrensperger, Kathy. *Searching Paul: Conversations with the Jewish Apostle to the Nations*. Tübingen: Mohr Siebeck, 2019.

Ellis, E. Earle. "Paul and His Co-workers." *NTS* 17 (1971): 437–52.

Emanuel, Sarah. *Humor, Resistance, and Jewish Cultural Persistence in the Book of Revelation: Roasting Rome*. Cambridge: Cambridge University Press, 2020.

Emmett, Grace. "'You Weakened Him': Jesus's Masculinity in *Mary Magdalene*." *Religion and Gender* 10 (2020): 97–117.

Esler, Philip F., and Ronald Piper. *Lazarus, Mary and Martha*. Minneapolis, MN: Fortress, 2006.

Falk, Daniel K. *Daily, Sabbath, and Festival Prayers in the Dead Sea Scrolls*. STDJ 27. Leiden: Brill, 1998.

Fee, Gordon D. *Paul's Letter to the Philippians*. Grand Rapids, MI: Eerdmans, 1995.

Feldman, Louis. "Josephus's Portrait of Joshua." *HTR* 82 (1989): 351–76.

Feldman, Louis. *"Remember Amalek!": Vengeance, Zealotry, and Group Destruction in the Bible according to Philo, Pseudo-Philo, and Josephus*. HUCM 31. Cincinnati, OH: Hebrew Union College, 2004.

Fenner, Chris. "What a Friend We Have in Jesus." *Hymnology Archive* (March 22, 2021). https://www.hymnologyarchive.com/what-a-friend-we-have-in-jesus.

Fetterley, Judith. *The Resisting Reader: A Feminist Approach to American Fiction*. Bloomington: Indiana University Press, 1978.

Fisch, Yael. "The Origins of Oral Torah: A New Pauline Perspective." *JSJ* 51 (2020): 43–66.

Fitzgerald, John T., ed. *Graeco-Roman Perspectives on Friendship*. RBS 34. Atlanta, GA: SBL Press, 1997.

Fitzgerald, John T. "Paul and Friendship." Pages 331–62 in vol. 1 of *Paul in the Greco-Roman World: A Handbook*. Edited by J. Paul Sampley. London: Bloomsbury T&T Clark, 2016.

Fitzgerald, John T. "Theodore of Mopsuestia on Paul's Letter to Philemon." Pages 333–63 in *Philemon in Perspective: Interpreting a Pauline Letter*. Edited by D. Francois Tolmie and Alfred Friedl. BZNW 169. Berlin: de Gruyter, 2010.

Fitzmyer, Joseph A. *The Acts of the Apostles: A New Translation with Introduction and Commentary*. AB 31. New York: Doubleday, 1998.

Fletcher, Michelle. *Reading Revelation as Pastiche: Imitating the Past*. New York: Bloomsbury, 2017.

Fletcher, Michelle. "Seeing Differently with *Mary Magdalene*." Pages 55–65 in *The T&T Clark Handbook of Jesus and Film*. Edited by Richard Walsh. London: T&T Clark, 2021.

Foucault, Michel. "The Subject and Power." Pages 208–26 in *Michel Foucault: Beyond Structuralism and Hermeneutics*. Edited by Hubert L. Dreyfus and Paul Rabinow. Chicago, IL: University of Chicago Press, 1982.

Fox, Kenneth A. "The Nicolaitans, Nicolaus, and the Early Church." *SR* 23 (1994): 485–96.

Fox, Richard Wightman. *Jesus in America: Personal Savior, Cultural Hero, National Obsession*. New York: HarperSanFrancisco, 2004.

Fox, Robin Lane. *Pagans and Christians*. New York: Alfred A. Knopf, 1987.

Frankfurter, David. "Jews or Not? Reconstructing the Other in Rev 2:9 and 3:9." *HTR* 94 (2001): 403–25.

Fredriksen, Paula. "'If It *Looks* Like a Duck, and It *Quacks* Like a Duck …': On *Not* Giving Up the Godfearers." Pages 25–34 in *A Most Reliable Witness. Essays in Honor of Ross Shepard Kraemer*. Edited by Susan Ashbrook Harvey, Nathaniel DesRosiers, Shira L. Lander, Jacqueline Pastis, and Daniel Ullucci. Providence, RI: Brown Judaic Studies, 2016.

Fredriksen, Paula. "Judaizing the Nations: The Ritual Demands of Paul's Gospel." *NTS* 56 (2010): 232–52.

Fredriksen, Paula. *Paul: The Pagans' Apostle*. New Haven, CT: Yale University Press, 2018.

Fredriksen, Paula. "Philo, Herod, Paul, and the Many Gods of Ancient Jewish 'Monotheism.'" *HTR* 115 (2022): 23–45.

Fredriksen, Paula. "What 'Parting of the Ways'? Jews, Gentiles, and the Ancient Mediterranean City." Pages 35–64 in *The Ways That Never Parted: Jews and Christians in Late Antiquity and the Early Middle Ages*. Edited by Adam H. Becker and Annette Yoshiko Reed. Tübingen: Mohr Siebeck, 2003.

Fredriksen, Paula. "Where Do We Go from Here? Conflict and Co-existence in Institutional Contexts." Pages 381–97 in *Negotiating Identities: Conflict, Conversion, and Consolidation in Early Judaism and Christianity (200 BCE–600 CE)*. Edited by Karin Hedner Zetterholm, Anders Runesson, Cecilia Wassén, and Magnus Zetterholm. CB. Lanham, MD: Lexington Books, 2022.

Fredriksen, Paula. "Who Was Paul?" Pages 23–47 in *The New Cambridge Companion to St. Paul*. Edited by Bruce Longenecker. Cambridge: Cambridge University Press, 2020.

Frey, Jörg. "The Relevance of the Roman Imperial Cult for the Book of Revelation: Exegetical and Hermeneutical Reflections on the Relation between the Seven Letters and the Visionary Main Part of the Book." Pages 213–55 in *The New Testament and Early Christian Literature in Greco-Roman Context*. Edited by John Fotopoulos. Leiden: Brill, 2006.

Froelich, Margaret. "Sacrificed Meat in Corinth and Jesus Worship as a Cult among Cults." *Journal of Early Christian History* 10 (2020): 44–56. doi.org/10.1080/22225 82X.2020.1779101.

Fürstenberg, Yair. "The Shared Image of Pharisaic Law in the Gospels and Rabbinic Tradition." Pages 199–219 in *The Pharisees*. Edited by Amy-Jill Levine and Joseph Sievers. Grand Rapids, MI: Eerdmans, 2021.

Gamble, Harry Y. *The Textual History of the Letter to the Romans: A Study in Textual and Literary Criticism*. Grand Rapids, MI: Eerdmans, 1977.

Gaventa, Beverly Roberts. *Our Mother St. Paul*. Louisville, KY: Westminster John Knox, 2007.

Gennep, Arnold van. *The Rites of Passage*. London: Routledge, 1960.

Gillihan, Yonder Moynihan. *Civic Ideology, Organization, and Law in the Rule Scrolls: A Comparative Study of the Covenanters' Sect and Contemporary Voluntary Associations in Political Context*. STDJ 97. Leiden: Brill, 2012.

Gillman, Florence Morgan. "Paul, His Nurse Metaphor (1 Thessalonians 2:7) and the Thessalonian Women Who Turned Against Idols." *CBQ* 84 (2022): 279–94.

Glad, Clarence E. "Frank Speech, Flattery, and Friendship in Philodemus." Pages 21–59 in *Friendship, Flattery, and Frankness of Speech: Studies on Friendship in the New Testament World*. Edited by John T. Fitzgerald. NovTSup 82. Leiden: Brill, 1996.

Goldsworthy, Adrian. *Philip and Alexander: Kings and Conquerors*. New York: Basic Books, 2020.

Goodman, Martin. *Judaism in the Roman World. Collected Essays*. Leiden: Brill, 2007.

Goodman, Martin. "A Note on Josephus, the Pharisees and Ancestral Tradition." *JJS* 1 (1999): 17–20.
Graetz, Heinrich. *History of the Jews*. Philadelphia, PA: Jewish Publication Society of America, 1893.
Greydanus, Steven D. "Through Other Eyes: Point of View and Defamiliarization in Jesus Films." Pages 77–88 in *The T&T Clark Handbook of Jesus and Film*. Edited by Richard Walsh. London: T&T Clark, 2021.
Gross, Heinrich. "Der Glaube an Mose nach Exodus (4. 14. 19)." Pages 57–65 in *Wort—Gebot—Glaube: Beiträge zur Theologie des Alten Testaments. Walter Eichrodt zum 80. Geburtstag*. Edited by Johann J. Stamm, Ernst Jenni, and Hans Joachim Stoebe. Zürich: Zwingli, 1970.
Grossman, Maxine L. "Cultivating Identity: Textual Virtuosity and 'Insider' Status." Pages 1–11 in *Defining Identities: We, You, and the Other in the Dead Sea Scrolls. Proceedings of the Fifth Meeting of the IOQS in Groningen*. Edited by Florentino García Martínez and Mladen Popović. STDJ 70. Leiden: Brill, 2008.
Gruen, Erich. *Diaspora: Jews amidst Greeks and Romans*. Cambridge, MA: Harvard University Press, 2002.
Gruen, Erich S. *Heritage and Hellenism: The Reinvention of Jewish Tradition*. HCS 30. Berkeley: University of California Press, 1998.
Haber, Susan. *They Shall Purify Themselves: Essays on Purity in Early Judaism*. Edited by Adele Reinhartz. Atlanta, GA: SBL Press, 2008.
Hanau, Shira. "German Dictionary Changes Definition of 'Jew' after Complaint from Local Jewish Community." *Jewish Telegraph Agency* (February 17, 2022). https://www.jta.org/2022/02/17/global/german-dictionary-changes-definition-of-jew-after-complaint-from-local-jewish-community.
Harrill, J. A. "The Use of the New Testament in the American Slave Controversy: A Case History in the Hermeneutical Tension between Biblical Criticism and Christian Moral Debate." *Religion and American Culture* 10 (2000): 149–86.
Harvey, Anthony E. *Alternative Approaches to New Testament Study*. London: SPCK, 1985.
Hasted, Nick. "Mary Magdalene and Christian Cinema's Resurrection." *The Independent* (March 15, 2018). https://www.independent.co.uk/arts-entertainment/films/features/mary-magdalene-film-rooney-mara-joaquin-phoenix-religion-a8258036.html.
Hempel, Charlotte. *The Community Rules from Qumran: A Commentary*. TSAJ 183. Tübingen: Mohr Siebeck, 2020.
Hempel, Charlotte. "The Long Text of the *Serekh* as Crisis Literature." *RevQ* 27 (2015): 3–23.
Hengel, Martin. *Judaism and Hellenism: Studies in Their Encounter in Palestine during the Early Hellenistic Period*. Translated by John Bowden. 2 vols. Philadelphia, PA: Fortress, 1974.
Hengel, Martin. *The Pre-Christian Paul*. London: SCM, 1991.
Hengel, Martin. "The Stance of the Apostle Paul toward the Law in the Unknown Years between Damascus and Antioch." Pages 75–103 in *The Paradoxes of Paul*. Vol. 2 of *Justification and Variegated Nomism*. Edited by D. A. Carson, Peter O'Brien, and Mark A. Seifried. Grand Rapids, MI: Baker, 2004.
Hengel, Martin. *The Zealots: Investigations into the Jewish Freedom Movement in the Period from Herod I until 70 A.D*. Translated by David Smith. Edinburgh: T&T Clark, 1989.
Henten, Jan Willem van. "Balaam in Revelation 2:14." Pages 247–63 in *The Prestige of the Pagan Prophet Balaam in Judaism, Early Christianity and Islam*. Edited by George H. van Kooten and Jacques van Ruiten. Leiden: Brill, 2008.

Henten, Jan Willem van. "Playing God in the Movies: *Bruce Almighty* and the Preposterous History of Genesis 1:26–27." Pages 125–41 in *Creation and Creativity: From Genesis to Genetics and Back*. Edited by Alastair Hunter and Caroline Vander Stichele. Amsterdam Studies in the Bible and Religion 1. Sheffield: Sheffield Phoenix, 2006.

Herzer, Jens. *Pontius Pilatus: Henker und Heiliger*. Biblische Gestalten 32. Leipzig: Evangelische Verlagsanstalt, 2020.

Heschel, Abraham J. *God in Search of Man: A Philosophy of Judaism*. New York: The Jewish Publication Society of America, 1959.

Heschel, Abraham J. "What Is Man?" Pages 33–41 in *Between God and Man: An Interpretation of Judaism from the Writings of Abraham J. Heschel*. Selected, edited, and introduced by F. A. Rothschild. New York: Free Press, 1997.

Heszer, Catherine. "The Rule of the Wise as an Alternative to Kingdom and Democracy in Ancient Rabbinic and Philosophical Thought." Lecture given at the University of Zürich. Zürich, September 23, 2019.

Hylen, Susan E. *Women in the New Testament World*. Essentials of Biblical Studies. Oxford: Oxford University Press, 2019.

Hodge, Caroline E. Johnson. "Married to an Unbeliever: Households, Hierarchies, and Holiness in 1 Corinthians 7:12–16." *HTR* 103 (2010): 1–25.

Holtz, Gudrun. "Inclusivism at Qumran." *DSD* 16 (2009): 22–54.

Horsely, G. H. R., ed. *New Documents Illustrating Early Christianity*. Vol. 3. Sydney: Macquarie University Press, 1983.

Horst, Pieter Willem van der. *Saxa iudaica loquuntur*. Leiden: Brill, 2014.

Houtman, Cees. *Exodus. Volume 2, Chapters 7:14–19:25*. HCOT. Peeters: Leuven, 1996.

Howard-Brook, Wes. "Why We Need to Translate *Ioudaioi* as 'Judeans.'" Pages 76–83 in *Jesus Wasn't Killed by the Jews: Reflections for Christians in Lent*. Edited by Jon M. Sweeny. Maryknoll, NY: Orbis Books, 2020.

Humphries-Brooks, Stephenson. *Cinematic Savior: Hollywood's Making of the American Christ*. Westport, CT: Praeger, 2006.

Hutson, Christopher Roy. "Was Timothy Timid? On the Rhetoric of Fearlessness (1 Corinthians 16:10–11) and Cowardice (2 Timothy 1:7)." *BR* 42 (1997): 58–73.

Ilan, Tal. *Silencing the Queen: The Literary History of Shelamzion and Other Jewish Women*. Tübingen: Mohr Siebeck, 2006.

Irshai, Oded. "'Include Me Out': Tertullian, the Rabbis, and the Graeco-Roman City." Pages 117–32 in *Identité à travers l'éthique: Nouvelles perspectives sur la formation des l'identités collectives dans le monde gréco-romain*. Edited by Katell Berthelot, R. Naiweld, and D. Stökl ben Ezra. Turnhout: Brepols, 2015.

Jaroš, Karl. *In Sachen Pontius Pilatus*. KAW 93. Mainz: von Zabern, 2002.

Jewett, Robert. *Romans*. Minneapolis, MN: Fortress, 2007.

Jewett, Robert. "Tenement Churches and Communal Meals in the Early Church." *BR* 38 (1994): 23–43.

Johnstone, William. *Exodus*. Old Testament Guides. Sheffield: Sheffield Academic, 1990.

Jokiranta, Jutta. *Social Identity and Sectarianism in the Qumran Movement*. STDJ 105. Leiden: Brill, 2013.

Joshel, Sandra R. "Nurturing the Master's Child: Slavery and the Roman Child-Nurse." *Signs* 12 (1986): 3–22.

Kaster, Robert A. *Guardians of Language: The Grammarian and Society in Late Antiquity*. Berkeley: University of California Press, 1997.

Katz, Steven T. "Issues in the Separation of Judaism and Christianity after 70 CE: A Reconsideration." *JBL* 103 (1984): 43–76.
Kaufman, Jane. "OSU Investigating Professor's 'Jewing Down' Comment." *Cleveland Jewish News* (December 22, 2021).
Kazen, Thomas. "Evolution, Emotion and Exegesis: Disgust and Empathy in Biblical Texts on Moral and Ritual Issues." Pages 191–218 in *Linnaeus and Homo Religiosus: Biological Roots of Religious Awareness and Human Identity*. Edited by Carl R. Bråkenhielm. Uppsala: Acta Universitatis Upsaliensis, 2009.
Kazen, Thomas. *Impurity and Purification in Early Judaism and the Jesus Tradition*. RBS 98. Atlanta, GA: SBL Press, 2021.
Kazen, Thomas. *Issues of Impurity in Early Judaism*. ConBNT 45. Winona Lake, IN: Eisenbrauns, 2010.
Kearsley, R. A. "Some Asiarchs of Ephesos." Pages 46–55 in *New Documents Illustrating Early Christianity: A Review of the Greek Inscriptions and Papyri Published in 1979*. Edited by G. H. R. Horsley. Sydney: Macquarie University, 1987.
Keener, Craig S. *Acts: An Exegetical Commentary*. Vol. 3. Grand Rapids, MI: Baker Academic, 2014.
Kelly, J. N. D. *A Commentary on the Pastoral Epistles*. Grand Rapids, MI: Baker, 1981.
Kennedy, George A. *Progymnasmata: Greek Textbooks of Prose Composition and Rhetoric*. WGRW 10. Atlanta, GA: SBL Press, 2003.
Kimelman, Reuven. "*Birkat ha-Minim* and the Lack of Evidence for an Anti-Christian Jewish Prayer in Late Antiquity." Pages 226–44 in *Aspects of Judaism in the Graeco-Roman Period*. Vol 2 of *Jewish and Christian Self-Definition*. Edited by E. P. Sanders. Philadelphia, PA: Fortress, 1981.
Kister, Menahem. "The Fate of the Canaanites and the Despoilation of the Egyptians: Polemics Among Jews, Pagans, Christians and Gnostics: Motifs and Motives." Pages 66–111 in *The Gift of the Land and the Fate of the Canaanites in Jewish Thought*. Edited by Katell Berthelot, Joseph E. David, and Marc Hirshman. Oxford: Oxford University Press, 2014.
Kittel, Gerhard, and Gerhard Friedrich, eds. *Theological Dictionary of the New Testament*. Translated by Geoffrey W. Bromiley. 10 vols. Grand Rapids, MI: Eerdmans, 1964–76.
Klauck, Hans-Josef. *Die antike Briefliteratur und das Neue Testament: Ein Lehr- und Arbeitsbuch*. UTB 2022. Paderborn: Ferdinand Schöningh, 1998.
Kloppenborg, John S. *Christ's Associations: Connecting and Belonging in the Ancient City*. New Haven, CT: Yale University Press, 2019.
Kobel, Esther. *Dining with John. Communal Meals and Identity Formation in the Fourth Gospel and Its Historical and Cultural Context*. BibInt 109. Leiden: Brill, 2011.
Koehler, Ludwig, Walter Baumgartner, Benedikt Hartmann, and Edward Y. Kutscher. *Hebräisches und Aramäisches Lexikon zum Alten Testament*. 4 vols. 3rd ed. Leiden: Brill, 1967–90.
Konstan, David. *Friendship in the Classical World*. Cambridge: Cambridge University Press, 1997.
Korner, Ralph J. *The Origin and Meaning of* Ekklēsia *in the Early Jesus Movement*. AJEC 98. Leiden: Brill, 2017.
Kozlovic, Anton Karl. "The Ten Commandments." Pages 252–8 in *The Bible and Cinema: Fifty Key Films*. Edited by Adele Reinhartz. London: Routledge, 2013.
Laes, Christian. *Children in the Roman Empire: Outsiders Within*. Cambridge: Cambridge University Press, 2011.

Lampe, Peter. "Paul, Patrons, and Clients." Pages 204–38 in vol. 2 of *Paul in the Greco-Roman World: A Handbook*. Edited by J. Paul Sampley. London: Bloomsbury T&T Clark, 2016.

Lang, Bernhard. "The Baptismal Raising of Lazarus: A New Interpretation of John 11." *NovT* 58 (2016): 301–17.

Lang, T. J. "Trouble with Insiders: The Social Profile of the ἄπιστοι in Paul's Corinthian Correspondence." *JBL* 137 (2018): 981–1001.

Langer, Ruth. *Cursing the Christians? A History of the Birkat ha-Minim*. New York: Oxford University Press, 2011.

Langer, Ruth. "Birkat Ha-Minim. A Jewish Curse of Christians?" Pages 653–4 in *The Jewish Annotated New Testament*. Edited by Amy-Jill Levine and Marc Zvi Brettler. 2nd ed. New York: Oxford University Press, 2017.

Last, Richard, and Philip A. Harland. *Group Survival in the Ancient Mediterranean: Rethinking Material Conditions in the Landscape of Jews and Christians*. London: T&T Clark, 2020.

Lebeau, Paul. *Le Vin Nouveau du Royaume: Étude Exégétique et Patristique sur la Parole Eschatologique de Jésus à la Céne*. Paris: Desclée de Brouwer, 1966.

Lehmann, Ann-Sophie. "Maria Magdalena und die feministische Kunstgeschichte." Pages 159–77 in *Doing Gender in Medien-, Kunst- und Kulturwissenschaften: Eine Einführung*. Edited by Rosemarie Buikema and Kathrin Thiele. Berlin: LIT, 2017.

Levine, Amy-Jill. "Christian Privilege, Christian Fragility, and the Gospel of John." Pages 87–110 in *The Gospel of John and Jewish–Christian Relations*. Edited by Adele Reinhartz. Lanham, MD: Lexington Books, 2018.

Levine, Amy-Jill. "Jesus and the Liberal Academy: From First Century Jew to Twenty-First Century Anti-Fascist." Forthcoming in *What Does Theology Do, Actually? Exegeting Exegesis*. Edited by Phillip A. Davis, Jr., Daniel Lanzinger, and Matthew R. Robinson. Leipzig: Evangelische Verlagsanstalt, 2023.

Levine, Amy-Jill. *The Misunderstood Jew: The Church and the Scandal of the Jewish Jesus*. San Francisco, CA: HarperOne, 2007.

Levine, Amy-Jill. "Supersessionism: Admit and Address Rather Than Debate or Deny." *Religions* 13 (2022): 155. doi.org/10.3390/rel13020155.

Levine, Lee I. *The Ancient Synagogue: The First Thousand Years*. New Haven, CT: Yale University Press, 2005.

Lewy, Hans. "Ein Rechtsstreit um den Boden Palästinas." *MGWJ* 77 (1933): 84–99, 172–80.

Lewy, Hans. *Studies in Jewish Hellenism*. Jerusalem: Bialik Institute, 1960 [Hebrew].

Lica, Vasile. "φιλορώμαιος oder φιλοκαίσαρ?" *BJ* 192 (1992–3): 225–30.

Licht, Jacob. "The Plant Eternal and the People of Divine Deliverance." Pages 49–75 in *Essays on the Dead Sea Scrolls in Memory of E. L. Sukenik*. Edited by Chaim Rabin and Yigael Yadin. Jerusalem: Shrine of the Book, 1961 [Hebrew].

Licht, Jacob. *The Rule Scroll: A Scroll from the Wilderness of Judaea*. Jerusalem: Bialik Institute, 1965 [Hebrew].

Lieberman, Saul. *Tosefta Ki-Fshuta: Part III, Oder Moed, Shabbat-Eruvin*. New York: Jewish Theological Seminary of America, 1962.

Linder, Amnon. *The Jews in the Legal Sources of the Early Middle Ages*. Detroit, MI: Wayne State University Press, 1997.

Linder, Amnon. *The Jews in Roman Imperial Legislation*. Detroit, MI: Wayne State University Press, 1987.

Louvish, Simon. *Cecil B. DeMille and the Golden Calf*. London: Faber and Faber, 2007.

Lowenthal, Leo. "Biographies in Popular Magazines." Pages 507–48 in *Radio Research: 1942–43*. Edited by Paul Lazarsfeld and Frank Stanton. New York: Duell, Sloan, and Pearce, 1944.

Lüderitz, Gerd. *Corpus jüdischer Zeugnisse aus der Cyrenaika*. Wiesbaden: L. Reichert, 1983.

Luz, Ulrich. *Matthew 8–20: A Commentary*. Translated by James E. Crouch. Hermeneia. Minneapolis, MN: Fortress, 2001.

Luz, Ulrich. *Matthew 21–28: A Commentary*. Translated by James E. Crouch. Hermeneia. Minneapolis, MN: Fortress, 2005.

MacDonald, Margaret Y. "The Thessalonian and the Corinthian Letters." Pages 56–91 in *The New Cambridge Companion to St. Paul*. Edited by Bruce W. Longenecker. Cambridge: Cambridge University Press, 2020.

Maier, Harry O. "Paul's Letter to Philemon: A Case Study in Individualisation, Dividuation, and Partibility in Imperial Spatial Contexts." Pages 519–39 in *Religious Individualisation: Historical Dimensions and Comparative Perspectives*. Edited by Martin Fuchs, Antje Linkenbach, Martin Mulsow, Bernd-Christian Otto, Rahul Bjørn Parson, and Jörg Rüpke. Berlin: de Gruyter, 2020.

Maier, Paul. "Sejanus, Pilate, and the Date of the Crucifixion." *CH* 37 (1968): 3–13.

Malbon, Elizabeth Struthers. "Gospel of Mark." Pages 478–92 in *The Women's Bible Commentary: Revised and Expanded Edition*. Edited by Carol A. Newsom, Sharon H. Ringe, and Jacqueline E. Lapsey. London: SPCK, 2012.

Manson, T. W., and Matthew Black, eds. *Studies in the Gospels and Epistles*. Manchester: Manchester University Press, 1962.

Marek, Christian. *In the Land of a Thousand Gods*. Princeton, NJ: Princeton University Press, 2016.

Marshall, I. Howard, and Philip H. Towner. *A Critical and Exegetical Commentary on the Pastoral Epistles*. Edinburgh: T&T Clark, 1999.

Marshall, John. "Apocalypticism and Anti-Semitism: Inner-Group Resources and Inter-Group Conflicts." Pages 68–82 in *Apocalypticism, Anti-Semitism and the Historical Jesus*. Edited by John S. Kloppenborg with John Marshall. London: T&T Clark International, 2005.

Martin, Michael W. "Progymnastic Topic Lists: A Compositional Template for Luke and Other *Bioi*?" *NTS* 54 (2008): 18–41.

Martínez, Florentino García. Review of *Discoveries in the Judaean Desert VII. Qumrân Grotte 4 III (4Q482–4Q520)*, by Maurice Baillet. *JSJ* 15 (1984): 157–64.

Martyn, J. Louis. *Galatians: A New Translation with Introduction and Commentary*. New York: Doubleday, 1997.

Martyn, J. Louis. *History and Theology in the Fourth Gospel*. 3rd ed. Louisville, KY: Westminster John Knox, 2003.

Mason, Steve. "Jews, Judaeans, Judaizing, Judaism: Problems of Categorization in Ancient History." *JSJ* 38 (2007): 457–512.

McAfee, Matthew. "The Heart of Pharaoh in Exodus 4–15." *BBR* 20 (2010): 331–53.

McDermott, Jim. "The Gospel of John Has Been Used to Justify Anti-Semitism—So We Should Stop Reading It on Good Friday." *America* (April 14, 2022). https://www.amer icamagazine.org/faith/2022/04/14/good-friday-gospel-john-jews-242822.

McFarlan Miller, Emily. "Episcopal Church Mulls Changes to Holy Week Readings Seen as Antisemitic." *Religion News Service* (April 14, 2022). https://religionnews. com/2022/04/14/episcopal-church-mulls-changes-to-holy-week-readings-seen-as-anti semitic/.

McGowan, Andrew Brian. *Ascetic Eucharists: Food and Drink in Early Christian Ritual Meals*. Oxford: Clarendon, 1999.

McNeel, Jennifer Houston. *Paul as Infant and Nursing Mother: Metaphor, Rhetoric and Identity in 1 Thessalonians 2:5–8*. ECL 12. Atlanta, GA: SBL Press, 2014.

Merton, Robert K. "The Matthew Effect, II." Pages 318–36 in *On Social Structure and Science*. Edited by Piotr Sztompka. Chicago, IL: University of Chicago Press, 1996.

Messner, Brian E. "'No Friend of Caesar': Jesus, Pilate, Sejanus, and Tiberius." *Stone-Campbell Journal* 11 (2008): 47–57.

Metso, Sarianna. *The Serekh Texts*. LSTS 62. London: T&T Clark, 2007.

Metzner, Rainer. "Exkurs 6: Freund des Kaisers." Pages 327–8 in *Die Prominenten im Neuen Testament: Ein prosopographischer Kommentar*. NTOA/SUNT 66. Göttingen: Vandenhoeck & Ruprecht, 2008.

Meyer, Stephen C. *Epic Sound: Music in Postwar Hollywood Biblical Films*. Bloomington: Indiana University Press, 2015.

Milgrom, Jacob. *Leviticus 1–16: A New Translation with Introduction and Commentary*. AB 3. New York: Doubleday, 1991.

Millar, Fergus. *The Emperor in the Roman World (31 BC–AD 337)*. Ithaca, NY: Cornell University Press, 1977.

Miller, Stuart S. *At the Intersection of Texts and Material Finds: Stepped Pools, Stone Vessels, and Ritual Purity among the Jews of Roman Galilee*. Göttingen: Vandenhoeck & Ruprecht, 2015.

Mitchell, Margaret M. *Paul and the Rhetoric of Reconciliation: An Exegetical Investigation of the Language and Composition of 1 Corinthians*. Louisville, KY: Westminster John Knox, 1991.

Moloney, Francis J. *The Gospel of John*. SP 4. Collegeville, MN: Liturgical Press, 2005.

Morgan, Teresa. "Ethos: The Socialization of Children in Education and Beyond." Pages 504–20 in *A Companion to Families in the Greek and Roman Worlds*. Edited by Beryl Rawson. Oxford: Blackwell, 2011.

Mustakallio, Katarina, and Christian Krötzl, eds. *De Amicitia: Friendship and Social Networks in Antiquity and the Middle Ages*. AIRF 36. Rome: Institutum Romanum Finlandiae, 2009.

Nanos, Mark D. *The Mystery of Romans. The Jewish Context of Paul's Letter*. Minneapolis, MN: Fortress, 1996.

Nanos, Mark D. "Re-Framing Paul's Opposition to Erga Nomouas 'Rites of a Custom' for Proselyte Conversion Completed by the Synecdoche 'Circumcision.'" *The Journal of the Jesus Movement in Its Jewish Setting* 8 (2021): 75–115.

Nasrallah, Laura. "1 Corinthians." Pages 446–7 in *The Letters and Legacy of Paul: Fortress Commentary on the Bible Study Edition*. Edited by Margaret Aymer, Cynthia Briggs Kittredge, and David A. Sanchez. Minneapolis, MN: Augsburg Fortress, 2016.

Newsom, Carol A. *The Self as Symbolic Space: Constructing Identity and Community at Qumran*. STDJ 52. Leiden: Brill, 2004.

Niebuhr, Karl-Wilhelm. "Jesus, Paul, and the Pharisees. Observations on Their Commonalities and Their Understanding of Torah." Pages 109–41 in *The Message of Paul the Apostle within Second Temple Judaism*. Edited by František Abel. Lanham, MD: Lexington Books, 2020.

Nirenberg, David. *Anti-Judaism: The Western Tradition*. New York: Norton, 2013.

Nitzan, Bilhah. *Qumran Prayer and Religious Poetry*. Translated by Jonathan Chipman. STDJ 12. Leiden: Brill, 1994.

Noam, Vered. "Pharisaic Halakha as Emerging from 4QMMT." Pages 55–79 in *The Pharisees*. Edited by Amy-Jill Levine and Joseph Sievers. Grand Rapids, MI: Eerdmans, 2021.

Noerdlinger, Henry S. *Moses and Egypt: The Documentation of the Motion Picture* The Ten Commandments. Los Angeles: University of Southern California Press, 1956.

Novenson, Matthew V., ed. *Monotheism and Christology*. Leiden: Brill, 2021.

Olsson, Birger. "'All My Teaching Was Done in Synagogues' (John 18,20)." Pages 203–24 in *Theology and Christology in the Fourth Gospel: Essays by the Members of the SNTS Johannine Writings Seminar*. Edited by Gilbert van Belle, Jan G. Van der Watt, and P. J. Maritz. BETL 184. Leuven: Leuven University Press, 2005.

Orrison, Katherine. *Written in Stone: Making Cecil B. DeMille's Epic: The Ten Commandments*. Lanham, MD: Vestal, 1999.

Orth, Wolfgang. "Seleukidische Hoftitel und politische Strukturen im Spiegel der Septuaginta-Überlieferung." Pages 65–77 in vol. 1 of *Septuaginta Deutsch: Erläuterungen und Kommentare zum griechischen Alten Testament*. Edited by Martin Karrer and Wolfgang Kraus. Stuttgart: Deutsche Bibelgesellschaft, 2011.

Ortlund, Dane C. "Phinehan Zeal: A Consideration of James Dunn's Proposal." *JSP* 20 (2011): 299–315.

Ortlund, Dane C. *Zeal without Knowledge. The Concept of Zeal in Romans 10, Galatians 1, and Philippians 3*. London: Bloomsbury, 2014.

Osiek, Carolyn. *Philippians, Philemon*. Nashville, TN: Abingdon, 2000.

Osiek, Carolyn, and Margaret Y. MacDonald (with Janet Tulloch). *A Woman's Place: House Churches in Earliest Christianity*. Minneapolis, MN: Fortress, 2006.

Parks, Sara, Shayna Sheinfeld, and Meredith J. C. Warren. *Jewish and Christian Women in the Ancient Mediterranean*. London: Routledge, 2022.

Parsons, Mikeal, and Michael Wade Martin. *Ancient Rhetoric and the New Testament: The Influence of Elementary Greek Composition*. Waco, TX: Baylor University Press, 2018.

Pattarumadathil, Henry. "Pharisees and Sadducees Together in Matthew." Pages 136–47 in *Pharisees*. Edited by Joseph Sievers and Amy-Jill Levine. Grand Rapids, MI: Eerdmans, 2021.

Paulsen, David. "Churches Consider Alternate Good Friday Liturgies, Bible Translations over Concerns of Anti-Jewish Interpretations." *Episcopal News Service* (April 12, 2022). https://www.episcopalnewsservice.org/2022/04/12/churches-eye-alternate-liturgies-bible-translations-amid-anti-jewish-concerns-on-good-friday/.

Pervo, Richard I. "With Lucian: Who Needs Friends? Friendship in the *Toxaris*." Pages 163–80 in *Greco-Roman Perspectives on Friendship*. Edited by John T. Fitzgerald. RBS 34. Atlanta, GA: Scholars Press, 1997.

Petropoulou, Maria-Zoe. *Animal Sacrifice in Ancient Greek Religion, Judaism, and Christianity, 100 BC to AD 200*. Oxford: Oxford University Press, 2008.

Poirier, John C. "Purity beyond the Temple in the Second Temple Era." *JBL* 122 (2003): 247–65.

Potter, David S. "Roman Religion: Ideas and Actions." Pages 113–67 in *Life, Death and Entertainment in the Roman Empire*. Edited by David S. Potter and David J. Mattingly. Ann Arbor: University of Michigan Press, 1999.

Price, Simon. *Rituals and Power: The Roman Imperial Cult in Asia Minor*. Cambridge: Cambridge University Press, 1984.

Prothero, Stephen. *American Jesus: How the Son of God Became a National Icon*. New York: Farrar, Straus and Giroux, 2003.

Rawson, Beryl. *Children and Childhood in Roman Italy*. Oxford: Oxford University Press, 2003.
Reinhartz, Adele. *Befriending the Beloved Disciple: A Jewish Reading of the Gospel of John*. New York: Continuum, 2001.
Reinhartz, Adele. *Bible and Cinema: An Introduction*. New York: Routledge, 2013.
Reinhartz, Adele. "The Bible Epic." Pages 179–93 in part 2 of *The Bible in Motion: A Handbook of the Bible and Its Reception in Film*. Edited by Rhonda Burnette-Bletsch. Berlin: de Gruyter, 2016.
Reinhartz, Adele. *Cast Out of the Covenant: Jews and Anti-Judaism in the Gospel of John*. Lanham, MD: Lexington Books, 2018.
Reinhartz, Adele. "A Fork in the Road or a Multi-Lane Highway? New Perspectives on 'The Parting of the Ways' between Judaism and Christianity." Pages 280–95 in *The Changing Face of Judaism, Christianity and Other Greco-Roman Religions in Antiquity*. Edited by Ian H. Henderson, Gerbern S. Oegema, Sara Parks Ricker, and James H. Charlesworth. Gütersloh: Gütersloher Verlagshaus, 2006.
Reinhartz, Adele. "The Gospel According to John." Pages 168–218 in *The Jewish Annotated New Testament*. Edited by Amy-Jill Levine and Marc Zvi Brettler. 2nd ed. New York: Oxford University Press, 2017.
Reinhartz, Adele, ed. *The Gospel of John and Jewish-Christian Relations*. Lanham, MD: Lexington Books/Fortress Academic, 2018.
Reinhartz, Adele. "Holy Words in Hollywood: DeMille's *The Ten Commandments* (1956) and American Identity." Pages 123–35 in *The Bible in the Public Square: Its Enduring Influence in American Life*. Edited by Mark A. Chancey, Carol Meyers, and Eric M. Meyers. Atlanta, GA: SBL Press, 2014.
Reinhartz, Adele. "Jesus in Film: Hollywood Perspectives on the Jewishness of Jesus." *Journal of Religion & Film* 2.2 (1998): Article 2. https://digitalcommons.unomaha.edu/jrf/vol2/iss2/2.
Reinhartz, Adele. *Jesus of Hollywood*. Oxford: Oxford University Press, 2007.
Reinhartz, Adele. "Judaism and Antisemitism in Bible Movies." Pages 777–91 in part 2 of *The Bible in Motion: A Handbook of the Bible and Its Reception in Film*. Edited by Rhonda Burnette-Bletsch. Berlin: de Gruyter, 2016.
Reinhartz, Adele. "To Love the Lord: An Intertextual Reading of John 20." Pages 53–69 in *The Labour of Reading: Desire, Alienation, and Biblical Interpretation*. Edited by Fiona C. Black, Roland Boer, and Erin Runions. Atlanta, GA: SBL Press, 1999.
Reinhartz, Adele. "Reflections on My Journey with John: A Retrospective from Adele Reinhartz." *Ancient Jew Review* (April 11, 2018). https://www.ancientjewreview.com/read/2018/2/24/reflections-on-my-journey-with-john-a-retrospective-from-adele-reinhartz.
Reinhartz, Adele. "The Vanishing Jews of Antiquity." Pages 10–23 in *Jew and Judean: A Marginalia Forum on Politics and Historiography in the Translation of Ancient Texts*. Edited by Timothy Michael Law and Charles Halton. *Marginalia/Los Angeles Review of Books* (June 24, 2014). https://themarginaliareview.com/vanishing-jews-antiquity-adele-reinhartz/.
Reinhartz, Adele. "Violence against the Jews: Anti-Judaism in the Jesus Movies." Pages 133–44 in *Religion und Gewalt im Bibelfilm*. Edited by Reinhold Zwick. FilTh 20. Marburg: Schüren, 2012.
Reinhartz, Adele, and Paula Fredriksen, eds. *Jesus, Judaism and Christian Anti-Judaism: Reading the New Testament after the Holocaust*. Louisville, KY: Westminster John Knox, 2002.

Ridinger, Robert. "From Moses to DeMille: Adapting the Bible to the Big Screen." *JRTI* 19 (2020): 129–47.
Rindge, Matthew S. *Bible and Film: The Basics*. London: Routledge, 2022.
Rives, James B. "The Decree of Decius and the Religion of the Empire." *JRS* 89 (1999): 135–54.
Rokeah, David. "Hypothetica." Pages 153–68 in *Historical Writings, Apologetic Writings*. Vol. 1 of *Philo of Alexandria*. Edited by Suzanne Daniel-Nataf. Jerusalem: Bialik Institute, 1986 [Hebrew].
Rosenblum, Jordan. "'Why Do You Refuse to Eat Pork?' Jews, Food, and Identity in Roman Palestine." *JQR* 100 (2010): 95–110.
Roth, Ulrike. "Paul, Philemon, and Onesimus: A Christian Design for Mastery." *ZNW* 105 (2014): 102–30.
Runesson, Anders. *Divine Wrath and Salvation in Matthew: The Narrative World of the First Gospel*. Minneapolis, MN: Fortress, 2016.
Runesson, Anders. *Judaism for Gentiles: Reading Paul Beyond the Parting of the Ways Paradigm*. In collaboration with Rebecca Runesson. WUNT 494. Tübingen: Mohr Siebeck, 2022.
Runesson, Anders. *The Origins of the Synagogue: A Socio-Historical Study*. ConBNT 37. Stockholm: Almqvist & Wiksell, 2001.
Runesson, Anders. "Placing Paul: Institutional Structures and Theological Strategy in the World of the Early Christ-Believers." *SEÅ* 80 (2015): 43–67.
Runesson, Anders, Donald D. Binder, and Birger Olsson. *The Ancient Synagogue from Its Origins to 200 C.E.: A Source Book*. AGJU 72. Leiden: Brill, 2007.
Runesson, Rebecca. "Dangerous Associations: Re-assessing Acts 16:13–15 in Light of the Bacchanalia Conspiracy." Paper presented at the Annual Meeting of the SBL. Houston, TX, November 20, 2021.
Ryan, Jordan J. *The Role of the Synagogue in the Aims of Jesus*. Minneapolis, MN: Fortress, 2017.
Saller, Richard P. "Patronage and Friendship in Early Imperial Rome: Drawing the Distinction." Pages 49–62 in *Patronage in Ancient Society*. Edited by A. Wallace-Hadrill. London: Routledge, 1989.
Saller, Richard P. *Personal Patronage under the Early Empire*. Cambridge: Cambridge University Press, 1982.
Sanders, E. P. "Jewish Association with Gentiles and Galatians 2:11–14." Pages 170–88 in *The Conversation Continues: Studies in Paul and John in Honor of J. Louis Martyn*. Edited by Robert T. Fortna and Beverly R. Gaventa. Nashville, TN: Abingdon, 1990.
Sanders, E. P. *Jewish Law from Jesus to the Mishnah: Five Studies*. Philadelphia, PA: Trinity Press international, 1990.
Sanders, E. P. *Paul, the Law, and the Jewish People*. Philadelphia, PA: Fortress, 1983.
Sandmel, Samuel. *We Jews and Jesus*. New York: Oxford University Press, 1965.
Sankey, Ira. *Gospel Hymns and Sacred Songs*. Chicago, IL: Biglow & Main, 1875.
Schaberg, Jane. "Fast Forwarding to the Magdalene." Page 33–45 in *Biblical Glamour and Hollywood Glitz*. Edited by Alice Bach. Semeia 74. Atlanta, GA: SBL Press, 1996.
Scheid, John. *The Gods, the State, and the Individual: Reflections on Civic Religion in Rome*. Philadelphia, PA: University of Pennsylvania Press, 2016.
Schellenberg, Ryan S. *Abject Joy: Paul, Prison, and the Arts of Making Do*. Oxford: Oxford University Press, 2021.
Schiffman, Lawrence H. *The Eschatological Community of the Dead Sea Scrolls: A Study of the Rule of the Congregation*. SBLMS 38. Atlanta, GA: Scholars Press, 1989.

Schnelle, Udo, Michael Labahn, and Manfred Lang, eds. *Texte zum Johannesevangelium. Vol. I.2 of Neuer Wettstein: Texte zum Neuen Testament aus Griechentum und Hellenismus*. Berlin: de Gruyter, 2001.

Schofield, Malcolm. "Political Friendship and the Ideology of Reciprocity." Pages 37–51 in *Kosmos: Essays in Order, Conflict and Community in Classical Athens*. Edited by Peter Cartledge, Paul Millett, and Sitta von Reden. Cambridge: Cambridge University Press, 1998.

Scholtissek, Klaus. "'Eine größere Liebe als diese hat niemand, als wenn einer sein Leben hingibt für seine Freunde' (Joh 15,13)." Pages 413–39 in *Kontexte des Johannesevangeliums: Das vierte Evangelium in religions- und traditionsgeschichtlicher Perspektive*. Edited by Jörg Frey and Udo Schnelle. WUNT 175. Tübingen: Mohr Siebeck, 2004.

Schottroff, Louise. "The Creation Narrative: Genesis 1.1–2.4a." Pages 24–38 in *A Feminist Companion to Genesis*. Edited by Athalya Brenner. Sheffield: Sheffield Academic, 1993.

Schramm, Michael. *Freundschaft im Neuplatonismus: Politisches Denken und Sozialphilosophie von Plotin bis Kaiser Julian*. BzA 319. Berlin: de Gruyter, 2013.

Schremer, Adiel. "'[T]He[y] Did Not Read the Sealed Book': Qumran Halakhic Revolution and the Emergence of Torah Study in the Second Temple Judaism." Pages 105–25 in *Historical Perspectives: From the Hasmoneans to Bar Kokhba in Light of the Dead Sea Scrolls: Proceedings of the Fourth International Symposium of the Orion Center for the Study of the Dead Sea Scrolls and Associated Literature, January 27–31, 1999*. Edited by David M. Goodblatt, Avital Pinnick, and Daniel R. Schwartz. STDJ 37. Leiden: Brill, 2001.

Schulz, Siegfried. *Gott ist kein Sklavenhalter: Die Geschichte einer verspäteten Revolution*. Zürich: Flamberg; Hamburg: Furche, 1972.

Schüssler Fiorenza, Elisabeth. *The Book of Revelation: Justice and Judgment*. Minneapolis, MN: Fortress, 1998.

Schüssler Fiorenza, Elisabeth. *Discipleship of Equals: A Critical Feminist Ekklēsia-Logy of Liberation*. London: SCM Press, 1993.

Schüssler Fiorenza, Elisabeth. "Discipleship of Equals." JEGTF 16 (2008): 67–90.

Segal, Alan F. *Paul the Convert. The Apostolate and Apostasy of Saul the Pharisee*. New Haven, CT: Yale University Press, 1992.

Sheinfeld, Shayna. "From *Nomos* to *Logos*: Torah in First-Century Jewish Texts." Pages 61–74 in *The Message of Paul the Apostle within Second Temple Judaism*. Edited by František Ábel. Lanham, MD: Lexington Books, 2020.

Shepherd, David J. *The Bible on Silent Film: Spectacle, Story and Scripture in the Early Cinema*. Cambridge: Cambridge University Press, 2013.

Sherk, Robert K., ed. *The Roman Empire: Augustus to Hadrian*. New York: Cambridge University, 1988.

Sievers, Joseph, and Amy-Jill Levine, eds. *The Pharisees*. Grand Rapids, MI: Eerdmans, 2021.

Simon, Marcel. *Verus Israël. A Study of the Relations between Christians and Jews in the Roman Empire, A.D. 135–425*. Oxford: Oxford University Press, 1986.

Smiles, Vincent M. "The Concept of 'Zeal' in Second Temple Judaism and Paul's Critique of It in Romans 10:2." CBQ 64 (2002): 282–99.

Smit, Peter-Ben, and Eva van Urk, eds. *Parrhesia: Ancient and Modern Perspectives on Freedom of Speech*. Leiden: Brill, 2018.

Smith, David. "Paul's 'Friends': Rethinking Paul in Light of His Social Network." Stone-Campbell Journal 22 (2019): 77–87.

Smith, Dennis Edwin. *From Symposium to Eucharist: The Banquet in the Early Christian World*. Minneapolis, MN: Fortress, 2003.
Söding, Thomas. "Einsatz des Lebens. Ein Motiv johanneischer Soteriologie." Pages 363–84 in *The Death of Jesus in the Fourth Gospel*. Edited by G. van Belle. Leuven: Leuven University Press, 2007.
Staley, Jeffrey L. "One Hundred Years of Cinematic Attempts at Raising a Stiff (Jn 11:1–46)." Pages 41–54 in *T&T Clark Handbook of Jesus and Film*. Edited by Richard Walsh. London: Bloomsbury, 2021.
Sterling, Gregory E. "Philo, *Hypothetica*." Pages 2501–24 in *Outside the Bible: Ancient Jewish Writings Related to Scripture*. Edited by Louis H. Feldman, James L. Kugel, and Lawrence H. Schiffman. Philadelphia, PA: Jewish Publication Society of America, 2013.
Stern, Menachem. *Greek and Latin Authors on Jews and Judaism*. 3 vols. Jerusalem: Israel Academy of Sciences and Humanities, 1974–84.
Stern, Richard C., Clayton N. Jefford, and Buerric Debona, O. S. B. *Savior on the Silver Screen*. New York: Paulist Press, 1999.
Stowers, Stanley K. *A Rereading of Romans: Justice, Jews and Gentiles*. New Haven, CT: Yale University Press, 1994.
Tajfel, Henri. *Differentiation between Social Groups: Studies in Social Psychology of Intergroup Relations*. London: Academic Press, 1978.
Tatum, W. Barnes. *Jesus at the Movies: A Guide to the First Hundred Years*. Santa Rosa, CA: Polebridge, 1997.
Taussig, Hal. *In the Beginning Was the Meal: Social Experimentation & Early Christian Identity*. Minneapolis, MN: Fortress, 2009.
Thatcher, Tom. "Aspects of Historicity in the Fourth Gospel: Phase Two of the John, Jesus, and History Project." Pages 1–6 in vol. 2 of *John, Jesus, and History*. Edited by Paul N. Anderson, Felix Just, and Tom Thatcher. Atlanta, GA: SBL Press, 2009.
Theophilos, Michael P. "John 15.14 and the ΦΙΛ-Lexeme in Light of Numismatic Evidence: Friendship or Obedience." *NTS* 64 (2018): 33–43.
Thomassen, Bjørn. "The Uses and Meanings of Liminality." *International Political Anthropology* 2 (2009): 5–28.
Tilborg, Sjef van. *Imaginative Love in John*. Leiden: Brill, 1993.
Tite, Philip L. "Roman Diet and Meat Consumption: Reassessing Elite Access to Meat in 1 Corinthians 8 and 10." *JSNT* 42 (2019): 185–222.
Tolbert, Mary Ann. *Sowing the Gospel: Mark's World in Literary-Historical Perspective*. Minneapolis, MN: Fortress, 1989.
Tolmie, D. Francois. "The Ethics of the Letter to Philemon." *Neot* 54 (2020): 47–66.
Tolmie, D. Francois. "Pontius Pilate: Failing in More Ways Than One." Pages 578–97 in *Character Studies in the Fourth Gospel. Narrative Approaches to Seventy Figures in John*. Edited by Steven A. Hunt, D. Francois Tolmie, and Ruben Zimmermann. WUNT 314. Tübingen: Mohr Siebeck, 2013. Repr., Grand Rapids, MI: Eerdmans, 2016.
Tolmie, D. Francois. "Tendencies in the Research on the Letter to Philemon since 1980." Pages 1–27 in *Philemon in Perspective: Interpreting a Pauline Letter*. Edited by D. Francois Tolmie and Alfred Friedl. BZNW 169. Berlin: de Gruyter, 2010.
Tuckett, Christopher, ed. *The Gospel of Mary*. Oxford: Oxford University Press, 2007.
Tupamahu, Ekaputra. "The Stubborn Invisibility of Whiteness in Biblical Scholarship." *Political Theology Network* (November 12, 2020). https://politicaltheology.com/the-stubborn-invisibility-of-whiteness-in-biblical-scholarship/.
Turner, Victor. "Liminality and Communitas." Pages 359–74 in *The Ritual Process: Structure and Anti-Structure*. Chicago, IL: Aldine, 1969.

Tzoref, Shani. "The Use of Scripture in the *Community Rule*." Pages 203–34 in *A Companion to Biblical Interpretation in Early Judaism*. Edited by Matthias Henze. Grand Rapids, MI: Eerdmans, 2012.

VanderKam, James C. *Jubilees 1: A Commentary on the Book of Jubilees Chapters 1–21*. Hermeneia. Minneapolis, MN: Fortress, 2018.

Vander Stichele, Caroline. "Mary Magdalene in Motion." Pages 93–114 in *Recent Releases: The Bible in Contemporary Cinema*. Edited by Geert Hallbäck and Annika Hvithamar. Sheffield: Sheffield Phoenix Press, 2008.

Vander Stichele, Caroline. "Mary Magdalene Portrayed on the Silver Screen." Pages 26–31 in *Mary Magdalene: Chief Witness, Sinner, Feminist*. Utrecht: Museum Catharijneconvent, 2021.

Vander Stichele, Caroline. "Talking Nonsense? The Disciples' Response to the Women in Luke 24:1–22 and Other Early Christian Texts." Forthcoming in *Themes and Texts in Luke-Acts: Essays in Honour of Bart J. Koet*. Edited by Bert Jan Lietaert Peerbolte, Caroline Vander Stichele, and Archibald L. H. M. van Wieringen. Leiden: Brill, 2023.

Veligianni, Chryssoula. "*Philos* und *philos*-Komposita in den griechischen Inschriften der Kaiserzeit." Pages 63–80 in *Aspects of Friendship in the Graeco-Roman World*. Edited by M. Peachin. Portsmouth: JRA, 2001.

Verboven, Koenraad. "The Associative Order: Status and Ethos among Roman Businessmen in Late Republic and Early Empire." *Athenaeum* 95 (2007): 1–33.

Viam, Mordechai. "Yodefat—Jotapata." Pages 109–26 in *The Archaeological Record from Cities, Towns, and Villages*. Vol. 2 of *Galilee in the Late Second Temple and Mishnaic Periods*. Edited by David A. Fiensy and James Riley Strange. Minneapolis, MN: Fortress, 2015.

Vlassopoulos, Kostas. "Greek Slavery: From Domination to Property and Back Again." *JHS* 131 (2011): 115–30.

Vos, Craig S. de. "Once a Slave, Always a Slave? Slavery, Manumission and Relational Patterns in Paul's Letter to Philemon." *JSNT* 23 (2001): 89–105.

Wallace, David R. "Friendship in Philemon." *BBR* 30 (2020): 561–82.

Walsh, Richard. "'My Kingdom Is Not of This World': Johannine Jesus Films and Christian Supersessionism." Pages 165–83 in *The Gospel of John and Jewish-Christian Relations*. Edited by Adele Reinhartz. Lanham, MD: Lexington Books, 2018.

Walsh, Richard. *Reading the Gospels in the Dark: Portrayals of Jesus in Film*. Harrisburg, PA: Trinity, 2003.

Walsh, Richard. *Three Versions of Judas*. London: Equinox, 2010.

Walsh, Richard. "The Zealots in the Jesus Film Tradition." Pages 105–32 in *Religion und Gewalt im Bibelfilm*. Edited by Reinhold Zwick. FilTh 20. Marburg: Schüren, 2012.

Walsh, Richard, and Jeffrey L. Staley. *Jesus, the Gospels, and Cinematic Imagination: Introducing Jesus Movies, Christ Films, and the Messiah in Motion*. London: T&T Clark, 2022.

Ward, Peter. *Picture Composition for Film and Television*. 2nd ed. Oxford: Focal Press, 2003.

Warren, Meredith J. C. "The Cup of God's Wrath: Libation and Early Christian Meal Practice in Revelation." *Religions* 9, 413 (2018): 1–13.

Warren, Meredith J. C. *Food and Transformation in Ancient Mediterranean Literature*. Atlanta, GA: SBL Press, 2019.

Wassén, Cecilia. "The Connection between Purity Practices and the Jerusalem Temple (the House of God) around the Turn of the Area." Pages 167–90 in *La Maison de*

Dieu/Das Haus Gottes. Edited by Christian Grappe. WUNT 471. Tübingen: Mohr Siebeck, 2021.
Wassén, Cecilia. "Do You Have to Be Pure in a Metaphorical Temple? Sanctuary Metaphors and Construction of Sacred Space in the Dead Sea Scrolls and Paul's Letters." Pages 55–86 in *Purity, Holiness, and Identity in Judaism and Christianity: Essays in Memory of Susan Haber*. Edited by Carl S. Ehrlich, Anders Runesson, and Eileen Schuller. Tübingen: Mohr Siebeck, 2013.
Wassén, Cecilia. "The (Im)Purity Levels of Communal Meals within the Qumran Movement." *JAJ* 7 (2016): 102–22.
Wassén, Cecilia. "The Jewishness of Jesus and Ritual Purity." *SIDA* 27 (2016): 11–36.
Wassén, Cecilia. "Stepped Pools and Stone Vessels: Rethinking Jewish Purity Practices in Palestine." *BAR* 45 (2019): 53–8.
Weiss, Zeev. *Public Spectacles in Roman and Late Antique Palestine*. Cambridge, MA: Harvard University Press, 2014.
Welton, Rebekah. "Yahweh the Wrathful Vintner: Blood and Wine-Making Metaphors in Isaiah 49.26a and 63.6." *Journal of Interdisciplinary Biblical Studies* 4 (2022): 19–41.
Wessels, G. Francois. "The Letter to Philemon in the Context of Slavery in Early Christianity." Pages 143–68 in *Philemon in Perspective: Interpreting a Pauline Letter*. Edited by D. Francois Tolmie and Alfred Friedl. BZNW 169. Berlin: de Gruyter, 2010.
Westermann, William L. *The Slave Systems of Greek and Roman Antiquity*. Memoirs of The American Philosophical Society 40. Philadelphia, PA: American Philosophical Society, 1955.
Williams, Margaret. *The Jews among the Greeks and Romans. A Diasporan Sourcebook*. Baltimore, MD: Johns Hopkins University Press, 1998.
Williams, Thaddeus J. *Love, Freedom and Evil: Does Authentic Love Require Free Will?* Amsterdam: Rodopi, 2011.
Wills, Lawrence M. "The Gospel according to Mark." Pages 67–106 in *Jewish Annotated New Testament*. 2nd ed. Edited by Amy-Jill Levine and Marc Zvi Brettler. New York: Oxford University Press, 2017.
Winsor, Ann Roberts. *A King Is Bound in the Tresses. Allusions to the Song of Songs in the Fourth Gospel*. New York: Peter Lang, 1999.
Winter, Sara C. "Paul's Letter to Philemon." *NTS* 33 (1987): 1–15.
Winterling, Aloys. "Freundschaft und Klientel im kaiserzeitlichen Rom." *Historia* 57 (2008): 298–316.
Wischmeyer, Oda. "Das Adjektiv ΑΓΑΠΗΤΟΣ in den paulinischen Briefen: Eine traditionsgeschichtliche Miszelle." *NTS* 32 (1986): 476–80.
Wright, Melanie J. *Moses in America: The Cultural Uses of Biblical Narrative*. Oxford: Oxford University Press, 2003.
Wright, N. T. *What Saint Paul Really Said: Was Paul of Tarsus the Real Founder of Christianity?* Grand Rapids, MI: Eerdmans, 1997.
Yadin, Yigael. *The Temple Scroll*. Jerusalem: Israel Exploration Society, 1983.
Young, Frances. *Biblical Exegesis and the Formation of Christian Culture*. Cambridge, MA: Cambridge University Press, 1997.
Zacharek, Stephanie, Eliana Dockterman, and Haley Sweetland Edwards. "The Silence Breakers: The Voices of the Launched Movement." *Time* (December 18, 2017). https://time.com/time-person-of-the-year-2017-silence-breakers/.
Zahn, Theodor. *Das Evangelium des Johannes*. Vol. 4 of *Kommentar zum Neuen Testament*. 6th ed. Leipzig: Deichert, 1921.

Zimmermann, Mirjam, and Ruben Zimmermann. "Freundschaftsethik im Johannesevangelium: Zur öffentlichen und politischen Reichweite eines ethischen Konzepts." Pages 163–83 in *Biblical Ethics and Application: Purview, Validity, and Relevance of Biblical Texts in Ethical Discourse, Contexts and Norms of New Testament Ethics 9*. Edited by Ruben Zimmermann and Stephan Joubert. WUNT 384. Tübingen: Mohr Siebeck, 2017.

Zimmermann, Ruben. "'Deuten' heißt erzählen und übertragen. Narrativität und Metaphorik als sprachliche Grundformen historischer Sinnbildung zum Tod Jesu." Pages 315–73 in *Deutungen des Todes Jesu im Neuen Testament*. Edited by Jörg Frey and Jens Schröter. WUNT 181. Tübingen: Mohr Siebeck, 2005.

Zwick, Reinhold. "The Book of Job in the Movies: On Cinema's Exploration of Theodicy and the Hiddenness of God." Pages 355–77 in *The Bible in Motion: A Handbook of the Bible and Its Reception in Film*. Edited by Rhonda Burnett-Bletsch. Berlin: de Gruyter, 2016.

Bibliography of the Works of Adele Reinhartz (1983–2022)

Compiled by Emily Victoria Hanlon

A. Doctoral Dissertation

"John 20:30–31 and the Purpose of the Fourth Gospel." PhD diss., McMaster University, 1983.

B. Monographs

1. *The Word in the World: The Cosmological Tale in the Fourth Gospel.* SBLMS 45. Atlanta, GA: Scholars Press, 1992. x, 156 pages.
2. *"Why Ask My Name?" Anonymity and Identity in Biblical Narrative.* New York: Oxford University Press, 1998. xii, 226 pages.
— Winner of 2000 Canadian Jewish Book Award for Biblical Scholarship.
3. *Befriending the Beloved Disciple: A Jewish Reading of the Gospel of John.* New York: Continuum International, 2001. 206 pages.
— Finalist of 2001 National Jewish Book Awards.
— Winner of 2003 F. W. Beare Award for Outstanding Book in Christian Origins (Canadian Society of Biblical Studies).
4. *Scripture on the Silver Screen.* Louisville, KY: Westminster John Knox, 2003. ix, 217 pages.
5. *Freundschaft mit dem Geliebten Jünger: Eine jüdische Lektüre des Johannesevangeliums.* Translated by Esther Kobel. Zürich: TVZ Theologischer Verlag Zürich, 2005. 245 pages.
— Translation of *Befriending the Beloved Disciple* (Item B3).
6. *Jesus of Hollywood.* New York: Oxford University Press, 2007. Paperback edition: 2009. xiv, 313 pages.
7. *Caiaphas the High Priest. Studies on Personalities of the New Testament.* Columbia: University of South Carolina Press, 2011. Minneapolis, MN: Fortress Press, 2013. x, 254 pages.
8. *The Bible and Cinema: An Introduction.* London: Routledge, 2013. xi, 286 pages. 2nd. ed. London/New York: 2022. xii, 409 pages.
9. ハリウッド映画と聖書 (*Hariuddo eiga to seisho*). Translated by Utako Kurihara. Tokyo: Misuzu Shobo, 2018. 430, 29 pages.
— Translation of *The Bible and Cinema* (Item B8).
10. *Cast Out of the Covenant: Jews and Anti-Judaism in the Gospel of John.* Lanham, MD: Lexington Books, 2018. 249 pages.
11. *The Bible and Cinema: An Introduction.* 2nd, rev., and enl. ed. London: Routledge, 2022. 422 pages.

C. Edited Volumes

1. *God the Father in the Gospel of John.* Semeia 85. Atlanta, GA: SBL Press, 1999.
2. *Frye and the Afterlife of the Word.* Edited with James Kee. Semeia 89. Atlanta, GA: SBL Press, 2002.
3. *Jesus, Judaism, and Christian Anti-Judaism: Reading the New Testament After the Holocaust.* Edited with Paula Fredriksen. Louisville, KY: Westminster John Knox, 2002.
4. *Common Judaism Explored: Explorations in Second-Temple Judaism.* Edited with Wayne McCready. Minneapolis, MN: Fortress, 2008.
   Collection of essays based on lectures given by an international group of scholars at an SSHRC-sponsored workshop at the Calgary Institute for the Humanities, 2005.
5. Haber, Susan. *"They Shall Purify Themselves": Essays on Purity in Early Judaism.* EJL 24. Atlanta, GA: SBL Press, 2008.
6. *The Oxford Encyclopedia of the Books of the Bible.* Edited with Michael Coogan, Marc Brettler, Daniel Schowalter, and Brent A. Strawn. 2 vols. New York: Oxford University Press, 2011.
7. *The Bible and Cinema: 50 Key Films.* London: Routledge, 2013.
8. *Son of Man: An African Jesus Movie.* Edited with Richard Walsh and Jeffrey Staley. Sheffield: Sheffield Phoenix Press, 2013.
9. *The Gospel of John and Jewish-Christian Relations.* Lanham, MD: Lexington Books/Fortress Academic, 2018.

D. Book Chapters

1. "To Catch a Thief: Jesus' Opponents in John 10:1–5." Pages 167–79 in *Self-Definition and Self-Discovery in Early Christianity: A Study in Changing Horizons. Essays in Appreciation of Ben F. Meyer from Former Students.* Edited by David J. Hawkin and Tom Robinson. SBEC 26. Lewiston, NY: Edwin Mellen Press, 1990.
2. "From Narrative to History: The Resurrection of Martha and Mary." Pages 161–84 in *"Women Like This": New Perspectives on Jewish Women in the Greco-Roman World.* Edited by Amy-Jill Levine. Atlanta, GA: Scholars Press, 1991.
3. "The Greek Book of Esther." Pages 286–92 in *Women's Bible Commentary.* Edited by Carol A. Newsom and Sharon H. Ringe. London: SPCK; Louisville, KY: Westminster John Knox, 1992 [Enl. ed., 1998].
4. "Parents and Children: A Philonic Perspective." Pages 61–88 in *The Jewish Family in Antiquity.* Edited by Shaye Cohen. Atlanta, GA: Scholars Press, 1993.
5. "Samson's Mother: An Unnamed Protagonist." Pages 157–70 in *A Feminist Companion to Judges.* Edited by Athalya Brenner. Sheffield: JSOT Press, 1993 (Reprint of item E8).
6. "Anonymous Female Characters in the Books of Kings." Pages 43–65 in *A Feminist Companion to Samuel and Kings.* Edited by Athalya Brenner. Sheffield: JSOT Press, 1994.
7. "A Feminist Commentary on the Gospel of John." Pages 561–600 in vol. 2 of *Searching the Scriptures.* Edited by Elisabeth Schüssler Fiorenza. New York: Crossroad, 1994.
8. "Feminist Criticism and Biblical Studies on the Verge of the Twenty-First Century." Pages 30–8 in *A Feminist Companion to Reading the Bible: Approaches, Methods and Strategies.* Edited by Athalya Brenner and Carole Fontaine. Sheffield: Sheffield Academic Press, 1997.

9. "The Greek Book of Esther." Pages 286–92 in *The Women's Bible Commentary*. Edited by Carol A. Newsom and Sharon H. Ringe. Enl. ed. Louisville, KY: Westminster John Knox, 1998.
10. "The Johannine Community and Its Jewish Neighbors: A Reappraisal." Pages 111–38 in *Literary and Social Readings of the Fourth Gospel*. Vol. 2 of *What Is John?* Edited by Fernando F. Segovia. Atlanta, GA: Scholars Press, 1998.
11. "On Travel, Translation, and Ethnography: The Gospel of John at the Turn of the Century." Pages 249–56 in *Literary and Social Readings of the Fourth Gospel*. Vol. 2 of *What Is John?* Edited by Fernando F. Segovia. Atlanta, GA: Scholars Press, 1998.
12. "To Love the Lord: An Intertextual Reading of John 20." Pages 56–69 in *The Labour of Reading: Essays in Honour of Robert C. Culley*. Edited by Fiona Black, Roland Boer, Christian Kelm, and Erin Runions. SemeiaSt 36. Atlanta, GA: Scholars Press, 1999.
13. "Better Homes and Gardens: Women and Domestic Space in the Books of Judith and Susanna." Pages 325–39 in *Text and Artifact: Judaism and Christianity in the Ancient Mediterranean World: Essays in Honour of Peter Richardson*. Edited by Michel Desjardins and Stephen G. Wilson. SCJud 9. Waterloo, ON: Wilfrid Laurier Press, 2000.
14. "Jesus of Hollywood: A Jewish Perspective." Pages 131–46 in *The Historical Jesus through Catholic and Jewish Eyes*. Edited by Leonard Greenspoon. Valley Forge, PA: Trinity Press International, 2000.
15. "The Greek Book of Esther." Pages 642–49 in *The Oxford Bible Commentary*. Edited by John Barton and John Muddiman. Oxford: Oxford University Press, 2001.
16. "'Jews' and Jews in the Fourth Gospel." Pages 341–56 in *Anti-Judaism and the Fourth Gospel: Papers of the Leuven Colloquium, 2000*. Edited by Reimund Bieringer, Didier Pollefeyt, and Frederique Vandecasteele-Vanneuville. Assen: Van Gorcum, 2001.
17. "John 8:31–59 from a Jewish Perspective." Pages 787–97 in *Ethics and Religion*. Vol. 2 of *Remembering for the Future 2000: The Holocaust in an Age of Genocide*. Edited by John K. Roth and Elisabeth Maxwell. London: Palgrave, 2001.
18. "The 'Bride' in John 3.29: A Feminist Rereading." Pages 230–41 in *The Lost Coin: Parables of Women Work and Wisdom*. Edited by Mary Ann Beavis. Sheffield: Sheffield Academic Press, 2002.
19. "The Colonized as Colonizer: A Postcolonial Reading of the Gospel of John." Pages 170–92 in *Postcolonialism and John*. Edited by Jeffrey Staley and Rasiah S. Sugirtharajah. Sheffield: Sheffield Academic Press, 2002.
20. "The Gospel of John: How the Jews Become Part of the Plot." Pages 99–116 in *Jesus, Judaism and Christian Anti-Judaism: Reading the New Testament after the Holocaust*. Edited with Paula Fredriksen. Louisville, KY: Westminster John Knox, 2002.
21. "Introduction." With Paula Fredriksen. Pages 1–7 in *Jesus, Judaism and Christian Anti-Judaism: Reading the New Testament after the Holocaust*. Edited with Paula Fredriksen. Louisville, KY: Westminster John Knox, 2002.
22. "The Old Testament/Hebrew Bible and the Apocrypha." Pages 15–27 in *The Biblical World*. Edited by John Barton. London: Routledge, 2002.
23. "Ruth: Introduction and Annotations." Pages 1578–86 in *The Jewish Study Bible*. Edited by Adele Berlin and Marc Brettler. New York: Oxford University Press, 2003.
24. "The Happy Holy Family in the Jesus Film Genre." Pages 123–42 in *Wisdom on the Cutting Edge: The Study of Women in Biblical Worlds*. Edited by Alice Bach and Jane Schaberg. New York: Continuum, 2003.

25. "Jesus on the Silver Screen." Pages 186–9 in *Revelation: Representations of Christ in Photography*. Edited by Nissan N. Perez. London: Merrell in association with the Israel Museum, 2003.
26. "Jewish Women's Biblical Scholarship." Pages 2000–5 in *The Jewish Study Bible*. Edited by Adele Berlin and Marc Brettler. New York: Oxford University Press, 2003.
27. "Some Reflections on Feminist Biblical Hermeneutics for Liberation." With Marie-Theres Wacker. Pages 34–47 in *Feminist Interpretation of the Bible and the Hermeneutics of Liberation*. Edited by Silvia Schroer and Sophia Bietenhard. JSOTSup 374. Sheffield: Sheffield Academic Press, 2003.
28. "Women in the Johannine Community: An Exercise in Historical Imagination." Pages 14–33 in vol. 2 of *A Feminist Companion to John*. Edited by Amy-Jill Levine. Sheffield: Sheffield Academic Press, 2003.
29. "The Grammar of Hate in the Gospel of Love: Reading the Fourth Gospel in the Twenty-First Century." Pages 416–27 in *Israel und seine Heilstraditionen im Johannesevangelium: Festgabe für Johannes Beutler SJ zum 70. Geburtstag*. Edited by Angelika Strotmann, Klaus Scholtissek, and Michael Labahn. Paderborn: Schöningh, 2004.
30. "Jesus of Hollywood." Pages 165–79 in *Perspectives on the Passion of the Christ: Religious Thinkers and Writers Explore the Issues Raised by the Controversial Movie*. New York: Miramax Books, 2004.
31. "Joodentum." Pages 95–108 in *Midden in de Cirkel: Vrouwen en leiderschap in diverse spirituele tradities*. Edited by Sabine Van den Eynde and Kristien Justaert. Antwerp: Halewijn, 2004.
— Translated into Flemish by Reimund Bieringer.
32. "Women at War: Gender and Leadership in Biblical and Post-Biblical Literature." Pages 35–54 in vol. 1 of *Jewish Religious Leadership: Image and Reality*. Edited by Jack Wertheimer. New York: Jewish Theological Seminary Press, 2004.
33. "Celluloid Saviors and the Gospels." Pages 161–5 in *Jesus in the World's Faiths: Leading Thinkers from the Five Religions Reflect on His Meaning*. Edited by Gregory A. Barker. Maryknoll, NY: Orbis, 2005.
34. "John and Judaism: A Response to Burton Visotzky." Pages 108–16 in *Life in Abundance: Studies of John's Gospel in Tribute to Raymond E. Brown, S. S.* Edited by John Donahue. Collegeville, MN: Liturgical Press, 2005.
35. "John, Gender and Judaism: A Feminist's Dilemma." Pages 182–95 in *Text, Ethik, Judentum und Christentum, Gesellschaft: Festschrift für Ekkehard W. Stegemann zum 60. Geburtstag*. Vol. 1 of *Kontexte der Schrift*. Edited by Gabriella Gelardini. Stuttgart: Kohlhammer, 2005.
36. "Love, Hate, and Violence in the Gospel of John." Pages 109–23 in *Violence in the New Testament*. Edited by Shelly Matthews and E. Leigh Gibson. New York: Continuum, 2005.
37. "A Fork in the Road or a Multi-Lane Highway? New Perspectives on 'The Parting of the Ways' Between Judaism and Christianity." Pages 278–93 in *The Changing Face of Judaism, Christianity, and Other Greco Roman Religions in Antiquity*. Edited by Ian H. Henderson and Gerbern S. Oegema. Studien zu den Jüdischen Schriften aus hellenistisch-römischer Zeit 2. Gütersloh: Gütersloher Verlagshaus, 2006.
38. "Aristotelian *Epigenesis* in the Gospel of John: The Next Generation." Pages 9–18 in *Gender and Body in the Gospel of John*. Edited by Gitte Buch-Hansen, Troels Engberg-Pedersen, and Lone Fatum. Working Papers 1. Copenhagen: Biblical Studies Section, University of Copenhagen, 2006.

39. "Conflict and Coexistence in Jewish Interpretation." With Miriam-Simma Walfish. Pages 101–25 in *Hagar, Sarah, and Their Children: Jewish, Christian, and Muslim Perspectives*. Edited by Phyllis Trible and Letty M. Russell. Louisville, KY: Westminster John Knox, 2006.
40. "Rodney Stark and 'The Mission to the Jews.'" Pages 197–212 in *Religious Rivalries in the Early Roman Empire and the Rise of Christianity*. Edited by Leif E. Vaage. SCJud 18. Waterloo, ON: Wilfrid Laurier University Press, 2006.
41. "Chaste Betrayals: Women and Men in the Apocryphal Novels." Pages 227–42 in *Heavenly Tablets: Interpretation, Identity and Tradition in Ancient Judaism*. Edited by Lynn LiDonnici and Andrea Lieber. JSJSup119. Leiden: Brill, 2007.
42. "'Jews' and Anti-Judaism: Reading John after *Nostra Aetate*." Pages 51–65 in *Nostra Aetate at 40: Achievements and Challenges in Christian-Jewish Relations*. Edited by Jean Duhaime. Montreal: Novalis, 2007.
43. "John's Pharisees." With Raimo Hakola. Pages 131–47 in *In Quest of the Historical Pharisees*. Edited by Jacob Neusner and Bruce Chilton. Waco, TX: Baylor University Press, 2007.
44. "Reading History in the Fourth Gospel: A Response to J. L. Martyn." Pages 191–4 in *What We Have Heard from the Beginning: The Past, Present, and Future of Johannine Studies*. Edited by Tom Thatcher. Waco, TX: Baylor University Press, 2007.
45. "Scripture on the Silver Screen." Pages 374–7 in *The Religion and Film Reader*. Edited by Jolyon P. Mitchell and S. Brent Plate. New York: Routledge, 2007.
46. "Who Cares about Caiaphas?" Pages 31–40 in *Identity and Interaction in the Ancient Mediterranean: Jews, Christians and Others. Essays in Honour of Stephen G. Wilson*. Edited by Zeba A. Crook and Philip A. Harland. Sheffield: Sheffield Phoenix Press, 2007.
47. "Building Skyscrapers on Toothpicks: The Literary-Critical Challenge to Historical Criticism." Pages 55–76 in *Anatomies of Narrative Criticism*. Edited by Tom Thatcher. Atlanta, GA: SBL Press, 2008.
48. "Caiaphas on Camera." Pages 131–48 in *Images of the Word: Hollywood's Bible and Beyond*. Edited by David Shepherd. SemeiaSt 54. Atlanta, GA: SBL Press, 2008.
49. "Crucifying Caiaphas: Hellenism and the High Priesthood in Life of Jesus Narratives." Pages 227–45 in *Redefining First Century Jewish and Christian Identities: Essays in Honor of Ed Parish Sanders*. Edited by Fabian E. Udoh, Susannah Heschel, Mark Chancey, and Gregory Tatum. CJAn Series 16. Notre Dame, IN: University of Notre Dame Press, 2008.
50. "Jesus of Hollywood." Pages 165–77 in *The Passion Story: From Visual Representation to Social Drama*. Edited by Marcia A. Kupfer. University Park: Pennsylvania State University Press, 2008 (Reprint of item D30).
51. "The Gospel according to Benedict: *Jesus of Nazareth* on Jews and Judaism." Pages 223–46 in *The Pope and Jesus of Nazareth: Christ, Scripture and the Church*. Edited by Adrian Pabst and Angus Paddison. London: SCM Press, 2009.
52. "Gospel Audiences: Variations on a Theme." Pages 134–52 in *The Audience of the Gospels: The Origin and Function of the Gospels in Early Christianity*. Edited by Edward W. Klink. London: T&T Clark, 2009.
53. "The Gospel of John." Pages 223–42 in *The Oxford Handbook of English Literature and Theology*. Edited by Andrew W. Hass, David Jasper, and Elisabeth Jay. Oxford: Oxford University Press, 2009.
54. "Jesus and Christ-Figures." Pages 421–39 in *Routledge Companion to Religion and Film*. Edited by John Lyden. London: Routledge, 2009.

55. "Jesus Movies." Pages 211–22 in *Continuum Companion to Religion and Film*. Edited by William Blizek. New York: Continuum, 2009.
56. "We, You, They: Boundary Language in 4QMMT and the New Testament Epistles." Pages 89–105 in *Text, Thought, and Practice in Qumran and Early Christianity: Proceedings of a Joint Symposium by the Orion Center for the Study of the Dead Sea Scrolls and Associated Literature, Jointly Sponsored by the Hebrew University Center for the Study of Christianity, January 11-13, 2004*. Edited by Ruth A. Clements and Daniel R. Schwartz. StTDJ 84. Leiden: Brill, 2009.
57. "'Who Am I? Where Am I Going?': The Sopranos on Life, Death and Religion." Pages 373–99 in *Small Screen, Big Picture: Lived Religion and Television*. Edited by Diane Winston and Jane Naomi Iwamura. Waco, TX: Baylor University Press, 2009.
58. "Automatic Text Segmentation for Movie Subtitles." With Martin Scaiano, Diana Inkpen, and Robert Laganiere. Pages 295–8 in *Advances in Artificial Intelligence: Proceedings of the 23rd Canadian Conference on Artificial Intelligence. Canadian AI 2010, Ottawa, Canada, May 31–June 2, 2010*. Edited by Atefeh Farzindar and Vlado Kešelj. Berlin: Springer, 2010.
59. "Repentance, Reconciliation and Relationship: The Book of Jonah as Case Study." Pages 9–27 in *Reconciliation in Interfaith Perspective: Jewish, Christian and Muslim Voices*. Edited by Reimund Bieringer and David Bolton. Leuven, MA: Peeters, 2010.
60. "'Common Judaism,' 'The Parting of the Ways,' and 'The Johannine Community.'" Pages 69–88 in *Orthodoxy, Liberalism, and Adaptation: Essays on Ways of Worldmaking in Times of Change from Biblical, Historical and Systematic Perspectives*. Edited by Bob Becking. Leiden: Brill, 2011.
61. "'The Gospel of John': Introduction and Annotations." Pages 152–96 in *The Jewish Annotated New Testament*. Edited by Amy-Jill Levine and Marc Zvi Brettler. New York: Oxford University Press, 2011.
62. "Jesus in Film." Pages 519–31 in *Blackwell Companion to Jesus*. Edited by Delbert Burkett. Malden, MA: Wiley-Blackwell, 2011.
63. "Foreword." Pages xv–xix in *Soundings in the Religion of Jesus: Perspectives and Methods in Contemporary Scholarship*. Edited by Bruce Chilton, Anthony Le Donne, and Jacob Neusner. Minneapolis, MN: Fortress Press, 2012.
64. "The Greek Book of Esther." Pages 396–403 in *The Women's Bible Commentary*. Edited by Carol A. Newsom, Sharon H. Ringe, and Jacqueline E. Lapsley. 3rd rev. ed. Louisville, KY: Westminster John Knox, 2012.
65. "Forging a New Identity: Johannine Rhetoric and the Audience of the Fourth Gospel." Pages 123–34 in *Paul, John, and Apocalyptic Eschatology: Studies in Honour of Martinus C. de Boer*. Edited by Jan Krans, L. J. Lietaert Peerbolte, Peter-Ben Smit, and Arie W. Zwiep. NovTSup 149. Leiden: Brill, 2013.
66. "The Temple Cleansing and the Death of Jesus." Pages 101–11 in *Purity, Holiness, and Identity in Judaism: Essays in Memory of Susan Haber*. Edited by Carl. S. Ehrlich, Anders Runesson, and Eileen Schuller. WUNT 305. Tübingen: Mohr Siebeck, 2013.
67. "Violence Against the Jews." Pages 133–44 in *Religion und Gewalt im Bibelfilm*. Edited by Reinhold Zwick. Marburg: Schüren Verlag, 2013.
68. "The Destruction of the Jerusalem Temple as a Trauma for Nascent Christianity." Pages 276–88 in *Trauma and Traumatization in Individual and Collective Dimensions: Insights from Biblical Studies and Beyond*. Edited by Eve-Marie Becker, Jan Dochhorn, and Else K. Holt. Studia Aarhusiana Neotestamentica (SANt) 2. Göttingen: Vandenhoeck & Ruprecht, 2014.

69. "Holy Words in Hollywood: DeMille's *The Ten Commandments* (1956) and American Identity." Pages 123–35 in *The Bible in the Public Square*. Edited by Carol Meyers, Eric Meyers, and Mark Chancey. Atlanta, GA: SBL Press, 2014.
70. "Jewish Women's Scholarly Writings on the Bible." Pages 2086–91 in *The Jewish Study Bible*. Edited by Adele Berlin and Marc Zvi Brettler. 2nd ed. New York: Oxford University Press, 2014.
71. "Philo's *Exposition of the Law* and Social History: Methodological Considerations." Pages 180–99 in *Reading Philo*. Edited by Torrey Seland. Grand Rapids, MI: Eerdmans, 2014.
72. "Ruth: Introduction and Annotations." Pages 1573–80 in *The Jewish Study Bible*. 2nd ed. Edited by Adele Berlin and Marc Zvi Brettler. New York: Oxford University Press, 2014.
73. "'Children of God' and Aristotelian Epigenesis in the Gospel of John." Pages 243–52 in *Creation Stories in Dialogue: The Bible, Science, and Folk Traditions*. Edited by R. Alan Culpepper and Jan G. Van der Watt. Leiden: Brill, 2015.
74. "Dying for Our Sins: Jesus' Passion on the Silver Screen." Pages 311–32 in *Engaging the Passion: Perspectives on the Death of Jesus*. Edited by O. Larry Yarbrough. Minneapolis, MN: Fortress Press, 2015.
75. "E.T. Phone Home: Exile and Gender in Postexilic Storytelling." Pages 243–51 in *A Most Reliable Witness: Essays in Honor of Ross Shepard Kraemer*. Edited by Susan Ashbrook Harvey, Nathaniel DesRosiers, Shira L. Lander, Jacqueline Z. Pastis, and Daniel Ullucci. BJSt 358. Atlanta, GA: SBL Press, 2015.
76. "Hook-Nosed Heebies: Brian, Jesus and Jewish Identity." Pages 207–20 in *Jesus and Brian: Exploring the Historical Jesus and His Times via Monty Python's Life of Brian*. Edited by Joan E. Taylor. London: Bloomsbury T&T Clark, 2015.
77. "The Bible Epic." Pages 175–92 in vol. 1 of *The Bible in Motion: A Handbook of the Bible and Its Reception in Film*. Edited by Rhonda Burnette-Bletsch. Handbooks of the Bible and Its Reception 2. Berlin: de Gruyter, 2016.
78. "Judaism and Antisemitism in Bible Movies." Pages 779–94 in vol. 2 of *The Bible in Motion: A Handbook of the Bible and Its Reception in Film*. Edited by Rhonda Burnette-Bletsch. Berlin: de Gruyter, 2016.
79. "Reproach and Revelation: Ethics in John 11:1–44." Pages 92–106 in *Torah Ethics and Early Christian Identity*. Edited by Susan Wendel and David Miller. Grand Rapids, MI: Eerdmans, 2016.
80. "A Rebellious Son? Jesus and His Mother in John 2:4." Pages 235–49 in *The Opening of John's Narrative: (John 1:19–2:22): Historical, Literary, and Theological Readings from the Colloquium Ioanneum 2015 in Ephesus*. Edited by R. Alan Culpepper and Jörg Frey. WUNT 385. Tübingen: Mohr Siebeck, 2017.
81. "LXX Esther: A Hellenistic Jewish Revenge Fantasy." Pages 9–28 in *Early Jewish Writings*. Edited by Eileen Schuller and Marie-Theres Wacker. Atlanta, GA: SBL Press, 2017.
82. "Das septuagintagriechische Esterbuch: Eine hellenistisch-jüdische Rachefantasie." Pages 13–32 in *Frühjüdische Schriften*. Edited by Eileen Schuller and Marie-Theres Wacker. Die Bibel und die Frauen 3. Pseudepigraphische und apokryphe Schriften 1. Stuttgart: Kohlhammer, 2017.
— Translation of "LXX Esther: A Hellenistic Jewish Revenge Fantasy" by Gerlinde Baumann (Item D81).

83. "The Gospel of John: Introduction and Annotations." Pages 168–218 in *The Jewish Annotated New Testament*. Edited by Amy-Jill Levine and Marc Zvi Brettler. 2nd, rev. and enl. ed. New York: Oxford University Press, 2017.
84. "The Lyin' King? Deception and Christology in the Gospel of John." Pages 153–69 in *Johannine Ethics: The Moral World of the Gospel and Epistles of John*. Edited by Christopher W. Skinner and Sherri Brown. Minneapolis, MN: Fortress Press, 2017.
85. "Story and History: John, Judaism, and the Historical Imagination." Pages 113–26 in *John and Judaism: A Contested Relationship in Context*. Edited by R. Alan Culpepper and Paul N. Anderson. Atlanta, GA: SBL Press, 2017.
86. "'And the Word Was God': John's Christology and Jesus's Discourse in Jewish Context." Pages 67–91 in *Reading the Gospel of John's Christology as Early Jewish Messianism: Royal, Prophetic, and Divine Messiahs*. Edited by Benjamin E. Reynolds and Gabriele Boccaccini. AGJU 106. Leiden: Brill, 2018.
87. "How Christianity Parted from Judaism." Pages 97–120 in *Early Judaism: New Insights and Scholarship*. Edited by Frederick E. Greenspahn. New York: New York University Press, 2018.
88. "The Jews of the Fourth Gospel." Pages 121–37 in *The Oxford Handbook of Johannine Studies*. Edited by Judith M. Lieu and Martinus C. de Boer. Oxford: Oxford University Press, 2018.
89. "Reversing the Hermeneutical Flow: Noah's Flood in Recent Hollywood Films." Pages 287–99 in *T&T Clark Companion to the Bible and Film*. Edited by Richard Walsh. London: T&T Clark, 2018.
90. "A Jewish Woman's Society of Biblical Literature Experience." Pages 223–9 in *Women and the Society of Biblical Literature*. Edited by Nicole Tilford. Atlanta, GA: SBL Press, 2019.
91. "Of Mountains and Messiahs: John 4:19–23 and Divine Covenant." Pages 187–98 in *Expressions of the Johannine Kerygma in John 2:23–5:18: Historical, Literary, and Theological Readings from the Colloquium Ioanneum 2017 in Jerusalem*. Edited by R. Alan Culpepper and Jörg Frey. WUNT 423. Tübingen: Mohr Siebeck, 2019.
92. "Wise Women in the Gospel of John." Pages 159–72 in *Re-making the World: Christianity and Categories: Essays in Honor of Karen L. King*. Edited by Taylor G. Petrey. WUNT 434. Tübingen: Mohr Siebeck, 2019.
93. "'Children of the Devil': John 8:44 and Its Early Reception." Pages 43–54 in *Confronting Antisemitism from the Perspectives of Christianity, Islam, and Judaism*. Edited by Armin Lange, Kerstin Mayerhofer, Dina Porat, and Lawrence H. Schiffman. An End to Antisemitism 2. Berlin: de Gruyter, 2020.
94. "Preface." Pages xv–xvii in *The Bible Onscreen in the New Millennium: New Heart and New Spirit*. Edited by Wickham Clayton. Manchester: Manchester University Press, 2020.
95. "Women and Gender in the Gospel of John." Pages 137–53 in *Gender and Second-Temple Judaism*. Edited by Shayna Sheinfeld and Kathy Ehrensperger. Lanham, MD: Lexington Books, 2020.
96. "The Apocrypha and Pseudepigrapha." Pages 19–32 in *The Biblical World*. Edited by Katharine J. Dell. 2nd ed. London: Routledge, 2021.
97. "Doing God's Work: John 5:17–18 from a Jewish Perspective." Pages 29–38 in *Signs and Discourses in John 5 and 6: Historical, Literary, and Theological Readings from the Colloquium Ioanneum 2019 in Eisenach*. Edited by Jörg Frey and Craig R. Koester. WUNT 463. Tübingen: Mohr Siebeck, 2021.

98. "Failed Christ Figures in Québec Films." Pages 249–60 in *T&T Clark Handbook of Jesus and Film*. Edited by Richard Walsh. London: T&T Clark, 2021.
99. "The Fourth Gospel and the First Century Outreach Campaign to the Gentiles." Pages 251–66 in *Social History of the Jews in Antiquity: Studies in Dialogue with Albert Baumgarten*. Edited by Michal Bar-Asher Siegal and Jonathan Ben-Dov. TSAJ 185. Tübingen: Mohr Siebeck, 2021.
100. "The 'Parting of the Ways' and the Criterion of Plausibility." Pages 147–56 in *Paul and Matthew among Jews and Gentiles: Essays in Honour of Terence L. Donaldson*. Edited by Ronald Charles. LNTS 628. London: Bloomsbury, 2021.
101. "The Pharisees on Film." Pages 344–60 in *The Pharisees*. Edited by Joseph Sievers and Amy-Jill Levine. Grand Rapids, MI: Eerdmans, 2021.
102. "Sexuality, Stoning, and Supersessionism in Biblical Epic Films of the Post-World War II Era." Pages 313–25 in *The Oxford Handbook of Feminist Approaches to the Hebrew Bible*. Edited by Susanne Scholz. Oxford: Oxford University Press, 2021.
103. "New Testament Origins of Christian Anti-Judaism." Pages 42–56 in *The Cambridge Companion to Antisemitism*. Edited by Steven T. Katz. Cambridge: Cambridge University Press, 2022.

E. Refereed Journal Articles

1. "The meaning of NOMOS in Philo's 'Exposition of the Law.'" *SR* 15 (1986): 337–45.
2. "On the Meaning of the Pauline Exhortation: '*mimētai mou ginesthe*—Become Imitators of Me.'" *SR* 16 (1987): 393–403.
3. "The New Testament and Anti-Judaism: A Literary-Critical Approach." *JES* 25 (1988): 524–37.
4. "Great Expectations: A Reader-Oriented Approach to Johannine Christology and Eschatology." *LitTh* 3 (1989): 61–76.
5. "Jesus as Prophet: Predictive Prolepses in the Fourth Gospel." *JSNT* 11 (1989): 3–16.
6. "Rabbinic Perceptions of Simon Bar Kosiba." *JSJ* 20 (1989): 172–94.
7. "Philo on Infanticide." *SPhiloA* 4 (1992): 42–58.
8. "Samson's Mother: An Unnamed Protagonist." *JSOT* 55 (1992): 25–37.
9. "Anonymity and Character in the Books of Samuel." *Semeia* 63 (1993): 117–41.
10. "Jewish Feminist Discourses." *Concilium* 263 (1996): 66–73.
11. "A Nice Jewish Girl Reads the Gospel of John." *Semeia* 77 (1997): 177–93.
12. "Jesus in Film: Hollywood Perspectives on the Jewishness of Jesus." *The Journal of Religion and Film* 2 (1998): 1–11.
13. "Midrash She Wrote: Jewish Women's Writing on the Bible." *Shofar* 16 (1998): 6–27.
14. "'And the Word Was Begotten': Divine Epigenesis in the Gospel of John." *Semeia* 85 (1999): 83–103.
15. "Introduction: 'Father' as Metaphor in the Fourth Gospel." *Semeia* 85 (1999): 1–10.
16. "Reflections on Table Fellowship and Community Identity." *Semeia* 86 (1999): 227–33.
17. "Margins, Methods, and Metaphors: Reflections on *A Feminist Companion to the Hebrew Bible*." *Proof.* 20 (2000): 43–60.
18. "Die 'Glückliche Heilige Familie' in den Jesus-Filmen." *lectio difficilior* 2 (2002). http://www.lectio.unibe.ch/02_2/reinhartz.htm.

— Translation by Irène Schwyn and Alison Sauer of "The Happy Holy Family in the Jesus Film Genre" (Item D24).
19. "Oscar Cullmann und sein Beitrag zur Johannes-Forschung." *ThZ* 57 (2002): 221–31.
— Translated by Esther Kobel.
20. "Contagion and Cure: A Response to 'The Disease of Postcolonial New Testament Studies and the Hermeneutics of Healing' by Amy-Jill Levine." *JFSR* 20 (2004): 111–15.
21. "Joh 8,31–59 aus jüdischer Sicht." *BK* 59 (2004): 137–46.
— Revised and translated version of "John 8:31–59 from a Jewish Perspective" (Item D17).
22. "History and Pseudo-History in the Jesus Film Genre." *BibInt* 14 (2006): 1–17.
23. "Le donne nell'ebraismo." *Conc(I)* 3 (2006): 20–9.
24. "Why Comment? Reflections on Bible Commentaries in General and Andrew Lincoln's *The Gospel according to Saint John* in Particular." *JSNT* 29 (2007): 333–42.
25. "'Juden' und Juden im vierten Evangelium." *KuI* 23 (2008): 127–42.
— Translation by Esther Kobel of "'And the Word Was Begotten': Divine Epigenesis in the Gospel of John" (Item E14).
26. "Playing with Paradigms: The Christ-Figure Genre in Contemporary Film." *Australian Religious Studies Review* 21 (2008): 298–317.
27. "Judaism in the Gospel of John." *Int* 63 (2009): 382–93.
28. "'Rewritten Gospel': The Case of Caiaphas the High Priest." *NTS* 55 (2009): 160–78.
29. "Josephus on Children and Childhood." With Kim Shier. *SR* 41 (2012): 364–75.
30. "Introducing the JBL Forum, an Occasional Exchange." *JBL* 133 (2014): 421.
31. "The JBL Forum, an Occasional Exchange." *JBL* 133 (2014): 647.
32. "The JBL Forum, an Occasional Exchange." *JBL* 133 (2014): 837.
33. "Rabbi Jesus im Johannesevangelium." *KuI* 29 (2014): 108–18.
34. "Editor's Foreword: *The Journal of Biblical Literature and the Critical Investigation of the Bible.*" *JBL* 134 (2015): 457–70.
35. "Incarnation and Covenant: The Fourth Gospel through the Lens of Trauma Theory." *Int* 69 (2015): 35–48.
36. "The JBL Forum, an Occasional Exchange." *JBL* 134 (2015): 849.
37. "Torah Reading in the Johannine Community." *Journal of Early Christian History* 5 (2015): 111–16.
38. "'E.T. nach Hause telefonieren': Exil und Gender in Erzählungen der nachexilischen Zeit." *lectio difficilior* 2 (2015). http://www.lectio.unibe.ch/15_2/reinhartz.html.
39. "Les saints héros d'Hollywood." *CinémAction* 160 (2016): 82–91.
40. "The Seal of the Confessional: Robert Lepage's *Le Confessionnal* in Social and Cultural Context." *Journal of Religion and Film* 20 (2016): 1–24.
41. "Snared by Words? (Proverbs 6:2): On the Perils of Editing." *JBL* 135 (2016): 441–5.
42. "The JBL Forum, an Occasional Exchange: Black Lives Matter for Critical Biblical Scholarship." *JBL* 136 (2017): 203.
43. "Editor's Foreword: Passing the Torch." *JBL* 137 (2018): 785–8.
44. "*Paul and Palestinian Judaism* in 20th Century Context." *Journal for the Jesus Movement in Its Jewish Setting* 5 (2018): 32–37.
45. "The Gospel of John and the 'Parting of the Ways.'" *EvT* 80 (2020): 465–71.
46. "Presidential Address: Introduction." *JBL* 139 (2020): 3–6. (Introduction to Gale Yee).
47. "A Long, Long Way: Hollywood's Unfinished Journey from Racism to Reconciliation." *Journal of Religion and Film* 25 (2021): 1–9.
48. "The Hermeneutics of Chutzpah: A Disquisition on the Values of 'Critical Investigation of the Bible.'" *JBL* 140 (2021): 8–30.
— SBL Presidential Address for 2020.

F. Popular Publications

1. "Jesus of Hollywood: From D. W. Griffith to Mel Gibson." Pages 26–9 in *The New Republic*. March 8, 2004.
2. "The Vanishing Jews of Antiquity." *The Marginalia Review*. June 24, 2014. https://themarginaliareview.com/vanishing-jews-antiquity-adele-reinhartz/.
— This article generated a Forum, subsequently published in eBook form by Marginalia on August 26, 2014.
3. "A Response to the Jew and Judean Forum." *The Marginalia Review*. August 26, 2014. https://themarginaliareview.com/response-jew-judean-forum-adele-reinhartz/.
4. "The Jewishness of Christianity: The Straddling of Two Eras." December 16, 2014. http://www.ancientjewreview.com/articles/2014/12/16/the-jewishness-of-christianitythestraddling-of-two-eras?rq=reinhartz.
5. "God, Israelites and Non-Israelites: Embracing Ambivalence: Parashat Ekev." August 26, 2016. http://thetorah.com/god-israelites-and-non-israelites-embracing-ambivalence/.
6. "Reflections on My Journey with John | A Retrospective from Adele Reinhartz." April 18, 2018. https://www.ancientjewreview.com/read/2018/2/24/reflections-on-my-journey-with-john-a-retrospective-from-adele-reinhartz.
7. "Caiaphas the High Priest." August 2018. https://www.bibleodyssey.org/en/people/main-articles/caiaphas.
8. "Jew/Judean (Word Study)." https://www.bibleodyssey.org/passages/related-articles/jew-judean-word-study.

G. Encyclopedia Articles

1. "John 4:7–42: Samaritan Woman," 454. "John 8:3–11: Adulterous Woman," 454–5. "John 9:2–3, 18–23: Mother of a Blind Son," 455. "John 16:21: Woman in Labor," 456, all in: *Women in Scripture: A Dictionary of Named and Unnamed Women in the Hebrew Bible, The Apocryphal/Deuterocanonical Books, and the New Testament*. Edited by Carol Meyers, Toni Craven and Ross S. Kraemer. Boston, MA: Houghton Mifflin, 2000.
2. "Jews in the New Testament." *NIDB* 3:311–12.
3. "Second Temple Period Jewish Life." *NIDB* 5:148–50.
4. "Anonymity." *EBR* 2:98–100.
5. "Jesus, Images of, in Movies." Pages 645–6 in *The Cambridge Dictionary of Christianity*. Edited by Daniel Patte. Cambridge: Cambridge University Press, 2010.
6. "John, Gospel." Pages 651–2 in *The Cambridge Dictionary of Christianity*. Edited by Daniel Patte. Cambridge: Cambridge University Press, 2010.
7. "Film." Pages 334–44 in vol. 1 of *The Oxford Encyclopedia of the Bible and the Arts*. Edited by Timothy Beal. New York: Oxford University Press, 2016.
8. "Caiaphas. IV. Literature." *EBR* 4:730.
9. "Caiaphas. V. Visual Arts." *EBR* 4:730–1.
10. "Caiaphas. VI. Film." *EBR* 4:731–2.
11. "Old Testament. Film." *EBR* 21:forthcoming.

H. Book Reviews

1. Review of *Jewish Spirituality from the Bible to the Middle Ages*, edited by Arthur Green. *SR* 16 (1987): 380.
2. Review of *Anti-Semitism in Times of Crisis*, edited by Sander L. Gilman and Steven T. Katz. *Shofar* 11 (1992): 126-8.
3. Review of *Searching the Scriptures: A Feminist Introduction*, edited by Elisabeth Schüssler Fiorenza. *JES* 31 (1994): 379.
4. Review of *Death of the Messiah*, by Raymond E. Brown. *JES* 32 (1995): 269-70.
5. Review of *Reconceiving Texts as Speech Acts: An Analysis of 1 John*, by Dietmar Neufeld. *SR* 25 (1996): 244.
6. Review of *The Crucifixion of Jesus: History, Myth, Faith*, by Gerard S. Sloyan. *JES* 33 (1996): 590.
7. Review of *The Place of Judaism in Philo's Thought: Israel, Jews, and Proselytes*, by Ellen Birnbaum. *JJS* 48 (1997): 366-7.
8. Review of *Found Treasures: Stories by Yiddish Women Writers*, by Frieda Forman, Margie Wolfe, and Sarah Silberstein Swartz. *Women's History Review* 6 (1997): 144-5.
9. Review of *Jewish Women in Greco-Roman Palestine: An Inquiry into Image and Status*, by Tal Ilan. *AJSR* 22 (1997): 114-16.
10. "Radical Dualism and the Reading of Paul." Review of *A Radical Jew: Paul and the Politics of Identity*, by Daniel Boyarin. *Proof* 18 (1998): 103-6.
11. Review of *Constructing Early Christian Families: Family as Social Reality and Metaphor*, edited by Halvor Moxnes. *VC* 52 (1998): 442-4.
12. Review of *Tasting the Dish: Rabbinic Rhetorics of Sexuality*, by Michael Satlow. *AJSR* 23 (1998): 116-18.
13. Review of *The Language and the Law of God: Interpretation and Politics in Philo of Alexandria*, by Francesca Calabi. *SPhiloA* 9 (1999): 168-70.
14. Review of *The New Testament and Hellenistic Judaism*, by Peder Borgen and Søren Giversen. *Shofar* 18 (1999): 161-3.
15. Review of *The Gospel and Letters of John*, by R. Alan Culpepper. *HeyJ* 40 (1999): 351-2.
16. Review of *Narrative Art and Act in the Fourth Gospel*, by Derek Tovey. *RBL* 2 (2000): 400-2.
17. Review of *Heritage and Hellenism: The Reinvention of Jewish Tradition*, by Erch Gruen. *HeyJ* 31 (2000): 332-3.
18. Review of *Traditions of the Bible: A Guide to the Bible as It Was at the Start of the Common Era*, by James L. Kulgl. *HeyJ* 31 (2000): 88-90.
19. Review of *Dying for God: Martyrdom and the Making of Christianity and Judaism*, by Daniel Boyarin. *HeyJ* 42 (2001): 81-3.
20. Review of *Colossians and Ephesians*, by Margaret Y. MacDonald. *SR* 30 (2001): 248-50.
21. Review of *Guardians of Letters: Literacy, Power, and the Transmitters of Early Christian Literature*, by Kim Haines-Eitzen. *JAAR* 71 (2003): 690-2.
22. Review of *Tales of the Neighbourhood: Jewish Narrative Dialogues in Late Antiquity*, by Galit Hasan-Rokem. *RBL* 6 (2004): 320-3.
23. Review of *Companions and Competitors*. Vol. 3 of *A Marginal Jew*, by John P. Meier. *HeyJ* 45 (2004): 70-1.

24. Review of *Are We Amused? Humour about Women in the Biblical Worlds*, by Athalya Brenner. *RBL* 58 (2005): 47–50.
25. Review of *Border Lines: The Partition of Judaeo-Christianity*, by Daniel Boyarin. *SPhiloA* 17 (2005): 217–23.
26. Review of *Judas: Images of the Lost Disciple*, by Kim Paffenroth. *CBQ* 67 (2005): 535–6.
27. Review of *The Jews and the World in the Fourth Gospel: Parallelism, Function, and Context*, by Lars Kierspel. *RBL* 9 (2007). https://www.sblcentral.org/home/bookDetails/5800?search=Kierspel%20AND%20reinhartz&type=0.
28. Review of *Becoming God's Beloved in the Company of Friends: A Spirituality of the Fourth Gospel*, by Mary Margaret Pazdan. *CBQ* 702 (2008): 385–7.
29. Review of *Lazarus, Mary and Martha: Social-Scientific Approaches to the Gospel of John*, by Philip F. Esler and Ronald Piper. *Int* 62 (2008): 209–10.
30. Review of *Israel's God and Rebecca's Children: Christology and Community in Early Judaism and Christianity, Essays in Honor of Larry W. Hurtado and Alan F. Segal*, edited by David Capes, April D. DeConick, and Helen K. Bond. *CBQ* 71 (2009): 451–2.
31. Review of *Animal Sacrifice in Ancient Greek Religion, Judaism, and Christianity, 100 BC to AD 200*, by Maria-Zoe Petropoulou. *RBL* 11 (2009): 310–12.
32. Review of *The Death of Jesus in the Fourth Gospel*, edited by G. Van Belle. *CBQ* 72 (2010): 419–20.
33. Review of *Law and Love*. Vol. 4 of *A Marginal Jew: Rethinking the Historical Jesus*, by John P. Meier. *CBQ* 72 (2010): 602–4.
34. Review of *Not God's People: Insiders and Outsiders in the Biblical World*, by Lawrence M. Wills. *Int* 64 (2010): 313.
35. Review of *Ignatius of Antioch and the Parting of the Ways: Early Jewish-Christian Relations*, by Thomas A. Robinson. H-Net Reviews. June 2010. http://www.h-net.org/reviews/showrev.php?id=29553.
36. Review of *Rhetoric and Theology: Figural Reading of John 9*, by William M. Wright IV. *RBL* 10 (2010). https://www.sblcentral.org/API/Reviews/7732_8425.pdf.
37. Review of *The Misunderstood Jew: The Church and the Scandal of the Jewish Jesus*, by Amy-Jill Levine. *Int* 19 (2011): 344–6.
38. Review of *The Apostle Paul in the Jewish Imagination: A Study in Modern Jewish-Christian Relations*, by Daniel Langton. *RBL* 13 (2/2011): 428–33.
39. Review of *The Ancient Synagogue from Its Origins to 200 C.E.: A Source Book*, by Anders Runesson, Birger Olsson, and Donald D. Binder. *RBL* 2 (2012): 199–202.
40. Review of *Kaiphas. Der Hohepriester jenes Jahres*, by Rainer Metzner. *JSJ* 43 (2012): 419–20.
41. "Was the Word in the Beginning? On the Relationship between Language and Concepts." Review of *Judaism: The Genealogy of a Modern Nation*, by Daniel Boyarin. *The Marginalia Review* (2019). https://themarginaliareview.com/word-beginning-relationship-language-concepts.
42. Review of *Jewish Glass and Christian Stone: A Materialist Mapping of the "Parting of the Ways,"* by Eric C. Smith. *RBL* 22 (2020): 240–4.
43. Review of *History, Theology, and Narrative Rhetoric in the Fourth Gospel*, by Harold W. Attridge. *RBL* 22 (2020). https://www.sblcentral.org/API/Reviews/13229_14758.pdf.
44. Review of *The Ways That Often Parted: Essays in Honor of Joel Marcus*, edited by Lori Baron, Jill Hicks-Keeton, and Matthew Thiessen. *RBL* 22 (2020): 236–40.

Index

abiding in Jesus 23, 175
Abraham 24, 69, 70, 88, 96
abuse
  physical (*see* punishment)
  verbal 21, 62, 68, 92, 127 n.35
affection
  adoration 176–7, 192
  comfort 83, 110, 115, 169–70
  concern 88, 90, 92, 95, 103, 120, 165
  devotion 90, 101, 167
  endearment 83–4, 90
  good will 60–1, 89
  joy 9, 27, 89–92, 113 n.37, 128, 189–92, 1945
  pride 25, 91–2
agape (*see* love)
alienation (*see* isolation)
alliance (political) 36
am-ha-aretz 72, 103
anointing 28–9, 31–2, 164, 167, 170, 177
antagonism/antagonists (*see also* hate) 2, 21–2, 68, 73, 75–6, 105, 170
anti-Judaism/anti-semitism 1–2, 14–22, 41, 68, 95, 144, 172, 192 n.12, 194, 196, 199
Aphthonius the Sophist 55
apocalyptic (*see* eschatology)
apologetics (*see* rhetoric)
aposynagōgos 2, 4–5, 14, 17, 19–20, 67–77
Apuleius 28
Aristotle 244, 37, 60–2, 173 n.5, 175
associations (*see also* church and synagogue) 46, 47 n.16
Athenaeus 28
Aulus Gellius 61, 109

banquet (*see* table fellowship)
baptism 5, 164, 170, 190, 193
Baruch 127–8
Belial (*see also* Satan) 151, 153–5, 157
Ben Sira 55, 59, 141–2, 147

betrayal 54–55, 177–9
biography (*bios*) 55–6, 172–3
birkat ha-minim (*see also* curse) 2, 20–21, 67–68
blessing 50 n.25, 57, 151–4, 157, 165
bride 26, 27–8, 31
bridegroom 23, 27–8, 31, 88
Bruce Almighty (film) 9–10, 181–8

celibacy 69, 172
children
  abandoned 107, 110
  birth 108, 110–12, 133–5
  infancy (metaphoric) 107–11, 113–15
  nurture 110, 135, 165
  orphans 107, 113
  parental affection 84, 94, 108, 115
  premature birth 107
  wet nurse 106–15
church/*ekklēsia*
  in Antioch 76
  building 176
  congregation 108, 112, 73–4, 99–102
  in Corinth 89, 93
  house 4, 80, 85, 93, 114
  institution 15, 21–2, 30–2, 44, 46 n.8, 47, 50, 52, 68–70, 163, 198
  modern 14–15, 20–2
  in Philippi 92
  in Rome 179, 93
Cicero 37, 60–62, 78
circumcision 4, 69, 72, 96
clients (*see* patron-client)
commensality (*see* table fellowship)
community
  boundaries 69, 101, 121, 124–6, 129, 151
  cohesion 6, 7, 78, 101 n.18, 121–9, 142, 150–8
  destabilization 21, 121, 125, 129
  formation 7, 106–15, 119–20, 150–8, 190

Index

contract 107, 110–12
conversion 90–4, 94, 101 n.18, 103, 146, 179
corpse (*see also* impurity) 29, 131, 133–9, 192, 197
covenant (*see also* contract) 13, 15, 69, 101, 150–8
co-worker 78–80, 83, 91–3, 107–8, 113–15
creation story 161, 184, 188
crucifixion (*see* punishment)
curse (see also *birkat ha-minim*) 73–4, 143–4, 151–4, 157 n.22

David and Jonathan 58
The Da Vinci Code (film) 170
Dead Sea Scrolls (*see under* Qumran)
death
 on behalf of another 61
 danger of 26–7, 112–13
 demise of an individual 55, 128, 131, 174, 189–99
 Jesus's 5, 163
 state 5, 77, 189–99
demon
 communion 123–6
 exorcism 50, 60, 163–5, 166
 possession 168
diaspora 4, 20, 47, 51–2, 56, 70–6, 102, 131, 155
dikaiosynē (*see* righteousness)
Dio Cassius 42
Diogenes Laertius 60
discipline (*see* punishment)
disrespect 26, 55, 121–6, 178–9, 187
diversity 20–32, 51–2, 72, 80, 96
Dogma (film) 175

enemies/foes 6, 87, 88–9, 145, 105, 121, 140–1, 145–8, 179
Epictetus 34–5, 37, 58
equality/egalitarianism 4, 16, 20, 24, 26, 37, 54, 58, 60, 82, 86, 163, 169, 173 n.6, 199
eschatology 2, 6, 15, 17, 50 n.25, 75, 96 n.3, 120 n.2, 157, 176
Essenes 47 n.15, 72
hetairos 53–63
ethics
 Christian 81–2

Greco-Roman 24, 55, 85–6
Jewish 69
modern 79, 81–2, 85–6, 173–4, 186–8
ethnic identity 6, 51, 69, 77, 967, 101, 151, 154, 156–8, 164 n.7, 172
ethnocentrism 3, 68, 100–1
Eusebius 41, 147
exclusion (see also *aposynagōgos* and isolation) 20 n.24, 51, 76, 119 n.2, 135

family (*see also* children and marriage)
 affection 89, 108
 divine 75, 87 n.1
 estrangement 165, 174
 fictive/spiritual kinship 4, 7, 79, 81–4, 89–92, 94, 107–8, 111
 life 106–7, 189
 members 110–11
 paterfamilias and authority 80, 120 n.5, 163, 165, 197
flattery/flatterer 58–9, 62–3
footwashing 24, 164, 170
forgiveness (*see* reconciliation)
fornication (see *porneia*)
frankness 2, 4, 21, 24, 37, 61, 63, 173
freedom (*see also* slavery) 8, 33–4, 42, 71, 85, 88, 92, 111
friendship
 absent 78
 affection (*see* affection)
 befriending 14, 78–86
 comradery (*see also* co-worker) 8, 57, 61
 cross-religious 87–8
 cultivation 8, 94, 106, 109, 119
 disciples 23–5, 27, 82, 88, 167, 175
 divine 23–4, 88, 175
 exclusivity 89, 170
 false 8, 53–63, 73
 Hellenistic ideals 23–5
 hierarchical 25, 170
 imperial 8–9, 33–40, 88, 178–80
 intergender 9, 80, 161–71
 philos/philia 27, 53, 57, 60, 87–8
 political 34–9
 true 8–10, 121, 171, 173–4
From the Manger to the Cross (film) 190–1

Index

gender (*see also* women)
    relations 9, 23–32, 51, 80, 82–4, 161, 170, 188
    roles 28, 32, 133, 135, 164, 170
generosity 27, 54–5, 61, 63, 73, 80, 88, 103, 119
gentiles (*see* non-Jews)
gifts 21, 24, 91–2, 97, 176
god-fearers 71, 73
Godspell (film) 175
The Gospel of John (film) 175
The Greatest Story Ever Told (film) 9, 176–8, 193–5
greetings 30, 36, 54–5, 62, 79, 88–9, 93
grief (*see also* mourning) 29–30, 55, 133–4, 166–7, 190, 195
guest (*see* host/guest)

halakah (*see* Torah)
hate (*see also* antagonism and anti-Judaism) 1, 2, 14–15, 19, 24, 61–2, 88, 125, 191
haver 103
Hellenization 23, 55, 72, 132, 143, 143, 146
hero/heroine 9, 25–7, 164 n.7, 172, 173 n.6, 174, 178 n.22, 179
hierarchy 25, 27, 75, 81, 170, 198–9
Hippocrates 58
Homer 57, 63, 143, 149
honor/shame 9, 24, 26, 33–43, 46, 59, 75, 93, 120, 164, 168, 183
hospitality 88, 92, 94, 176
host/guest 8, 54–6, 61, 80, 88, 94, 119, 125, 176, 199
hypocrisy/insincerity (*see also* flattery) 29, 61–2, 152–4, 194, 199 n.11

idolatry 46, 62, 69, 120–9, 153, 155–6
immorality (*see* sin)
imperial cult 120, 128–9
impurity (*see* purity)
infancy (*see* children)
intimacy
    sexual 121, 127, 133, 167
    social 7, 9, 23–32, 62, 108–9, 112, 115, 167
invective (*see* abuse)
Ioudaioi
    historical community 15, 67, 140, 146
    identity 16–17, 22
    narrative device 5, 68, 76–7, 173
    pejorative 15, 17–19, 21
isolation 50, 130, 134–9, 172–6

Jesus Christ Superstar (film) 169–70
Jesus of Montreal (film) 170, 180
Jesus of Nazareth (film) 9, 178–80, 193
Jews (see *Ioudaioi*)
Job 59, 181 n.1
John the Baptist 23, 27, 88, 176–8
Josephus 39, 42, 59, 72, 74, 96–9, 103, 134–9, 141–2, 144, 147, 185 n.20
Jubilees, Book of 144 n.17
Judas 8–9, 29, 53–63, 162, 169, 173–9, 192, 195
judaize 69, 71–2
Justin Martyr 67
justice 10, 16 n.11, 17, 49, 61, 155–6, 187

King of Kings (1927 film) 191–2
kingdom of heaven/God 17, 49, 50 n.25, 70, 88–9, 162, 166, 176, 197–8
kiss (*see* greetings)

The Last Temptation of Christ (film) 161, 166, 169–70, 195–6
law/nomos νόμος (*see* Torah)
Lazarus 5, 9, 23, 26, 28–9, 88, 164, 167, 176–7, 189–99
labor/work 109–15, 135, 175, 187
laborer 54–6, 108
libation (*see under* table fellowship)
liminality (*see also* isolation) 190, 193–9
Longinus 58
love
    agape 27, 32
    beloved 29, 31, 78, 80–1, 87–94
    brotherly (*see under* Family)
    of enemies 89, 178
    eros 27–32
    paternal (*see under* children)
    philia (*see under* friendship)
    romantic 30–1, 161, 169, 172
loyalty 9, 39, 42, 58, 61–2, 88–9, 91, 93
Lucian 25–6

Maccabees (books of) 36, 38, 59, 101, 122, 141, 147
marriage
  chaste 69
  metaphor 107
  patriarchs 28
  with unbeliever 103
  wedding 21, 54–6
  wedding at Cana 21, 27–8, 31, 195
martyr stories 112–13, 126
Mary (film) 170
Mary Magdalene 8, 29–30, 161–71, 173, 194, 198
Mary Magdalene (film) 8, 161–71, 196
meals (*see under* table fellowship)
mentor 4, 80–2, 173, 175, 177, 180, 182
messiah/messianic
  age 3, 15, 22, 51, 102, 128
  claims for Jesus 28, 31, 45–7, 50–2, 70, 95, 102, 104, 161, 177–9, 194
  community 103
  crucified 70, 73–5
  Davidic warrior 69, 162, 178
  return 15, 75–6
metaphor
  literary 6–7, 54, 78, 84, 106–15, 132 n.10
  visual 197
monotheism 74
Monty Python's the Life of Brian (film) 175
Mosaic law (*see* Torah)
Moses 21, 24, 28, 135, 140–1, 146, 175, 182–6
mourning (*see also* grief) 29, 133–4, 177, 189–99
Musonius Rufus 58

neighbors 6, 14, 45, 58, 70, 125, 129, 140–9
Nicolaus the Sophist 55
noli me tangere 30–2, 161
nomos (*see* Torah)
non-Jews 50 n.25, 69, 74, 97, 102, 140–9

oath (*see also* contract) 26, 62, 144
Onesimus 4, 80–6, 92
oppression 7, 83, 113, 156
otherness 84, 76, 173–7

parable 53–5, 56, 88, 133, 162 n.6
parody 127 n.35, 175

"parting of the ways" 1–2, 4, 68
The Passion of the Christ (film) 168
patronage
  client kings 35–6, 39, 67 n.2
  God as patron 46, 174
  relations 37–8, 80, 91 n.8, 94
persecution 38, 75, 100–1, 113
Pharisee
  association 17, 21–2, 49 n.18, 72, 95–6, 131, 138
  Christ-following 51
  Paul 3, 69, 95–105
Philemon 4, 78–86, 92
Philo of Alexandria 6, 39–40, 42, 55, 59, 72, 97–8, 103, 108, 137–9, 144–9
Phlegon of Tralles 29
Pilate 8–9, 33–43, 88, 176
Plato 37, 57–8, 60, 62
Plutarch 55–6, 60, 62–3, 119, 143
porneia 69, 121, 127
priesthood
  chief priests 3, 17, 36, 72, 176–7, 191, 194
  priests and Levites 131, 133–6, 152–5
Proverbs 58–9
punishment 98–9
  capital 22, 54, 56, 122, 178
  corporal 73, 74, 76
  crucifixion 74, 163
  divine 153, 183
  ostracism 49–50, 55
  placation of gods 75–6
purity/impurity 6, 16, 21–2, 54, 120, 130–9
purification rites 7, 21, 131–3, 137–9

Qumran
  community 6, 98, 103, 136, 138, 150–9
  excavations 47
  scrolls 6, 47, 97–9, 131–2, 134–7, 150–9
Quo Vadis (film) 179

Rabbinic literature 67, 97, 99, 103–4, 133, 135–6, 143–6, 185 n.20
reader response 78–86, 173
reciprocity 9, 24, 37, 60, 174
reconciliation 3, 89 n.4, 92, 104–5, 155, 178, 198
Reinhartz, Adele
  anti-Judaism 17, 19, 68

Index

Befriending the Beloved Disciple 1–3, 13–22, 78–86, 173, 180
The Bible in Motion 190 n.5
Cast Out of the Covenant 1–2, 5, 13–4, 19–22, 66 n.3, 67
ecclesiological tale 79
"Introduction to the Gospel of John" in The Jewish Annotated New Testament 13
Jesus of Hollywood 8, 161, 167–8, 172–9, 178 n.23
"The Vanishing Jews of Antiquity" 13
reader-response criticism 78–86, 175
rhetorical analysis 68, 76
"To Love the Lord: An Intertextual Reading of John 20" 161–71
renunciation of relationships (*see also* "parting of the ways") 69, 193
The Robe (film) 179
replacement theology 3, 13–15, 21
responsibility/duty 25, 29, 82, 119, 123, 155, 182, 186–8
reversals
  of fortune 28, 53–5
  role 42, 115, 170
rhetoric (*see also* anti-Judaism)
  apologetics 2, 16–19, 140–9
  disaffiliation 2, 5, 68
  expropriation 5
  syncrisis 8, 55–7, 63
  topoi (*see* friendship)
righteousness 54, 88, 97, 100, 102, 125, 156

Sadducees 15, 17, 21–2, 72, 97–8, 138
Samaritan
  ethnic group 5, 19, 22, 52, 136
  good 133
  woman at well 18, 21, 28, 31
Satan (*see also* Belial) 12, 19, 22, 77, 125–7, 169
Scaevola 61
sectarian 6, 47, 98, 131–8, 150–8, 180
sensuality (see *eros*)
shame (*see* honor/shame)
The Sign of the Cross (film) 179
slaves/slavery 4, 7, 46, 80–6, 92, 106–7, 110–15, 143, 148
Song of Songs 28–9, 31, 59, 161
stoicism 148–9

Strabo 146
supersessionism 2–3, 5, 15, 172, 178–9, 193 n.4, 198
synagogue (see also *aposynagōgos*) 2, 4–5, 20–2, 46–52, 67–77, 98
syncrisis (*see* rhetoric)

table fellowship
  banquet 24, 26, 28, 54, 128
  deipnon 24
  eucharist 126
  meat 119–25
  last supper 28, 163–4, 167–70, 179, 193, 195
  libation 120, 126–9
  sacrificial meal 130–1, 133, 136
  service 28
  symposium 24
Tacitus 25–6, 38–41
temple (Jerusalem) 16–17, 48, 130–4, 136, 145, 148, 178, 193–4, 198
The Ten Commandments (1923 film) 185
The Ten Commandments (1956 film) 9–10, 182, 185–8
Themistios 37
Theognis 57
Theophrastus 61
Tobit (book of) 131, 137
Torah
  books/laws of Moses 98, 135, 138, 148, 154, 190
  law/halakah/traditions 3, 49, 95–104, 131–4, 138
  laxity 74, 125
  leniency 98–9
  observance/piety 54, 72, 95–6, 102–3, 120, 134, 153, 190
  rabbinical 99

virtue (*see* ethics)

weddings (*see under* marriage)
work (*see* labor)
women (see also intergender under friendship)
  association membership 46, 51
  childbirth (*see also under* children) 112, 134–5
  church roles 80, 82, 89–90, 164

equality 20–1
menstruation 7, 130–8
as property 112
reproduction 110–11, 114
work 109–10, 162

Xenophon 57–8

zeal 3, 99–103
Zealots/insurrectionists 72, 179

www.ingramcontent.com/pod-product-compliance
Lightning Source LLC
Chambersburg PA
CBHW051519230426
43668CB00012B/1667